Women in Classical Antiquity

Women in Classical Antiquity

From Birth to Death

Laura K. McClure

WILEY Blackwell

This edition first published 2020
© 2020 John Wiley & Sons, Inc.

The right of Laura K. McClure to be identified as the author of this work has been asserted in accordance with law.

Registered Office
John Wiley & Sons, Inc., 111 River Street, Hoboken, NJ 07030, USA

Editorial Office
101 Station Landing, Medford, MA 02155, USA

For details of our global editorial offices, customer services, and more information about Wiley products visit us at www.wiley.com.

Wiley also publishes its books in a variety of electronic formats and by print-on-demand. Some content that appears in standard print versions of this book may not be available in other formats.

Library of Congress Cataloging-in-Publication Data

Names: McClure, Laura, 1959– author.
Title: Women in classical antiquity from birth to death / Laura K. McClure.
Description: Hoboken, NJ : Wiley-Blackwell, 2019. | Includes index. |
 Identifiers: LCCN 2018050273 (print) | LCCN 2018051516 (ebook) | ISBN 9781118413647
  (Adobe PDF) | ISBN 9781118413654 (ePub) | ISBN 9781118413517 (hardcover) |
  ISBN 9781118413524 (pbk.)
Subjects: LCSH: Women–Greece–Social conditions. | Women–Rome–Social conditions.
Classification: LCC HQ1134 (ebook) | LCC HQ1134 .M35 2019 (print) | DDC 305.40938–dc23
LC record available at https://lccn.loc.gov/2018050273

Cover Design: Wiley
Cover Image: © PRISMA ARCHIVO/Alamy Stock Photo

Set in 10/12pt Warnock by SPi Global, Pondicherry, India

10 9 8 7 6 5 4 3 2 1

For my parents

Contents

List of Figures

List of Charts

List of Boxes

Preface

It has been almost three decades since a new textbook on women in classical antiquity has appeared. Since then, much has changed in the field. New areas of inquiry, new discoveries, new critical approaches, new technologies, and new research have radically modified and expanded what we know about the lives of women in the ancient world and how we understand their representation. This book is an attempt not only to communicate these advances to a general audience but also to convey just how rapidly and dynamically our view of the classical past is evolving. At the same time, it must be acknowledged at the outset that it is impossible to do justice to this escalating body of scholarship and the countless primary sources, many fragmentary or obscure, on which they rely in just one book. Instead, in what follows, I aim to isolate key texts and objects, events and concepts that best represent important ancient Greek and Roman perspectives on women and gender. What makes this book unique, however, is its focus on the life course. This approach not only helps to organize a complex body of evidence by means of an overarching narrative, it also shows how the source materials tend to engage with women and gender at moments critical to formulating social identity, such as birth, adolescence, marriage, childbirth, and death.

Throughout I have tried to strike a balance between a chronological and topical methodology. The book begins with the assumption that readers are unfamiliar with ancient Greek and Roman history and cultural institutions. To provide this necessary context, the book is divided into three chronological periods: Part I: Greece; Interlude: The Hellenistic World; and Part II: Rome. Each part begins with a brief overview of historical events, values, and institutions critical for understanding male identity to lay the foundation for the consideration of women and gender in subsequent chapters. The introduction to ancient Greece examines the rise of the polis during the archaic period and then considers the events and ideas that shaped classical Athens and masculine ideals of heroism, citizenship, and self-control. The Roman chapter explores the foundation of the Republic, the expansion of Roman power throughout the Italian peninsula and beyond, the collapse of the Republic and the foundation of the Empire. It further examines how the Romans constructed male identity around notions of military courage, political ambition, and family lineage. Although the book attempts to integrate material and visual elements in the form of painting, sculpture, architecture, numismatics and inscriptions, the primary focus remains throughout on literary representations of women and gender.

Because the life cycle begins with birth, Chapters 3 and 10 explore the incorporation of the female infant into the family and household and the ways she acquired the gendered characteristics necessary for adulthood. Chapters 4 and 11 examine female adolescence, including concerns about virginity, medical views of the female body, religious roles, and education, culminating with reconstructions of the wedding ceremony. Ancient views of marriage and motherhood, as exemplified by virtuous wives, form the subject of Chapters 5 and 12. Deviations from this norm, typically expressed by female sexual activity outside of marriage in the form of adultery and prostitution, are considered in Chapters 6 and 13. The last chapter of each section examines evidence for women as figures of authority and the possibilities for female civic engagement, whether in the form of religious activity, as in Greece, or as benefactors and businesswomen in the Roman world. This structure has the advantage of allowing students to easily compare the situation of women across both cultures.

Each chapter begins by isolating a fundamental aspect of the life stage to be examined through the introduction of the deity who governs it, as with Greece, or through an exemplary female, as with Rome. Given divergences in source materials and cultural practices, corresponding Greek and Roman chapters do not always contain the same topics. For example, Chapter 10 discusses the education of Roman girls whereas Chapter 3 does not, because we do not have any reliable evidence of this practice among the Greeks. Boxes introduce students to methodological discussions, such as the types of evidence important for the study of women in classical antiquity, including Athenian vases and Roman wall painting. Others cover cultural institutions, such as the Greek theater or the Roman baths, and topics central to female life, including cosmetics, hairdressing, and dolls. Questions for review and reflection are given at the end of each chapter, along with a list of suggestions for further readings, both primary and secondary. The latter consists of a small selection of recent scholarly books and online resources accessible to students and useful for conducting undergraduate research. Many of these works have been indispensable to framing the discussion within their respective chapters. Pedagogical features such as timelines, maps, and charts are provided at the front of this book to help students navigate the ancient evidence and historical periods. Greek or Latin words introduced in each chapter appear in bold type and are also collected in a full glossary at the back of the book. Translations of the Greek and Latin text have been adapted from the Loeb Classical Library series.

The book has been designed for maximum flexibility in the classroom. It can be used alone as a general introduction to women and gender in the classical world, in support of a course on women in ancient art or similar topic, or in conjunction with a selection of primary sources. Individual chapters can also be used separately. For instance, those on the organization of the family and household might provide a useful introduction to a course on women in Greek or Roman literature in translation.

Acknowledgments

A great many people contributed to this book over the course of several years. I am grateful first to the Blackwell editorial team, and in particular, Haze Humbert, for encouraging this project at all stages. Anonymous referees read and commented on the manuscript over several stages. All of their suggestions for revision and expansion have been invaluable to shaping my progress on this book. At the University of Wisconsin, I am fortunate to be able to teach and work in a supportive and collegial environment. Thanks are owed to former chair Jeff Beneker for his steadfast encouragement and recognition of the research aspect of this project. My Latinist colleagues, Nandini Pandey, Grant Nelsestuen, and Alex Dressler, patiently endured my hallway conversations about all things Roman, answering questions, providing bibliography, and reading chapters. Credit is owed to Alex for the idea of using exemplarity to structure the Roman chapters. Lively conversations with Claire Taylor have helped me think about forms of women's empowerment in classical Athens, particularly how they participated in social networks. Archeology colleagues Nicholas Cahill, William Aylward, and Mark Stansbury-O'Donnell have been immensely generous with their knowledge of material culture and assistance with images. Beyond UW, conversations with Lin Foxhall, Kathryn Gutzwiller, Sharon James, Allison Keith, Andromache Karanika, Esther Eidinow, Lisa Maurizio, Melissa Mueller, Nancy Sultan, Angeliki Tzanetou, and Lisl Walsh have been a great source of knowledge, inspiration, and support. Many thanks to Machi, in particular, for organizing a Classical Association of the Middle West and South presidential panel, "Constructions of Girlhood in Greco-Roman Antiquity," in 2018, which grew directly out of research for this book. Graduate assistants, Amy Hendricks and Rebecca Moorman, combed the manuscript for errors and omissions during the revision and proofreading stages. Lastly, special thanks to Sandra Kerka for her expert help with copyediting.

Madison, Wisconsin   *Laura K. McClure*
December 2018

Abbreviations

The abbreviations used here are mostly those used in the third edition of the Oxford Classical Dictionary.

General

BCE   Before Common Era, used in place of BC ("Before Christ")
c.   *circa*, "approximately"
CE   Common Era, used in place of AD (Latin *Anno Domini*, "in the year of our Lord")
Cf.   *confer*, "compare"
e.g.   *exempli gratia*, "for example"
fl.   *floruit*, "s/he flourished," the general period in which a person lived
Fr.   Fragment (*pl.* Frr.)

Collections of Sources and Reference Works

AE   *L'Année Épigraphique*, published in *Revue Archéologique* and separately (1888–)
CEG   *Carmina Epigraphica Graeca*
CIL   *Corpus Inscriptionum Latinarum*
CMG   *Corpus Medicorum Graecorum*
IG   *Inscriptiones Graecae*
P. Oxy   *Oxyrhynchus Papyri*
SEG   *Supplementum Epigraphicum Graecum*
TLE   *Thesaurus Linguae Etruscae*, a collection of Etruscan tomb inscriptions.
WO   U. Wilcken (ed.), *Griechische Ostraka aus Aegypten und Nubien* (Leipzig and Berlin, 1899)

Greek and Roman Authors and Texts

Aesch.	Aeschylus	
	Ag.	*Agamemnon*
	Cho.	*Choephori*, "Libation Bearers"
	Eum.	*Eumenides*
Anth. Gr.	*Greek Anthology*	
Alc.	Alcman	
Ap. Rhod.	Apollonius of Rhodes, *Voyage of the Argo*	
App.	Appian	
	B Civ.	*Civil Wars*

Ar.	Aristophanes	
	Ach.	*Acharnians*
	Eccl.	*Ecclesiazusae*, "Women of the Ecclesia"
	Lys.	*Lysistrata*
	Nub.	*Nubes*, "Clouds"
	Thesm.	*Thesmophoriazusae*, "Women of the Thesmophoria"
Arch.	Archilochus	
Arist.	Aristotle	
	Eth. Eud.	*Eudemian Ethics*
	Eth. Nic.	*Nichomachean Ethics*
	Gen. An.	*Generation of Animals*
	Pol.	*Politics*
	Rhet.	*Rhetoric*
Ath.	Athenaeus, *Deipnosophistae*, "Dining Sophists"	
Aug.	Augustus	
	RG	*Res Gestae*, *"The Deeds of Divine Augustus"*
Aul. Gell.	Aulus Gellius, *Attic Nights*	
Catull.	Catullus	
Cic.	Cicero	
	Att.	*Letters to Atticus*
	Brut.	*Brutus*
	Cael.	*In Defense of Caelius*
	Har. resp.	*On the Responses of the Haruspices*
	Mur.	*In Defense of Murena*
	Phil.	*Philippics*
	Tusc.	*Tusculan Disputations*
	Verr.	*Against Verres*
Dem.	Demosthenes	
[Dem.]	Pseudo-Demosthenes	
Dio	Dio Cassius, *Roman History*	
Dion. Hal.	Dionysius of Halicarnassus	
	Ant. Rom.	*Roman Antiquities*
Eur.	Euripides	
	Alc.	*Alcestis*
	Andr.	*Andromache*
	Cap. Mel.	*Captive Melanippe*
	Hec.	*Hecuba*
	Hipp.	*Hippolytus*
	IA	*Iphigenia in Aulis*
	IT	*Iphigeneia in Tauris*
	Med.	*Medea*
	Pho.	*Phoenician Women*
	Tro.	*Trojan Women*
Hdt.	Herodotus	

Hes.	Hesiod	
	Op.	*Works and Days*
	Theog.	*Theogony*
Herod.	Herodas	
Hippoc.	Hippocrates	
	Mul.	*Diseases of Women*
	Nat. Puer	*On the Nature of the Child*
	Ster.	*On Infertility*
	Virg.	*On Virgins*
Hom.	Homer	
	Il.	*Iliad*
	Od.	*Odyssey*
Hom. Hymn Aphr.	*Homeric Hymn to Aphrodite*	
Hom. Hymn. Dem.	*Homeric Hymn to Demeter*	
Hor.	Horace	
	Carm. saec.	*Carmen Saeculare,* "Secular Hymn"
	Ep.	*Epistles*
Juv.	Juvenal	
Luc.	Lucian	
	Dial. Meretr.	*Dialogue of the Courtesans*
Lys.	Lysias	
Macr.	Macrobius	
	Sat.	*Saturnalia*
Mart.	Martial	
Men.	Menander	
	Per.	*Perikeiromene,* "The Girl Who Gets Her Hair Cut Short"
Nep.	Cornelius Nepos, *On Famous Men*	
Ov.	Ovid	
	Am.	*Amores*
	Ars	*Art of Love*
	Fast.	*Fasti*
	Met.	*Metamorphoses*
	Trist.	*Tristia*
Pers.	Persius	
Pl.	Plato	
	Tim.	*Timaeus*
Plaut.	Plautus	
	Amph.	*Amphitryo*
	Aul.	*Aulularia*
	Cas.	*Casina*
	Men.	*Menaechmi*
	Mil.	*Braggart Soldier*
Plin.	Pliny the Elder	
	NH	*Natural History*

Plin.	Pliny the Younger	
	Ep.	*Letters*
Plut.	Plutarch	
	Alex.	*Alexander*
	Ant.	*Antony*
	Caes.	*Caesar*
	Cic.	*Cicero*
	Lyc.	*Lycurgus*
	Mor.	*Moralia*
	Num.	*Numa*
	Pyrrh.	*Pyrrhus*
	Quaest. Rom.	*Roman Questions*
	Tib. Gracch.	*Tiberius Gracchus*
Polyb.	Polybius, *Histories*	
Poseid.	Poseidippus	
Prop.	Propertius	
Sen.	Seneca	
	Ben.	*On Benefits*
	Controv.	*Controversies*
	Helv.	*Consolation to Helvia*
Sor. *Gyn.*	Soranus, *Gynecology*	
Soph.	Sophocles	
	Ant.	*Antigone*
	Ter.	*Tereus*
	Trach.	*Trachiniae,* "Women of Trachis"
Tac.	Tacitus	
	Ann.	*Annals*
	Dial.	*Dialogue on Oratory*
Thuc.	Thucydides, *Peloponnesian Wars*	
Theoc.	Theocritus	
	Id.	*Idyll*
Tib.	Tibullus	
Tyrt.	Tyrtaeus	
Val. Max.	Valerius Maximus	
Verg.	Vergil	
	Aen.	*Aeneid*
	Ec.	*Eclogues*
Vitr.	Vitruvius, *On Architecture*	
Xen.	Xenophon	
	Hier.	*Hiero*
	Oec.	*Household Economy*
	Mem.	*Memorabilia*
	Symp.	*Symposium*
Zonar.	Zonaras	

Timeline of the Classical World

This timeline is a very abbreviated overview intended to provide a historical context for the material in this book. Dates are often approximate, particularly for the Greek period, and follow established opinions. Only frequently mentioned authors have been included. Not all Roman emperors are listed.

GREECE (BCE)	
3000–2100	EARLY BRONZE AGE: Beginning of Minoan Civilization on Crete
2100	Greek Speakers enter Greece
2100–1600	MIDDLE BRONZE AGE: MINOAN PERIOD
1800	Earliest writing in Linear A
1600–1150	LATE BRONZE AGE: MYCENAEAN PERIOD
1600–1500	Mycenean Shaft Graves
1450	Destruction of palace at Knossos
1400	Earliest writing in Linear B
1184	Traditional Date of the mythic Trojan War
1200	Destruction of Mycenaean palaces
1150–750	IRON AGE
800	First Olympian games
750–490	ARCHAIC PERIOD
750–25	Homer's *Iliad* and *Odyssey*
fl. 600	Sappho
535	Invention of Drama at Athens
c. 525–456	Aeschylus
508	Democratic Reforms at Athens
c. 496–406	Sophocles
490–323	CLASSICAL PERIOD
490–79	PERSIAN WARS
c. 480–406	Euripides
469–399	Hippocrates
444–385	Aristophanes
431–404	Peloponnesian War
430–354	Xenophon
399	Trial and execution of Socrates
384–322	Aristotle
340	Pseudo-Demosthenes, *Against Neaera*

HELLENISTIC PERIOD (BCE)	
359	Philip II becomes king of Macedon
357	Marriage of Philip and Olympias
356	Birth of Alexander III to Philip and Olympias
336	Assassination of Philip II, ascent of Alexander
334	Alexander begins campaign against Persia
323	Death of Alexander in Babylon
	Birth of Alexander IV to Roxane
316	Death of Olympias
316–268	Arsinoe II
298/7	Founding of Mouseion and Library in Alexandria
277	Establishment of three Hellenistic kingdoms
ca. 266–221	Berenice II
69–30	Cleopatra VII
30	Augustus conquers Egypt and becomes first Roman emperor

ROME	
753 BCE	Legendary Foundation of Rome
753–509 BCE	Monarchy
509 BCE	Beginning of the Republic
494–287 BCE	Conflict of the Orders
450 BCE	Law of the Twelve Tables
264–241 BCE	First Punic War
c. 254–184 BCE	Plautus
218–201 BCE	Second Punic War
195–159?	Terence
149–146 BCE	Third Punic War
146 BCE	Invasion of Greece
133–121 BCE	Gracchi Reforms
107–100 BCE	Marius
106–43 BCE	Cicero
90–88 BCE	Social Wars
83–70 BCE	Civil War: Sulla
70–19 BCE	Vergil
73–71 BCE	Spartacus' Slave Revolt
59 BCE	Formation of First Triumvirate: Pompey, Caesar, Crassus
59 BCE-17 CE	Livy
58–51 BCE	Caesar conquers Gaul
44 BCE	Death of Julius Caesar
43 BCE	Formation of Second Triumvirate: Antony, Octavian, Lepidus
43 BCE-17 CE	Ovid
31 BCE	Battle of Actium
30 BCE	Death of Antony and Cleopatra
27 BCE	Senate Decrees Octavian Princeps
c. 4 BCE-65 CE	Seneca
12–41 CE	Caligula
14 CE	Death of Augustus

14–68 CE	Julio-Claudian Emperors
37–68 CE	Nero
c. 50–120 CE	Plutarch
68–69 CE	Civil War
69–96 CE	Flavian Dynasty
96–180 CE	Five Good Emperors
117–138 CE	Hadrian
161–192 CE	Commodus
193 CE	Year of the Five Emperors
212 BCE	All Free Men in the Roman Empire Granted Citizenship
476 BCE	Traditional Date for the Fall of Rome

Maps

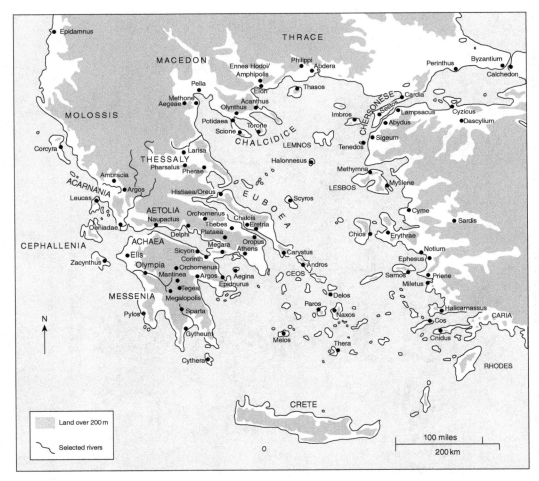

Map 1 Greece and the Aegean. Source: P.J. Rhodes, *A History of the Classical Greek World*, 2nd ed., Blackwell, 2011, p. xxiv.

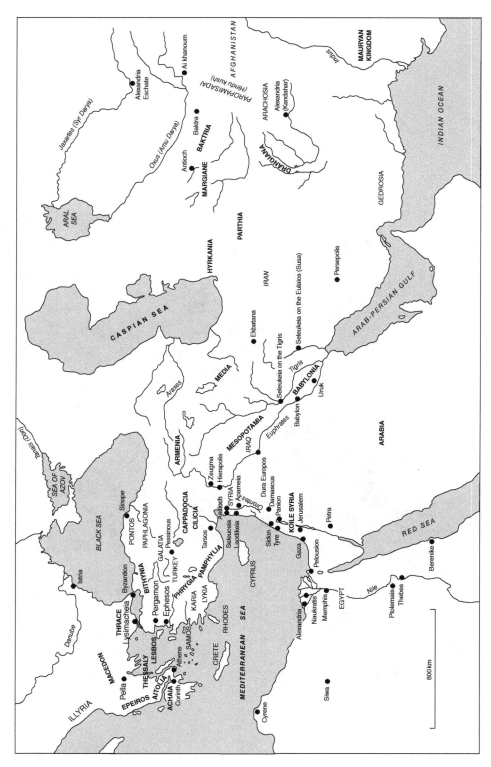

Map 2 The Hellenistic Kingdoms. Source: *A History of the Hellenistic World*, Blackwell, 2008, p. xv.

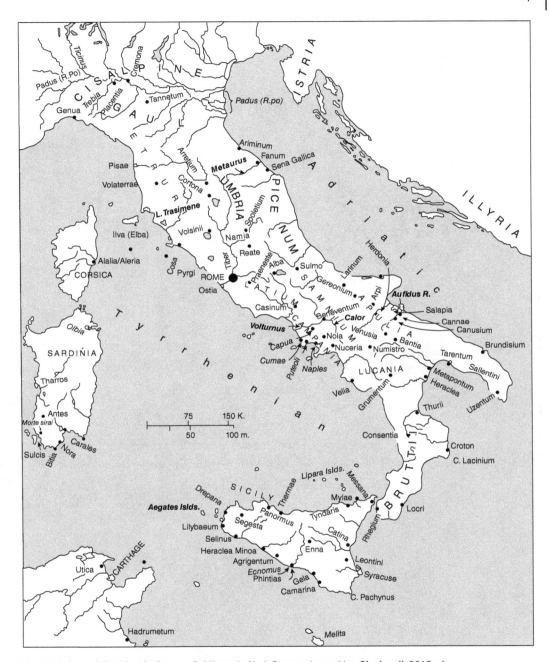

Map 3 Italy and the Islands. Source: B. Mineo (ed.), *A Companion to Livy*, Blackwell, 2015, xiv.

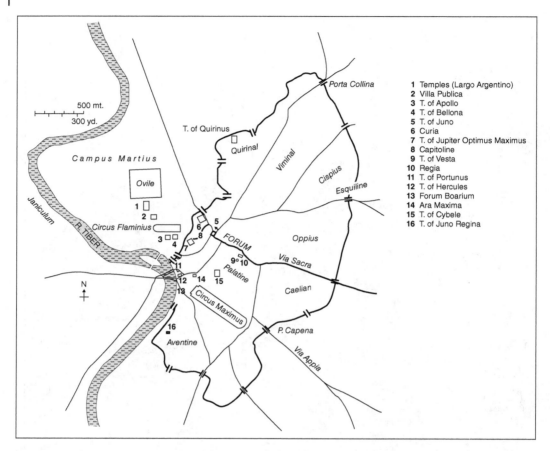

1 Temples (Largo Argentino)
2 Villa Publica
3 T. of Apollo
4 T. of Bellona
5 T. of Juno
6 Curia
7 T. of Jupiter Optimus Maximus
8 Capitoline
9 T. of Vesta
10 Regia
11 T. of Portunus
12 T. of Hercules
13 Forum Boarium
14 Ara Maxima
15 T. of Cybele
16 T. of Juno Regina

Map 4 City of Rome (Second to Third centuries CE). Source: B. Mineo (ed.), *A Companion to Livy*, Blackwell, 2015, xii.

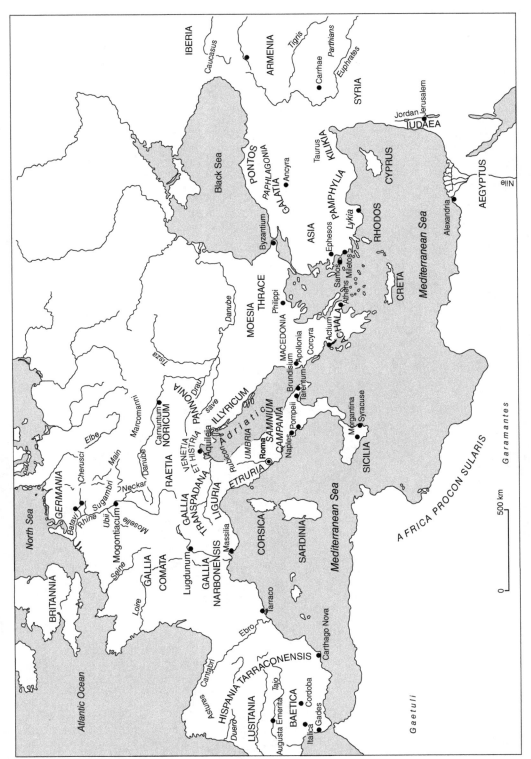

Map 5 The Roman Empire in the Time of Augustus. Source: A. Erskine (ed.), *A Companion to Ancient History*, Blackwell, 2009, p. xxxvii.

Introduction

1

Approaches to Women and Gender in Classical Antiquity

Hospes, quod deico paullum est: asta ac pellege. Heic est sepulcrum hau pulcrum pulcrai feminae. Nomen parentes nominarunt Claudiam. Suom maritum corde dilexit suo. Gnatos duos creavit; horum alterum in terra linquit, alium sub terra locat. Sermone lepido, tum autem incessu commodo. Domum servavit, lanam fecit. Dixi. Abei.

Stranger, what I have to say is little; stand near and read it through. Here is the tomb, not lovely, of a lovely woman. Her parents named her Claudia. Her husband she loved with her heart. Two sons she bore; of these, one she leaves on earth, the other she placed under the earth. She was of charming speech and graceful movement as well. She kept house, she worked in wool. I have spoken. Go your way.

Epitaph of Claudia, Rome, second century BCE (CIL VI 15346)

If you happened to run across this inscription without any background information, what would you think? Of course, you would not be able to read it unless you knew Latin, the language in which this inscription was written over 2000 years ago. Nor would you be able to view the original stone on which these words were written because it no longer exists. Rather, these words are recorded on copies made much later, in the fifteenth and sixteenth centuries CE. It does not specify the author nor does it tell us much about its subject. What then can we infer from the writing? The inscription is funerary: it commemorates a woman named Claudia after her death. It is also public, addressed to a nonfamily member. Someone, probably her husband or other relative, cared enough about this woman to memorialize her and could afford to do so. She was a wife and mother, attractive, affectionate, refined, and industrious.

This inscription illustrates some of the complexities involved in the study of women and gender in classical antiquity. Who was Claudia? When did she live? What were the names of her husband and parents? Why did one of her sons die? Did she give birth to any other children? How would she describe herself? What did she think of her world? The stone seems to raise as many questions as it answers. Discovering Claudia involves a tantalizing process of piecing together a wide array of evidence produced over two millennia ago, both literary and visual, and much of it fragmentary. To find out more about her life and the lives of other women, we must dig deeper, delving into the historical, political, and religious contexts of the sources and using the interpretive approaches available to modern students and scholars.

From this very short text, we can deduce a few general points about ancient conceptions of women and gender. First and most importantly, it calls attention to the fact that men have produced most of the artifacts and documents about women that survive from classical antiquity. The result is that these sources almost always convey a male perspective. For instance, the inscription emphasizes the female attributes and qualities most important to husbands:

physical attractiveness, a loving nature and charming personality, household management, and the ability to bear male children. The inscription also suggests that views of women in antiquity are in large part conditioned by the source or genre in which they appear, not to mention accidents of history. Such perspectives are mediated, that is, they do not provide direct evidence for the lives of women but rather often give a distorted view. Whoever set up this inscription probably commissioned a professional who in turn borrowed from a stock set of phrases for the commemoration of the dead. The result is a generic portrait of a virtuous Roman matron, with little individualized information about the woman herself. Another important point to be gleaned from this example is that representations of women and gender often intersect with how a society constructs the stages of the life course. Here death is viewed as a critical moment for fashioning social identity and ensuring its perpetuation through time.

Before going any further, it is important to distinguish the concept of "sex" from "gender." "Sex" refers to the biological sex of a person at birth, whereas "gender" is the culturally defined and culturally specific male or female social identity assigned to an individual. Concern with gender in ancient societies typically aligns with the major phases of the life course, such as birth, adolescence, marriage, parenthood, and death. Although many of these stages are linked to biological growth, they are all critical moments for the development and reinforcement of social identity. In this respect, the concept of age does not pertain simply to biological age and physical development but to a socially recognized life phase. Gender and age are thus linked processes: through socialization during the life course, which archeologist Roberta Gilchrist calls the "gender clock," the individual gradually acquires gender traits until adulthood, when male and female roles are fully differentiated. Women's lives in classical antiquity are often described in terms of the life cycle of personal and family events, beginning with birth and education, moving to marriage and motherhood, and ending with sickness and death. As we see in subsequent chapters, the literary and material record largely focuses on the middle stage for women, on their roles as wives and mothers, and their transition to this stage rather than on infancy, childhood, and old age. This book therefore seeks to elucidate aspects of women's lives in classical antiquity that were particularly formative to the establishment of their social identity through an exploration of the female life course, from birth and childhood, to adolescence and the transition to marriage, to childbirth and motherhood, and finally death. Along the way, our journey also requires us to attend to the dynamic processes by which contemporary scholars construct their knowledge of the remote past, the nature of their sources, and the methodologies and approaches that have informed their work.

1.1 Ancient Greek and Roman Sources

"Classical antiquity" is a very broad term that applies to a long period of cultural history centered on the Mediterranean Sea and consisting of two interrelated civilizations, ancient Greece and Rome. The period spans approximately 1300 years, from the eighth century BCE to the fifth century CE, starting with the appearance of the Homeric poems and ending with the decline of the Roman Empire and the rise of Christianity. Although we often think of these two civilizations as separate political and social entities, it is important to remember that they overlapped and interacted for more than 1000 years, whether through archaic Greek settlements in Italy, where the Greeks encountered the Etruscans; the influence of Greek poetic models on Roman literature during the Hellenistic period; or the final Roman conquest of Greece in the Republican period (see Timeline).

Gender pervaded all aspects of life in the ancient world. Although Greek and Roman views of women diverged in important ways, as we will see, many of the symbolic, social, and legal categories that defined women and their literary and artistic representations remained relatively constant throughout all periods of classical antiquity. This stability is in part the result of the influence of Greek mythology, educational models, and poetic and artistic forms on Roman literature and society. Life in ancient Mediterranean towns did not change significantly for hundreds of years, as compared to radical shifts found in later historical periods, such as the industrial revolution, or our own rapidly evolving information age. Class and social status were much more important determinants in the lives of individuals, for both men and women, in Greco-Roman antiquity than they are in most Western societies today. As a result, an individual's social identity tended to be fixed from birth. Moreover, the male-centered perspective that dominates the written and visual sources emphasizes the female qualities and attributes, similar across both cultures, that best served the aims of men, such as obedience, fertility, industry, and piety, while repudiating characteristics that contradicted these ideals, such as independence, intelligence, public visibility, and sexual self-expression.

So the first challenge in interpreting ancient sources on women is the problem of male bias. Another obstacle is the loss of so much material from the ancient world: as little as 5% of the art, architecture, literature, and other documents produced in classical antiquity is extant today. The sources that have survived pose numerous questions about language, dating, production, performance, and even author and genre. Often, we do not have an author's complete body of work: for instance, we have only around 5% of the work of the female poet Sappho (c. 600 BCE, see Box 1.1), most of it fragmentary (see Figure 1.1). The absence of much important

---

Box 1.1 A Poem's Journey from Antiquity to Modernity

How were classical texts transmitted to the modern era? Some sources, like the inscription that opens this chapter, were written in stone, but most Greek and Roman texts were originally inked on papyrus sheets, which were glued together to form a roll. As books became popular during the Hellenistic period, commercial dealers produced and circulated multiple copies for libraries and private collections. Alexandria in Egypt housed the largest library in the ancient world: somewhere between 200 000 and 490 000 volumes during the third century BCE, many of which were subsequently destroyed in a major fire. The demand for books in the Roman period further ensured that numerous copies of Latin texts were in circulation, thereby increasing the odds that such works would be preserved. By the medieval period, however, many Greek and Roman texts had been lost due to war, Christian censorship, and changes in manuscript production. The recopying of Greek texts by Byzantine scholars resulted in the loss of countless works that were judged not worth preserving.

An exciting story of transmission and discovery involves the work of the Greek female poet Sappho. Her surviving poetry largely consists of quotations preserved by other ancient authors, along with a few fragmentary papyrus scraps. Indeed, only one complete poem has survived, a playful hymn to Aphrodite. The recent identification of a papyrus scroll at the University of Cologne in Germany as part of a roll containing the poems of Sappho (Figure 1.1) has expanded the number of complete poems to two or three. The text, preserved as part of the funerary wrapping on an Egyptian mummy, is the earliest known manuscript of her poems, copied just 300 years after her death. It contains three poems, all in a fragmentary state; the second one, however, had already been identified on another Egyptian papyrus in 1922. By piecing the two fragments together, scholars were able to come up with an almost complete poem, which is translated here:

[You for] the fragrant-blossomed Muses' lovely gifts [be zealous,] girls, [and the] clear melodious lyre: [but my once tender] body old age now [has seized;] my hair's turned [white] instead of dark; my heart's grown heavy, my knees will not support me, that once on a time were fleet for the dance as fawns. This state I oft bemoan; but what's to do? Not to grow old, being human, there's no way. Tithonus once, the tale was, rose-armed Dawn, love-smitten, carried off to the world's end, handsome and young then, yet in time grey age overtook him, husband of an immortal wife. (trans. M. L. West)

Astonishingly, Sappho's story continues to evolve: in 2014 two more fragments were identified, the so-called "Brothers Poem," in which the poet writes about the safe return of her seafaring brother, and the "Kypris Poem," which considers the suffering inflicted by unrequited love.

Figure 1.1 A fragment of Sappho preserving 12 lines of the Tithonus poem, Cologne papyrus, P. Köln XI 429.

material makes it difficult to judge whether gender was the main concern of a particular genre or whether the views espoused in the extant works are atypical. Vanished texts might provide a much different picture from that presented by the surviving sources.

Ancient sources for the study of women in antiquity cover a broad spectrum of genres, including epic, lyric and erotic poetry, drama, history, biography, satire, legal and medical texts, and visual evidence such as painted pottery, sculpture, architecture, wall paintings, and inscriptions. These sources frequently provide conflicting and even contradictory views of women. In addition to being male authored, they often represent an elite perspective and as such tend not to be concerned with ordinary people and marginal groups, such as slaves and foreigners. In the case of Greece, much of our literary evidence comes from Athens and reflects an Atheno-centric worldview. Roman sources, on the other hand, are often influenced by political ideology and the battle for dominance in the Mediterranean and beyond. Although this book primarily focuses on ancient literary sources, it also considers aspects of material and visual culture especially as it engages with women and gender. Like ancient texts, most of our visual images from antiquity have been lost. Bronze statues have been melted down, marble sculptures, broken, and wall paintings eroded. Even pottery, our best artistic source for women in ancient Greece, has not escaped the ravages of time (see Box 3.1 in Chapter 3). Although 50 000 vases produced in Athens during the archaic and classical periods have managed to survive, this number represents probably only a fraction of the original production. At first glance, these images may seem easy to interpret to the modern viewer; however, it is often actually quite difficult to reconstruct their original context and accurately identify their stories. Other aspects of material culture, including sculptural reliefs, inscriptions (as Claudia's cited previously), burial sites and archeological remains of houses, brothels, temples, and ancient towns, all provide important information about gender and sexuality. For example, the excavation of Pompeii, an ancient Roman town located on the bay of Naples and buried by the eruption of Mt. Vesuvius in 79 CE, affords a rare glimpse into the lives of its female inhabitants, as we see in Chapter 10.

Despite the diversity of ancient sources, there is nonetheless a major gap between the fictional portrayal of women and their lived realities. Consider the difference between the images of women in contemporary television, film, and video games and the actual lives of real women today. The same principle applies to the ancient world: literary sources cannot be taken as an objective mirror of reality but rather as an imaginative reconstruction of human experience by a given author during a particular period of time. Even history, a genre that we tend to view as more accurate in its portrayal of people and events, contains numerous biases and distortions, not least of which is the lack of interest among ancient authors in women and girls as historical subjects. Another challenge is the fact that representations of women in antiquity tend to cluster in certain genres, which further distorts our picture of women. For instance, the surviving Greek tragedies perhaps contain the largest number of fully developed female characters in classical literature, and yet they are notorious for their crimes. Any conclusions drawn about women and gender from this genre must be tempered by the knowledge that these females are often represented as acting in defiance of social norms.

Although these external factors pose a challenge, it is still possible to glean significant insights into the lived realities of women in classical antiquity and to understand ancient constructions of gender from the primary sources. A good example is found in the comedy *Lysistrata* by Aristophanes (444–385 BCE) in which the women of Greece stage a sex strike and occupy the sacred center of the city in an attempt to stop the war, a play to which we return several times in Part 1. The plot is as implausible as it sounds: women from all parts of Greece would not have been able to band together without their husbands' knowledge, and their sexual abstinence would not have had the intended effect, because Athenian men had ready access to sexual partners outside of marriage. Nor could women have exclusively occupied the Acropolis, the holy precinct of the goddess Athena, by sheer force. However, despite its fictive premise, the play provides a wealth of reliable information about the everyday lives of women in classical Athens. When Lysistrata wonders aloud where all of the women are after they fail to appear at the appointed time, her friend Calonice explains:

> Don't worry, they will come, dearest. It is very difficult for women to get away from the house. One woman works at her husband, another has to wake the slave, still another puts her baby to sleep, another has to wash and feed it. (Ar. *Lys.* 16–20)

Although imaginary, this passage gives us a good sense of the routine domestic activities of citizen women in fifth-century Athens: largely confined to the house, they worked in close proximity with their female slaves and were responsible for caregiving. At the same time, the bit about the husband, which probably contains a sexual innuendo, reminds us that the purpose of the conversation, and the play, is male entertainment. As these examples suggest, discovering women and gender in classical antiquity is a complex process best undertaken from a variety of perspectives.

1.2   Gender in Context: Social Identity in the Ancient World

Although there is no doubt that free citizen men exerted much more control over their lives and identities than their female counterparts at all periods in the classical world, it is important to note that ancient conceptions of the self differed markedly from modern Western ideas. For instance, slaves comprised between 30 and 40% of the population in classical antiquity. This meant that a large part of the community had little autonomy and familial identity apart from that of their owners. Further, regardless of gender, an individual's social status derived from familial, religious, and political affiliations that operated within a complex social network. Therefore individual identity was almost always constituted through connections within a group and between groups. Indeed, the philosopher Aristotle (384–322 BCE) defined a human being as a "political animal," implying that an individual cannot exist apart from his city-state. Belonging is thus a central idea in many ancient literary texts, starting with the *Odyssey* of Homer (eighth century BCE), a poem that chronicles Odysseus' quest to return home after the Trojan War. Declining the beautiful nymph Calypso's offer to remain on her island as her immortal consort, the hero explains the importance of returning home to his mortal wife:

> Mighty goddess, do not be angry with me for this. I myself know full well that wise Penelope is inferior to look upon than you in form and in stature, for she is a mortal, while you are immortal and ageless. But even so I wish and long every day to reach my home and to see the day of my return. (Hom. *Od*. 5.215–21)

This passage suggests that Odysseus' identity is contingent upon his return to Ithaca, where he will reclaim his position in his community and family. And although Penelope does not have the same freedom to experience adventure as her husband, she clearly exerts a powerful influence on him as his wife, to the extent that he refuses to live his life without her.

In Roman culture, identity was also inextricably bound to family and political status. For example, in the *Aeneid* of Vergil (70–19 BCE), a reworking of Homer's epics, the hero Aeneas describes the necessity of abandoning personal love for the higher goal of founding Rome, "But now to great Italy Apollo's power commands me to go; his Lycian oracles resound for Italy. This is my love, this is my fatherland" (Verg. *Aen*. 4.345–7). Odysseus and Aeneas not only must operate within their social framework, they must also obey the external imperative of the gods. Although fictive, these two Greek and Roman heroes exemplify important ancient ideas about identity and the self. Absent are modern values of radical individualism, self-determinism, and autonomy. Indeed, actions driven by these concepts often spell disaster for the male hero. As explored further in Chapters 2 and 8, individual male identity in the Greco-Roman world was largely the product of birth and external circumstance rather than an internal concept of the self as autonomous and detached from the larger community. The idea of individual freedom in classical antiquity was simply much more restricted than it is today. This difference is particularly significant for our discussion of gender, for it suggests that women's agency and personhood in classical antiquity, although obviously more limited in scope than that of men, nonetheless occurred in a social, political, and religious context much different from our own.

As today, gender intersected with other aspects of social identity in the ancient world, including social status, age, and ethnicity. Because elite members of ancient societies controlled most public discourse, the foundational works of art and literature almost exclusively feature aristocrats and royalty while rendering invisible slaves and the lower classes. This book, like most scholarship on gender and women in classical antiquity, focuses primarily on upper-class women, real women from ancient and prestigious families, and their mythic and literary counterparts. Although a large portion of the population consisted of slaves, they are seldom given more than a passing reference in literary and visual sources. Nonetheless, it is possible to imagine that even marginal members of ancient Greek and Roman communities, whether slaves, freed persons, or foreigners, participated in social networks and overheard and discussed the important events of the day, even if they had no direct political impact on their outcome. Some scholars have even speculated that free women of the lower classes in Rome may have been more emancipated or more equal to their male counterparts than elite women because they may have been less constrained by legal definitions of marriage or legitimacy and less subject to a sexual double standard. Perhaps they had a different attitude toward normative values, though it is hard to tell as their voices have disappeared. Because of the constraints imposed by the literary sources, however, the ancient constructions of gender and representations of women discussed in this book focus mainly on elite and aristocratic women, although attention is given to slaves and the lower classes whenever possible.

1.3 Critical Approaches

Although the following methodological approaches mostly pertain to the analysis of literary texts, some of them, like structuralism and feminist theory, have been equally influential in the interpretation of visual representations of women. Until the late twentieth century, the primary method for the study of classical texts both in the United States and Europe was philological, a form of linguistic analysis. Classical philology developed out of the nineteenth-century belief that literary and historical studies should employ an objective scientific methodology parallel to that of the physical sciences. This practice involves extensive training in ancient Greek and Latin in order to analyze individual words in literary texts, taking into account their historical context, to arrive at one correct interpretation. This type of scholarship has resulted in the foundational critical tools employed by classicists and students today, such as dictionaries, commentaries, and editions of ancient texts. Although this methodology has given us a thorough understanding of the Greek and Latin languages and literary genres, it does not readily help us understand aspects of gender in classical antiquity. Instead, contemporary critical approaches borrowed from other disciplines have proven invaluable for allowing feminist classical scholars to ask, and answer, a different set of questions from those a philologist might pose.

Whereas a philological reading concentrates on understanding the language of a text and its historical context, a feminist reading considers how it portrays women and reflects issues of gender and sexuality during the period of its production. As we saw previously, the limited number of extant primary sources and their fragmentary or corrupt state make the study of gender and women in antiquity more challenging in many ways than modern studies of the subject and explain the importance of the philological foundation of classical scholarship. Even with these combined methodologies, many, many questions about women and gender in classical antiquity remain unanswered, and some will never be fully resolved. Sometimes scholars looking at the same evidence come to radically different conclusions! Ongoing debates continue about issues such as whether women attended the Athenian theater or whether a woman or a male impostor actually wrote Sulpicia's lyrics, questions that even sophisticated theoretical approaches cannot always help to answer.

In contrast to philology, which aims to arrive at the "correct" interpretation of a text, modern critical theory assumes that there cannot be one true reading, because any interpretation necessarily involves assumptions and biases on the part of the reader. Critical theory is a way to make explicit the concerns and questions the reader brings to a text. For instance, Marxist theory could help her think about how literature reflects issues of class, ideology, and economic disparities. The remainder of this chapter briefly sketches a few of the main approaches employed by classicists over the last several decades to study questions of women and gender in antiquity: structuralism, psychoanalytic criticism, feminist theory, and, as a general catch-all, cultural criticism. These critical methodologies are not mutually exclusive; different approaches often overlap and inform scholarly interpretations without explicit acknowledgement. Just as the study of the past is a dynamic process of discovery and reinterpretation, as this book emphasizes, so, too, the history of women and the representation of gender are continually changing in response to new evidence, new approaches, and changing attitudes toward male and female roles and sexuality. Only two decades ago the study of women and gender in the classical world was a new and controversial field; today it is a standard part of the humanities curriculum at most colleges and universities in the United States and United Kingdom. Indeed, debates on gender more generally have moved extremely fast in recent years thanks to the contributions of trans people.

1.4 Structuralism

Developed in the early twentieth century, structuralism is an attempt to understand in a systematic way the fundamental cognitive structures that organize human experience. It is thus a method of systematizing perceptions that can be applied across disciplines, and it has been particularly influential in the field of classics. Structuralist theory holds that the structure of language itself produces reality. Linguistic structures, not individuals, produce and determine meaning, because we can think only through language. The structures that underlie surface phenomena, that is, the objects and activities that we observe and participate in, are actually relatively few. For example, whereas the English language consists of over a million words, the structure of its vocabulary consists of just 31 phonemes, or individual sounds. Structuralists attempt to define the invisible structuring mechanisms generated by the human mind and projected upon the world in order to understand that world. The theory does not suggest there is no factual reality, but rather that there are too many facts to be perceived without some way to limit and organize them. The order we see in the world is one that we impose upon it. A structuralist framework therefore focuses on how innate symbolic structures in the human mind, such as language, influence our understanding of reality.

As developed by Ferdinand de Saussure (1857–1913), two concepts central to structuralism have been particularly important for the study of women and gender in classical antiquity. First, the emphasis on overarching systems has freed classical scholars from the nineteenth-century philological emphasis on historical development to look at larger structuring concepts, such as gender, across genres, media, and time periods. For instance, the close association of women with the body and the natural world is a concept that pervades all of classical literature. A second important structuralist concept taken up by classicists is the idea that components of a structure have meaning only in relation to each other, because they cannot exist in isolation. The human mind is best able to distinguish difference through these differences, or binary oppositions, such as nature and culture, female and male, and divine and human. The emphasis on difference has been particularly productive for Hellenists, because the ancient Greek language and much of Greek thought is organized around polarities, to which gender is central.

Structuralist anthropology as developed by Claude Lévi-Strauss (1908–2009) represents another key development for the study of gender and women in classical antiquity. Lévi-Strauss believed that all cultures share the same social structures regardless of differences in surface phenomena. All cultures participate in rites of passage, such as coming-of-age ceremonies, that mark the movement from childhood to adulthood, even though the individual cultural expressions of this transition vary (for example, from the compulsory period of military service for adolescent males in classical Athens to obtaining a driver's license in the United States today). Lévi-Strauss concentrated on classical mythology in an attempt to show that different myths are actually variants of the same story and thus demonstrate that individuals across cultures share the same structures of consciousness. As an example, he analyzed the ancient Greek myth of Oedipus, which he argues shows the conflict between our knowledge that we are born of sexual union and the persistent belief in Greek myth that people are born from the earth. Mythology represents the human attempt to make sense of an otherwise chaotic world by reconciling oppositions. Lévi-Strauss further posited that each myth consists of a limited set of universal motifs, such as the hero slaying a monster. Because structuralism emphasizes language and narrative, it has been an important tool for literary analysis among classicists, influencing the work of classical scholars Jean-Pierre Vernant (1914–2007) and Pierre Vidal-Naquet (1930–2006), which focuses on the frameworks underlying ancient Greek myth, ritual, and Athenian drama. Of particular significance for the study of women in antiquity have been the writings of Nicole Loraux (1940–2003) whose explorations of sexual difference in ancient Greek literature and mythology have stimulated some of the most interesting research today.

1.5 Psychoanalytic Criticism

Psychoanalytic criticism represents one of the earliest approaches to the study of women and gender in the classical world. Developed by Sigmund Freud (1856–1939) at the turn of the twentieth century, psychoanalytic concepts are widespread today: most of us are familiar with terms like "defense mechanism," "sibling rivalry," and "inferiority complex." Although psychoanalysis was in origin a psychological method and Freud was not a literary critic, the focus on understanding family relationships and individual behavior and the emphasis on the complexity of meanings produced by the unconscious mind are readily applicable to literary interpretation.

Freud drew extensively on Greek myth and tragedy in developing his new science of the mind. Indeed, he also gravitated toward the myth of Oedipus in naming the central concept of psychoanalytic theory the Oedipus complex. According to Freud, infants can experience the world only through a symbiotic relationship with the mother. Once aware of himself and his mother as separate entities, normally at the stage of language acquisition, the male infant directs his desire toward the mother. The presence of the father as his mother's lover threatens him symbolically with castration. This anxiety forces him to renounce his desire for his mother and repress this drive and to enter the paternal world of authority, rules, and prohibitions. The repression of Oedipal feelings establishes the unconscious, an area of the mind inaccessible to our normal mental activities. Another important concept for literary studies is dreamwork. Freud considered dreams to be an expression of unconscious drives and emotions. He suggested that they are usually sexual in nature and have their origins in emotions, anxieties, or desires experienced in childhood. Because direct expression of these forbidden feelings would be overwhelming, dreams use a form of encryption or dreamwork. Decoding dreams systematically through psychoanalysis helps patients access this hidden material. A similar technique can be used with literary texts to access the deeper meanings that lie beneath the surface.

In classical studies, psychoanalytic theory has played an important role in research on women in antiquity and their representation in literature because of its focus on the family and the capacity of literary texts, like dreams, to contain multiple and often hidden meanings. For example, Philip Slater in *The Glory of Hera* (1968) explained the seemingly hostile relationship between mothers and sons in Greek mythology as the reflection of the psychological and social reality of the Greek city-state. He speculated that mothers in ancient Greece, frustrated by their lack of domestic and political power, displaced their ambitions onto their male children, and yet because of their own thwarted desires remained emotionally ambivalent toward them. This psychological dynamic, in Slater's view, explains the pervasive misogyny of ancient Greek culture. The subsequent work of French psychoanalytic critics Jacques Lacan (1901–1981) and Julia Kristeva (1941–) have also facilitated feminist interpretations of ancient literature and has been used to explain, for example, the interplay of erotic desire and politics in Latin love elegy.

1.6 Feminist Criticism

Feminist literary criticism, which dates to the social movement of the 1960s, has also had a major impact on the development of the study of women in classical antiquity. Feminist theory is not really a distinct critical approach but rather a set of beliefs and practices that borrows from multiple theories, including structuralism and psychoanalysis. Feminist critics consider the ways in which literature, art, and other media reinforce or undermine the economic, political, social, and psychological oppression of women. A core tenet is that patriarchal ideology, the underlying assumption that males control society, oppresses women economically, politically, socially, and psychologically. A feature of patriarchy is biological essentialism, the belief that one's nature and social role are conditioned by biological sex and thus cannot be changed. Patriarchy also establishes women as other by objectifying and marginalizing them. Under patriarchy, men are the standard by which everything is measured. All of Western culture is deeply rooted in patriarchy, and although it is found in cultures that predate the civilizations of ancient Greece and Rome, their literary and visual representations of gender dynamics played a formative role in the later tradition. Feminist criticism, in contrast, seeks to view culture outside the framework of patriarchy. Feminism is also a form of political activism, in that it attempts to promote social change through increasing awareness of sexism and advocates for gender equality.

As discussed previously, feminism distinguishes between sex as a biological condition and gender as the cultural programming that shapes human identities as masculine or feminine. Feminism and gender studies are closely related, as evidenced by the recent trend of renaming women's studies programs to include the term "gender." As a social construction, gender is the process by which we give meaning to the perceived biological differences between men and women. Indeed, all societies represent gender through a system of codes that identify an individual as male or female. Despite the fact that most extant texts from classical antiquity were written by men, it is nonetheless possible to examine how gender as a construct operates within them because of advances in feminist and gender theory in other disciplines.

A major challenge for feminist critics is the fact that men almost exclusively have constructed and transmitted the Western intellectual and cultural tradition from classical antiquity onward. For this reason, much of feminist scholarship has focused on recovering the voices and experiences of women that have been marginalized in history and literature. Feminist scholars have highlighted neglected female authors and historical figures to demonstrate the importance of their contributions. Scholars of English literature, for example, have helped broaden the traditional canon to include female writers such as Emily Dickinson, George Eliot, and Virginia Woolf, many of whom were not only influenced by classical literature, but in fact helped shape its reception in the nineteenth and twentieth centuries. Feminist classical scholars engage in similar work, restoring the lives of forgotten women to the historical record, drawing attention to conceptions of gender in the literary and visual record and bringing to light the contributions of women to their societies.

1.7 Cultural Criticism

Cultural criticism includes theories that have a political and sociological emphasis important to research on women and gender in antiquity. Perhaps the most influential critic in this category for classical scholars has been French philosopher Michel Foucault (1926–1984), who had close intellectual ties with ancient historians Peter Brown (1935–) and Paul Veyne (1930–). Foucault's diverse writings defy categorization. His affinities with structuralism are evident in his emphasis on language as a factor in limiting our ideas and what we are able to think about. He also believed that the autonomous subject cannot be the source of meaning and coherence. Unlike structuralists, however, Foucault was interested in the social conditions of language use. He referred to the social use of language as "discourse," which he viewed not as free and unconstrained but as strictly controlled, reflecting the distribution of social and political power in human societies. Foucauldian theory is thus concerned with questions of discourse and power: how the uses of language privilege certain individuals, while excluding others, and what institutional frameworks, such as medicine and law, make discourse possible.

The ancient world forms the subject of two volumes of Foucault's work, *The History of Sexuality* (1978), which explores the emergence of the individual in classical antiquity. As in psychoanalytic theory, sexuality is central to Foucault's view of the development and definition of the self. In *The Use of Pleasure* (1985), Foucault examines Greek sexual norms in the classical period with a view to later Christian values and proposes that the Greeks linked sexuality to issues of power rather than morality. Sexual restraint and moderation formed the core of self-identity for elite Athenian males, as well as for Romans, as we shall see in Chapters 2 and 8, and laid the foundation for Christian morality. Foucault believed that philosophical concepts such as "truth" and "knowledge" are culturally determined, change over time, and cannot exist outside of history. His main contribution was to show that power is distributed diffusely through every aspect of society rather than operating from the top down. Power in this regard is an all-encompassing and inescapable feature of social life. Although gender is not central to Foucault's work, his ideas about the self, sexuality, society, and power have inspired new and fruitful ways of viewing women, gender, and sexuality in classical antiquity. In particular, Foucault's focus on how sexuality was controlled and regulated in classical Athens has led to further explorations, including further investigations of ancient prostitution and its intersection with gender and politics.

Although this book does not deal explicitly with the burgeoning discipline of gender diversity in the ancient world and its intersection with contemporary transgender discourse because of space constraints, it is important to recognize the contributions of this movement to our changing views of women and gender in the ancient world. Although Greek and Latin texts clearly articulate gender norms based on biological sex and represent them as critical to the construct and maintenance of social and political hierarchies, they also feature characters who do not conform to gender categories. We find masculinized women who live apart from men in the form of the Amazons, effeminate and even transgender males, like the followers of the goddess Cybele whose initiation in her cult involves self-castration, and ambiguously sexed hermaphrodites. In Ovid's *Metamorphoses* (8 CE), a Latin epic that chronicles over two hundred myths, we find several gender-fluid figures that challenge the boundaries of anatomical sex and socially constructed gender. The blind prophet Teiresias, for instance, transforms from a man into a woman and back again, experiencing two sexualities in the process. Conversely, the woman Caenis requests to be turned into a man after her brutal rape by the god Apollo so that she may never be sexually violated again. Ovid's poem also includes multiple instances of transvestism as a means of manipulating the outer appearance of gender identity in order to conceal or deceive others concerning one's true sex. These real and mythical figures challenge in surprising ways the very binaries of sex and gender that underpinned Greco-Roman antiquity and promise to contribute new insights into ancient ideas of selfhood, sexuality, and gender with the help of contemporary transgender discourse.

1.8 Conclusion

The study of women and gender in the classical world involves many challenges. The first is the fact that so many of our primary sources, whether literary or visual, no longer survive or exist in a fragmentary state. Most of this evidence is authored by men and as such reflects a male bias. Female characteristics desirable to men, such as fertility, industry, and beauty, are emphasized, whereas independence, intelligence, and sexual self-expression are derided. Representations of women and gender are further influenced by genre: a funerary inscription delivers standard praise for a good wife, whereas satire enumerates all of women's negative characteristics in order to poke fun at contemporary society. Most of these sources do not reflect social reality in a straightforward fashion but rather combine fact and fiction to entertain and educate. It is also important to remember that in both Greek and Roman societies, personal identity for both men and women derived largely from social status, with less opportunity for social mobility than today. Lastly, critical approaches such as psychoanalysis, structuralism and, above all, feminism have provided important interpretive tools for exploring representations of ancient women in both literary and material sources.

Questions for Review

1 What are some questions we might ask of a text, image, or artifact in order to understand how it represents ideas about gender?

2 What are some of the difficulties posed by our ancient sources for the study of women and gender?

3 Give an example of how women are represented in contemporary media and discuss to what extent these images reflect reality.

4 How did ancient views of the individual differ from today?

5 What is feminist theory and how might it help us understand ancient representations of women?

References

Foucault, Michel (1978). *History of Sexuality: An Introduction*, vol. 1. New York: Vintage Books (reissue edition, 1990).

Foucault, Michel (1985). *History of Sexuality: The Use of Pleasure*, vol. 2. New York: Vintage Books (reissue edition, 1990).

Slater, Philip (1968). *The Glory of Hera: Greek Mythology and the Greek Family*. Princeton, NJ: Princeton University Press (reissue edition, 2014).

Further Reading

Beard, Mary and Henderson, John (2000). *Classics: A Very Short Introduction*. Oxford: Oxford University Press.

    Beginning with a walk through the classical art collection at the British Museum, the authors discuss the significance of the study of classics and its influence on Western culture.

Foxhall, Lin (2013). *Studying Gender in Classical Antiquity*. Cambridge: Cambridge University Press.

    The author investigates how gender shaped people's lives and experiences in ancient Greece and Rome and shows its link to wealth, status, age, and life stage. The introduction provides an overview of the history of the study of women in antiquity.

Gannon, Meghan (2015). "Sappho's New Poems: The Tangled Tale of Their Discovery." *Live Science* (January 23). https://www.livescience.com/49543-sappho-new-poems-discovery.html (accessed 10 October 2018).

    Discusses the discovery of two fragments by Sappho, the so-called "Brothers" and "Kypris" poems and the difficulty of authenticating such finds.

Gilchrist, Roberta (2007). Archaeology and the life course: a time and age for gender. In: *A Companion to Social Archaeology* (ed. L Meskell and R Preucel), 142–160. Oxford: Blackwell.

    Provides a general overview of the life course approach and discusses its usefulness for archeology.

Reynolds, Leighton (2013). *Scribes and Scholars: A Guide to the Transmission of Greek and Latin Literature*, 4e. Oxford: Clarendon Press.

    Provides a wonderful introduction to how classical texts have survived to the present day, from the preservation of books by ancient libraries to the transmission of texts by medieval copyists.

Schmitz, Thomas (2007). *Modern Literary Theory and Ancient Texts*. Oxford: Blackwell.

    A clear overview of the main forms of literary theory and how they have been used to uncover the meanings of ancient texts. The author employs a balanced approach, highlighting objections and limitations where relevant.

Tyson, Lois (2006). *Critical Theory Today: A User Friendly Guide*, 2e. New York and London: Routledge.

    An excellent, highly readable introduction to contemporary critical theory. In addition to providing synopses of each approach, the author applies them to *The Great Gatsby* as an example.

West, Martin (2005). "A New Sappho Poem." *Times Literary Supplement* (June 21).

    Discusses the discovery of a new papyrus containing one of Sappho's poems and the process by which scholars came to identify it. Includes the text in the ancient Greek original, translation, and a brief interpretation.

Greece

2

Introduction to Ancient Greece

Why do you foretell my death? This is not your business. I myself know well it is my destiny for me to die here far from my beloved father and mother. But for all that I will not stop until my enemies have had enough of my fighting.

(Hom. *Il.* 19.420–4)

Who were the Greeks? When and how did they live? An understanding of their history, culture, and values is critical to interpreting the place of women and gender within their society, from Bronze Age settlements to cosmopolitan Hellenistic cities (see Timeline). The opening passage, taken from Homer's story of the Trojan war, points to warfare as a primary concern of this culture. The story begins with the emergence of small agricultural settlements in the Mediterranean basin around 3000 BCE within the shadows of the vast and powerful kingdoms of the ancient Near East and Egypt. Although much remains unknown about the earliest period of Greek history, the evidence suggests a radical shift from the relatively egalitarian, peaceful society of the non-Greek Minoans to the war-driven culture of the Mycenaeans, which played a formative role in the shaping of subsequent Greek civilization. Within this framework, we also consider some key ideas central to male identity in the Greek world, including heroism, citizenship, self-control, and the pursuit of pleasure in the symposium and the theater.

The term "the Greeks" is a bit misleading because they did not know themselves by this name, but rather called themselves Hellenes and their country Hellas. Nor was Greece in antiquity ever a unified nation-state with a centralized government. Instead, it consisted of several separate political units, kingdoms in the late Bronze Age and city-states in the archaic and classical periods. By the fifth century BCE, the Greeks inhabited a vast area that included the Greek peninsula, Asia Minor on the coast of Turkey, the set of islands known as the Cyclades, Crete, parts of Italy known as Magna Graecia, and North Africa (see Map 1). Although the independent Greek city-states never considered themselves an integrated political entity, they shared common beliefs and practices and occasionally banded together at moments of military crisis, such as during the Persian invasion in 480 BCE. What united them was their language, which they believed distinguished them from all other peoples. They referred to these non-Greeks as *barbaroi* because of their seemingly unclear speech – what sounded like babbling, or *barbar*, to them. Panhellenic religion in the form of sanctuaries and festivals further provided a sense of shared cultural identity.

The geography also contributed to the lack of political unity among the Greeks, as a glance at Map 1 attests. The combination of mountainous terrain, rugged coastlines, and scattered islands contributed to the relative isolation of many city-states. The sea, rather than mainland roads, provided the easiest way to navigate between cities; indeed, most mainland Greeks lived no further than 40 miles from the sea. About one-fifth of the land was cultivated, mostly with

Women in Classical Antiquity: From Birth to Death, First Edition. Laura K. McClure.
© 2020 John Wiley & Sons, Inc. Published 2020 by John Wiley & Sons, Inc.

grain, vines, and olive trees. The climate of Greece explains much about its culture: mild winters and moderate annual rainfall facilitated agriculture and created a temperate environment in which much of life, for men at any rate, was conducted outdoors, including exercise at the gymnasium, public meetings, legal trials, and theatrical performances. Then as today, the summer heat in Greece could be brutal, as the poet Hesiod (c. 700 BCE) describes:

> When the artichoke flowers and the chirping cicada sits in the tree and pours down its sweet song continually from under its wings in the time of tiring heat, then goats are the fattest and wine at its best, women are most lustful, but men the most desiccated, because the dog star parches both head and knees, and the skin is withered by the heat. (Hes. *Op.* 582–88)

Although the poem was composed almost three thousand years ago, we can still imagine the languid summer heat of the rural countryside. It also helps to explain how summer, not winter, represented the barren season for the Greeks, whose main form of work was agricultural. And although the Greeks eventually produced some of the most spectacular literary and artistic monuments of Western civilization, their lifestyle, even for the wealthy, was quite modest by modern standards throughout all periods of their history. Most Greeks lived in small communities as peasants, farming small plots, in which they planted a mix of cereals, mainly barley, but also wheat, along with olives, grapevines, and figs. Animal husbandry was also practiced, and most rural estates included oxen for plowing, mules, sheep, goats, and pigs. Mud-brick houses constructed around an inner courtyard with dirt floors provided shelter and a center for economic activity. Within this domestic space, agricultural resources were converted into products for domestic use – grapes into wine, olives into oil, and wool into clothing – all of which could serve as the basis of trade.

2.1 Greece in the Bronze Age: Minoan and Mycenaean Civilizations

We can trace the Greeks back to two Bronze Age cultures, the Minoans and the Mycenaeans. The Minoans represent the earliest Bronze Age civilization of the Mediterranean basin. They were the descendants of immigrants of unknown origin who settled around 7000 BCE in the central and eastern parts of the island of Crete, where they practiced farming and raised livestock. The term Minoan comes from the mythic king of Crete, Minos, and designates the prehistoric civilization that flourished on the island from around 3000 to 1100 BCE, reaching its apex at around 1600. The Minoans spoke a non-Indo-European language linguistically distinct from later Greek. Apart from their mythology, they left few traces on subsequent Greek civilization. Their geographical location – the large island of Crete that marks the southern boundary of the Greek islands – further isolated them from developments on the mainland. At the same time, it meant they were advantageously situated for trade, which eventually helped them gain wealth and power.

The primary distinguishing feature of Minoan civilization was its huge building complexes, referred to as palaces, which began to appear on Crete around 2000 BCE. The main purpose of these buildings was not simply to provide a residence for the ruling families but to centralize and administer the economic, political, and religious activities of the surrounding community. Excavated by the archeologist Sir Arthur Evans in 1899, the palace at Knossos was the largest and most impressive of these complexes. The original building consisted of a large rectangular central court surrounded by many smaller rooms, including halls, stairways, and storage areas on multiple levels. This layout reflects the role of the palace in a redistributive economy: it gathered raw materials, perhaps as a form of taxation, to use in manufacturing goods, which could then be reallocated to the local population. Surpluses allowed the Minoans to engage in trade with the Near East and Egypt, thereby increasing the wealth of the various court centers and contributing to their expansion and enhancement. Administering this complex economy required a new form of technology, writing, in order to keep track of inventories and commercial transactions. The Minoans employed a syllabic writing system called Linear A, which appeared around 1800 BCE and remains undeciphered today.

The resources the Minoans amassed in overseas trade financed a sophisticated artistic culture that drew on Near Eastern and Egyptian influences, yet expressed a distinct outlook. Minoan wall paintings, or frescos, feature vivid depictions of birds, fish, flowers, and human figures, all rendered in bright colors. The jewelry, pottery, and metal and ivory work reveal an equally high level of technical skill that later influenced Mycenaean artistic production. Interestingly, the visual record contains few images of warfare and many female figures (see Box 2.1). This fact, combined with the lack of fortifications and weapons uncovered in the archeological excavations, led Sir Arthur Evans to posit what he called the "Minoan Peace." Given the small amount of evidence for internal armed conflict, he believed the Minoans were a peace-loving society with little interest in warfare until the arrival of Mycenaeans. Although recent archeological finds have modified this view, it nonetheless remains an intriguing hypothesis not completely contradicted by the archeological record.

Around 2100 BCE, a new group of people, the Mycenaeans, settled in the Greek mainland just as Minoan culture began to emerge. They exerted a formative influence on later Greek civilization through their religion, mythology, values, and language, which was an early form of ancient Greek. For instance, the account of the Trojan War described in Homer's epic poems, the *Iliad* and *Odyssey*, has its origins in the oral storytelling traditions of the Mycenaeans. Although Mycenaean civilization reached its prime much later than that of the Minoans, the two cultures interacted with and influenced one another for several generations. Whereas the Minoans prospered through trade, the Mycenaeans advanced through conquest. When they first encountered the Minoans, the palace complex had already been perfected as a model for centralized administration. They adapted this system of organization to the mainland, where they constructed monumental structures to serve as centers of religious, political, and economic activity.

Despite the strong influence of the Minoans, the Mycenaeans diverged in a few important ways. First, their palaces were considerably smaller, often located on hilltops, and heavily fortified by high, thick walls, suggesting a defensive function. Another notable departure was Mycenaean burial customs. Whereas the Minoans buried their dead simply, in communal fashion, with few grave goods, the Mycenaeans created elaborate tombs, filling them with a stunning array of gifts. In 1876, a wealthy German businessman and amateur archeologist, Heinrich Schliemann, first excavated the citadel at Mycenae. What survived apart from the ruined palace walls was a series of shaft graves, deep rectangular pits cut into the rocky ground into which the bodies were lowered and grouped together inside a circular wall at the edge of the citadel, just beyond the lion gate. The shafts contained numerous grave goods of exceptional quality, including scores of bronze weapons, exquisitely wrought gold jewelry, and other luxury artifacts constructed of imported materials.

The Mycenaeans also invented a new syllabic writing system, Linear B, which they adapted from Minoan Linear A. Thousands of small clay Linear B tablets have been discovered at the building complexes of Knossos in Crete and Pylos on the mainland. Originally intended as a temporary form of accounting, these objects have survived because of fires that baked them hard at both sites. Although they are not literary texts, which did not appear until the eighth

Box 2.1 The Myth of Matriarchy

Just as the absence of references to warfare prompted the idea of a "Minoan Peace," so the large number of artistic representations of women in both the frescos and terracotta figurines similarly led to the conclusion that Minoan culture was matriarchal in origin. In the wall paintings, female figures are often depicted as larger than their male counterparts and occupy prominent spatial positions. These compositional features suggest that women held a high position within their society: those represented may be divinities or public officials such as priestesses, or they may be performing important ritual activities. A fresco from Thera, home of a Minoan colony, shows a young girl picking crocus flowers, possibly as an offering to a goddess represented by a female figure shown elsewhere on the fresco (Figure 2.1). The girl wears a richly colored and textured skirt and bodice, as well as a large amount of jewelry – several bracelets, pendants from her upper arms and sleeves, and large hoop earrings. Her hair is elaborately arranged in what is believed to be a youthful style, with most of the head shaved except for a single curl at the back

Figure 2.1 Girl gathering crocus flowers; based on the snakelike locks of hair, the girl is believed to be an adolescent; fresco from Room 3, House Xeste 3, Thera, c. 1700–1450 BCE. Thera, Greece, Santozeum, Thera Foundation, Petros M. Nomikos.

of her head and wispy bangs at the front. This image, along with the other frescos in the room, has been interpreted as depicting a female puberty rite marking the transition from adolescence to the adult role of wife and mother. Whatever the status and role of the figures, the size and complexity of the fresco series suggest that the Minoans placed a great deal of emphasis on women's religious and social contributions to their society.

Given that depictions of women in Minoan art vastly outnumber those of men, scholars have speculated that their presence may reflect a matriarchal religion or society. In 1861, Johann Bachofen published *Mother Right: An Investigation of the Religious and Juridical Character of Matriarchy in the Ancient World*, in which he postulated that the earliest human civilizations were not male governed but rather matriarchal. In ancient agrarian societies, the elevated status of the mother was closely linked to the importance of the earth, which people worshipped in the form of a goddess. Female figurines and the worship of maternal deities thus predominate in these societies, particularly representations of motherhood, as exemplified by mother and child terracotta figurines commonly found in Bronze Age Aegean communities. Matriarchy, in Bachofen's view, gradually yielded to patriarchy when new social and religious institutions were introduced during the Mycenaean period, particularly monogamous marriage and the worship of male sky gods, such as Zeus. Although Bachofen's theories have long been discredited, they influenced the modern study of women in antiquity which began in the late 1960s, when feminism as a social movement in the United States and Europe began to influence scholarly discourse in classics and other academic disciplines. The influence of his work can still be seen today in the Goddess movement that emerged out of second wave feminism.

century BCE, they nonetheless afford a glimpse into the Mycenaean social and political structures. At the top rung of society was the "master," followed by various other elite functionaries, including priests. Slaves, many of them female, occupied the lowest rung of the social ladder. For example, tablets from Pylos indicate that over 600 slave women – the same number as children – worked as weavers, grinders of grain, bath attendants, and flax workers. The tablets depict a highly gendered society, delineating a clear division of labor for men and women both in the domestic and palatial contexts. They also reveal a nascent form of Greek religion: in addition to a goddess designated as ***potnia*** ("mistress"), which may refer to the mother goddess of the Minoans or a variety of local female deities, we can also recognize the names of other gods important to later Greek life, including Zeus, Hera, Athena, and Hermes.

War was a recurring theme in the Mycenaean world. The preponderance of weapons and armor found among the grave goods at Mycenae attests to the great value they placed on warfare. The use of heavy fortification to protect the palace complexes, as well as their hilltop locations, further suggests the anticipation of repeated skirmishes with outsiders. The visual record similarly reflects a strong interest in war, as depicted by the warriors, outfitted with helmets, spears, shields, and greaves (armor to protect the shins), departing for war on the vase in Figure 2.2. Mycenaean frescos also show a taste for violence: instead of the animated scenes of religious ritual, athletic activity, and finely drawn female figures of the Minoans, these paintings reveal a marked preference for battle and hunting motifs with few representations of women. These warlike sensibilities became one of the hallmarks of ancient Greek civilization to be celebrated in the art and literature of later periods.

Around 1200 BCE, the Mycenaeans suffered a devastating blow: almost every settlement was attacked, plundered, and burned by invaders. This onslaught sparked a downward spiral from which they never fully recovered. Palatial sites such as Pylos were abandoned and never again inhabited; Mycenae was quickly reoccupied and rebuilt but later succumbed to new attacks.

Figure 2.2 Warrior vase from Mycenae depicting helmeted soldiers marching with spears and helmets, c. 1600 BCE. Athens, National Archaeological Museum, 1426.

The entire region appears to have been on edge. Linear B tablets at Pylos allude to the dispatch of rowers and guards to the coast. Elsewhere inhabitants strengthened their fortifications and improved their water supply systems, as if readying themselves for a long siege. The collapse of Mycenaean civilization reflected a wider catastrophe affecting the entire eastern Mediterranean. Egyptian records from the New Kingdom speak of "Sea Peoples," marauders who attacked and burned Troy between 1250 and 1200, the approximate date the Greeks assigned to the Trojan War. Although scholars today do not think the Trojan War actually happened, it provided an important cultural touchstone for Greek civilization in subsequent periods. The Hittite empire also fell around 1200 BCE, and many cities in Anatolia and Syria were destroyed. Whereas scholars have long theorized the downfall of Mycenaean civilization resulted from the so-called Dorian invasion from the north, current thought points rather to a "systems collapse," a complete breakdown of political, social, environmental, and economic processes. Whatever the cause, these events essentially erased Mycenaean culture and forever changed the course of Greek civilization.

2.2 Iron Age

After 1200 BCE, the Greek world plunged into a period of cultural isolation and poverty. For almost five centuries, no monumental stone structures were constructed on the mainland or on the islands. Population levels declined, writing disappeared, supplies of bronze and other metals dwindled, and trade ties were severed. Even contact between neighboring communities became difficult. Instead of palace complexes, Greeks of this period resided in modest huts in rudimentary villages. Yet daily life continued much as it always had. Greeks worshipped the same gods, cultivated traditional crops, worked wool, and engaged in the crafts of pottery and metalwork, although at much less technically advanced levels than before. Indeed, the same rhythm and activities of agricultural life would remain unchanged for many centuries. Despite the loss of technology and the reduced standard of living, it was during this period that Greek civilization as we know it today began to coalesce. Virtually cut off from contact with other cultures in the Mediterranean, the Greeks turned inward, establishing new settlements, developing a new style of pottery, and formalizing their tradition of oral storytelling, which perpetuated the memory of the heroes and kings from the late Bronze Age.

Greek civilization reached its lowest ebb and then began to recover around 1000 BCE. One sign was the smelting and working of iron, a harder metal than bronze and an ore native to Greece. The population began to slowly increase. Around 900, a new form of pottery called Protogeometric emerged in Attica and quickly spread to other regions. As discussed in the introduction, pottery is a vital source for understanding Greek culture and values from the Bronze Age through the Classical period. Protogeometric ornamentation utilized a ruler brush and compass, rather than relying on freehand painting, to create straight lines and circular patterns around the base of the vase. Gradually, these motifs yielded to detailed linear and angular designs, such as meander, zigzags, and triangles, and the clearly defined zones or bands of Geometric pottery that developed around 900 BCE in Attica. At this time, vases also began to feature living creatures, first animals and birds and eventually humans, for the first time since the collapse of Mycenaean civilization. As an example, the Dipylon amphora (Figure 2.3), juxtaposes bands of small, precise geometric patterns with a central narrative panel that shows mourners grouped around a corpse, a scene appropriate to the vase's function as a funerary

Figure 2.3 Late Geometric amphora from the Dipylon cemetery in Athens, c. 750 BCE. Athens, National Archaeological Museum, inv. 804.

marker. The presence of this type of pottery as far away as Syria, Jordan, Israel, and parts of Italy during the ninth and eighth centuries BCE attests to the return of Greek trade during the late Iron Age.

Trade and travel also brought to Greece another important invention, the Phoenician alphabet, which the Greeks adapted to their own language; this ended an almost four-hundred-year period of illiteracy. The development of Greek poetry paralleled advances in pottery and coincided with the invention of the Greek alphabet. The epic poems attributed to Homer, the earliest poetic texts in the Western tradition, appeared around the middle of the eighth century BCE. Although legend identifies Homer as a blind bard from Ionia, on the coast of modern-day Turkey, scholars continue to debate by whom, when, and where the *Iliad* and *Odyssey* were composed. The poems represent the culmination of an oral tradition that extended back into the late Bronze Age, but they do not directly reflect that early society. Instead, they involve a mix of language, cultural practices, and social structures from the late Bronze Age. The warrior society depicted in the poems revolves around a communal structure known as a kingdom, a simplified version of the Mycenaean kingdoms, over which a king rules, but with limited control. Because the office was hereditary, passing from father to son, one of the most important markers of social identity in the poems is the **patronym**, the use of the father's name to establish the importance of the hero. He must also possess courage in battle or **andreia** ("manliness") and the ability to persuade others, or as Homer puts it, he must be a "speaker of words and doer of deeds" (Hom. *Il.* 9.443). A competitive ethic governs the life of the king: his main objective is to compete and win, to "always be the best," whether in athletics or warfare. The hero thus continually engages in a struggle to win honor, the public recognition of his skills and achievement, often in the form of material goods. The Trojan warrior Glaucus reinforces the importance of these values when he relates the story of his ancestry to his Greek counterpart, Diomedes:

> But Hippolochus was my father, and I say that I was begotten by him, he sent me to Troy, and he ordered me often to always be the best and to be pre-eminent above all others, and not to disgrace the clan of my fathers, who were the best men by far in Ephyre and wide Lycia. I boast that I came from such a lineage and bloodline. (Hom. *Il.* 6.206–11)

As this passage indicates, the defining feature of Glaucus' identity is his paternal lineage, which, as we learn earlier in the speech, links him to the mythological past. Moreover, his father instilled in him the heroic values necessary to compete with others and ultimately enhance the reputation of his clan. A similar ideology is at work in the exchange between the Trojan hero, Hector, and his wife, Andromache, when he prays that his frightened baby son will someday become an outstanding warrior who will surpass even his father in excellence:

> Zeus and you other gods, grant that this my child become pre-eminent among the Trojans, as I am, and that he possess might and rule in strength over Ilion. And may someone one day say, "he is better by far than his father," as he goes into battle. And when he kills a man may he bear the bloody spoils and delight the heart of his mother. (Hom. *Il.* 6.476–80)

For these men, war represents the main way not only to surpass one's peers but also to transcend the human condition and achieve everlasting **kleos** ("glory") in the form of commemoration through poetry and funerary honor. The quest for immortality, whether through death in battle or philosophical reflection, is central to Greek constructions of masculinity. In contrast, the body, with its uncontrollable appetites and propensity for death, is always gendered as feminine. Unheroic or cowardly behavior invites comparison of the hero to a woman, as when a warrior in the *Iliad* rebukes the Greek army by calling them, "Weaklings, cowards worthy of reproach, you women, not men, of Achaia" (Hom. *Il.* 2.235). The importance of warfare for male identity and the gendering of the mind and soul as masculine and the body as feminine are themes that will recur in subsequent representations of women and gender in the Greek tradition.

By the end of the eighth century, Greek religion had assumed the form it would take throughout the rest of pagan antiquity. Some of the gods recorded in Linear B tablets disappeared while others were added, such as Aphrodite, the Greek version of the Near Eastern fertility goddess known variously as Ishtar, Astarte, and Inanna. The gods appear as fully developed characters in both the *Iliad* and the *Odyssey*, immersed in their own petty rivalries and intervening in squabbles among their mortal favorites. In another epic from the same period, the *Theogony*, the poet Hesiod sets forth the first comprehensive account of the gods, their origins, their powers, and their genealogies. The work, however, does not represent religious doctrine, but rather attempts to systematize a broad range of myths while telling an entertaining story. The centrality of the gods to eighth-century archaic epic shows that the pantheon at this time had become more or less fixed (see Chart 2.1).

A key difference between Greek religion and Christianity is its emphasis on practice rather than belief. The Greeks considered the correct performance of a ritual action more important than personal conviction about the existence of the gods and their powers. Further, they did not have a concept of a deity as a creative power but believed the cosmos, the earth, and its natural features all came about through acts of sexual reproduction, starting with the coupling of the earth and sky gods, Gaia and Uranus. Greek religion was polytheistic, involving the acknowledgment of many gods, all of whom correspond to a specific aspect of the natural world or represent a particular facet of human experience. Ares, for instance, as the war god encompasses the human impulse for violence and aggression; he is both a personification of warfare and a character capable of committing adultery with Aphrodite. The Greek gods are also anthropomorphic, that is, they look like mortals, possess human attributes, and behave as scandalously as, if not worse than, humans. To explain how they can occupy bodies and yet still be immortal, the Greeks attributed to them divine blood and a heavenly form of nourishment.

Chart 2.1 The Greek and Roman Gods.

Greek Name	Roman Name	Spheres
Apollo	Apollo	Sickness and healing, prophecy, music
Aphrodite	Venus	Female and male sexuality, female beauty
Ares	Mars	War, blood lust, aggression
Artemis	Diana	Wilderness, hunting, virginity, childbirth
Athena	Minerva	Weaving, military strategy, wisdom
Demeter	Ceres	Agriculture, grain, harvest cycle
Dionysus	Bacchus	Wine, vegetation, male fertility, madness
Hades	Pluto	Death, underworld, hidden wealth of the earth
Hephaestus	Vulcan	Fire, metalworking, craft
Hera	Juno	Monogamy, marriage
Hermes	Mercury	Messenger, trade, travel
Hestia	Vesta	Hearth, virginity
Poseidon	Neptune	Sea, earthquakes
Persephone	Proserpina	Underworld, vegetation
Zeus	Jupiter/Jove	Sky, weather, male fertility

The literary and visual traditions depict the gods as closely interacting with humans; indeed, many of the gods mate with humans and thus spawn mortal offspring, including important heroes like Achilles in the *Iliad*. The attributes and powers of deities usually reflect gender distinctions in the human sphere. Female deities tend to govern the female life cycle, from virginity to marriage, sexuality, and childbirth, as well as feminine realms and characteristics, such as the household, domesticity, and beauty.

2.3   The Rise of the *Polis* in the Archaic Period

By the beginning of the eighth century BCE, the ***polis*** ("city-state") had emerged as one of the most important achievements of the ancient Greeks. It was to serve as the model for social and political organization in Greece until the Roman period and as a political ideal for many nations after the decline of classical antiquity. In contrast to the earlier civilizations of the Near East, Egypt, and Bronze Age Greece, the polis was small in size and regionally based. The polis in its most basic form consisted of a community of adult male citizens, citizens without political rights such as women and children, and noncitizens such as foreigners and slaves. In contrast to Rome, the Greek polis was a relatively closed society, with little interest in assimilating outsiders. A clear expression of this idea is found in myths of autochthony, which depict the original inhabitants of a city, such as Thebes and Athens, as born directly from the earth. These stories legitimized a community's political control of geography by claiming descent from the land rather than by occupying it as settlers. The polis encompassed a defined geographical region that included a city and neighboring territory to form a single, self-governing unit. The city included a walled citadel, later called the ***acropolis***, and a central marketplace or ***agora***, where civic business was conducted. By modern standards, the size of the average polis was small, consisting of only a few thousand inhabitants. This scale allowed for its male citizens to engage in meaningful political activity at its center. Hundreds of independent city-states existed at any given time in ancient Greece, most quite small and many of them colonies, with the result that their institutions differed in significant ways. Nonetheless, a few generalizations are possible.

According to the historian Thucydides (c. 460–400 BCE), "men are the polis" (Thuc. 7.77.7). That is to say, the polis was a citizen-state to which the community of male citizens was central. At all periods, citizenship, defined as having a share in the public and religious life of the polis, was restricted to men. Women could not participate in public life, with one very important exception, religious activities, a point that is more fully developed in Chapter 7. Slaves occupied the bottom rung of society, and although they were excluded from many of the social and political institutions of the polis, they also could participate in communal religious life. Smaller networks of affiliation based on kinship, cult, and locality existed within the larger polis (see Chapter 3). The polis was thus not only a political community but a religious one as well, obligating its citizens to perform military and economic service to the state, to obey its laws and to worship its gods. The fierce spirit of independence that characterized each Greek polis meant that the main way the early city-states interacted was through regular warfare.

In the seventh century, many city-states underwent a brief period of tyranny in which one individual seized control of the government and ruled in defiance of existing laws. The tyrant maintained his power through force of arms and personality, although seldom for longer than two generations. And while the title originally did not have negative connotations, it eventually came to have strong pejorative associations as cities like Athens trended toward democracy. In the sixth century BCE, beneficent tyrants such as Pisistratus in Athens were responsible for instituting new public institutions that both honored the gods and fostered civic pride, such as the procession in honor of Athena called the ***Panathenaia*** and the dramatic festival known as the **City Dionysia** (see Box 4.1).

Another important development was the creation of a new military formation, the ***hoplite*** phalanx. Because hoplites had to finance their own equipment, which included a bronze helmet, body armor, greaves, and a shield, they symbolized the increasing wealth and power of the nonaristocratic class, particularly prosperous farmers and craftsmen. In battle, each hoplite used his own shield to protect his neighbor on the left side. This formation contrasted aristocratic fighting methods, which were highly individualistic, and, by extension, represented a rejection of aristocratic control in the polis. Although the wealthiest citizens continued to use expensive horses in warfare and the poor, unable to afford hoplite armor, served as light-armed troops or on warships, the hoplite became the dominant political symbol of the archaic period, as expressed by the lyric poet Tyrtaeus (seventh century BCE):

This is the common good both for the polis and the people, whenever a man stands in the forefront of battle without cease, and pays no heed at all to shameful escape, but rather emboldens his heart and soul with daring, and encourages his neighbor with words as he stands by. (Tyrt. Fr. 12.15–19 West)

Here the hoplite marks a cultural shift from an emphasis on individual valor and glory, as represented by the Homeric hero, to a more cooperative model of warfare that emphasized collective identity and eroded traditional distinctions of birth and wealth. This change in military practice points to a transition from oligarchy and tyranny to a more broad-based form of rule in which the majority of polis members participated and which would eventually evolve into a system of democratic government at Athens.

Another important development of the archaic period closely linked to the rise of the polis was the ***symposium*** or banquet. The symposium took place in the ***andron*** ("men's quarters"), where men in the family dined and entertained their male guests. There a visitor to the Greek house would encounter only male members of the family. When strangers entered, the women would retreat to the private parts of the house, possibly even to a women's quarters (see Chapter 3). The andron was the most lavishly decorated and expensively furnished room in the house. Closest to the entrance, it mediated the space between the household and the city. The typical layout accommodated several couches, on which male guests reclined, leaning on their left elbows, one or two to a couch (Figure 2.4). The symposium was regulated by a symposiarch who determined the quantity and the order of the drinking. The wine was diluted with water and served by slaves. The partygoers wore garlands on their heads as they listened to songs accompanied by the lyre or aulos (a flutelike reed instrument), watched performances of dancers and mimes or played drinking games.

The symposium was an aristocratic institution that served as a means of transmitting traditional values and promoting male homosocial and homoerotic bonds within the polis. Citizen women were not allowed to participate. Only female noncitizens, such as dancers, musicians, prostitutes, and courtesans, most of whom were slaves, could attend. One such woman is depicted in Figure 2.4. Standing unclothed between two couches, she plays the aulos as one of the celebrants reaches out to grope her at right. More is said about the lives of these women in Chapter 6. Even as males enjoyed the sexual services of these women, they also engaged in homoerotic activity among themselves. The mythic prototype was Ganymede, a boy so beautiful that Zeus abducted him and installed him at his court on Olympus to serve as his immortal wine-pourer. The Greeks used the word ***paiderastia*** ("boy love") to refer to the sexual pursuit of adolescent boys by adult men. They considered boys just before the growth of the first beard to be at their most attractive.

Figure 2.4 A female aulos-player entertains men at a symposium on this Attic red-figure kylix attributed to the Foundry Painter, c. 500–450 BCE. Cambridge, Fitzwilliam Museum, no. 204353.

Custom differentiated the sexual roles assigned to men and boys: the senior partner was called the subject of desire, ***erastes*** ("lover"), whereas the boy was considered the object of desire, ***eromenos*** ("beloved"). The youth determined whether to gratify his lover's sexual advances and might comply for a number of reasons, including material and social advancement. At the same time, he ran the risk of harming his reputation if he complied too readily, or for the wrong reasons. Like the symposium, this homoerotic form of engagement was highly ritualized, and scholars continue to debate its structure and social function. What is clear, however, is that sexual activity between older men and youths on the verge of adulthood was not only socially acceptable but also encouraged in certain contexts. Another venue that brought the two together was the gymnasium, an open space for exercise often located in connection with a sanctuary. It was not a gym or sports club in the modern sense but rather a place for education and intellectual exchange in addition to exercise. The institution of paiderastia can thus be understood as the product of a homosocial environment: Greek men spent most of their time together, whether in warfare, training in the gymnasium, or participating in the symposium, with few opportunities for contact with women of citizen status. The fact that the Athenian lawgiver Solon (c. 640–558 BCE) forbade male slaves to exercise in the gymnasium or to engage in homoerotic relationships attests to the importance of these activities for defining the social parameters of free male citizens in the Athenian polis.

Despite their divisiveness, the Greek city-states came together both through Panhellenic institutions, such as festivals, shrines, and oracles, and through their shared mythological and literary tradition. Delphi, home of the oracle of Apollo, represents one of the most important religious sites during the Archaic period, consulted throughout the ancient world by Greeks and foreigners alike, particularly for political advice. We meet its priestess, the Pythia, in Chapter 7. Beginning in the early eighth century BCE, athletic contests provided another opportunity for both individual competition and Panhellenic unity. The most famous occurred every four years at Olympia. Held over a period of five days, the festival required the cessation of all military activity and brought together hostile factions in a communal celebration of Olympian Zeus. These and other religious activities contributed to a shared Greek consciousness, despite the near continuous warfare among city-states.

2.4   Athens and the Classical Period

Whereas the development of the polis represents the crowning achievement of the archaic period, the invention of democracy at Athens marks the signal accomplishment of the subsequent epoch. This radical new form of government would have a lasting impact on Western civilization and still serves as an ideal for many nations today. Although tyrants ruled Athens throughout much of the sixth century, their reforms, patronage, and institutions paradoxically proved decisive for the democratic revolution that was to take place in 508 BCE at Athens. Three men in particular set in motion this momentous course of events. The Athenian poet, philosopher, and statesman Solon laid the foundation for democracy when he introduced reforms in 594 BCE aimed at reducing the power of the aristocracy and increasing the participation of citizens in the main political body, the **Assembly**. Another key reform was elimination of debt bondage, the practice of selling an individual into slavery as a form of repayment for a debt, in 594 BCE. According to the historian Herodotus (c. 484-425 BCE), soon after passing his laws, Solon left Greece for 10 years, visiting king Croesus in Sardis, to prevent the Athenians from repealing his legislation. Although his reforms ultimately failed, they were viewed both by successive generations of Athenians as well as modern-day scholars as important precursors to democratic society.

Another pivotal figure in the transition to democracy was the tyrant Pisistratus, who came to power about forty years after Solon's legislation and is known for his benevolent reign. Although Pisistratus was a successful ruler who aided the poor, built aqueducts and temples, and expanded civic festivals, particularly encouraging the development of drama, his tyranny deteriorated in the second generation, when his son Hippias came to power. This cruel regime incited a third important figure of this period, Cleisthenes, to take action. After overthrowing Hippias, he reorganized the Athenian government around city districts, called *demes*, rather than around aristocratic families, as it had in the past. From this point on, males used the name of their deme, in addition to the patronym to identify themselves. The effect of these reforms was to emphasize the importance of belonging to the city over the clan or family and to increase opportunities for political participation among nonaristocratic members of the polis.

Both the formation and dissolution of the Athenian empire was influenced by two major events that flank the fifth century: the Persian wars and the Peloponnesian war (see Timeline). Whereas the Persian invasion gave rise to a rare show of unity among the Greek city-states as they joined forces against a common enemy, the Peloponnesian war accomplished quite the opposite, pitting cities against one another and eventually weakening them. The Persian wars were a series of conflicts between east and west that began in 560 BCE, when Croesus ascended the throne at Lydia (in modern-day Turkey) and conquered the Greek cities along the coast of Asia Minor. Croesus was conquered by the Persian army, led by Cyrus the Great, as it moved westward and conquered lands that eventually extended as far away Babylon. Cyrus's son, Cambyses II, although less successful as a leader, nonetheless managed to annex Egypt. Under his successor, Darius I, the Persian Empire stretched from the Black Sea to the Persian Gulf and from the Mediterranean to the edge of India. Given the broad swath of territory under their control, it was inevitable that they would turn their gaze to Greece.

In 499 BCE, the revolt of the Greek city-states along the coast of Asia Minor provoked responses from both sides (see Map 1). The fierce independence of the Greek city-states compelled them to rebel from the crushing oppression of the Persian-appointed tyrants who ruled them. The Athenians soon entered the fray, routing the Persians at the battle of Marathon in 490 BCE with the help of their allies, the Plataeans. After this temporary victory, the Athenians, under the leadership of Themistocles, focused on strengthening their navy, a move that would prove decisive in their subsequent Persian encounters. In 480 BCE, Xerxes, the son of Darius, led a massive Persian force across the Hellespont, which connects the Aegean Sea to the sea of Marmara, and onto Greek soil with the intention of subjugating all of Greece. After key victories at Artemisium and Thermopylae, the army pressed forward and gained control of the Isthmus of Corinth, a situation that led many of the Greek city-states to defect to the side of Persia. Soon after, Themistocles lured the Persians into a naval battle at Salamis, where their multitude of ships were trapped in the narrow straits. Although vastly outnumbered, the Greeks triumphed, forcing Xerxes and his troops to retreat. After two other battles, the Greeks secured their victory over the Persians, which became a source of admiration and pride for generations to come.

Despite the fact that the Athenians and Spartans fought side by side in the Persian Wars, contributing to important Greek successes, within 50 years the two city-states were engaged in a devastating war that went on for almost three decades. A brief discussion of ancient Sparta and its unique social and political system will help us to understand the origins of this conflict as well as provide further insight into the construction of masculinity during the classical period. Located in the region of Laconia in the southern Peloponnese, ancient Sparta emerged as the dominant military power in this region around 650 BCE. From the beginning, its form of government was staunchly oligarchic, led by two hereditary kings with equal authority, and never adopted democratic ideals. The Spartans practiced a form of public slavery in which they subjugated their non-Spartan neighbors, called helots, to a life of physical labor, an arrangement that necessitated constant military vigilance to ensure internal political stability. The fear of helot uprisings transformed early Sparta, under the leadership of Lycurgus, into a regime quite different from that of other aristocratic city-states, particularly with regard to childrearing and education, institutions that in Sparta had the exclusive aim of preparing males for war. Indeed, only those men who had undergone a rigorous Spartan education could achieve citizenship status.

The process began at birth: sickly children were abandoned, often with the expectation that they would die. Those deemed worthy of survival underwent a strict regime intended to harden them against pain and suffering. Once a boy reached the age of 7, he entered the state-supervised educational system, where he underwent training to develop the skills necessary for a life of military service, including physical discipline and mental courage, in addition to music and poetry. A late anecdote, not to be taken too literally, suggests that even mothers had a role to play in instilling these core values in their sons:

> Another mother, when her sons had run away from battle and come to her, said, "Why have you come here having run away like common slaves? Or do you intend to crawl back in to your mother's womb from which you were born?' To emphasize her point, she hiked up her skirts and exposed herself to them. (Plut. *Mor.* 241b)

Upon reaching adulthood, Spartan males sought to be elected to a communal dining hall where they would take all of their meals with other men, as a sort of military camp. Husbands resided with their dining comrades, visiting their wives only at night under the cloak of secrecy. These arrangements point to a familial structure radically different from that of other city-states and a unique understanding of the role of women in their society, which is considered in more detail in the next chapter.

The triumph over the Persians inspired Greek confidence and emboldened the Athenians, in particular, to build and strengthen their power base by forming a league of Greek states to protect against further Persian incursions. In exchange, these city-states paid hefty taxes to Athens, with which they financed major architectural projects such as the rebuilding of the Acropolis, which had been devastated by the war. Even as Athens became increasingly imperialistic toward other city-states, at home its democratic form of government became more open to all classes of citizen men. Signs of this shift include the decline in political importance of the aristocratic council of Areopagus, the opening up of the office of chief magistrate or **archon** to any Athenian citizen and the introduction of pay for the performance of state duties, such serving on a jury. The net effect of these reforms meant that an increasingly wider sector of society could participate in governance. A popular leader of the time, Pericles, also enhanced the prestige of Athens and inspired patriotism during the 15 years he served as general by rebuilding important buildings, such as the Parthenon on the Acropolis and the temple of Poseidon at Sounion, as well as by promoting new learning and ideas through the teachings of the sophists. In the words of Thucydides, the Athenian system of government under Pericles served as "a model to others," respected for the values of equality, tolerance, and respect for the laws.

Despite this ideology, Athens was becoming increasingly aggressive toward other city-states, particularly Sparta. Their constant struggle for control of central Greece led to a treaty in 445 BCE, but it was short lived. Athens continued to press for supremacy, subjecting its allies to increasingly restrictive measures aimed at collecting tribute and forcing them to use Athenian measures and coinage. This arrogant foreign policy finally provoked the Spartans to break the truce and wage war on Athens with the help of their allies. Just after the war started, however, a mysterious plague hit Athens in successive waves between 430 and 427 BCE, killing a third of its population, including Pericles. The loss of his leadership sparked a downward political spiral from which Athens never really recovered, as unscrupulous politicians vied for the popular vote and eventually lost control over internal affairs. A failed military expedition to Sicily in 415 BCE, followed by the revolt of many allies, further weakened the polis, with the result that the city eventually capitulated to the Spartans in 404 BCE.

These historical events help to explain Athenian expectations about manhood during the classical period. First of all, democratic reforms reconfigured male social identity along political lines, reducing the importance of birth and genealogy. Second, warfare was a predominant feature of life for all citizen males, and sometimes even for male slaves. Lastly, Athenian imperialism required absolute loyalty to the aims and goals of the polis on the part of male citizens in exchange for its freedoms and protections. Herodotus provides insight into these values in his account of an exchange between Solon and the Lydian king Croesus. After displaying the magnificent treasures of the palace, Croesus asks his guest:

> Athenian friend, we have heard a lot about you because of your wisdom and your wanderings, how as one who loves learning you have traveled much of the world for the sake of seeing it. Now I desire to ask you, "Who is the happiest man you have seen?" Croesus asked this question expecting that he was the happiest of men, but Solon, refusing to flatter him, told him the truth, "O King, it is Tellus the Athenian." Croesus was taken aback at what he had said and replied sharply, "Why do you think Tellus to be the happiest?" And Solon said, "Tellus was from a prosperous city and his children were good and noble. He saw children born to them all and all of these survived. His life was prosperous by our standards and his death was most glorious: when the Athenians were fighting their neighbors in Eleusis, he came to their aid, routed the enemy and died very finely. The Athenians buried him at public expense on the spot where he fell and gave him much honor." (Hdt. 1.30)

With his question, the king fishes for a compliment, but Solon refuses take the bait. Instead, he singles out an obscure citizen of good birth, who exemplifies, anachronistically, classical Athenian values. Tellus prizes his polis above all, to the point that he is willing to sacrifice his life for it. He has sired male children who will ensure the continuity of his family line. In exchange for courage in battle, he receives eternal recognition from the Athenians in the form of a funerary monument. Tellus's life contrasts the materialism of the Persians and their monarchical system of rule, in which all the wealth accrues to one man, with the collective and democratic values of the Athenians, who emphasize honor, patriotism, and valor, rather than wealth. When Croesus goes on to ask who the second happiest man is, Solon adduces the example of Cleobis and Biton, brothers who died after hauling their mother to a religious festival in a wagon. This second story adds another value to the mix, respect for the gods. From Solon's speech, which imbues an archaic leader with contemporary values, we can infer that male identity in classical Athens derived from citizen status combined with birth, heroic action on behalf of the polis and piety.

One last facet of male identity not mentioned in this account but important for understanding both Greek and later Roman conceptions of gender was self-control, or mastery over the emotions and the body. Although this idea is first developed most fully in Greek philosophical and legal treatises during the fourth century BCE, it has its roots in heroic conceptions of the body, suffering, and death, as found in the *Iliad*. Surprising from a modern standpoint is the connection between sexual morality and political ideology. For instance, a male citizen who had prostituted himself could not legally participate in civic life because he allowed his body to be used by others. Because such men lacked sexual self-control, they could not be entrusted with managing the city's affairs. The *Symposium* of Plato (c. 429–347 BCE) further illustrates the importance of mind over body in its portrait of the philosopher, Socrates, who exhibits such self-control that he appears immune to all physical discomfort, the disorienting effects of wine, and even erotic desire. The privileging of mind over body evident in philosophical works had important implications for conceptions of the female, as we see in subsequent chapters.

Although democratic ideology dictated civic and martial values in the classical polis, the images of masculinity encountered in popular entertainment, such as the theater, often contradicted them. Tragedy was introduced into Athens around 535 BCE under the rule of the tyrant Pisistratus in the form of the City Dionysia, an annual five-day festival in honor of the god Dionysus (see Box 4.1). Recently it has been argued that the invention of theater coincided with the democratic revolution in 508 BCE. Either way, the development of tragedy paralleled democratic reforms and the rise of Athenian imperialism. The festival involved various religious and civic ceremonies, including processions, choral performances, and parades. Only men seem to have attended, with the possible exception of priestesses and courtesans. Scholars in recent years have called attention to the political aspects of the festival; seating seems to have been assigned by political district, whereas the clever rhetoric of tragic characters had parallels in the assembly and law courts. In both theater and government spheres, Athenians were "spectators of speeches."

The theater can also be understood as a large-scale, public version of the symposium, a ritualized form of male recreation in honor of Dionysus where poetry served to transmit and reinforce traditional values. But the male characters the spectators encountered on the Athenian stage were often far from heroic in the Homeric sense: in tragedies like *Oedipus the King* by Sophocles (c. 497–406 BCE), the title character learns he has killed his father and committed incest with his mother; in the final scene, he gouges out his eyes with his wife's brooch pins. Aeschylus (c. 525–456 BCE) in *Agamemnon* portrays the king being stabbed to death in the bath by his wife upon his return from the Trojan War. At the end of *Medea* by Euripides (c. 480–406 BCE), we hear how the great hero, Jason, who captured the golden fleece, will die when a chunk of the rotting ship that made him a hero falls off and hits him on the head. None of this fits with the heroic model, nor does it exemplify the civic values praised by Solon. Although the purpose of and meanings of these representations of masculinity continue to be debated by scholars, they do suggest that Greek tragedy may have served as a safety valve, allowing the male spectators the opportunity to experience unmasculine emotions in a ritual environment.

The story of Greek civilization does not end with the classical period but rather continues on for several hundred more years, even under Roman rule. We return to the subject in Chapter 8, when we look more closely at the Hellenistic era and its function as a bridge between Greek and Roman cultures.

2.5   Conclusion

This brief summary attempts to outline the major historical events of Greek civilization, beginning with its origins in the Bronze Age, and to convey some basic ideas of masculinity. At all periods, the warrior, whether the Homeric hero or a hoplite soldier, represented the ideal for Greek men. Such an individual might come from an aristocratic family, could command great wealth in the form of property, and exerted authority over all of the members of his household. His task was to die a glorious death on the battlefield and to achieve everlasting fame for either himself or his polis. As a citizen, he participated in the city's business, a task that became increasingly important with the advent of democracy at Athens. During the classical period, moral qualities such as self-control also served to distinguish free Greek males from women, slaves, and foreigners. Through the domestic labor of his wife and slaves, he had the leisure to engage in his city's political life and to enjoy drinking parties and the theater, among other pursuits, largely apart from the company of respectable women. Of course, this picture of Greek manhood derives from elite literary sources such as epic and tragedy, and especially philosophy, which had little interest in portraying the average person. The reality was certainly more complex, and possibly more colorful, than we can even imagine.

Questions for Review

1   How did climate and geography influence the development of Greek civilization?

2   What was the polis?

3   What attributes and values were important for Greek men?

4   What are some of the characteristics of Greek religion?

5   What was the symposium and what values did it instill?

Reference

Bachofen, Johann Jakob (1992). *Myth, Religion, and Mother Right.* trans. R. Manheim. Princeton, NJ: Princeton University Press.

Further Reading

Primary Sources

Homer, *Iliad*
Plato, *Symposium*

Secondary Sources

Burkert, Walter (1985). *Greek Religion*. Cambridge, MA: Harvard University Press.
  A comprehensive treatment of ancient Greek religion from 800 to 300 BCE that deals with a
  number of complex issues such as beliefs about the dead, mystery religions, and civic festivals.
Dover, Kenneth (1989). *Greek Homosexuality: Updated and with a New Postcript*. Cambridge, MA:
  Harvard University Press.
  A landmark study that explores Greek views of homosexuality and establishes the framework for
  understanding the cultural institution of *paederastia*.
Finley, Moses (2002). *The World of Odysseus*. New York: New York Review of Books (a new edition
  of the original work published in 1954).
  An influential account of the representation of Iron Age society in the Homeric poems, covering
  ancient economics, the household and family, and morals and values.
Hansen, Moses Herman (2006). *Polis: An Introduction to the Ancient Greek City-State*. New York:
  Oxford University Press.
  Focusing on Athens, this introduction to the ancient Greek city-state covers its emergence, size,
  and population, along with its political organization.
Hanson, Victor (2006). *Wars of the Ancient Greeks*. New York: Harper Perennial.
  Provides an accessible discussion of Greek beliefs about warfare, the type of weapons and
  equipment they used, and the major battles fought. Includes many illustrations.
Hobden, Fiona (2013). *The Symposion in Ancient Greek Society and Thought*. Cambridge:
  Cambridge University Press.
  Explores the cultural phenomenon of the ancient Greek drinking party through its visual and
  literary representations. Chapter 4 includes a discussion of the symposium and political life.
Olsen, Barbara (2014). *Women in Mycenaean Greece. The Linear B Tablets from Pylos and Knossos*.
  London and New York: Routledge.
  Examines the role of women in the social structure of two Mycenaean communities, Pylos and
  Knossos, as reflected in Linear B tablets, focusing on their labor and control over property.
Pomeroy, Sarah, Burstein, Stanley, Donlan, Walter, and Roberts, Jennifer (1999). *Ancient Greece: A
  Political, Social, and Cultural History*. Oxford and New York: Oxford University Press.
  A chronological and comprehensive account of ancient Greek history from the Bronze Age to
  Alexander the Great that attempts to capture its complexity and variety. Integrates recent
  research in archeology, anthropology, and social history into a traditional historical narrative.

3

The Greek Family and Household

> It is more honorable for a woman to remain indoors rather than to be outside, but for the man it is more shameful to remain indoors than to take care of affairs outside the house.
>
> (Xen. *Oec.* 7.30.6–31.1)

What was it like to grow up female in ancient Greece? For girls, as for boys, gender expectations shaped every facet of experience. Although brothers and sisters mingled and played together in their earliest years, enjoying many of the same toys and games, their paths quickly diverged as they learned the skills and behaviors necessary to assume their adult roles. As the opening passage suggests, men and women occupied distinct spheres where they perform gender-differentiated tasks: women belonged to the house and family and men to the outside world. Males separated from the house through rituals of political affiliation and incorporation, athletic participation and, eventually, military service, and females remained mostly at home, close to the family and domestic concerns. Thus both inside and outside of the house gender served as a way to reinforce social hierarchies and boundaries. This chapter first explores the structure of the ancient Greek family and the organization of domestic space to understand the ideology of physical separation for women and its influence on gender-differentiated labor within the family. It then looks at textile manufacture as the primary domestic task for women, its contribution to the household economy, and the significance of weaving in literature. As a fundamental female activity, woolworking comes to represent in myth and literature a symbolic form of empowerment that enables women to help or harm those closest to them. The remainder of the chapter focuses on recovering from scattered and fragmentary evidence the lived realities of girls in ancient Greece and the ritual activities in which they participated.

It has been argued that that concept of childhood is a particularly modern, Western notion. To be sure, few representations of children and childhood are found in the ancient world. Nonetheless, it is clear that both the ancient Greeks and the Romans recognized childhood as a distinct life stage. Children underwent birth rituals that recognized their membership in the family, played with special toys and miniature versions of adult objects, and wore distinctive clothing and ornaments. Funerary archeology and visual evidence allow us to identify the following four preadult stages: infancy from birth to the third year; young childhood from the fourth to around the seventh year; older childhood until puberty; and adolescence, which began at the onset of puberty, probably around age 13 or 14 for girls. During each of these periods, ancient Greek children "learned" gender.

Women in Classical Antiquity: From Birth to Death, First Edition. Laura K. McClure.
© 2020 John Wiley & Sons, Inc. Published 2020 by John Wiley & Sons, Inc.

3.1 *Oikos*: Family and Household

The ancient Greek definition of the family is broad and often hard to pin down. The main term the Greeks used for family is ***oikos***. It includes not only human beings but also property and therefore is best translated as "household" or "estate." The oikos refers to a group of people related by blood, marriage, and adoption and to the property held by the family. A main difference between the term oikos and the modern, Western model of the nuclear family is that it includes human and nonhuman possessions. Slaves were not considered members of the family but rather formed part of the property of the oikos. Their contributions to its labor are discussed more fully at the end of this section. Freed men and women could also reside in the household of their former masters. The aim of the household was economic self-sufficiency through the production and processing of raw materials into goods to be used by the family or traded for what they could not produce for themselves at home.

According to Aristotle, quoting Hesiod, the oikos consists of "a house, a woman, and an ox for ploughing" (Arist. *Pol.* 1252b10–12). In other words, the main purpose of the oikos was economic, to provide sustenance for the family through the raising of food and the acquisition and management of possessions. The productive aspects of the oikos can be seen in the derivation of the English word "economics" from the Greek *oikonomikos*, which means "management of the household." The social structure of the household was hierarchical: the male head had authority over everyone within the oikos in his capacity as father, husband, and slave master. Through him, the oikos was linked to the polis and its various forms of male affiliation. He also connected the female members of the household to the city as their **kyrios** ("guardian"), because his wife and daughters could not legally represent themselves. The term, however, did not designate a formal assignment or permanent role but rather empowered the man to serve as the mediator between the private life of the household and the public world of politics. In this regard, the guardian did not possess the legal or social authority of the Roman head of household and thus did not have the right of life or death over the free members of his household.

The oikos was permanent, whereas its members were transient. The composition of the family was constantly changing. Girls separated from their natal families upon marriage around the age of 14, whereas boys remained in the paternal oikos. When sons married, new women joined their household. Whereas the groom normally remained in his ancestral home, women lived out their lives in two or more households and may have been perceived as outsiders. It was not uncommon for three generations to live in the same house. The oikos continued only through marriage and the production of legitimate children, preferably males, because familial descent was traced through the father and property was directly inherited only by sons. On her marriage, a daughter received a dowry, which represented her share of the estate. The dowry could be used to attract a husband and also provided economic leverage within the marriage, because it had to be returned to the woman's family if the marriage did not work out. It is estimated that approximately two-thirds of households contained up to two children, and about a third, three to four. Large nuclear families were thus a rarity during the classical period. We have evidence of very few families that raised more than one daughter.

Membership in the oikos took several forms, all of which were geared toward its perpetuation. The formal recognition and acceptance of the newborn child into the oikos by the male head of household represented the first step in granting membership in the family for both boys and girls. The next step was a ritual that involved carrying the baby around the hearth. A lack of male offspring created a crisis for the family because it posed inheritance problems and introduced the possibility that the oikos could die out. Solutions included the adoption of a male heir or the marriage of daughters to the nearest male relative on the paternal side. Adoption was less common in archaic and classical Athens than among the Romans. Adopted sons in Greece had less control over their father's estate than biological sons in that they could not make a will.

Despite the overwhelming preference for boys in ancient Greece, a daughter could provide an important safety net for her family's property in the event that no sons were born or they did not survive. Upon the death of her father, such a daughter was designated an *epikleros*, a term that means "attached to the estate." Although a daughter could not legally inherit her father's wealth, she could transmit it to another. Athenian law required that the male guardian of a fatherless daughter, usually a paternal uncle or other close kin, marry her or arrange for her marriage to another. In turn, her sons from this marriage would inherit her father's estate. The institution of epikleros thus had two functions: to ensure that fatherless daughters, rich or poor, married and to make possible the transmission of the oikos when there was a break in the family line. A better insurance policy for the continuation of the household was the birth of a son and few families would have greeted an epikleros with much enthusiasm. The oikos thus served as a mechanism for perpetuating the paternal line and ensuring its permanence. Without the birth of male children, the family could vanish and the oikos expire. One of the worst imprecations that could be uttered against an opponent in the Athenian law court was the wish that his oikos die out.

For Aristotle, the oikos represents the building block of the polis (Arist. *Pol.* 1253b.2–3), but it is prior and more necessary (Arist. *Eth. Nic.* 1162a17–19). That is, the oikos is the most basic social unit required for human survival, and without it, there can be no larger human community. It intersected with the polis during the classical period in several important ways. First, the household belonged to the larger kinship group represented by *genos* that included not just the nuclear family but also more distantly related family members, all tracing their lineage back to a single ancestor and potentially comprising several households. After a male baby was accepted into his father's oikos, he was introduced to the genos. Later, he needed to gain admission to his local political association, the *phratry* ("brotherhood") and deme, both inherited through the father. Admission to these two groups amounted to a public declaration of the boy's legitimacy and represented the first step in gaining citizenship status in Athens. The father enrolled his young son, as a toddler and perhaps again at 16, into the phratry, acknowledging him to be legitimate and his own, and presented him as part of the annual festival of Apatouria. Conversely, the city had a vested interest in perpetuating the oikos because of its religious role in maintaining family cult.

Girls in classical Athens were largely excluded from this process, with the result that the social identity of male and female children began to diverge at around age six. Although there is some evidence that girls could be presented to the phratry, they were not registered with the deme. Their citizen status would thus be known only to family members and to other women in the community. The girl's identity in turn revolved around the oikos: she became a member of the oikos at the hearth, in the presence of family and close friends. Boys, on the other hand, underwent additional ceremonies witnessed by a larger group of unrelated or loosely related adult males as they gradually gained citizen status. The fact that girls did not undergo as many rituals of incorporation during childhood as their brothers suggests a weaker bond to the paternal oikos, allowing them to transition more easily to the homes of their husbands upon marriage.

3.2 Greek Domestic Space

Although ancient Greek houses lacked the sumptuousness and ostentation of aristocratic Roman villas, those of wealthy families sought to organize their space with a view to gender. Houses were small, usually no more than 800 square feet. A single entrance led to a series of rooms organized around a central, unroofed interior courtyard. The entryway restricted access to the house and the organization of interior space facilitated the separation of the sexes. Athenian literary sources from the classical period repeatedly refer to the physical separation of elite women within a specific sector of the house, called the **gynaikonitis.** The main purpose of this arrangement was to prevent the household's women – daughters and wives and even female slaves – from sexual contact with unrelated males. One source describes the illicit intrusion of a drunken man into this space, "breaking down the door, he entered the women's quarters: within were my sister and nieces, who have lived such orderly lives that they were ashamed to be seen even by their own male relatives" (Lys. 3.6). In the gynaikonitis, elite citizen women worked and slept together with their female slaves. When Ischomachus in a treatise on household economy by Xenophon (c. 430–354 BCE) shows his bride around her new home, he describes this segregated space:

> The bedroom, because in a secure spot, called for the most valuable bedding and furniture, while the dry storage rooms are appropriate for grain, the cool ones for wine, and the bright ones for whatever products and utensils require light. Then I showed her the living rooms designed to be cool in the summer and warm in the winter. And I pointed out to her that the whole house has its front facing south, so that it was clearly sunny in the winter and shaded in the summer. I also showed her the women's quarters, separated from the men's by a bolted door, so that nothing should be carried outside from within that should not and so that the slaves would not procreate without our knowledge. (Xen. *Oec.* 9.3–5)

In this account, the interior bedroom serves as the bridal chamber for the newly married pair; later, the couple typically slept apart, with the wife occupying the separate women's quarters with her female servants. It is noteworthy that gender trumps free status as the most important criterion for determining the organization of domestic space. In Xenophon's account, the first floor contains both the andron and the gynaikonitis. He specifies that the door between these two spaces includes a lock to prevent the slaves from sleeping together without their owner's permission. The movements of Ischomachus' wife, in contrast, are not restricted to this quarter but extend throughout the spaces of the house, unless, one presumes, other men are present.

The orator Lysias (c. 445–380 BCE) also describes a women's quarters as separate from that of men and located on the second story of Euphiletus' house:

> My house occupies two floors: the upper floor, which contains the women's quarters, is the same size as the lower, with the men's quarters. When a child was born to us, his mother breastfed him. So that she might not run the risk of going downstairs every time she had to give him a bath, I myself took over the upper story and let the women have the ground floor. (Lys. 1.9)

With the birth of their first child, Euphiletus relocates his wife and her quarters to the first floor. Although intended to address the needs of the new mother, this exchange actually facilitates his wife's adultery by allowing easy access to her lover. This passage further indicates that the division of the house into male and female areas may have been temporary and not necessarily an architectural feature of the Greek house.

Clear evidence of a dedicated space set aside for women in the Greek house has not been corroborated by the archeological record. We cannot know for certain whether women occupied the second story, as in the case of Euphiletus' wife, because such a space would have been constructed of wood and therefore is not preserved. The diagram of a Greek house from the

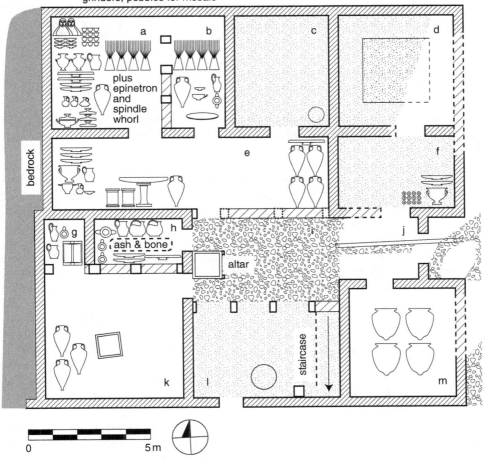

rooms under construction:
amphoras of sand and lime;
red and blue pigment &
grinders; pebbles for mosaic

plus
epinetron
and
spindle
whorl

bedrock

ash & bone

altar

staircase

0   5 m

Figure 3.1 Diagram of the House of Many Colors, in the villa section of Olynthos, c. 432–348 BCE. *Source:* Courtesy of Nicholas Cahill.

late fifth- or early fourth-century BCE from Olynthos (Figure 3.1), a town in central Macedon, seems to indicate a specialized female space. The rooms at the upper left contain weaving utensils, a special type of vase used for women in carding wool, called an epinetron (see Box 3.1), and a couple of other vases featuring women's scenes. These objects suggest that this space may have constituted the women's quarters, although we cannot be sure. The persistence of references to a women's quarters in a wide variety of literary contexts suggests, however, that it was a well-known and desirable feature of domestic space for elite Athenians of the classical period. Indeed, it would have been a sign of great wealth and high status for a citizen to be able to provide a dedicated space for the women of his family. But it was probably more common for domestic spaces to serve a variety of purposes. Individual rooms could thus be repurposed according to the family's needs. When male guests entered the oikos, for instance, a segregated space for women could be achieved through the strategic placement of textiles or other coverings and then converted back again to a more public space after their departure. Whether or not the gynaikonitis actually existed, the literary allusions reflect an ideology of spatial separation for well-born women and a widespread association of females with the inside of the oikos. Indeed, interior space is always gendered as feminine in both the literary and artistic traditions, where women are depicted as engaging in female activities such as wool working, adornment, and childcare.

3.3   Textile Production: Women's Work

> A home is required for the rearing of infant children, and a home is required for making food out of the harvest. Similarly a home is required for the making of cloth from wool. (Xen. *Oec.* 7.21)

Because respectable women in the archaic and classical periods spent the majority of their time inside the house, their labor took place indoors, in contrast to that of adult males, whose work took them outside, whether in the form of farming, politics, or warfare. As stated previously, the main aim of the oikos was economic. Before exploring the mechanics of textile production and its symbolic meanings, it is necessary to understand ancient attitudes toward labor. Both Greece and Rome were slave societies whose economies depended upon unfree labor. Freedom from the compulsion to work distinguished upper-class free citizens from everyone else. At the bottom were the slaves who served them, followed by free individuals forced to earn a living through trade and other pursuits. Within this economic structure, respectable citizen women contributed their work as household managers, caregivers, and most important, textile workers, providing men with the leisure to pursue other things. The production and management of cloth constituted the primary form of both domestic and commercial labor for women of all social classes in ancient Greece. Although men manufactured certain types of industrial cloth, such as sails for ships, women almost without exception controlled cloth production within the oikos and managed the circulation of woven objects inside and outside of the house in literary and artistic representations.

The virgin goddess Athena governed the art of weaving in female life, as well as the military sphere of men. An Athenian inscription from a dedication to the goddess after 350 BCE attests to weaving as one of the few commercial skills by means of which women could earn a living:

> By her handiwork and skill, and with just daring, Melinna raised her children and set up this memorial to you, Athena, goddess of handiwork, a share of the possessions she has won, in honor of your favor. (*CEG* 774)

The making of textiles was one of the most important contributions made by women to the oikos in ancient Greece. It involved a multistage and often physically demanding process that began with the cleaning and combing of raw wool that was then spun into thread and woven into finished garments. Women fashioned all of the garments worn by the members of their family, as well as household textiles. Textiles could also represent a form of portable female wealth as they featured prominently in the trousseaux girls brought with them when they married. One non-Athenian law from Gortyn on the island of Crete even stipulates that upon divorce a woman was entitled to take with her half of whatever she had woven during her marriage when she left her husband's house. In Athens, however, textiles produced by women became the property of the oikos (Xen. *Mem.* 2.7.7–10).

A black-figure lekythos (Figure 3.2) shows women engaged in various stages of textile production (see also Box 3.1). To the right, a woman spins wool into a fine thread using a distaff,

spindle, and whorl while her companion produces a coarser thread with a primitive distaff, drawing the combed wool from the wool basket at their feet. The other two women at left fold the finished cloth and place it on a low stool. On the other side of the vase (not shown), two women work at an upright loom. Weights tied to the bottom, which archeologists have found in abundance in the excavation of Greek houses, hold down the ends of the warp threads. Loom weights were of such personal value that women seem to have taken them with them when they married. One woman separates the warp threads with a heddle rod while her companion runs the weft threads through with a shuttle. The finished portion of the textile is then rolled up at the top of the loom. The small size of the weavers in comparison to the other female figures may suggest their status as domestic slaves. If you look closely at the shoulder of the vase, you will see four maidens holding hands and dancing, engaged in a sort of choral performance associated with female adolescence, as we see in the next chapter.

In the comedy *Lysistrata*, the title character gives a detailed description of textile manufacture and uses it as a metaphor for achieving political unity in democratic Athens during a period of dissension:

> Imagine the polis as a newly shorn fleece. First, put it in a bath, and wash out all the dung; spread it on a bed and beat out the scoundrels with a stick and pick out the burrs. As for those who clump and knot themselves together to gain government positions, card them out and pluck off their heads. Then comb everything into a wool basket of unity and goodwill, mixing in everyone ... So take all these flocks and bring them together here, joining them all and making one great ball. And from this weave a fine new cloak for the people. (Ar. *Lys.* 573–86)

Box 3.1 Athenian Vases

As one of the most extensive and well preserved of all of the artistic media from ancient Greece, Athenian figured pottery offers a rich resource for the study of women, gender, and sexuality. The genre is particularly important for our subject because the vases contain a large number of representations of women participating in familiar everyday activities often too mundane to occasion comment in literature, such as fetching water, dressing, wool working, infant care, and performing rituals related to weddings and funerals. Although in some ways these images seem far more accessible to the modern viewer than literary texts, their interpretation is in fact complex. Take, for example, the vase by the Amasis painter discussed previously (Figure 3.2). Although it appears to be a fairly straightforward depiction of women engaged in textile manufacture, the vase tells us nothing about its context. Are the smaller figures slaves or children? Is this a genre scene of women's daily work or ritual girl weavers preparing the Panathenaic peplos, as perhaps indicated by the enthroned goddess on the shoulder? Both arguments have been advanced but there is no scholarly consensus.

As noted earlier, ceramic production characterizes every period of Greek civilization, extending as far back as the Minoans. The bulk of surviving Athenian vases belong to the archaic and classical periods and conform to one of two styles, called black- and red-figure painting. Both types of vases were made of iron-rich clay that turned a deep orange-red when fired. The paint consisted of the same type of clay thinned out with water. Black-figure painters outlined their scenes on the surface of the vases, filled them in with the clay paint, and then incised details with a sharp instrument. The red-figure technique, introduced around 530 BCE, involved a reverse process: the painter first outlined his figures, then painted in interior lines and filled in the background. When fired, the surface paint remained black while the unpainted background turned orange. Vases were produced for domestic use, for dedication at sanctuaries and for funerary ritual, to be placed on tombs or in graves alongside the deceased. Before 500 BCE, we find few domestic scenes or representations of women; when evident, they normally adorn vase shapes associated with women (Figure 3.3), such as the *loutrophoros* ("ritual water holder") used for weddings, and the *epinetron*, which women wore over their thighs to protect them while carding wool. The *hydria* ("water vessel") often represents women drawing water at the fountain house. Images of wives and courtesans proliferate in the early fifth century. The *pyxis* ("cosmetic jar") shows images of women connected with beauty and adornment. Later in the century, painters attempted to attract a female market by depicting female rituals as well as mythological and garden scenes. Another important vase for the study of women and gender is the white-ground *lekythos* used in funerary ritual and produced in large numbers between 470 and 420 BCE. Many of these depict female figures visiting a tomb, usually an adult woman with a smaller figure, either a child or servant.

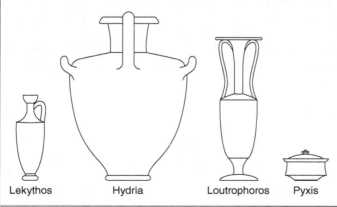

Figure 3.3 These vase types are all vessels associated with women's ritual and domestic activities. *Source*: Smith and Plantzos (2012), Figure 3.1.

Lekythos   Hydria   Loutrophoros   Pyxis

This description parallels the process of textile production depicted on the vase discussed previously, from the cleaning of raw wool, to carding and combing in preparation for spinning thread and finally, the weaving of finished cloth.

Girls learned aspects of wool preparation and weaving at an early age and assisted their mothers in the manufacture the clothing worn by the members of their oikos. Because work at the standing loom required strength and dexterity, some scholars believe that girls did not contribute to the large-scale manufacture of cloth until the age of 11 or 12. They may have practiced making smaller, sometimes even elaborate, weavings on miniature, hand-held looms. This skill allowed them to participate in civic rituals such as the Arrhephoria, discussed later, and prepared them for the management of their own households as married women. In Greek literature, scraps of cloth woven by girls often serve as the basis for the recognition of long-lost relatives. In Aeschylus' *Libation Bearers* (458 BCE), for instance, the adolescent Electra becomes convinced of her brother's identity only when he shows her the patterned piece of cloth she wove for him as a young girl: "And see this piece of weaving, the work of your hand, the strokes of the batten and the beasts in the design. Control yourself! Do not go mad with joy!" (Aesch. *Cho.* 231–3). In an emotional scene of reunion in Euripides' *Ion* (414–13 BCE), a bit of cloth similarly authenticates the identity of a mother to the son she had abandoned at birth:

CREUSA: Look! The textile that I wove as a girl!
ION: What sort? Maidens weave many things.
CREUSA: Unfinished, a sort of practice piece from the loom...
ION: What is its shape? You will not trick me in this way.
CREUSA: A Gorgon in the middle threads of the robe...
ION: O Zeus, what fate hunts me down!
CREUSA: Edged with snakes, like an aegis.
ION: Look! This is the robe, we are discovering the oracle.
CREUSA: O long lost weaving of my girlhood! (Eur. *Ion* 1417–1425)

These two passages suggest that young girls learned the art of weaving at home and could even produce quite elaborate textiles showing animal figures and characters from mythology. They practiced their craft with such pieces before they were deemed ready to produce full-scale garments for their households. The importance of training girls in wool working is attested by another passage from Xenophon, where the speaker describes his new bride's skills, "Are you not content that she had come to me knowing only how to take wool and produce a cloak, and had seen how the wool-spinning is distributed to the maids?" (Xen. *Oec.* 7.6).

Greek mythology is full of stories in which women's weaving features prominently. Textiles created and circulated by women have an ambiguous symbolic status, sometimes beneficial to men, at other times deadly. In Homer's *Odyssey*, women's work has a positive value, suggesting industry, intelligence, and marital fidelity. Penelope remains faithful to her absent husband for 20 years by weaving a funerary garment for her father-in-law. By means of this stratagem, which we discuss more fully in Chapter 5, she successfully manages to keep other men at bay until her husband returns. Women are also depicted as giving gifts of textiles to guests as signs of friendship and to foster ties between unrelated households. Helen offers to Odysseus' son, Telemachus, the most beautiful and largest of the richly patterned garments she has woven, the one that "shone like a star" (Hom. *Od.* 15.109). Such highly skilled work brought kleos to women in the same way as victory in battle to men. Clothing fashioned by women serves another positive social function as the signifier of male identity in the world beyond the oikos. So Odysseus' fine tunic and cloak bear his wife's unmistakable signature, as Penelope exclaims, "I myself gave him this clothing, which you describe; I folded it in my chamber, and I too attached the shining pin, as an ornament" (Hom. *Od.* 19.255–7). The hero's clothing in turn advertises to the world the wealth and status of his household and the skill of its women in producing it.

As remarked in the opening chapter, different literary genres provide divergent views of the same subject. In contrast to epic, women's textiles in Greek tragedy often have sinister associations, even serving as instruments of murder and revenge. We take a closer look at many of these plays in Chapter 6. For instance, the queen Clytemnestra wraps her husband in a large piece of cloth before killing him, declaring "I cast around him a garment entangling like a fishing net, an evil wealth of cloth, so that he would not be able to flee or ward off death" (Aesch. *Ag.* 1381–3). Similarly, Heracles dies as a result of contact with a garment onto which his wife, Deianira, has rubbed what she believes to be a love potion but what turns out instead to be a corrosive poison (see Box 6.1). The sorceress Medea also uses a garment infused with a terrible toxin to kill her rival, her faithless husband's new bride. After trying on the gifts of a crown and dress sent by Medea and admiring herself in the mirror, the young wife suddenly cries out in pain:

> The golden wreath around her head shot forth a terrible stream of all-devouring fire, and the finely woven dress, the gift of your children, was eating away at the pale flesh of the wretched girl. She stood up and fled, all on fire, shaking her hair this way and that to put out the flames. (Eur. *Med.* 1186–91)

In all of these contexts, textiles represent a negative form of female agency; instead of strengthening ties between members of the oikos and forging ties with others, as in Homer, they destroy the family and its reputation. The symbolic power of wool working is also seen in the myth of the three Fates, who determine each individual life span at birth. Clotho spins the thread, Lachesis weaves it into a piece of cloth that determines the pattern of destiny, and Atropos tears it apart at death. It has been suggested that this myth arose from the practice of female attendants at work at their spinning while their mistresses labored in childbirth.

Female slaves assisted citizen women, even those in modest households, with their daily domestic duties. Slavery was a fact of Greek life during all periods. They were typically foreigners, often the captives of war. Removed from their families and communities and transported to an alien country, they were treated as property without legal rights. The status of slaves varied. They could be publicly owned like the slaves who worked in the silver mines or belong to an individual family. As we have already seen, female domestic slaves occupied the same quarters as the free women of the house, where they worked alongside them at textile production and even slept with them in the same room. A passage from Xenophon describes the responsibility of the wife for training and supervising female slaves in wool working, "But there are other pleasant duties for you to perform, such as when you take a woman unskilled in spinning wool and make her competent in the craft, thereby making her twice as valuable to you" (Xen. *Oec.* 7.41). Elsewhere we learn that the woman of the household was also in charge of caring for any slave who fell ill. Within the household, slaves performed the more arduous domestic tasks such as cleaning, fetching water, and processing, preparing, and cooking food.

Despite their status as property, female domestic slaves are often represented as cherished members of the family, especially as nannies in charge of children. In this capacity, they developed close bonds with their wards, as evidenced by their frequent representation in literature as maternal surrogates. In Homer's *Odyssey*, the old servant Eurycleia first discerns a physical resemblance between the disguised stranger and her master, discovering his true identity even before his wife. When washing the stranger's feet, she touches a scar and recognizes it as the one Odysseus received during a childhood hunting accident. Eurycleia's uncanny instinct about the hero's identity results from the fact that she has known him since birth. Indeed, she was the one who placed the newborn in his maternal grandfather's lap for naming. The tragic character Cilissa further elicits the close connection between nurse and child. She alone feels genuine sorrow at the news of Orestes' death and recalls how she cared for the child in his infancy:

> Dear Orestes, for whom I wore out my life, whom I took from his mother and nursed, for whom I endured many thankless tasks when his shrill cries disturbed my rest. For of course one must nurse a senseless infant like a mere beast, by way of instinct. For a baby cannot communicate his needs while still in swaddling clothes, whether he is hungry, or thirsty, or needs to pee, a child's immature body has a rule of its own. Even though I often predicted these things, sometimes, miscalculating, I had to wash his swaddling clothes, such that I was both laundress and nurse. Expert in these two activities, I received the infant Orestes from his father. (Aesch. *Cho.* 749–62)

This passage provides an interesting perspective on the duties performed by the nurse in the Greek oikos. In wealthy families, care of the infant appears to have been turned over to her once the father had officially accepted him. Thereafter the nurse was responsible for feeding, dressing, changing, and soothing the newborn child and even washing his clothes. The nurse was thus an invaluable member of the household and integral to its ability to function successfully. In one court case, the male speaker describes with affection his childhood nurse who had returned to live with him and his family after the death of her husband, even though she was now a freedwoman:

> My wife happened to be eating breakfast with the children in the courtyard and with her was an elderly woman who had been my nurse, a kindly and trustworthy woman, who had been given her freedom by my father. After her manumission, she lived with her husband, but after his death, when she herself was an old woman and there was nobody to care for her, she came back to me. (Dem. 47.55)

3.4   Growing Up Female in the Greek Family

Gender socialization in ancient Greece began at birth, when a wreath of olive branches, a reference to athletic victory, was placed on the door to mark the arrival of a boy, and a garland of tufted wool, a symbol of wool working, for the birth of a girl. Upon delivery, the midwife evaluated the general health of the child and inspected it for any abnormalities. If healthy, on the fifth day after birth, both male and female infants were accepted into the cult of the household hearth in the ritual of the **Amphidromia** and thereby gained admittance into the family and assumed a legal social identity. This ritual involved carrying the baby around the household hearth, the sacred center of the oikos, and the place where new members of the oikos were introduced, particularly wives and slaves. For example, Clytemnestra instructs Cassandra, as her husband's slave concubine and outsider, to join the family at the hearth where they will perform sacrifices in celebration of Agamemnon's homecoming. Because fire is a form of purification, one theory is that the ritual of the Amphidromia may have been intended to purge the newcomer of pollution. The relation of the hearth and women is looked at in more detail in Chapter 4. After the ceremony relatives brought gifts for the baby, especially amulets that were slung around his neck and across his body to protect him from bad luck, illness, and the evil eye.

On the tenth day, the father gave the child a name to indicate family membership. The reason for the delay, according to Aristotle, was the belief that babies who survived this period were more likely to live to adulthood. Relatives and friends attended this event and gave gifts. Women danced all night long in celebration of the birth and ribbons, apples, and kisses were offered as prizes. Athenians had only one personal name and were distinguished from others, when necessary, by the use of a patronym, and by the name of deme to which they belonged. It was Athenian practice, however, not to mention the name of respectable women in public. The names of boys connected them to their male ancestors, usually on the father's side; first-born sons often received the name of their paternal grandfather, and second-born sons, the name of the maternal grandfather. Even girls' names came from the father's side of the family, with the name of the first daughter following that of her paternal grandmother. The infrequency of patronyms associated with women in funerary inscriptions further underscores their detachment from their natal family upon marriage.

The rate of infant mortality in classical Greece has been estimated at around 30%, although it is impossible to know the reality. The deaths of children under the age of 2 were so common that they are hardly ever described as untimely in funerary epitaphs. Indeed, infant death is rarely mentioned in literature or commemorated in art; unlike adults, babies could be buried within the city walls, sometimes even within the house. The graves of young children frequently contain child-specific objects such as baby feeders, miniature drinking cups, terracotta animals, and rattles. Deformed infants were widely viewed as inauspicious and were typically exposed by placing them in a terracotta pot or other container and left far from home, although material evidence for this practice largely dates from the Hellenistic period. A well in the Athenian agora containing the bodies of at minimum 449 infants and fetuses seems to have served as a repository for the bodies of children rejected by the family because of birth defects. It is possible that the midwives who assisted women in labor disposed of such babies at places like this, possibly known only to women. The practice of infant exposure also may have been widespread among prostitutes, for whom a child spelled economic ruin.

A question that has received much attention from historians is whether female babies were exposed at a greater rate than males. It has been argued that female infants were more likely to be left to die than males, at a rate estimated at around 20% in classical Athens. The main reason cited is the high cost of dowries for daughters. This view, however, has been recently challenged. The infant mortality rates for both sexes were so high that it is hard to imagine citizen parents actively seeking to get rid of healthy children. Recall from Chapter 2 the story Solon tells about Tellus the Athenian: part of his status as the happiest man derives from the fact that all of his sons survived to adulthood and he lived long enough to see them produce living offspring. As one Athenian orator remarks, "It is a very rare and very difficult thing to have both fine and many children" (Isocrates 9.72). A family consisting of even three living children would have been considered large. Thus infanticide is not likely to have been practiced except in extreme cases such as physical deformity, illegitimacy, or dire poverty. Whatever the reality, the sources nonetheless indicate a bias against the rearing of female children.

Once born and accepted into her father's oikos, a little girl underwent the ritual of the Amphidromia and received a name, just like her brothers. Until the age of 3 or 4, male and female children were considered more or less genderless, as the lack of gender-specific items found in the graves of children this age suggests. Indeed, the ancient Greek language uses the same word to refer to both male and female children, adding a masculine or feminine article to distinguish gender. As children approached puberty, however, the grave objects tend to be more gender specific and the bodies treated more like those of adults. Ancient medical writings show a similar disregard for sexual differentiation in children prior to puberty. The Hippocratic corpus, a collection of medical treatises from the late classical period (c. 420–350 BCE), rarely alludes to the sex of children whereas Aristotle's statement that a woman's body resembles that of a boy similarly further underscores the similarity of the two sexes prior to puberty

(Arist. *Gen. An.* 728a17). Despite this lack of differentiation, childhood in ancient Greece was nonetheless a period of socialization that prepared the individual to assume the gender roles appropriate to his or her biological sex upon adulthood.

Babies and children in general are not frequently represented in Greek art and literature. Those depicted are usually male, as to be expected given the concern for male heirs. Infants are usually shown naked and immobile in the arms of their caregivers, a string of protective amulets strung across their chest to ward off untimely death. Even as scenes of boys and their activities become increasingly popular on Athenian vases during the fifth-century BCE, images of girls remain scarce. Attic gravestones from a slightly later period, in contrast, contain many images of children of both sexes. The special regard for children during this period displayed both in the gravestones and in tragedy may reflect the immense loss of population brought about by a mysterious epidemic and the Peloponnesian war, which killed about a quarter of Athenian males. A beautifully carved funerary stele (Figure 3.4) shows a little girl clasping two pet doves to her chest and gazing down at them with sorrow and affection. She wears a high-waisted ***peplos***, a loose outer garment, partly opened at the side, and her long, wavy hair falls over her shoulder. Birds and other pets are often shown on gravestones as a reminder of the child's youth and her connection to her former life and home.

Another important source of evidence about children is a type of Athenian drinking vessel known as a ***chous***. This vessel was used in connection with the Anthesteria, an annual 3-day festival in honor of Dionysus that all Athenians celebrated, slaves, adult citizens, and both male and female children. On the first day, jars of new wine were opened, and on the second, known as the Choes, or feast of the jugs, a drinking competition took place. Miniature replicas of these

Figure 3.4 Attic gravestone depicting a little girl holding a pair of doves, c. 450–440 BCE. New York, Metropolitan Museum of Art, Fletcher Fund, 1927 (27.45).

drinking cups were given to both male and female children at the age of 3 or 4, perhaps containing their first taste of wine. Thousands of these vases have survived, some as grave-goods buried with Athenian children. The exterior of these pots represent a range of children's activities. Although they focus more on boys, several contain images of girls. Babies are shown with choes and cakes, playing with roller carts and balls. Toddlers and older children appear with pets, drive carts, interact with younger children, and play in mixed-sex groups. Fitting with the thesis that to the Greeks children under the age of 4 were not fully gendered, little distinction is made between male and female activities. Both sexes play with carts, animals, and balls. On the chous in Figure 3.5, a girl flanked by two boys holds a cake while her pet dog jumps at her feet. Girls are not segregated by gender on these vases but participate alongside the boys. The only distinction is in their costume and skin coloring, with the boys more frequently depicted as naked with a darker skin tone and the girls clothed and white-skinned, reflecting Greek conventions governing female modesty and beauty, discussed more fully in the next chapter. The mixed-gender interactions found on these pots underscore the idea that gender for the ancient Greeks was largely determined by social roles. Until children had completed the transition to adulthood and assumed gender-specific responsibilities, childbirth and warfare respectively, gendered characteristics were often less defined.

The relationship between brother and sister seems to have been particularly close, because siblings from the same family must have spent a lot of time together at home in their early years. In Greek literature, reunions between mixed-gender siblings occasion profound joy, and gravestones often depict brothers and sisters together. But the experience of boys and girls diverged during the period of older childhood (Pl. *Laws* 7.794C). Whereas boys received formal education, girls, especially those of good birth, normally stayed at home with their mothers, shielded from contact with the outer world. They did not compete in athletic contests like their brothers nor did they attend school. In New Comedy, a character warns about the dangers of

Figure 3.5 A girl holds a cake with two boys; Attic red-figure chous, c. 400 BCE. Athens, Agora Museum, P7685.

female education, "A man who teaches a woman to write should know that he is providing poison to an asp" (Men. Fr. 702 K). Several Attic vases show scrolls being handled and read by women, implying that some achieved literacy, although there is no literary evidence for the teaching of reading and writing to girls. These women are probably the Muses or the celebrated female poet Sappho. Other women depicted with books are possibly courtesans, who were known for their erudition and used their knowledge of poetry and conversational skills to entertain at the symposium, as we see in Chapter 6. Most respectable girls came into contact only with family members and neighbors.

Despite the extremely low rates of female literacy in ancient Greece, there was a tradition of female poets, beginning with Sappho. Another famous female poet Erinna (fl. 350 BCE) paints a vivid picture of girlhood in her poem, *The Distaff*. The 300-line fragment, only four lines of which were known until 1928, is a lament for her friend Baucis, commemorating their separation entailed by her marriage and subsequent death. The first part describes a game played among girls only, called "tortoise-little tortoise," a cross between a question-and-answer game and tag. The girl who is "it" plays a tortoise who crouches in the middle of a circle of girls who run around her chanting, "Tortoise, little tortoise, what are you doing in the middle?" The tortoise answers, "I'm weaving wool and Milesian thread." The girls pose another question, "What was your son doing when he died?" and the tortoise answers, "From white horses into the sea he jumped!" At the word "jumped," the tortoise leaps up and tries to capture another girl, who in turn becomes "it." In another part of the poem, Erinna describes how she and Baucis played with dolls together as young girls. The nostalgia for the toys and games of youth contributes to the poem's overwhelming sense of loss. The Greeks associated this feeling of loss with the transition to marriage for girls, underscoring the divergent experiences of boys and girls as they approached adulthood.

3.5 The Ritual Activities of Girls

Citizens, we will begin to say a few useful words for the polis, which makes sense, for it reared me in splendor. When I was seven years old straightaway I was an *arrephoros*. At the age of ten, I served as a grain-grinder for Athena. Then wearing a yellow gown, I played the bear at the rites of Brauron. And I once carried the basket as a beautiful girl, wearing a necklaces of figs. (Ar. *Lys.* 639–47)

Through participation in domestic and civic religion, children became socialized into their adult and gender-specific roles. As we saw earlier, both boys and girls participated in the ritual of the Choes at around three years of age. Around puberty, girls from elite families appear to have participated in numerous civic rituals. In contrast to their brothers, whose ritual socialization might span more than two decades, the ritual education of girls seems to have been compressed into a period of a few years due to the imperative of marriage. The passage from comedy above affords a rare glimpse into girls' ritual activities and provides a starting point for our discussion. Here a chorus of elderly Athenian women argue for their right to speak because of their cultic service to the city. They begin with the Arrhephoria, a ritual open only to young girls from among the best Athenian families. Two or four girls between the age of 7 and 11 were selected to live as an **arrephoros** on the Acropolis, a walled sacred precinct in the heart of the city and site of the Parthenon, where they played a ritual ball game and helped to weave the peplos presented to Athena as part of the annual procession of the Panathenaia. To mark the end of their service, they carried covered baskets on their heads containing secret objects and descended to an underground chamber. There they left what they were carrying and brought up other covered objects to the Acropolis. Although little is known about this last rite, it has been interpreted as a rite of passage or initiation. The festival of the Arrephoria also included the sacred grain grinder, the office referred to in the next line of the text. This position was open only to virgins, who may have been involved in preparing the special bread for the festival. The basket bearers in the procession in honor of Athena alluded to in the final line were probably adolescent girls at the age just before marriage and are discussed in the next chapter.

We know much more about the other sacred duty mentioned by the chorus, the rites of Brauron, a sanctuary of Artemis located on the eastern coast of Attica. According to the myth, a bear scratched a young girl while playing with her. The girl's brothers killed the bear, inciting the anger of Artemis. To punish the boys, she sent a plague that could be stopped only by the service of young girls "playing the bear" for the goddess before marriage, a rite known as the Arkteia. Every four years a select group of girls between the ages of 5 and 10 was chosen from each Athenian tribe to live in this sanctuary as Little Bears. Our understanding of this ritual derives from two types of sources: myths connected with Artemis and her rites and artifacts found at the precinct of Brauron, including records of dedications made by women. Fragments of pottery vessels in the shape used for dedications to Artemis excavated in the sanctuary provide visual evidence for the ritual of "playing the bear." These show girls naked or wearing short tunics as they dance, run, or process to an altar. They often hold wreathes or torches and the occasional presence of a palm tree points to the worship of Artemis. Some girls wear their hair loose. There is no visual example, however, of the saffron-colored garment mentioned in the comic passage as central to the rite. In addition to the ritual activities of girls, we find older women helping to prepare the girls for their ritual activities, as well as the priestess herself playing the role of bear. Scholars have interpreted these activities as a rite of passage that marked the physical maturation of girls and prepared them for marriage by expunging their wildness. Women also made dedications to Artemis at Brauron in celebration of successful childbirth, as we see in Chapter 5.

Although only girls from elite families could have participated in the civic cult rituals outlined previously, involvement in domestic rituals was common for girls of all ages, even the very young. A sphere of activity that we do not often associate with children is death. Given high mortality rates and the close quarters in which most Athenians lived, children could not be spared from the reality of death. Both male and female children on Attic pottery are shown visiting the tombs of relatives, where they accompany their mothers and present offerings. Young girls also helped their mothers with preparing the body for burial and performing lamentations, as evident on an Attic red-figure loutrophoros (Figure 3.6). A little girl at bottom right stands in the midst of adult women, wearing a black funerary mantle and striking her head in a gesture of lament just beneath the garlanded head of the male corpse. She appears to be looking to the woman at left as if to mimic her movements.

Childhood in ancient Greece prepared girls for marriage and adulthood by training them in domestic skills such as textile manufacture, caregiving, and ritual practices, involving them in duties necessary for the survival of the family and city. Death ritual represents a primary obligation for the women of the family, as Chapter 7 shows, and seems to have involved young girls from an early age. The transition from childhood to adulthood for females was often abrupt. Because girls were expected to leave their families in early adolescence and take up residence in the households of their husbands, rituals of incorporation were deemphasized. During early childhood they participated in the same games as their brothers and used the same toys, but their path gradually diverged as they approached adolescence. The next chapter focuses on representations of female adolescence and the often traumatic transition to adulthood entailed by marriage.

Figure 3.6 Detail, Attic red-figure loutrophoros with female mourners, including a little girl, around the bier of the deceased, c. 430 BCE. London, British Museum, 1930,0417.1.

3.6   The Family in Ancient Sparta

A very different form of family structure is found in ancient Sparta and provides an important counterpoint to the Athenian focus of our primary sources. A major problem is a lack of reliable sources: most are not by Spartan authors and are either very late or involve an Athenian bias. As a communal society, the state regulated many aspects of domestic life, downplaying blood ties and the private family unit. Indeed, the state was envisioned as one large, artificial family, which held property in common. The decision about whether to rear babies resided with the state, which evaluated the vitality of newborn males with a view to their potential as soldiers. Fathers did not decide how to raise sons but rather all boys received the same education under state supervision. Marriage and the family served the sole purpose of producing warriors for the state. Women were thus valued primarily as mothers. A late anecdote sums up this view. When a foreign woman remarked to Gorgo, the wife of Leonidas, "You Spartan women are the only ones who can rule men," she replied, "That is because we are the only ones who give birth to men" (Plut. *Lyc.* 9). The Spartans prepared girls for motherhood through extensive physical conditioning, because it was believed that strong and vigorous bodies would better endure the challenge of childbirth and be more like to produce healthy and athletic offspring. Girls participated in athletic training competitions out of doors and purportedly appeared nude in public processions, just like boys. They also engaged in choral performances before male spectators, as we see in the next chapter. In contrast to their Athenian counterparts, Spartan girls do not seem to have been secluded within the house or held to the same standard of physical modesty.

3.7 Conclusion

The oikos is a broad concept that encompasses not only the nuclear family but also its property, including land, livestock, and slaves. Although male and female family members lived together in close proximity, their experiences diverged sharply, especially as they progressed through the stages of childhood. The birth of children contributed to the stability of the oikos, although daughters eventually left to join the households of their husbands. As boys underwent a gradual process of civic incorporation, girls remained at home, learning the domestic skills and ritual practices necessary for their future lives as wives and mothers. Domestic space reinforced these segregated gender roles in its designation of a men's and women's quarters, whether as a temporary or permanent space or social ideal. Within this structure, women performed domestic labor with the help of female slaves, principally textile production. In the literary sources, weaving represents a source of female agency and power both beneficial and detrimental to men. The evidence for ancient Sparta suggests a social structure radically different from that of classical Athens, in which girls seem to have enjoyed more freedom and equality, reminding us that even in ancient Greece conceptions of gender were not absolute but culturally determined.

Questions for Review

1   What was the structure of the Greek household?

2   What role did women's textile production play in Greek literature and society?

3   How did the lives of boys and girls differ in ancient Greece?

4   How did the ritual activities of girls prepare them for marriage and adulthood?

5   How did the lives of Spartan girls differ from their Athenian counterparts?

Reference

Smith, Tyler Jo and Plantzos, Dimitris (2012). *A Companion to Greek Art*. Wiley-Blackwell.

Further Reading

Primary Sources

Erinna, "The Distaff"
Euripides, *Medea*
Homer, *Odyssey*
Sophocles, *Women of Trachis*

Secondary Sources

Barber, Elizabeth Wayland (1994). *Women's Work: The First 20,000 Years. Women, Cloth, and Society in Ancient Times*. New York and London: Norton.
  Looks at the role of women in textile production from 20,000 to 500 BCE. Chapter 10 considers the symbolic associations of cloth in Greek myth.

Beaumont, Leslie (2012). *Childhood in Ancient Athens: Iconography and Social History*. New York: Routledge.
  A comprehensive study of the representation of children and childhood in Athenian art and literature, from birth and infancy to the development of the child through nurture, work, play, and education.

DuBois, Page (2008). *Slaves and Other Objects*. Chicago: University of Chicago Press.
  An unorthodox exploration of slaves in material culture and literature that seeks to make visible these often overlooked figures and to understand their importance. Considers the body, gender, and conceptions of the slave in Greek philosophy.

Goff, Barbara (2004). *Citizen Bacchae: Women's Ritual Practice in Ancient Greece*. Berkeley and Los Angeles: University of California Press.
  A theoretically informed account of the role of women in ancient Greek religion that seeks to emphasize ritual as a venue for alternative roles and identities. Draws on a wide range of evidence, including inscriptions, vase-paintings, and literary and historical texts.

Golden, Mark (1990). *Children and Childhood in Classical Athens*. Baltimore and London: Johns Hopkins University Press.
  A comprehensive overview of children and childhood in Athenian life from 500 to 300 BCE, with a focus on the age prior to marriage. Includes subjects such as siblings, parent–child relations, and outsiders.

Lewis, Sian (2002). *The Athenian Woman: An Iconographic Handbook*. London and New York: Routledge.
  A stimulating analysis of the representation of women on Greek pottery that provides several new and provocative interpretations of old debates. Topics covered include domestic labor, working women, the Greek house, and gender relations.

Morgan, Janett (2010). *The Classical Greek House*. Exeter: Bristol Phoenix Press.
  Combines textual analysis and material culture to offer new perspectives on the layout of ancient Greek domestic space.

Neils, Jennifer and Oakley, John (eds.) (2003). *Coming of Age in Ancient Greece: Images of Childhood from the Classical Past*. New Haven, CT: Yale University Press.
  Originally an exhibition catalogue, this book brings together a multitude of images of children and youths from ancient Greek vase painting and sculpture. The accompanying essays provide interesting insights into the main facets of Greek childhood.

Nevett, Lisa (1999). *House and Society in the Ancient Greek World*. Cambridge: Cambridge University Press.
  Explores the architecture of ancient Greek houses as a source of information about broader cultural issues.

4

Female Adolescence in Greece

Before her marriage, Timareta dedicated her drums, her lovely ball and the flowing veil for her hair, her dolls and their clothing, to Artemis of the marshes, a virgin to a virgin, as is appropriate.

(Anonymous, *Anth. Gr.* 6.280)

Adolescence in the ancient world was a time not only of momentous physical change, just as it is today, but also of heightened responsibility and new social roles. Whereas boys prepared for war through military training, girls anticipated the journey from the protected realm of their natal families to the alien households of their future husbands. Childhood came to an end not at a chronological age but when a girl had reached puberty and transitioned to her adult social role as a wife and mother. The onset of puberty confirmed that a girl had the potential to bear children and transformed her status from a child into that of a ***parthenos***, an unmarried, adolescent girl eligible for marriage. Because girls married so young – around 14 – the span of adolescence, known as ***partheneia***, was quite brief compared to modern standards. Until male and female teenagers achieved their adult social roles, they occupied a liminal state in which their gendered attributes could be considered somewhat fluid. Boys at this stage could assume a feminine or submissive role in a homoerotic relationship with an adult male, whereas girls, at least as imagined in literature, could engage in heroic actions often described in masculine terms. In contrast to children, we find many images of female adolescence in Greek literature and art from the archaic and classical periods. They emphasize not only the purity and desirability of adolescent girls on the cusp of marriage but also their erotic and religious power.

As with other life stages, girls underwent specific rituals that marked the transition to marriage and motherhood, many revolving around the goddess Artemis. In the epigraph above, Timareta offers her playthings to the goddess and renounces her childhood with this symbolic act. To understand Artemis' involvement with this phase of female life, it is necessary to grasp her range of powers and meanings. First, Artemis incarnates the wildness and purity of uncivilized nature. She is often represented as the queen of wild animals or as their hunter, wielding a bow and quiver. In the human realm, she represents the sexual inviolability of girls and their latent procreative power fundamental to the institution of marriage. These associations explain why the Greeks often used animal terms drawn from agriculture to refer to adolescent girls, like "filly" and "heifer." They continued the metaphor by referring to marriage as a "yoking together" and a spouse as a "yoke-mate." This vocabulary reflects the widespread idea that through marriage girls submitted to the authority of their husbands and became tame. Paradoxically, Artemis was also the goddess of childbirth. In myth, she assists with the delivery of her younger brother, Apollo, just minutes after her own birth. In the precinct of Brauron discussed in the previous chapter, women dedicated fine clothing to the goddess in gratitude

Women in Classical Antiquity: From Birth to Death, First Edition. Laura K. McClure.
© 2020 John Wiley & Sons, Inc. Published 2020 by John Wiley & Sons, Inc.

for the safe delivery of their babies. Artemis therefore oversaw the female reproductive cycle, from menarche and the release of blood that enables conception to childbirth, a process by which the adolescent girl is transformed from a wild creature to reproductive wife and mother. But the goddess could also be dangerous and threatening: not all teenage girls reached adulthood and not every maternal delivery went well.

4.1   Medical Views of Female Adolescence

The primary sign of the transformation of an adolescent girl into an adult woman was pregnancy and childbirth, a stage facilitated by the onset of menstruation. Because of their focus on female fertility, we find extensive discussion of menstruation and few references to menopause in ancient medical writings. Most of what we know of ancient Greek views of the female body during the classical period comes from a set of around 70 treatises known as the Hippocratic corpus (c. 450–350 BCE). Eleven focus on women's reproductive health and many of the other writings deal with female patients. Although Hippocrates (469–399 BCE) and his followers relied on traditional lore gathered and transmitted orally by midwives in their recommendations for the treatment of women, the corpus nonetheless reflects a male perspective on the female body. The natural philosopher Aristotle is the other main source for theories of sex and reproduction in the classical period. Although the Hippocratics and Aristotle had different scientific aims, both sets of writings argue that fundamental differences between the sexes did not become apparent until puberty. In the case of females, this meant the development of breasts and the onset of the menses. The Hippocratic authors attempt to account for menstruation through the nature of female flesh, which they view as soft and spongy by the time of puberty:

> I say that a woman's flesh is more sponge-like and softer than that of a man. For this reason, the woman's body draws moisture both with more speed and in greater quantity from the belly than does the body of a man. (Hippoc. *Mul.* 1.1)

This porous flesh more readily soaks up the excess blood produced by unused nourishment in the stomach, in turn releasing it as the menstrual flow. The ability of the female body to absorb moisture represents a healthy state for women as it facilitates the reproductive cycle. In pregnancy, the retained menstrual fluid nourishes the fetus, and after birth, the moisture provides milk for lactation. Although men also have an unused residue of blood, according to Aristotle, their ability to produce heat allows them to convert it into semen, whereas women, because colder by nature, can produce only menstrual fluid.

The release of excess matter through menstruation prevents the female body from becoming diseased in the absence of pregnancy, whereas its retention is especially dangerous for unmarried girls. Another Hippocratic treatise, *On Virgins*, describes how prolonged virginity poses risks to a girl's health. The writer attributes fevers, insanity, and even murderous and suicidal impulses to the failure of a girl to achieve marriage and pregnancy:

> When young women in the season of marriage remain without a husband, they suffer in particular at the time of the downward passage of their menses, this evil to which before they were not very subject. For at this later time in their life, blood collects in the uterus, destined to run out, but when the mouth of the exit does not open up, more blood keeps being added from food and the growth of the body, and then, left with nowhere to flow out, the blood springs up in its excess to the heart and the diaphragm. Now when these

parts are filled, the heart becomes stupefied, then from the stupefaction numb, and finally from the numbness these women become deranged …. She names strange and frightful things, and these urge the women to take a leap and to throw themselves down wells, or to hang themselves, as being better and in every way advantageous. When there are no visions, there is a pleasure from which the woman loves death as some kind of good. When there is a return to the senses, women dedicate many different things to Artemis, including the most costly cloaks of the female sort …. (Hippoc. *Virg.* 1, trans. P. Potter)

If menstruation does not take place, blood flows back out of the womb through the girl's body and accumulates in various places, causing different illnesses, both physical and mental. Without the intervention of sexual intercourse, virgins are susceptible to suicide. The male author, however, rejects the customary female solution to this problem, the dedication of clothing to Artemis at her sanctuary in Brauron, instead recommending that virgins "cohabit with a man as quickly as possible. If they become pregnant, they will be cured." This passage communicates many important Greek attitudes toward women and gender. First, it suggests because of their reproductive cycle, women are more prone to irrationality. Second, it legitimates the practice of marrying off girls at a young age, at menarche. It also promotes female sexual activity within marriage in order to ensure the passage from the uterus remains open. The idea of female adolescence as a dangerous transition and its association with death were widespread in Greek literature, recurring in many myths connected with Artemis, as discussed later in this chapter.

The virginity of unmarried girls nonetheless remained an important Greek value because it was essential to maintaining the integrity of the male family line, a concept embodied by the goddess Hestia (hearth). The importance of her Roman counterpart, Vesta, to the welfare of the Roman state is discussed more fully in Chapter 14. As a divinity, she is more or less a colorless abstraction rarely appearing in mythology or the visual arts. And yet she was central to family life in ancient Greece, because, from the Bronze Age on, the household was organized around the hearth. According to Hesiod, "Zeus the father gave her [Hestia] a high honor instead of marriage, and she has her place in the middle of the house" (*Hom. Hymn Aphr.* 30–32). The hearth anchored the house to the earth and therefore served as a symbol of permanence. The spatial fixity of Hestia and her purity represented the continuity of the male family line into the future. Before marriage, daughters maintained loyalty toward their father's house and so the duty of tending the paternal hearth fell to them. Once incorporated into the new household of her husband as a wife, a girl moved away from the fixed space of her ancestral home and worshipped at his family hearth, the very place where any children born to them were introduced and recognized as a member of the family. The virginity of maidens and the sexual fidelity of wives thus worked in tandem to ensure that only legitimate family members were accepted into the cult of the family's hearth.

4.2 *Aidos:* Protecting Purity

Because it was important for men to control the sexuality of their wellborn wives and daughters, they took measures to protect them from the advances of other men, such as spatial seclusion and prohibitions against showing the body. Hesiod specifies the interior rooms of the house as the proper space for maidens:

And [the wind] does not blow through the tender maiden who stays indoors with her dear mother, not yet experienced in the works of golden Aphrodite, and who washes her soft body and rubs herself with oil and lies down in the innermost part of the house, on a winter's day.... (Hes. *Op.* 420–4)

This passage pairs the domestic seclusion of girls with their burgeoning sexuality. By washing and anointing her body, the maiden makes herself attractive to potential suitors and prepares herself for marriage. At the same time, she is confined to the hidden part of the house, where she can be shielded from inappropriate contact with men. As we saw in the last chapter, literary texts often assert the presence of a women's quarters that kept females safely out of the view of unrelated males and prevented illicit sexual contact. Occasionally this space is also called the **parthenon** ("maiden chambers"), an age-specific term suggesting the desirability of segregating marriageable adolescent girls. Girls who ventured outdoors, away from the house, rendered themselves vulnerable to sexual assault and abduction, as in the case of Persephone discussed later.

Closely connected to the spatial segregation of adolescent girls was the custom of veiling. Veils served to shield the female body from the gaze of men, a practice still found today in many Islamic societies. Whereas the naked male body was celebrated as the heroic ideal in Greek art, respectable girls and women were always represented as clothed, with the notable exception of the goddess Aphrodite. This gender distinction can be seen in the freestanding sculptures of teenage boys and girls from the archaic period. The female version, known as a **kore**, another word for maiden, appears draped and stands erect with feet close together, arms either resting at the side or clasping an object close to the body, her mouth relaxed into a soft smile. One kore figure marks the tomb of Phrasiclea (Figure 4.1), a young woman who died before marriage (c. 530 BCE). An inscription on the base reads, "Gravestone of Phrasiclea. I shall always be called maiden, instead of marriage having been given this name by the gods. Aristion of Paros made me" (*IG* I^3 1261). The girl wears ornate clothing and a conical headdress associated with goddesses and decorated with flowers in the manner of a bride. Originally painted in vivid colors, her dress conceals the swelling contours of her adolescent body as she extends her left arm to make an offering.

Figure 4.1 Statue of Phrasiclea, marble, 550–40 BCE. Athens, National Archaeological Museum, 4889.

The act of veiling worked together with the lowering of the eyes to convey the important female virtue of **aidos** ("modesty"). Conversely, uncovering the face and directly gazing at a man showed sexual availability. Both women and girls were expected to cover their bodies completely while in public and to keep their eyes downcast when in the presence of men, as we learn from Euripides' *Hecuba*: "Custom dictates a woman should not gaze into the eyes of men" (Eur. *Hec.* 974-5). For an unmarried girl, these gestures were especially important as they protected her from the prying eyes of strangers and made a display of modesty. At the onset of puberty, girls adopted two age-specific garments, the veil and the sash that secured the peplos. In addition to covering the body, these items signified sexual maturity. The removal of these items symbolized male access to the female body upon marriage.

4.3   Nausicaa: A Teenage Girl in a Heroic World

A charming portrait of female adolescence is found in Homer's *Odyssey* when the hero encounters the plucky Phaeacian princess, Nausicaa. After almost drowning at sea, the exhausted man washes up on the shore of Phaeacia and crawls into a thicket to sleep. The next day Athena rebukes the princess for sleeping late instead of attending to her washing, potentially ruining her chances for marriage:

> Nausicaa, how did your mother bear such a thoughtless child? Your bright clothing is lying about uncared for; yet your marriage is soon and not only must you wear beautiful clothes yourself, but provide them for those who attend you. (Hom. *Od.* 6.26–30)

The girl swiftly gathers her garments and heads to the beach with her servants to wash the clothes. After spreading them out to dry, they throw off their veils and play ball while the princess leads them in song. Because the mythic model for a band of maidens and their leader is Artemis and her nymphs, the poet likens Nausicaa to the goddess to highlight not only her marriageable status but also her youthful beauty: "So amid her handmaidens the unwed parthenos distinguished herself" (Hom. *Od.* 6.110).

The sound of the girls playing awakens Odysseus, who emerges from the wood holding a spindly branch in front of his body in an attempt to cover his nakedness. In keeping with her exceptional status, only Nausicaa from among the girls dares to confront the wild-looking man, who supplicates her for his life:

> By your knees, lady, are you a goddess or a mortal? If you are a goddess, among those who hold broad heaven, then I deem you most like Artemis, daughter of great Zeus, in respect of your beauty, your stature and your form. But if you are a mortal, among those who dwell on earth, thrice-blessed is your father and queenly mother, and thrice-blessed your brothers, for their heart is always warmed with happiness because of you, when they watch their child enter the chorus. But most blessed beyond all others in his heart is that one who laden with wedding gifts leads you home. (Hom. *Od.* 6.149–59)

Odysseus' flattering speech continues the theme introduced earlier in the poem: Nausicaa as an eligible maiden embodies Artemis and the transitional stage of female adolescence – partheneia – that she governs. She is physically alluring but innocent of sex. She will not remain a maiden for long, for soon she will be married, as Odysseus predicts.

4.4   Choruses of Young Girls

The assimilation of Nausicaa and her companions to Artemis and her followers and their activities – attending to their appearance, playing games and singing – suggests a prototype for an important ritual activity of adolescent girls, choral performance. The impact of the chorus on ancient Greek life should not be underestimated, as difficult as it is for us to understand today. Readers of Greek tragedy will notice immediately the presence of a chorus in each play, a collective same-sex group who sing and dance in response to dramatic events (see Box 4.1). Indeed, it is believed that the tragic genre developed out of an early form of choral performance. The chorus also played a central role in social and religious life from the earliest period.

Box 4.1 Athenian Drama

Athenian drama comprises one of the richest resources for representations of women and gender in classical antiquity. Although hundreds of tragedies and comedies were staged, only 33 plays survive by the three main tragic poets, Aeschylus, Sophocles, and Euripides. Drama originated in a type of choral performance known as a **dithyramb**, a hymn to Dionysus sung by as many as 50 men or boys. In the late sixth century BCE, the form of this choral performance changed. The chorus leader began to engage in a rudimentary form of dialog with the members of the choral group. Gradually, what had been a unified choral performance became an alternation of choral odes with lines spoken by actors. The chorus, consisting of 12 members in tragedy and 24 in comedy, is a regular feature of Athenian drama that sets it apart from later dramatic conventions. The tragedies took their subject matter from heroic myths, such as the Trojan War and its aftermath. A few told of historic events, such as Aeschylus' *Persians* (472 BCE), which portrays the return home of the Persian king, Xerxes, after the Greek defeat of his army in 479 BCE. Comedy, in contrast, revolves around everyday characters and situations set in contemporary Athens and fantastical realms.

The development of drama closely paralleled the rise of Athenian democracy. Tragedies and comedies were performed at an annual Athenian festival for the god Dionysus called the City Dionysia. A state official in charge of the festival chose three tragedians to compete at the dramatic festival with the performance of three tragedies and one tragicomedy. Each day ended with the performance of a comic play. Three wealthy Athenians sponsored the training and outfitting of the chorus, which could be quite an expense given its size. This practice further highlights the importance of choral elements such as costume, dance, and song, for the audience. All actors were male and wore masks to portray stock characters, such as king, queen, herald, maiden, or slave.

Given the context and conventions of the tragic theater, one might wonder why it represents such a good source for understanding Greek constructions of gender. Although concerned with heroic myth, many extant plays focus on complex family dynamics in which women play a critical role as wives, mothers, and daughters. It shows us a world in which gender roles are often destabilized, with women sometimes acting like men and men like women, and the implications of these inversions for the larger community. The plays suggest that the male heroic model celebrated by Homer was incompatible with contemporary political ideals of citizenship, which required cooperation and collective identity. Female characters thus contribute important perspectives on the relation of the household to the democratic state and other contemporary social and political issues.

Typically composed of members of the same age and sex, the chorus celebrated important aspects of myth and ritual through their words and movements. Girls on the brink of marriage played a special role in such choruses, especially those connected with marriage. One tragic chorus composed of unmarried women recalls with pleasure and longing the choral dances of their youth performed at weddings:

> I wish I could take my place in the choruses where once as a maiden at important weddings whirling my foot alongside companies of my dear mother's friends, in rivalry of grace and luxurious finery urging myself to compete I wrapped myself in richly embroidered robes with my hair darkening my cheeks. (Eur. *IT* 1142–50)

Notice the attention to physical appearance given by this chorus: they describe the graceful movement of their feet, their fine clothing as well as their flowing hair. Given the importance of modesty and concealment for unmarried girls, this description may seem surprising.

Figure 4.2 Interior of an Attic white-ground phiale showing a maiden chorus dancing around an altar by the Painter of London D12, c. 450–440 BCE. Boston, Museum of Fine Arts 65.908.

However, choral performance represented one of the few appropriate venues for the public display of young women. In this context, wellborn girls could advertise their beauty and eligibility for marriage. The exterior of a shallow bowl used for pouring libations depicts one such chorus (Figure 4.2). Their hair bound with ribbons, they hold hands as they dance around an altar to the accompaniment of flute player. To the left of the altar is a wool basket, recalling the work of girls and women in domestic textile production discussed in the last chapter.

The script, as it were, for such a performance is found in a fragmentary text of a type of poem known as a ***partheneion*** by the Spartan poet Alcman (mid-late seventh century BCE). This type of poem was composed especially for performance by a chorus of adolescent Spartan girls and gives a sense of their concerns and activities. Although the poem poses many textual and interpretive difficulties, it probably represents a cult song composed to accompany a specific religious ritual. The focus appears to be the dedication of an object, perhaps a garment, to an unnamed goddess, possibly Artemis. Throughout the poem, the girls call attention to their dress, their jewelry, and their dance while praising each other's physical beauty:

> And so I sing the brightness of Agido: I see her like the sun which she declares to shine on us. But our renowned chorus leader permits me neither to praise nor blame her. For she seems distinguished to me, just as if someone were to put a horse among beasts, a strong, prize-winning horse with thundering feet of winged dreams.
>
> Do you not see her? The race-horse is from the northern Adriatic. But the hair of my cousin Hagesichora blooms bright as unmixed gold, and her silver face – why do I tell you openly?
>
> This is Hagesichora here. And the second in beauty after Agido will run like a Scythian horse against a Lydian. For the Doves, as we carry a robe to Orthria, rise through the ambrosial night as the star, Sirius, and fight against us.

> For neither is there abundance of purple to protect us, nor intricate golden snake ban-
> gles, nor Lydian headband, nor delight of violet-eyed maidens, nor the hair of Nanno,
> nor godlike Areta, Thylacis nor Cleësithera, nor will you go to Ainesimbrota's to say:
> May Astaphis be mine, if only Philylla would look our way, Damareta and the lovely
> Ianthemis. But Hagesichora guards me. (Alc. Fr. 1.39–77)

Although much remains mysterious about this poem, it is nonetheless possible to glean from it insights into the nature and function of the maiden chorus. The poem repeatedly calls atten-tion to the individual members of the chorus and their beauty, first by singling out Agido, perhaps an assistant or priestess, then their leader Hagesichora, and finally by naming several other girls. The fragment is rich with the imagery of light and luxury, with its references to the sun, stars, and precious metals. The emphasis on costume and adornment – headbands, brace-lets, purple-dyed cloth – evokes the wealth and marriageability of the young girls. The com-parison of Hagesichora and Agido to sleek horses recalls the association between adolescent girls and animals in need of taming. The last stanza implies a homoerotic attachment between the girls, perhaps customary for them at this life stage as it may have been for boys. Many believe the poem depicts a rite of adolescent initiation that both proclaims and accomplishes a change of social status. In the ceremony, the young girls of Sparta are being presented to the community at their moment of transition from childhood to womanhood, signaling their eligi-bility for marriage. Although the poem predates the classical period and this type of song is found elsewhere, the confidence and authority of these female voices perhaps reflect the public role of women at Sparta, as discussed in the last chapter.

Adolescent girls also participated in other ritual contexts as well. In the period before mar-riage, wellborn Athenian girls could serve in a variety of sacred capacities. Religious proces-sions provided frequent opportunities to put on display the beauty and grace of marriageable girls. A good example is the basket-bearer or ***kanephoros***, a position mentioned in the religious resume of the female chorus members in Aristophanes' *Lysistrata*, which we considered in Chapter 3. At this and other local processions, she had the conspicuous honor of carrying a special basket that contained ritual paraphernalia, including the knife, ribbons, garlands, and grains necessary for animal sacrifice. This basket, made of wicker or precious metal, is easily identifiable in the visual record. A kanephoros is shown leading a procession at Delphi on a red-figure jar (Figure 4.3). She wears an elaborately woven tunic and a heavy mantle that falls from her shoulders to her feet and jewelry, signifying both her importance and her modesty. She carries the basket on her head, as was the custom for women in ancient Greece, and her long hair falls loosely down her back. Because every religious festival required a basket carrier, there were many more opportunities for girls to participate in this capacity than, for example, in the rites at Brauron. As with maiden choruses, this sacred office put the parthenos on display and showed off her marriageable status to all who viewed her. A comic passage explicitly con-nects this ritual activity with attracting a husband when a father instructs his daughter to make sure she looks good bearing the basket: "Come, daughter, carry the basket prettily and wear a pretty and sour expression on your face; how happy will be the man who marries you!" (Ar. *Ach.* 245). To be chosen to serve as a basket-bearer brought great honor to a girl and her family, whereas to be passed over brought disgrace. When the unnamed sister of Harmodius suffered this humiliation in 514 BCE, he retaliated by killing the tyrant, Hipparchus. The elevated status of the basket-carrier is further attested by the fact that she received a portion of the sacrificial meat that culminated the procession and later became the subject of comic plays.

Although the female poet, Sappho, whom we met in Chapter 1, did not compose any poems in the genre of the partheneion, her lyric fragments frequently celebrate the beauty and allure of girls just before marriage, employing some of the same imagery. What we know of the poet's

Figure 4.3 Depiction of a kanephoros bearing a metal basket on her head; Attic red-figure volute krater by the Kleophon Painter, c. 430 BCE. Ferrara, Italy, Museo Nazionale di Spina 44 894 T. 57C.

life derives from her extant poems, most of which are fragmentary. Called the "Tenth Muse," she was widely admired and imitated in classical antiquity. Most of her poems were intended for solo rather than group choral performance and are addressed to a circle of adolescent female companions. Controversy still reigns as to the identity and function of these young women. For many years, it was believed that Sappho served as a sort of "school mistress," preparing girls for the transition to marriage and motherhood. That view has long been discredited as scholars have increasingly embraced the perspective that the fragments portray homoerotic attachments between Sappho and her companions, much as we saw in the Alcman fragment. The frequent references to partings and absence in the poems suggest that most of her circle shared their lives for only a brief period of time before marriage. Fragment 31, a poem later imitated by the Roman poet, Catullus (84–54? BCE), expresses in exquisite detail the powerful erotic response sparked by the sight of a beautiful girl:

> Equal to the gods seems that man to me who sits opposite you and nearby listens to your sweet voice and amorous laughter. Then the heart within my breast trembles, for when I look at you, even for a moment, it is no longer possible for me to speak, my tongue has snapped into silence, straight away a delicate fire runs under my skin. There is no sight in my eyes, my ears ring, a cold sweat flows over my body and trembling seizes all of me – for I am greener than grass and I seem close to death.... (Sappho Fr. 31)

By the second stanza, the focus turns from the girl and her male companion to the physical effects of her presence on the poet, which have rendered all of her senses except touch useless.

Because the poems describe her passions as a mature woman rather than that of her young associates, the goddess most frequently referenced is Aphrodite rather than Artemis. Sappho's poetry offers a rare and fascinating glimpse into a female-only world in which speech and poetry are addressed exclusively to women and represent uniquely female concerns.

4.5 Brides of Death

Despite the emphasis on beauty, charm, and eroticism in Greek depictions of female adolescence, the transition to marriage and motherhood must have been abrupt and even violent for many girls. A character in a lost play by Sophocles describes the period just before marriage for girls as bittersweet. The innocence and happiness of childhood yields to a sense of loss, fear, and uncertainty about the future:

> For as young girls, I think, we live the sweetest life among mortals in our father's house. Innocence always rears girls in delight. But when we mature and reach the age of marriage, we are thrust out and sold away from our paternal gods and our parents, some to strangers, some to barbarians, some to a good house, others to an abusive one. (Soph. *Ter.* Fr. 585 Radt)

It is not difficult to understand how frightening this transition must have been in real life if we consider how sheltered were girls from elite families and how young they were at marriage. Under these circumstances, it makes sense that marriage is often represented as a form of death for the girl in the literary sources.

An archetypal myth for marriage is found in the *Homeric Hymn to Demeter* (c. 600 BCE). The hymn relates a bride kidnapping in the form of Hades' abduction and rape of Persephone, daughter of the agricultural goddess, Demeter. Bride capture is also a theme in Roman foundation myth in the story of the Sabines. The groom and the girl's father had arranged this violent act without her knowledge, in keeping with Greek custom. The marriage, however, is literally a form of death since the groom is the god of the underworld. The opening scene of the poem describes a group of adolescent girls at play, much like Nausicaa and her friends, when Hades suddenly appears:

> Apart from Demeter, lady of the golden sword and giver of fruit, she was playing with the deep-bosomed daughters of Oceanus, picking flowers in a soft meadow – roses and crocuses and beautiful violets, irises and hyacinth and narcissus, which Earth produced as bait for the flower-faced girl, by the plan of Zeus to delight the god of Death, an amazing, glittering thing, a wonder to look upon both for all the immortal gods and mortal men: from its root a hundred heads grew, and it smelled incredibly sweet, so that all of heaven and wide earth and the salty swell of the sea laughed. And she, amazed, reached out her hands to take the beautiful toy, but the wide-pathed ground gaped open along the Nysian plain, and the lord, host of many, son of famous Cronos, sprang out upon her with his immortal horses. He snatched her unwilling onto his golden car and led her away, lamenting. She cried out loudly with her voice, calling upon her father, the son of Cronos, highest and best. But no one of the immortals nor mortals heard her voice. (*Hom. Hymn Dem.* 4–23)

The extended description of the flowers represents by turns the carefree pleasures of girlhood and the apprehensions of sexual maturity. Without the protections of her home and parents, Persephone is vulnerable to assault. The flower the girl reaches out to touch ultimately entraps her. The violence of the scene and the complicity of the male gods in the girl's abduction remind us that women in ancient Greek society had little control over whom they married. Rather they were circulated among men in order to establish links between their households.

Although Demeter hears her daughter's cries, she does not know about the abduction. Overcome with grief, she wanders for days trying to find news of her daughter. When she learns that Hades with the help of Zeus had arranged the kidknapping, she leaves the company of the gods and travels to the town of Eleusis. There she meets the daughters of King Celeus and offers to serve as the nurse to their newborn brother. Thwarted in her attempt to make the baby immortal by placing him in the fire, she commands the townspeople to build her a temple and departs. Still angry at the other Olympian gods, she causes a famine that threatens to wipe out the entire human race. To appease her, Zeus sends the messenger god, Hermes, to escort Persephone back to the upper world. But before she goes, Hades forces her to eat some pomegranate seeds, thereby guaranteeing her return to the underworld a third part of every year. Joyfully reunited with her daughter above ground, Demeter restores the crops to the earth and imparts the knowledge of her rites to the local people. The myth provides an explanation for the harvest cycle: when Persephone goes underground, it is winter and the earth lies fallow. When she returns in the spring, things start to grow again until the harvest is complete. Some feminist interpretations of the myth have emphasized how Demeter successfully challenges the male system of marriage by forcing Zeus to allow the girl to remain with her mother for part of the year instead of separating her completely from her natal family. Persephone nonetheless represents the archetypal bride: wrenched away from childhood innocence and the company of her mother and girlfriends, she is forced to dwell in a strange new home and submit to the will of its master. She is literally a "bride of death," a phrase commonly applied to girls who died before marriage in ancient Greece. The connection between Persephone and wedding imagery can be seen in a red-figure vase that depicts Hermes leading the girl back from the underworld (Figure 4.4). She ascends at left through a rocky outcrop, her way illuminated by two torches held by Hecate, goddess of magic and the crossroads. Persephone gazes across the surface of the vase at her mother, Demeter, who stands at right. She is lavishly adorned with a diadem and necklace in the manner of a bride.

The bride of death motif frequently appears in Greek tragedy, especially in scenes of voluntary sacrifice in which teenage girls are called upon to die on behalf of family, country or the gods. In Euripides' *Iphigenia at Aulis* (405 BCE), the goddess Artemis demands the death of Iphigenia, daughter of the Greek king, Agamemnon. Without her sacrifice, the Greek army will not be able to sail to Troy but will remain stranded on the island of Aulis. Agamemnon deceives the girl as to the purpose of her journey, telling her instead he plans to marry her to Achilles, greatest of the Greek heroes. When she learns the truth, she begs at first for her father to spare her life, but then undergoes a change of heart and heroically embraces her death:

> Mother, hear what thoughts have come to me: it is resolved that I must die. I wish to do this very thing with glory and to thrust aside cowardice. Consider with me how well I speak: hear my words, mother. In vain are you angry at your husband. It is not easy for us to endure impossible things. All of mighty Hellas now looks to me, in me alone are the passage of the ships and the sack of Troy .... If Artemis wishes to take my body, shall I, a mere mortal, stand in the way of a goddess? But that is impossible. I give my body to Hellas: sacrifice me, destroy Troy. This will be my memorial through the ages, this my children, my marriage, and my reputation. (Eur. *IA* 1374–1400)

Iphigenia acts almost as male warrior in her resolve to sacrifice her life to further the Greek cause. She argues that she has no claim on her body but rather that it belongs to Artemis.

Figure 4.4 Hermes leading Persephone back from the underworld; Attic red-figure bell-krater attributed to the Persephone Painter, c. 400 BCE. New York, Metropolitan Museum of Art, Fletcher Fund 28.57.23.

Instead of the rewards of marriage and children, she will win enduring fame for her bravery. Indeed, her heroic actions elicit praise from Achilles: "I envy you because Greece has chosen you, not me, to die" (Eur. *IA* 1407). Her sham wedding in truth will become a marriage to death, like that of Persephone. At the last minute, however, Artemis spares her life, replacing her with an animal sacrifice and transporting her to the remote land of Tauris to serve as her priestess.

That a Greek poet might plausibly portray an adolescent girl as a hero capable of dying for her country or some larger ideal reinforces the idea of the fluidity of ancient Greek gender roles prior to adulthood. Euripides' *Hecuba* (424 BCE) offers a similar account of a heroic maiden, the Trojan princess, Polyxena. The Greeks have conquered Troy, killing all its male inhabitants, and now prepare to divvy up the captive Trojan women. Achilles, now dead, has demanded that the virgin be sacrificed on his tomb in order to appease his insatiable lust for honor. Her mother, Hecuba, once a queen and now a slave, has no choice but to comply. Euripides provides an arresting portrait of Polyxena's final moments:

> "O Argives who destroyed my city, I die of my own free will. Let no one touch my body, for bravely I will offer my neck. But kill me allowing me to be free by the gods, that I might die free. For among the dead I am ashamed to be called a slave when I am royal" .... And when she heard the words of her master, taking her gown from the top of her shoulder, she tore it from the middle of her side to her navel, and revealed her breasts and chest, beautiful as a statue, and planting her knee to the earth, made the most heroic speech of all: "See here, young man, if you desire to strike my chest, strike away; but if you desire the place under my neck, my throat is ready for you." (Eur. *Hec.* 547–66).

Like Iphigenia, Polyxena publicly welcomes the opportunity to die. But as she unflinchingly confronts her sacrificer, she puts aside all modesty, stripping off her clothing like a male warrior. She displays uncommon courage by practically taunting him with her proud words. She turns what would have been an act of submission – voluntary sacrifice – into a form of suicide as she reasserts her royal status and takes control of her death. Her sacrifice does not contribute to a larger political goal, like that of Iphigenia, but rather disturbingly serves only to appease the arrogant ego of a dead hero.

Perhaps the most famous heroic virgin in tragic drama is Sophocles' Antigone. Although not technically a sacrificial victim like Iphigenia and Polyxena, she similarly embraces her own death in pursuit of a larger principle. When her two brothers die in single combat, the king decrees one of them, Polyneices, to be an enemy of the state and forbids burial of his body. Antigone disobeys his orders by casting handfuls of dust over his exposed corpse and performing the requisite funerary rites. She argues in her defense that divine laws should take precedence over those of mortals, a passage discussed more fully in Chapter 7. Condemned to die for her crime, Antigone equates her death to marriage in her final speech. "O tomb, O bridal chamber, eternal dwelling dug deep in the ground, where I go to find my family" (Soph. *Ant.* 892–3). The double suicide of the girl and her fiancé together in a remote cave at the end of the play literally renders Antigone a bride of death. But as compensation for the loss of marriage and motherhood, she will receive instead eternal fame and glory. The close association of marriage and death in these myths suggests that this life transition entailed a profound change of identity for women in ancient Greece. Like Persephone, the Greek bride left behind her childhood home to take up residence in a new house, where she submitted to the physical control of an unknown man. In this regard, she experienced a symbolic form of death as she relinquished her former identity. We should also not underestimate the very real risks of childbirth, discussed more fully in the next chapter, that also might have contributed to this equation.

4.6 The Greek Wedding

The brief period of adolescence concluded for a Greek girl when she married. In the ancient world as today, marriage was a social process rather than simply a legal moment. The wedding marked this transition in three stages: separation from childhood, usually through dedications to Artemis, transition to the new home with a nocturnal torchlight procession, and incorporation into the hearth of her husband's family. Weddings were a communal event from the earliest period of Greek history. On Achilles' shield in Homer's *Iliad*, the wedding procession comprises one of two scenes of the city at peace:

> In one, there were marriages and feasting; they led brides from their chambers by the light of blazing torches through the city, and loud bridal songs arose; young men whirled about, dancing, and in their midst flutes and lyres resounded. And there women stood by their doors and marveled. (Hom. *Il.* 18.491–6)

Although only family members participated in wedding celebrations, they attracted the interest of the entire community. Wedding rituals not only formed bonds between individual families, they also epitomized the social order necessary for peace and prosperity.

The wedding ceremony initiated the sexual relationship between the bride and the groom, distinguishing it as legitimate in the view of the community. Fathers were obligated to see that their daughters were suitably betrothed, married, and provided with a dowry. The process began with the engagement, signified by the term *engye*, which means to "place in the hand." It refers to the promise made by the bride's father to the groom, as well as the transference of his physical control over her to him, sealed by a handshake. Marriage involved a formal arrangement between the father of the bride and her prospective groom without consultation of the girl. The reproductive purpose of the union is evident in the formulas used in literary representations of betrothal, such as this one found in New Comedy:

FATHER: I give you my daughter to sow for the purpose of cultivating legitimate children.
GROOM: I take her.
FATHER: I also give you a dowry of three talents.
GROOM: I take it, too, happily. (Men. *Per.* 1012–5)

Note that the vows here take place between two men rather than between the future husband and wife, as today. The agricultural language recalls the association of adolescent girls with untamed nature while underscoring that the primary goal of marriage was the production of children. The formula also emphasizes that children born from this union will be legitimate, entitled to citizenship and to inherit property. The dowry that the father provided for his daughter represented the fulfillment of his final parental duty. In the absence of a father, the kyrios or closest male relative, such as brother or uncle, made the arrangements. The betrothal period could last quite a long time because it could be enacted even when a girl was still a child. The marriage, however, did not take place until the bride-to-be reached the age of sexual and reproductive maturity, around age 14. The term ***nymphe*** indicates this transitional period of marital eligibility, until the birth of her first child, when her transformation to adult woman was complete. The age of the groom, in contrast, was probably around 30, when a man might inherit his father's estate. Because girls married at such a young age, only just postpubescent, they married men almost old enough to be their fathers.

The wedding ceremony itself took place over 3 days, from the day before the wedding night to the day after. Prenuptial sacrifices, usually to Artemis, preceded the wedding ceremony. A passage from Euripides' *Iphigenia in Aulis* describes some of the ritual activities that took place:

They are presenting the maiden to Artemis, queen of Aulis, as a preliminary to marriage. What groom will lead her home? But come, begin the rites, get the baskets ready, crown your heads, and you, king Menelaus, prepare the wedding song, and throughout the tents let the flute resound and let there be the sound of dancing. (Eur. *IA* 433–39)

Sacrifices to Artemis marked the end of childhood and the transition of the girl from her sphere to that of Aphrodite, goddess of female sexuality. One passage describes these offerings as obligatory: "Before a bride goes into the bedchamber, she must bring a sacrifice to Artemis as a penalty" (*SEG* IX 72.8.84–85). The sacrifice in a sense substituted for the virginity of the bride, which she left behind upon marriage. Often this took the form of toys, as in the epigram that opens this chapter. The offering could also consist of a veil: "Alcibia dedicated the sacred veil for her hair to Hera, when she reached the time of her lawful wedding" (Arch. *Anth. Gr.* 6.133). The veil mentioned here and elsewhere refers to the one donned at puberty, to be replaced by the wedding veil. Sashes could be dedicated at this time, and symbolized the loss of virginity, because to "untie the sash" was a common euphemism for sexual intercourse. Hair could also be given, as the cutting of hair is a common coming-of-age ritual in many cultures, for both boys and girls. Euripides describes this custom at Troezen, where brides offered their shorn hair to Hippolytus, a follower of Artemis:

Unyoked girls before marriage will cut their hair for you who will reap the deep mourning of their tears through the ages. This will be forever the theme of the maidens who celebrate you in song, nor will Phaedra's love for you fall nameless and obscure. (Eur. *Hipp.* 1425–30)

The dedication of premarital hair physically marked a girl's transition to marriage as well as symbolized the loss of childhood, because hair was often dedicated at the tomb as a sign of mourning.

After the offerings, the bride, along with her groom, participated in several other rituals before the marriage could be accomplished. Both underwent a nuptial bath the night before the wedding to purify the body and to promote fertility with water drawn from a spring, which was believed to have generative power. After the bath, the bride adorned herself in preparation for her appearance at the wedding feast under the supervision of the ancient equivalent of a wedding planner, the *numpheutria*. Like today, the dressing of the bride was the focus of much attention and is a frequent scene on Attic vases. She most likely wore a purple gown, a color known for its costliness, and one associated with the goddess, Aphrodite, into whose sphere she would soon pass. Anointing herself with perfume, she covered her head and face with a veil and donned a crown. Hesiod's account of the creation of the first woman, Pandora, gives a glimpse into how such a bride might have looked:

> For the famous god with the crooked feet fashioned from earth a thing like a modest maiden according to the plan of the son of Cronus. And the grey-eyed goddess Athena clothed and adorned her with silvery garments. And from her head she spread with her hands an intricately embroidered veil, a wonder to look at. And she placed around her head a golden crown which the god with the crooked feet himself had made working it with his own hands to please his father Zeus. (Hes. *Theog.* 571–80)

In this passage, the goddess Athena acts as the bride's helper, outfitting her for the wedding. Pandora's exquisite clothing, veil, and crown, suggest her irresistible power of seduction and her transition to a sexual role. The bride's costume not only served to enhance her beauty but could also advertise her family's high social status to the guests. A character in Euripides' *Andromache* describes her bridal costume as follows:

> With a crown of rich gold around my head and a sheath of embroidered cloth on my body, I arrived here having these offerings not from Achilles nor Peleus, but from the land of Laconian Sparta my father gave these things to me along with many wedding gifts, so that I might speak freely. (Eur. *Andr.* 148–54)

She argues that her lavish dowry puts her in charge of her husband's house, a theme that recurs in Roman literature. Only after being carefully outfitted did the bride meet her groom. On a vessel used in the nuptial bath (Figure 4.5), a young man leads his wife to his house, grasping her by the wrist in a gesture signifying marriage and showing male control over the bride. Behind the bride stands the numpheutria, who adjusts her veil. The mother of the groom appears in the doorway at right, holding two torches, as she welcomes the bride into their home. A miniature Eros figure adjusts the bride's crown, representing her sexual allure. The vessel itself, called a loutrophoros, was used only for nuptial baths and for bathing the dead in preparation for burial, further highlighting the symbolic connection between wedding and death ritual for the ancient Greeks.

The wedding proper began with a feast that brought together friends and relatives of both the bride and the groom to celebrate, usually held at the home of the bride's family. The format resembled that of the symposium, only with a major difference: men and women dined together, each in a separate part of the room. The menu could be elaborate but always included traditional sesame cakes, which, with their many seeds, symbolized the fertility of the married couple. The guests participated in dances and sang songs, some of which resemble those found at

Figure 4.5 A young man leads the bride by her wrist to his house in a wedding procession; Attic red-figure loutrophoros, c. 425 BCE. Boston, Museum of Fine Arts, 03.802.

the symposium, but also songs specific to the occasion that praised the bride and groom and wished them future happiness. An example is found in a fragment of Sappho, "To what, O bridegroom, do I compare you? To a slender sapling, I compare you, most of all" (Sappho Fr. 115). In the evening, the father of the bride handed over his daughter to the groom before the assembled guests, bringing them together for the first time. It is believed that the unveiling of the bride, called the ***anakalypteria***, occurred then. The lifting of the veil that covered her face, especially her eyes, allowing her to look directly into the eyes of her husband, signified the bride's sexual availability to husband. In removing the veil, the bride put aside her aidos or modesty and expressed her erotic desire for her husband.

The wedding culminated with the procession of the bride at night to her new home, another scene widely depicted in art and literature. The cry, "Get up! Make way! Carry the torch!" initiated the journey. Mothers played an important role in the transfer of the bride from one home to the other. The mother of the bride accompanied her daughter to her new home carrying torches. Children who still had both parents living, signifying the health and fertility of the new couple, may have also participated in the procession. Upon arrival at groom's house, her new mother-in-law welcomed her at the door holding a torch in honor of Hymen, the god of marriage. The bride in effect was transferred from her biological mother to her mother-in-law, with whom she resided along with her husband. The ritual responsibility of torch bearing was so important to mothers that queen Clytemnestra refuses to return home from Aulis without her daughter, as her husband urges, for fear of missing out on this part of the ceremony, "And leave my child? Who will raise the torch?" (Eur. *IA* 732). Jocasta, another tragic queen, similarly laments not being able to do this for her son, "I did not light for you the torch fire that custom ordains in weddings, as a happy mother should" (Eur. *Pho.* 344–6). Once at her new home, the bride was conducted to the hearth as the newest member of the household, where she underwent a ritual of incorporation called the **katakhysmata**, the showering of the newlyweds with nuts, dried fruit, and coins. The ritual underscores the status of the bride as an outsider, as a virtual suppliant at her husband's hearth. Like an infant or newly bought slave, she had to undergo rituals at the hearth to integrate her into the family.

Before entering the bedroom where the union was consummated, the bride ate a quince or apple (Plut. *Mor.* 138d). This act recalls the pomegranate seeds that Persephone consumed in the underworld and represents her new bond with her husband. Her loyalties now belong to him, not to her natal family. After the couple entered the chamber, a friend of the groom closed the door and stood guard to ensure they were not disturbed. Sappho provides a comic description of this figure: "The doorkeeper's feet are seven fathoms long; his sandals are five ox-hides, and ten cobblers labored to finish them" (Sappho Fr. 110). Guests held a night-long vigil outside the door, singing a special type of song associated with weddings, the **epithalamium**, originally one sung outside the nuptial chamber, perhaps to disguise the cries of the bride, as the Hellenistic poet, Theocritus (fl. 270 BCE) suggests: "Maidens sing the epithalamium before the bridal chamber so that the voice of the virgin might not be heard as she is violated by her husband, but might go unnoticed, covered by the maidens' voices" (Theoc. *Id.* 18.3.42). This type of song later develops into a distinct poetic genre associated with weddings. The next day the wedding guests awoke the bride and groom at dawn for the final day of celebration and the giving of gifts. With these rituals completed, the life of the young woman had changed forever: no longer a virgin and no longer a member of her natal family, she adopted a new role as wife and mother and began to learn the customs of this alien household.

At Sparta, the nuptial process took a very different form. Because the Spartan regime required women's physical training to ensure they became healthy mothers, girls married only when fully mature and ready for motherhood. They practiced marriage by capture, a custom that probably had died out by the classical period. A girl designated the "bridesmaid" shaved the head of the captured bride, then dressed her in a man's cloak and shoes and placed her alone on a mattress in a darkened room. After dining at the public mess with other males, her groom would enter the room, have sex with her, and leave quickly, rejoining his peers in the barracks. This pattern of furtive conjugal visits could continue for more than a year, such that a man might even father children without ever having seen his wife in daylight. The Spartans believed this custom helped instill moderation and self-control, while stimulating the desire for sexual intercourse, thereby maximizing the odds that a child would be born from their union.

4.7 Conclusion

Adolescence for girls in ancient Greece marked the end of childhood and the beginning of adulthood, but in contrast to today, it was extremely brief. It coincided with the onset of menstruation, a primary concern of the medical writers, for whom it constituted the primary biological distinction between men and women. As the goddess who governed this transition, Artemis was the focus of much of the ritual activity of maidens. Because of their sexual maturation, access to well-born adolescent girls was strictly controlled; inside the house, she kept to the women's quarters, and outside she donned a veil and kept her gaze downcast to avoid attracting the notice of men. At the same time, her beauty could be appropriately displayed in ritual contexts such as processions and choral dancing in the hope of attracting a suitable husband. Marriage could occasion great fear and anxiety in a girl as she left the comfort of her natal family to join the bed of a stranger. Greek literature links this transition to death, beginning with the abduction of Persephone, who literally marries death but is allowed to evade it for a brief period each year. The examples of Antigone and Iphigenia show how unmarried girls can act heroically, receiving public acclaim in place of marriage and children. By means of the wedding ceremony, the girl shed her childhood identity and assumed membership in her husband's household. The next chapter explores various aspects of this new life stage, from conjugal sexuality governed by the goddess Aphrodite to pregnancy, childbirth, and motherhood.

Questions for Review

1 Why did Artemis govern female adolescence?

2 What are some ancient medical views of the female body during adolescence?

3 Why is marriage a symbolic form of death for girls?

4 What are the stages of the Greek wedding ceremony and what function do they serve?

5 How do Spartan views of female adolescence and marriage differ from those of the Athenian?

Further Reading

Primary Sources

Alcman, *Partheneion*
Euripides, *Iphigeneia at Aulis*
Hippocrates, *On Virgins*
Homeric Hymn to Demeter
Sappho

Secondary Sources

Calame, Claude (2001). *Choruses of Young Women in Ancient Greece: Their Morphology, Religious Role and Social Function.* trans. D. Collins and J. Orion. New York: Rowan and Littlefield.
 Develops a model for understanding the maiden chorus as a rite of passage, with special attention to the genre of the partheneion.
Dean-Jones, Lesley (1991). The cultural construct of the female body in classical Greek science. In: *Women's History and Ancient History* (ed. S Pomeroy), 111–137. Chapel Hill, NC: University of North Carolina Press.
 A clear and concise summary of ancient medical views of the female body, focusing on the Hippocratic writings and Aristotle, with an extensive treatment of their theories of menstruation.
Foley, Helene (ed.) (1993). *The Homeric Hymn to Demeter.* Princeton: Princeton University Press.
 Provides versions of the text in Greek and English with extensive commentary, followed by interpretive essays.

Llewelyn-Jones, Lloyd (2003). *Aphrodite's Tortoise: The Veiled Woman of Ancient Greece*. Swansea, Wales: Classical Press of Wales.

Explores the practice of veiling in ancient Greece from a cross-cultural perspective. Chapter 6 contains an interesting discussion of the concept of aidos.

Oakley, John and Sinos, Rebecca (1993). *The Wedding in Ancient Athens*. Madison, WI: University of Wisconsin Press.

Reconstructs the stages of the Greek wedding through an examination of literary and visual sources, with emphasis on the latter. Numerous vase images are included.

Pinney, Gloria Ferrari (2008). *Alcman and the Cosmos of Sparta*. Chicago: University of Chicago Press.

Sets forth a new interpretation of Alcman's *Partheneion* through a detailed analysis of the fragment.

Pinney, Gloria Ferrari (2002). *Figures of Speech: Men and Maidens in Ancient Greece*. Chicago: University of Chicago Press.

Examines the representations of gender in art to understand Greek ideals of femininity, masculinity, and marriage.

Vernant, Jean-Pierre (1969). Hestia-Hermes: the religious expression of space and movement among the Greeks. *Social Science Information* 8 (4): 131–168.

An exploration of the religious and mythological meaning of the hearth in Greek thought.

5

Greek Marriage and Motherhood

Courtesans we keep for pleasure, concubines for daily attendance upon our person, but wives for the procreation of legitimate children and to be the faithful guardians of our households.

([Dem.] 59.122)

The ancient Greeks and Romans were unusual for their practice of monogamy. Most ancient cultures were polygamous, with men having multiple female partners in various forms of official and unofficial relationships. As the opening passage implies, only one woman was recognized as a legitimate marriage partner in ancient Greece, although men expected to be sexually involved with others. They might keep concubines, engage in sexual activity with their slaves, or frequent prostitutes outside of the house. At the same time, the ancient Greeks held complex and often contradictory views toward their wives. On the one hand, they recognized the necessity of wives as economic partners and caregivers, as well as the importance of their biological role in the production of legitimate male heirs. On the other, they felt deep suspicion toward their wives, especially toward their sexuality. Chaste girls, with their unrealized sexual potential, were not threatening because they remained under the control of their fathers and guardians, strictly supervised within the house, whereas wives, for whom marriage necessitated the activation of sexuality, provoked male ambivalence. Their position as wives and mothers gave them greater freedom than daughters, potentially allowing them to subvert male control and ultimately posing troubling questions about paternity and mortality. The Greeks used the same word, *gyne*, for both woman and wife. The equation of woman with wife implies that adulthood for females in ancient Greece could not be achieved apart from marriage and reproductive sexuality. This chapter explores the positive role of women in the Greek household and family and their contributions as wives and mothers. The next chapter looks at negative representations of female sexuality and its repercussions for men.

5.1 Pandora: The Ambiguity of Wives

The story of the creation of the first human female, Pandora, briefly touched upon in the last chapter, provides fundamental insights into the bifurcated view of wives in ancient Greece. Two slightly different accounts survive from Hesiod. In the first, Zeus creates Pandora as a punishment for the trickery of Prometheus, who first disguises ox bones as choice cuts of meat and offers them to the god, misleading him into choosing the inferior portion. When Zeus punishes him by removing fire from mortals, he smuggles it back into the human world, hiding it inside a hollow stalk. Both acts involve defiance and trickery, two qualities also

Women in Classical Antiquity: From Birth to Death, First Edition. Laura K. McClure.
© 2020 John Wiley & Sons, Inc. Published 2020 by John Wiley & Sons, Inc.

found in the newly created female. For the second offense, Zeus retaliates by instructing the god of craft, Hephaestus, to shape from earth the likeness of a modest maiden, a punishment that fits the crime. Pandora's exquisite clothing, veil, and crown of flowers, although likening her to a bride about to be given to her new husband, also suggest a deceptive surface that easily misleads. She is a "beautiful evil" whose seductive exterior conceals an untrustworthy, thievish nature. From her springs "the deadly race and tribe of women, a great curse who live among mortal men, not helpful in wretched poverty, but only in wealth" (Hes. *Theog.* 591–3). Nonetheless, the poet informs us that it is better for men to marry than to remain single. The man who does not marry reaches old age without anyone to care for him and dies without offspring to inherit his property. This parable points to the necessity of women and their integration into the community through marriage, despite the pain and misery they purportedly bring to men.

The other account is probably more familiar to modern readers as it includes the first reference to "Pandora's box," which, in the original story, is actually a large terracotta jar of the type commonly found in Minoan civilization. This creation story provides a few more details about Pandora's character:

> And [Zeus] ordered the famous Hephaestus to mix earth with water as swiftly as possible, and to implant the voice and strength of a human, to make the lovely, beautiful shape of a maiden, with a face like the immortal goddesses; and Athena to teach her crafts, to weave a skillful web; and golden Aphrodite to shed grace on her head, and painful desire and limb-loosening sorrows. And he instructed Hermes, guide and slayer of Argus, to place in her the mind of a dog and a thievish character. So he spoke. And the gods obeyed the lord Zeus, son of Cronos. Straight away the famous lame god Hephaestus fashioned from earth the likeness of a modest maiden according to the counsels of Zeus. Grey-eyed Athena clothed and adorned her. The divine Graces and queenly Persuasion placed golden necklaces around her skin, while the lovely-haired Seasons crowned her head with spring flowers. Then the guide and slayer of Argus, Hermes, crafted within her heart lies and tricky words and a thievish character, according to the plan of deep-thundering Zeus. And the herald of the gods put a voice in her, and they called this woman, Pandora, because all the gods who inhabit the halls of Olympus, gave her a gift, the curse of hard-working men. (Hes. *Op.* 60–82)

As in the other Hesiodic account, Pandora is a "modest maiden" who embodies all of the desirable qualities of female adolescence described in the last chapter – beauty, modesty, sex appeal, and skill at weaving. To these are added clearly negative characteristics – lies, deception, and craftiness. She is passive and beautiful on the outside but scheming and destructive on the inside. Pandora thus exemplifies the dual nature of women in the Greek imagination: as a maiden, she is pure, circumspect, and obedient, but as a wife, she cannot be trusted. Passed from one man to the next – Hermes, the guide, delivers her to Epimetheus, the brother of Prometheus, who has been warned not to accept gifts from the gods – Pandora moves from maiden to wife. Once welcomed into Epimetheus' home, symbolically as a wife, she spreads destruction:

> Before the tribes of men lived on earth without troubles and without hard labor and terrible sicknesses, which bring death upon men. But the woman took the great lid off the jar with her hands and scattered them. She contrived wrenching anxiety for mortals. Hope alone remained there in an unbreakable home under the rim of the jar .... (Hes. Op. 90–7)

Like the biblical Eve in Genesis, the actions of Pandora introduce human suffering in all its various forms into the male world. Just as Eve's eating of the fruit leads to the expulsion from Eden and human mortality, so Pandora alienates men from the gods and introduces the certainty of old age and death. Hesiod's two accounts of the creation of Pandora provide a template for this chapter and the next. On the one hand, men in ancient Greece needed women to contribute to the economic welfare of their households as well as to bear offspring who could ensure its continuity. At the same time, they viewed wives with suspicion, because as outsiders they did not fully belong to their households. Many of these anxieties centered around female sexuality as an essential ingredient of marriage but an aspect difficult to control, as we see in Chapter 6. The two faces of Pandora, as it were, are further reflected in divergent literary representations of women in ancient Greece. On the one hand, we find virtuous wives and mothers praised in funerary inscriptions and exemplified in myth by characters such as Penelope, Alcestis, and Andromache. Contrasted are the adulterous, unfaithful, and even murderous spouses, such as Helen, Clytemnestra, and Medea, who are the targets of blame and invective, as we see in the next chapter.

5.2 Aphrodite: The Power of Female Sexuality

Many goddesses governed adult female life in ancient Greece. Demeter as goddess of grain promoted agrarian and female fertility and ensured the stability and continuity of the community. Despite her association with virgins, Artemis also ministered to women in childbirth. Women prayed to her to facilitate a painless and successful delivery. Athena directed the industry of women within the house in their capacity as weavers. Hera represented the principle of monogamy within marriage, as reflected by her antagonism toward Zeus' many mistresses in myth. But probably the most important goddess for female married life was Aphrodite. One story of her birth is instructive for understanding her powers. When the sky god, Ouranus, refused to uncouple from his wife, Gaia, thereby preventing their children from being born, Gaia enlists the help of her son, Cronos. By castrating his father with a scythe, he forces the pair to separate. Ouranus' penis, flung into the sea, gives birth to Aphrodite, who arises from the foam fully formed. Emerging from a context of violence and desire, Aphrodite, like Pandora, possesses ambivalent powers, seductive charm, irresistible desire, the instinct to procreate, and a knack for deception. The Greeks worshipped her in her capacity as goddess of female sexuality and fertility.

Aphrodite's importance for the continuation of the family and community is attested by the presence of her cults in every region of Greece. At Athens, the cult of Aphrodite Pandemos ("belonging to the people") and her companion Peitho ("persuasion") recognized her as a goddess who unites individuals in both the political and social spheres. The sanctuary of Aphrodite in the Gardens evoked her power of growth and fertility in the form of fruit, crops, and other vegetation. Aphrodite Ourania ("heavenly") was worshipped by brides, wives, and courtesans alike, because she governed their relationships with men. A sculptural relief from the Ludovisi throne illustrates this concept (Figure 5.1). It depicts the birth of Aphrodite from the sea, attended by two nymphs, who hold a garment before her naked body to protect her modesty. The panel belongs to a larger monument, probably an altar, which shows on one side a nude flute-girl and on the other, a fully veiled woman. These two figures represent the two sides of Aphrodite's worship, sex within marriage and its procreative purpose, and recreational sex outside of marriage for pleasure. Girls said goodbye to childhood through dedications to Artemis and anticipated their role as sexual partners by sacrificing to Aphrodite before marriage. Indeed, her various epithets, such as *Kypris*, the home of her most famous cult, could

Figure 5.1 Central panel of the Ludovisi throne, probably taken from the sanctuary of Aphrodite at Locri, c. 460 BCE. Rome, Museo Nationale, inv. 85702.

serve as a euphemism for sex. For this reason, the goddess also had a special importance as the patron of courtesans and prostitutes.

Within marriage, Aphrodite embodies the sex appeal of wives. She makes them so irresistible that their husbands cannot resist sleeping with them. Several amusing examples are found in Greek literature, beginning with Hera's seduction of Zeus in Homer's *Iliad*. Desperate to distract her husband from the battle in order to help the Greek army, Hera dresses up in the hope that her husband "might desire to lie in love with her next to her skin and she might be able to drift a harmless gentle sleep across his eyelids and conscious mind" (Hom. *Il*. 14.164–66). To that end, she undergoes an elaborate makeover, cleansing her body with ambrosia and anointing it with perfume. After combing and braiding her hair, she puts on a richly patterned robe woven by Athena, along with a tasseled sash, glistening veil, and a golden pin and earrings. To ensure the success of her plan, Hera then enlists the help of Aphrodite, requesting that she provide her with the characteristics of beauty and desirability by which the goddess subdues gods and men. Aphrodite in response lends her a special object: "The goddess spoke and from her chest loosened the elaborate, embroidered breast band, containing every sort of magic – on it is figured love, passionate desire, intimate sharing, and persuasion, which steals away the sense of even the most intelligent" (Hom. *Il*. 14.214–217).

The object described is not a sash of the type donned by girls at puberty but rather a sort of strap that crossed between the breasts. It functions not so much as lingerie but rather as a love charm intended to work its magic on the object of desire, compelling him to surrender to the woman's sexual advances. Erotic magic is frequently attributed to women in Greek literature and practice, particularly as a last resort of wives and as the purview of courtesans (see Box 6.1). The story of Hera's seduction of Zeus demonstrates the importance of female sexuality within marriage. Although the Greeks placed strictures on women's movements, segregated them spatially within the household, and prohibited the public display of the female body, as we have seen, a woman's ability to arouse and seduce her husband was essential to marriage and procreation. The power of Aphrodite is that of sexual attraction, which binds together a couple and leads to the birth of children. As a form of erotic capital, a woman's sexuality involved a certain amount of danger for a man as it meant that he could potentially lose control in the throes of passion or that she could choose to sleep with another man. In the case of Zeus and Hera, the love charm puts Hera temporarily in charge of the war and leads to a fleeting Greek victory over the Trojans.

The power of Aphrodite permeates Aristophanes' *Lysistrata,* in which the women of Greece stage a sex strike to persuade their husbands to stop the long war between Athens and Sparta. In order to accomplish the strike, the leader Lysistrata instructs the young wives to make themselves as attractive as possible through the use of cosmetics, filmy dresses, and the ancient version of a bikini wax:

> For if we women should sit inside all made up, skimpily clad in garments of sheer silk, our pubic hair plucked, our husbands would then be aroused and desire to have sex with us, we would not comply but would staunchly resist, until they negotiate a swift treaty. (Ar. *Lys.* 149–54)

Though it may surprise modern readers, it was common practice among adult women in ancient Greece – both respectable wives and prostitutes – to remove pubic hair by either plucking or singeing. The use of cosmetics by women was also widespread (see Box 5.1). Clothing comprised an important weapon in a wife's erotic arsenal, as we saw in the story of Hera's seduction of Zeus, and could take the form of a saffron-dyed yellow gown, or one made of finely spun linen or silk fabric that revealed the body beneath, and a special kind of slipper.

Like Hera in Homer's *Iliad,* these wives use their sex appeal to interfere with the male business of war. They too are empowered by Aphrodite to bring their plan to fruition, using their seductiveness to overcome the wits of men: "Eros who delights the mind and Cypris-born Aphrodite may you breathe desire upon our breasts and thighs, and cause the strained pleasure of erections in our husbands" (Ar. *Lys.* 551–3). Lysistrata's prayer is soon answered as one husband capitulates, approaching the sequestered women to bring home his wife, Myrrhine. He is obviously feeling the effects of sexual deprivation: "A man! A man! I see a man approaching, stricken, seized by the rites of Aphrodite!" (Ar. *Lys.* 831–2). Instead of offering relief, however, Lysistrata counsels his wife to lead him on, "to roast him and turn him on, to flatter him, to love him and not to love him, and to give him anything he wants – except what you swore over the bowl not to" (Ar. *Lys.* 839–41). A humorous scene ensues in which the wife again and again defers sexual gratification by insisting on the comforts of home before their union can be consummated. Myrrhine's successful delay tactics show the sex strike at work and foreshadow the women's ultimate victory over the men as they surrender to sexual desire and agree to end the war. The erotic power of women in this play, although obviously exaggerated for comic effect, nonetheless suggests the centrality of Aphrodite and female sexuality within marriage.

As these passages indicate, clothing played a major role in enhancing female beauty. Indeed, clothing and jewelry in the ancient world were prized possessions and could comprise a substantial portion of a woman's personal wealth. Most Greek garments were made of wool, although linen was widely used for some kinds of tunics and for undergarments, whereas silk was worn by wealthy women. Women's clothing tended to be more colorful than that of men. Many featured geometric motifs and figurative elements woven, and only very rarely embroidered, in contrasting purple, a costly dye made from sea snails. Clothes consisted of large pieces of cloth with simple contours woven to shape on traditional looms. Surprisingly, there was not much difference between Greek and Roman clothing in terms of material and cut. The traditional Greek woman's garment was the peplos, a square piece of fabric worn with the top third folded down and pinned at the shoulders. By the late classical period, however, the main costume for both men and women was the **chiton** ("tunic") topped with a **himation** ("cloak").

Box 5.1 Ancient Cosmetics

Ischomachus then said, "One time, Socrates, I saw that she had painted her face with thick white lead, so that she seem paler than she really is, and put on a lot of rouge, so that her cheeks would seem rosier than normal, and high boots, so that she would seem taller than she naturally was." (Xen. *Oec.* 10.2)

Here a husband criticizes his wife's use of cosmetics as a form of deception that violates the trust of marriage. Despite this disapproval, cosmetics were widely used among women in ancient Greece and Rome. Traces have been found in a pyxis, a special type of cosmetic jar produced exclusively for women (see Figure 3.3). Although laws at various periods restricted the number and types of garments women could wear, few explicitly prohibited the use of cosmetics. A husband in a law court speech notices the white lead on his wife's face when he encounters her in the middle of the night, a clue that she had just returned from a visit with her lover (Lys. 1.10, 17). A passage from Aristophanes suggests that the basket-bearer in the procession of the Panathenaia probably painted her face with white lead (Ar. *Eccl.* 732). These examples confirm that respectable women regularly applied cosmetics to enhance their appearance.

A white lead foundation and a form of rouge made from the alkanet root, two substances often found together, were the primary forms of makeup. Applied to the face, and sometimes to the neck and arms, lead carbonate produced a paler complexion, a desirable physical trait among Greek women from the earliest times. Goddesses and mortal women are described positively as "white armed," and many noble women in Greek tragedy are portrayed as having white hands, cheeks, throats, or necks. Pale skin was associated with wealth and high social status because it indicated that a woman did not need to leave the house but could rely on servants for any external business.

Although references to eye makeup are rare, women did enhance their eyes using a black ink or soot, a practice more often associated with prostitutes than with proper wives. A comic passage that lists the ways courtesans might hide their physical deficits discusses the use of cosmetics: "One has light eyebrows – she paints them black with soot. Another happens to be dark – she slathers on the white lead. One is too pale-skinned – she paints her face with rouge" (Alexis, Ath. 568b). Another comic anecdote distinguishes respectable married women from common prostitutes by their excessive use of makeup, especially eyeliner (Eubolus, Ath. 557f). Strange as it may seem, a slang term for prostitutes was "Anchovy," because of their pale skin, slenderness, and large eyes. As we have seen, the Greeks closely connected eroticism with the eyes: as discussed in Chapter 4, the virtuous maiden keeps her eyes downcast whereas the bride, once unveiled, gazes forthrightly at her husband, acknowledging her sexual availability to him. The use of eyeliner encouraged the male gaze and advertised the sexual availability of its wearer.

Most tunics lacked sleeves, consisting of two pieces of cloth joined at the sides and on the shoulders. On special occasions, such as religious festivals, women wore a special kind of garment called the **krokotos**, dyed yellow with saffron.

Visual sources suggest that most women did not wear undergarments beneath the peplos and chiton, although there are literary references to breast binding. Women enhanced their conservative and simple costume with elaborate jewelry, hairstyles, and makeup. Although women mainly wore leather sandals, they could also don special types of shoes to enhance their attractiveness. Brides, for instance, may have worn a special type of sandal. In Aristophanes' *Lysistrata*, the wives put on a special kind of soft boot to attract their husbands. The erotic appeal of women's feet and their coverings is also evident when a husband is imagined consulting a shoemaker about "stretching" his wife's sandal straps to alleviate pain: "Shoemaker, about my wife's foot: the thong is squeezing her little toe, where she's tender. So why don't you drop by some afternoon and loosen it up so there's more play down there?" (Ar. *Lys.* 416–19). Herodas (third century BCE), a Hellenist poet discussed more fully in Chapter 8, bases one of his comic sketches on the association of female footwear with sex (Herod. 7.57–64).

5.3   Virtuous Wives: Penelope and Alcestis

Although depictions of conjugal love are rare in Greek art and literature, one of the earliest and most compelling is that of Penelope and Odyssey in Homer's *Odyssey*. Parted from her husband for over 20 years, Penelope deftly manages to keep her husband's household intact. Indeed, many real Greek women would have found themselves in a similar position, left alone for months at a time while their husbands went away on military campaigns. Pressed by her suitors to remarry, she manages to resist them through a clever stratagem involving weaving, the primary economic contribution of women to the household, as we saw in Chapter 2. She promises the crowd of suitors who gather at her house each day that she will choose one of them to marry upon completion of a shroud for her father-in-law. But each night she secretly unravels her work:

> For she instills hope in all and makes promises to each man, sending us messages, but her mind is intent upon other things. For she has devised in her heart this further scheme: she set up a great loom in the palace and began to weave a very large and fine web, addressing us as follows: "Young men, suitors now that godlike Odysseus is dead, though eager for this marriage with me, wait until I complete this weaving, a shroud for the hero Laertes. For when destructive fate of remorseless death closes his eyes the spun thread will not be wasted in vain, and no local Achaean woman will criticize me, for not providing a man of many conquests with a winding sheet." So she spoke and the manly heart in us was persuaded. By day she worked at the great loom, but at night she undid it by the light of torches. So for three years she did this in secret, and deceived the Achaeans. But when the fourth year came and the seasons returned, one of her women, who knew clearly what was going on, confessed, and we caught her unraveling the splendid weaving. (Hom. *Od.* 1.91–109)

Penelope uses her domestic skills to suspend time until Odysseus returns. Her weaving represents the crafty intelligence that matches that of her husband. Although duplicitous, the stratagem serves a positive purpose. It preserves Odysseus' household and affirms Penelope's loyalty to him by effectively thwarting the possibility of a new marriage. Although she rarely leaves the women's quarters, Penelope exerts agency and independence through her weaving, paving the way for her husband's return home and the restoration of his political power. A red-figure vase depicts Penelope in a posture of grief seated on a stool below her loom with her son, Telemachus, holding a spear at left (Figure 5.2). The loom and the tapestry dominate the visual composition, emphasizing Penelope's fidelity and agency in the poem's narrative.

Penelope's fidelity and intelligence are further evident upon Odysseus' return home. Even after he identifies himself and provides convincing evidence that he is who he says he is, Penelope refuses to believe him. Instead, she finds her own way to test him, using "signs which we two alone know, signs hidden from others" (Hom. *Od.* 23.109–10). She orders the nurse to move their marriage bed, built by Odysseus, into the hall. Because only one other person, a female servant, has actually seen the bed apart from the couple, a stranger would not know that

Figure 5.2 Penelope with Laertes shroud; Attic red-figure skyphos by the Penelope Painter, c. 440 BCE. Chiusi, Italy, Museo Nazionale.

one of the bedposts is actually carved from a tree that grows in the middle of the bedroom and cannot be moved. Odysseus, knowing the secret of the bed, immediately expresses outrage at the mere suggestion that someone might move it. His reaction instantly confirms the hero's identity to his wife so the couple can be reunited. The bed carved into the tree symbolizes the permanence of their marriage and the continuation of the male line through their union.

Penelope's skepticism, like her weaving, preserves her marriage, even in their long years of separation. Otherwise, she might have inadvertently ended up sleeping with another man, as she explains to Odysseus, "For this reason I did not embrace you when I first saw you, always the heart in my breast was full of dread lest some man should come and beguile me with his words" (Hom. *Od.* 23.214–6). In contrast, Helen has committed the "shameless act" of sleeping with a foreigner because she did not have this skepticism. Whereas Penelope has refused to share her bed with another despite mounting evidence that Odysseus will never return home, Helen violated her marriage in the erroneous belief that the Greeks would never rescue her (Hom. *Od.* 23.218–25). The poem and the later tradition repeatedly juxtapose and contrast the virtuous wife, Penelope, with adulterous wives like Helen and her sister Clytemnestra, characters who are discussed more fully in the next chapter. Penelope wins fame among men for "remembering her husband well." Indeed, the Greek general Agamemnon congratulates Odysseus on his wife's ***arete*** ("virtue"), the female equivalent of male excellence in battle:

> Happy son of Laertes, Odysseus of the many devices, you possess a wife of great virtue, so good was the mind of blameless Penelope, the daughter of Icarius, she remembered Odysseus well, her wedded husband. Not ever will the fame of her virtue perish, but the immortal gods will make a lovely song for wise Penelope among men on earth. (Hom. *Od.* 24.192–8)

Penelope's heroism, in contrast to that of a warrior who earns glory from courage in battle, has a more passive quality. Through memory, she maintains a connection to her husband and keeps his presence alive in the household despite his long absence. Her weaving stratagem keeps the suitors at bay and protects Odysseus' property until his return. Her skepticism as to the true identity of her disguised husband safeguards her from becoming an unwitting participant in adultery.

Another mythic wife famous for her virtue is Alcestis, who is mentioned for her beauty and children in Homer but is not fully developed as a character in literature until Euripides' same-name play (438 BCE). Although Alcestis' heroism also benefits her husband's oikos, it assumes a form quite different from that of Penelope. Given the chance to die in place of her husband and save his life, she accepts. As Euripides tells the story, Zeus forced Apollo, god of healing, to serve as the slave of the mortal, Admetus. In exchange for treating him well, Apollo grants him a reprieve from death, as long as he can find someone else to die for him. When his elderly parents refuse, he asks his wife, Alcestis. She agrees, as she explains:

> Giving your life precedence over my own, so that you will continue to look upon the light, I am dying. I had the option not to die for you, for I could have married any Thessalian man I wished, and lived amid wealth in a royal house. But I refused to live life torn away from you with orphaned children, and I did not spare my prime, though I had much to enjoy. (Eur. *Alc.* 282–9)

Throughout her long speech, Alcestis never once mentions love for her husband as a motivation for her sacrifice but rather stresses that she dies to prevent her children from becoming orphans, a condition defined by the Greeks as the absence of a father but not of a mother. She further extracts a promise from Admetus never to remarry so that her children will not be subject to the unpredictable whims of a malicious stepmother. The male chorus repeatedly praise her for her action, singling her out as the best of wives: "Let her know that she dies glorious and the best wife under the sun by far" (Eur. *Alc.* 150–1). Like Penelope, she will be immortalized in song: "For you alone dear among women, you have dared to give your life for your husband and save him from death" (460–2). The language of the play casts Alcestis as a hero, who instead of dying for country, dies to save her family. Her virtue, however, is ultimately rewarded. At the end of the play, the superhero Heracles, another guest of Admetus, wrestles with death and restores Alcestis in the guise of a bride to the upper world and her husband.

Penelope and Alcestis are two examples from Greek myth of women who earn the praise of men for their exemplary actions. In everyday life, however, Athenians avoided publicly naming respectable women, identifying them instead by their male relatives. Public acclaim for a model wife and mother occurred only after death, when her name might appear on a grave marker. This type of funerary monument, called a ***stele***, began to appear around the mid-fifth century in Athens. It often contains a central relief framed by pilasters on the sides with a pediment above. The reliefs frequently depict the deceased in a scene of farewell with family members. Many focus on women. These gravestones lined the major roads that ran through the cemeteries just outside the gates of the city. They were thus highly visible to a broad sector of society. One gravestone commemorates a young woman named Mnesarete (Figure 5.3), whose name means something like "she who remembers virtue." She is seated at right on a plain stool without a cushion. She wears sandals, a chiton, and a himation draped over her shoulder, her left arm, her back, and lower body. She pulls her veil across her chest with her right arm. Her hair is gathered in a low bun at the nape of her neck and bound by a ribbon. On the left a young woman, probably a slave but possibly a sister, stands with eyes downcast. The inscription on the monument reads:

Figure 5.3 Grave relief of Mnesarete, daughter of Socrates, shown seated at right and attended by a girl at left, c. 380 BCE. Munich, Glyptothek Museum, inv. 491.

Mnesarete, daughter of Socrates, this woman left a husband and brothers, and grief to her mother, a child and a reputation for great virtue that will never age. Here one who reached the goal of all virtue is held in Persephone's chamber.

The inscription situates Mnesarete exclusively within the family context: she is defined by relationships with her father, siblings, mother, and child. Although her virtue is unspecified, it is indicated by her name and the repetition of the word arete, suggesting beyond the stories of myth that real women could hope to win acclaim only through their invisible work of fostering ties within the family.

5.4 How to Train a Wife

The *Household Economy* of Xenophon (c. 430–354 BCE), a work that has already been mentioned several times, provides another perspective on the attributes of an exemplary wife. Framed as a conversation between the philosopher Socrates and a gentleman farmer named Ischomachus, the dialog discusses how best to manage one's estate. A central part of this conversation revolves around the proper training of a wife. As we have seen, female domestic labor was a necessary component of male leisure. In other words, Ischomachus is able to philosophize with Socrates only because he has a trustworthy and competent wife managing his household. In keeping with convention, the woman is never named, although we know from other sources that she was called Chrysilla. A primary ingredient for a successful marriage and household, according to Ischomachus, is to choose a young and inexperienced girl. His own wife "was not yet fifteen when she came to me, and had spent her previous years under careful supervision so that she might see and hear and speak as little as possible" (Xen. *Oec.* 7.5–6). Her lack of exposure to the outside world means that she will be more easily trained and obedient to her husband's instructions. It also results, one presumes, from her spatial segregation within her father's house, where she was kept away from male view. A good wife had to take care not to be seen by other men, especially outside of the house, or people would gossip. The character Andromache takes pride in the fact that she seldom left her house while married: "Whether or not reproach attaches to a woman, if she does not remain at home, she is criticized; relinquishing my desire to go outside, I stayed at home" (Eur. *Tro.* 647–50).

Xenophon outlines the duties of Ischomachus' wife as follows: organizing and distributing agricultural products within the house, baking, teaching slaves to weave, caring for clothes and linens, arranging supplies and utensils in an orderly fashion, and keeping track of inventories. Tending to the sick was another important responsibility of women in an age before hospitals and nursing: "One of your proper concerns, however, may seem the most thankless: you will have to be concerned about nursing any of the slaves who fall ill" (Xen. *Oec.* 7.37). In another text, we hear of a dying man who takes back the pregnant young wife whom he had earlier cast off in order to have someone attend to his sick bed:

> He was won over in his illness by the attention of Neaera and her daughter – for they came to him while he was sick and without anyone to care for him, bringing remedies for his disease and looking after him. You yourselves know what value a woman has in the sick-room, when she waits upon a man who is suffering. ([Dem.] 59.56)

The age difference between husband and wife – around 15 years – is clearly seen in Xenophon's dialog. The husband is much older and already well established in his estate. He imparts detailed instructions about how to arrange the household while the wife strives to comply, eagerly seeking his approval at each turn. The text envisions marriage as an economic and reproductive partnership in which the respective duties of husband and wife are differentiated by gender. Such differences, according to the author, are rooted in nature and divinely ordained:

> For [the god] made the body and mind of the man better able to endure cold and heat and walking and military campaigns and thus enjoined him to do outside work. Since he made the female body by nature less capable in respect of these things, he thought fit to prescribe for her the inside work …. And knowing that he created in the woman and enjoined upon her the nurture of newborn children, he allotted to her a greater measure of affection for infants than to the man. (Xen. *Oec.* 7.23–4)

The goal of marriage is to preserve and increase the estate not only through agricultural production and stewardship but also through the birth of children. In the Greek view women are better equipped to rear children because they are more affectionate by nature than men. This cultural logic justifies the gendered division of labor within the oikos as well as points to the primary importance of women as mothers in the classical polis.

5.5 The Legal Status of Athenian Women

The epitaph that introduces this chapter distinguishes between courtesans, concubines, and wives, dividing them into two groups: those who tend to men's physical needs and those who bear them legitimate children. Setting aside the observation that the male speaker of this passage views women only in terms of their physical use for men, it nonetheless provides a good starting point for understanding the role of wives and mothers in the classical polis. The concept of legitimate children refers not only to a man's biological offspring but specifically to those recognized by the state as citizens. Because courtesans and concubines were usually foreigners, as we see in the next chapter, their children could not become citizens. In contrast, citizen women were those born from Athenian parents and entitled to participate in the communal ritual activities of the state. In 451 BCE, the statesman Pericles persuaded the assembly to change the citizenship laws such that only males born of both an Athenian father *and mother* could qualify as citizens. This reform gave women an important, if indirect, role in legitimating male citizenship in the Athenian polis. Indeed, challenges to a man's citizenship often took the form of questioning the political status of his mother. For instance, in the oration from which the epigraph is taken, the speaker demands that the courtesan, Neaera, be condemned for passing off her daughter as an Athenian citizen when she was, in fact, the product of unknown parentage.

Although Athenian women shared in citizenship as wives and mothers, they did not possess political rights. They did not attend, speak at, or vote in political assemblies nor could they hold public office. They could not represent themselves in court or probably even go to the theater. A law quoted in Isaeus (c. 420–340s BCE) further states, "For a child is not allowed to make a will; the law forbids either a child – or a woman – to negotiate any contract beyond the value of one measure of barley" (Isaeus 10.10). In contrast to their Spartan counterparts, Athenian women could not make a will, inherit or own property, or engage in commercial transactions in excess of enough grain to feed a family for four or five days. When we do hear of citizen women selling their wares – usually those who have fallen on hard times – they are small items, such as woolen ribbons, wreathes, and vegetables. Despite these restrictions, the Athenian legal system put into place certain protections for women that addressed their vulnerabilities. First, it protected them through the institution of guardianship. A woman's kyrios was her protector rather than master and was both legally and morally obligated to attend to her welfare, much like the relationship of parents to children today. The guardian provided a woman with domestic support and representation outside of the house. However, there was no guarantee that he would always act in her best interests. The law further safeguarded girls and women from crimes of sexual violence, called *hybris*. Although its meaning has been much debated, it was a powerful term of moral condemnation and treated as a serious crime. Whether rape or seduction, an act of hybris shamed not only the victim but also her male family members. The law authorized prosecution whenever someone committed an act of hybris against another person and stipulated that the legal system determine the penalty.

An important economic protection was the dowry. When a woman married, she contributed to her husband's household a dowry, which had been previously negotiated between her future husband and her father, as discussed in Chapter 4. Indeed, it was a matter of pride for an Athenian father or guardian to be able to provide a generous dowry, consisting of cash, furniture and housewares, or real estate. The dowry represented the woman's share of the paternal estate. It was intended primarily for her maintenance and thus served as a continual source of protection for her within the marriage. Although managed by her husband, the dowry legally belonged to the wife and had to be returned to her father or other guardian if the marriage dissolved. Even widows upon remarriage received dowries just like young girls. This practice ensured that women were not completely financially dependent during the marriage and guaranteed them financial support regardless of their marital status. It also provided a measure of economic control within the household. Because the dowry could be difficult to disentangle from the overall finances of her husband's oikos, it operated as a disincentive to divorce. Poor girls lacked a dowry and therefore had a hard time finding a marriage partner, driving some into prostitution or other professions for support. Sometimes family friends, or very occasionally the state, would provide them with dowries.

5.6   Pregnancy and Childbirth

Once a woman became a mother, she was likely to be treated less as a child by her husband and recognized as an adult. She may have had more freedom to do as she wished and more authority within the household, especially if she had given birth to a boy. Then as today, this transformation did not always go as planned. Some women experienced infertility, others conceived but succumbed to the risks posed by becoming pregnant and giving birth at too young an age. And death from childbirth was always a very distinct possibility for women in the Greco-Roman world.

When confronted with infertility, a woman or her husband might turn first to the gods. One of the most popular appeals to Asclepius, son of the god Apollo and the leading medical divinity in the late fifth century, was to cure infertility. The god dealt with all sorts of health problems but was particularly popular with women. Anatomical votive offerings of breasts and wombs were dedicated to the god in gratitude for pregnancy or in the hope of becoming pregnant or of producing a good milk supply. At Epidaurus, women anxious for children slept in Asclepius' temple where they awaited dreams that revealed the cure for their infertility. One inscription from the fourth century BCE describes how a woman named Ithmonice dreamed she asked the god to give her a daughter. When she conceived and remained pregnant for three years, she returned to Epidaurus to ask the god why she had not yet delivered. In sleep he informed her that she had not been specific enough in her request. As soon as she left the sanctuary, she purportedly gave birth. Elsewhere on the stone we even hear of a five-year pregnancy! Indeed, requests for intervention in infertility were second only to remedies for eye trouble or blindness. People also consulted the oracle of Zeus at Dodona, inscribing on lead tablets the question, "Will there be children for me?"

Another option was to consult a doctor. Although both men and women turned to the gods for children, only women sought out medical treatment. Indeed, the basic responsibility for fertility in the medical texts lies with the female, not the male. Conception and pregnancy is a major topic in the Hippocratic corpus, not only because men needed their wives to produce sons in order to continue the oikos but also because pregnancy is considered the precondition for female health. The Hippocratic writings thus repeatedly emphasize the importance of sexual intercourse and pregnancy for women. According to Hippocrates, women who have never given birth suffer from a greater range of female maladies than those who have and are even prone to other illnesses, such as, inexplicably, lameness. A constant refrain is, "If she becomes pregnant, she will be healthy." Although Hippocrates and his followers relied on traditional lore gathered and transmitted orally by midwives in their recommendations for the treatment of women, the corpus nonetheless reflects a male perspective on female reproduction.

One Hippocratic treatise, *On Infertility*, deals exclusively with the causes of infertility in women. First, it advises tests to ascertain whether the female patient could become pregnant. The determination of infertility and its treatment rested on the anatomical belief that a tube passed through the diaphragm connecting the vagina to the nostrils. If the passage is open, a woman will be able to conceive:

> Apply a suppository of a little oil of bitter almonds wrapped in wool: then at dawn examine whether the suppository has given off an odor through the woman's mouth: if it has, she will become pregnant, but otherwise not. (Hippoc. *Ster.* 2.2)

Once the physician diagnoses infertility in the woman patient, he applies various remedies, ranging from the merely disgusting to the downright dangerous. Some of these are simple, some long and complicated, requiring multiple drugs, regimens of purging, bathing and restrictive diets, and the use of lead or tin probes. One such recipe instructs the patient to sit over a vapor bath infused with cypress and bay leaves. A series of catheters of increasing thickness are then applied to open the cervix while the patient avoids food and drinks only sweet white wine, for as many days as she wants. (No doubt the woman remained in a pleasantly tipsy state for those few days.) She should then eat "fat, well-steamed meat of puppy together with octopus boiled in very sweet wine" (Hippoc. *Ster.* 5). Another prescribes:

> Boil bull's gall and brine, mix with fine sulfur, give this an elongated form the size of a large nut, and insert it without any covering directly against the uterus for two days and nights. Again after this, sprinkle on mercury herb … mixing pure myrrh, dissolve … anoint the mouth (sc. of the uterus) as far in as possible with the best grade of rose and iris unguent. (Hippoc. *Ster.* 23.2)

The treatise also stipulates that proper conditions must be met to ensure conception: for instance, spring is the best time to become pregnant. This brief discussion shows how medical texts construct and reinforce differentiated gender roles within classical Greece by emphasizing the importance of reproductive success in women.

A comic solution to the problem of female reproductive failure is a form of surreptitious adoption. In one comic play, we hear how an infertile wife contrives with the help of a midwife to pass off another woman's baby as her own in order to provide her husband with a son. She fakes a pregnancy and then introduces the supposititious child into the oikos as her husband's, as described in this humorous account:

> And I know another woman who alleged she was in labor for ten days, until she could purchase a baby; her husband ran around buying drugs to speed up labor, meanwhile an old woman brought in a baby in a pot, plugging his mouth with honeycomb so he wouldn't cry. Once she brought him in and gave a nod, the woman immediately shouted, "Go away, go away, husband! I think I am about to give birth!" Then she kicked the belly of the pot, while her husband ran out, overjoyed. The old woman removed the wax from the baby's mouth, and he started crying. Then the sneaky old woman picked up the baby and ran out, smiled at the husband and said: "A lion, a lion has been born to you, in your exact likeness! Absolutely everything about him resembles you, even his crooked penis!" (Ar. *Thesm.* 501–16)

Delivered by a male character disguised as a woman, the speech is deliberately provocative in its portrayal of women as devious, difficult to control, and in collusion with one another. It also suggests that such babies were readily available and easy to procure. But such a scenario could be plausible only in a society largely organized around gender segregation. Notice the husband is not present for the birth and that the wife relies on other women for assistance. In a play by the comic poet Menander (c. 344–292 BCE), another old woman serves a similar function: when she happens on abandoned twin infants, she gives the boy to a woman in need of a baby and keeps the girl for herself (Men. *Per.* 133–40).

Both Greek myth and medical texts tend to downplay the contribution of women to the reproductive process. Indeed, some stories bypass female reproduction altogether, as in the case of Zeus and his first wife, Metis, whose name means "cleverness." After lying with her, Zeus immediately fears the consequence, for he has heard a prophecy that she will bear extremely powerful children who in turn might overthrow him. To avoid this fate, Zeus promptly turns Metis into a fly and swallows her. A little while later, he suffers a terrible headache. Hephaestus splits open his head with an ax and out pops Athena, fully formed and dressed as a warrior. Another myth attributes a second birth to Zeus. When his mortal lover, Semele, becomes pregnant with his child and questions his divinity, he strikes her with a thunderbolt. As she dies consumed by the fire the god rips the unborn child from her womb and sews him into a pouch in his thigh. A few months later, Dionysus is born. In both of these stories, Zeus appropriates female reproductive power – the only form of power he himself does not possess by nature – to strengthen his position and ensure the continuity of his rule. These stories of male birth suggest great ambivalence toward female reproduction and the desire to control it. In a famous speech from Aeschylus' *Eumenides* (458 BCE), Apollo takes this view one step further:

> The mother is not the one who conceives what is called her child, but rather she is only the nurse of the newly sown embryo. The father, the one who mounts, begets the child, while the mother, like a stranger to a stranger, preserves the young plant, if no god harms it. (Aesch. *Eum.* 658–61)

He argues that the mother contributes no genetic material to her child but serves only as a kind of incubator for the fetus. He uses this argument to exculpate his "client," Orestes, from the crime of matricide by asserting that mother and child have no biological connection, or to put it in modern terms, that they share no DNA. Aristotle provides a similar account. Although in his view both the man and woman contribute genetic material to the formation of the fetus, the male provides the principle of movement and generation and the female only pure matter, that which nourishes the fetus. He restricts procreative agency to men while viewing women as the substrate for generation. In contrast, the Hippocratic writings state that conception results from the mingling of both male and female seeds in the womb, with the sex of the fetus determined by the stronger of the two.

The medical view of the labor process similarly downplays the agency of the mother. The Hippocratic writings conjecture that the baby fights her way out of the womb during labor like a chick pecking its way out of an egg. Contractions represent the consequence, rather than the cause, of this struggle. Because male children were considered stronger and more vigorous, they were thought to produce an easier birth for their mothers. For help in labor, women propitiated the goddesses Artemis and Eileithyia. Originally a Minoan goddess, the latter had numerous cults throughout Greece. In myth, she is the daughter of Hera and frequently associated with Artemis. She can help or hinder childbirth as she wishes. A Hellenistic epigram invokes Eileithyia and promises a dedication after a successful delivery: "Once again, Eileithyia, come when Lycaenis calls, you who help in childbirth to ease the pains of labor" (Callimachus, *Anth. Gr.* 6.146). We also find numerous dedications to Eileithyia, whether inexpensive terracotta figurines or costly votive reliefs such as Figure 5.4, demonstrating that women of all classes sought divine aid in birth. At Brauron, we have extensive lists of dedications made to Artemis in gratitude for a successful delivery. Although bronze objects such as mirrors are mentioned, most are garments, some quite elaborate: "an embroidered, purple tunic," "a spotted, sleeved tunic in a box," "a short tunic, scalloped and embroidered with letters woven into it," and "a woman's cloak with a deep, wavy border in purple." Euripides also mentions the practice of dedicating textiles at this sanctuary in connection with birth, although they are offered at the tomb of Iphigenia to commemorate women who had died in childbirth (Eur. *IT* 1464–7).

Most doctors in ancient Greece were male. They probably would not have been summoned to attend a birth unless there were complications, a decision that ultimately resided with the husband. To call on a physician may have been the mark of prestige, a luxury only the very wealthy could afford. More often, women turned to other women for advice in reproductive

Figure 5.4 Marble votive stele showing a mother after childbirth, late fifth century BCE, Athens. New York, Metropolitan Museum of Art, Fletcher Fund, 1924, 24.97.92.

matters and assistance in childbirth. Literary sources refer to the mothers of women in labor as acting as midwives, along with friends and neighbors who offered assistance. The comic character Praxagora uses the excuse of assisting a friend in childbirth to explain her mischievous absence to her husband: "A girlfriend in the throes of labor sent for me" (Ar. *Eccl.* 528). Professional midwives assisted in labor as well as provided advice about fertility, contraception, abortion, and even sex determination. According to Plato, they were normally older women, usually citizens, who had given birth themselves but were no longer of childbearing age. A funerary inscription for one midwife, however, suggests that some might have received medical training: "Phanostrate, a midwife and physician, lies here. She caused pain to nobody and will be missed after her death by all" (*CEG* 569).

Although it is impossible to give an exact figure, maternal mortality rates were extremely high in classical antiquity compared to modern Western societies. The peril and pain of childbirth are encapsulated by Medea's statement, "I would rather stand in battle three times than give birth once" (Eur. *Med.* 250–51). Many women died from exhaustion and hemorrhage after a difficult delivery, especially in the case of very young women, or if in poor health. Eclampsia and puerperal fever also occurred, though it is not believed infection played a major role in home births. A votive stele that served as an offering to a healing deity, either Asclepius or Hygieia ("Health"), in gratitude for a safe delivery depicts a woman just after birth (Figure 5.4). Her sinking posture and loosened clothing and hair indicate the physical hardship of childbirth. The figure behind her holds a swaddled infant in her left arm. On the left, two women carry torches and possibly represent gods, either Hygieia and Asclepius or Eileithyia and Artemis. Both mother and child have survived the ordeal, despite its dangers.

Childbirth brought ritual pollution, known as ***miasma***, upon anyone entering the house because it involved the shedding of blood. It was therefore forbidden to give birth on sacred ground, such as in a temple. A fourth-century BCE law from Cyrene states pollution afflicted those present at the birth for three days. The mother's own pollution probably lasted until the name-giving ceremony on the tenth day after the birth. However, childbirth was not considered as contaminating as death. The mother usually nursed the newborn herself. Recall that the young mother in Lysias' oration quoted previously moves to the first floor from the women's quarters upstairs in order to nurse her newborn son. If the family could afford it, a wet nurse might be employed, a woman who herself had recently given birth. Usually such a woman was a slave but she could also be a poor freeborn woman. Because it was believed that the nurse transmitted character through her milk, her personal qualities and habits were an important consideration for both the Greeks and the Romans.

Because of their focus on helping women to conceive and successfully carry a pregnancy to term, the Hippocratic writings have little to say about methods of contraception or abortion. They do mention a substance called misy, a form of copper ore, as effective in preventing conception for up to a year. Many of the recommended gynecological cures, such as pennyroyal, in fact may have hindered conception or acted as abortifacients. Substances used as barriers, such as sponges soaked in vinegar or oil, might have acted as spermicides. Withdrawal before ejaculation was probably widely practiced, although not directly attested in literary sources. Medical writers distinguished between contraception and abortion but often confused the two. Many modern opponents of abortion have cited the famous tenet of the Hippocratic oath, "I will not give to a woman a pessary to cause abortion," as evidence that the Greeks did not support the practice. In fact, this statement prohibits only abortifacients in the form of suppositories, possibly allowing for other forms of termination, such as surgical intervention or drugs taken orally. One Hippocratic account of an abortion seems to suggest that early intervention in a pregnancy did not count as an abortion but almost as the ancient equivalent of emergency contraception:

> A female relative of mine owned a very valuable singing girl, who had relations with men, but was not to conceive lest she lose her value. The singing girl had heard the sorts of things women say to one another, that when a woman is about to conceive, the seed does not leave her but rather remains within. She understood what she had heard and always kept a watch. But when she noticed one day that the seed did not go out of her, she told her mistress, and the case came to me. When I heard [the story], I ordered her to jump up and down so as to kick her heels against her buttocks, and when she had jumped for the seventh time, there was a noise and the seed ran down to the ground. And the girl, on seeing it, gazed at it and looked amazed. (Hippoc. *Nat. Puer* 2)

This implausible account has much to tell us not only about medical conceptions of the female body but also about Greek society as a whole. First, the girl's pregnancy is considered inconvenient for her owner, whose livelihood it might jeopardize. She herself is never consulted about the decision to terminate. We also see firsthand how gynecological information circulated among women and helped inform them about their bodies. This passage further suggests that it was socially acceptable under certain circumstances to end an unwanted pregnancy in classical Athens. Almost all of the other allusions to abortion in the Hippocratic writings refer not to elective termination of pregnancy but rather to spontaneous miscarriage. A fragment from Attic oratory, however, suggests that abortion was a crime against the husband, if his wife was pregnant when he died, because the unborn child could have inherited the estate. Temple inscriptions state that a woman incurred pollution for 40 days after an abortion. These scattered references indicate that although abortion may have been strictly a female concern, perhaps carried out in secret, it does not appear to have been widespread. At least, the practice does not generate as much public attention as it later does in Rome. Moreover, a woman could choose infant exposure over abortion as an alternative means of getting rid of an unwanted child and this seems to have been the more likely scenario. But again, we have no firm data for the popularity of either practice.

Whereas sexual intercourse and pregnancy promoted female health, the Greeks believed that an idle womb could pose a major threat to a woman's well-being. If a wife did not regularly engage in sex, her womb could become dry and light and start to gravitate toward other, moister parts of the body, such as the liver, heart, or brain. A woman so afflicted might become mute, lose consciousness, or even suffocate, suffering a form of hysteria, a term that derives from the Greek word for womb:

> If suffocation occurs suddenly, it will happen especially to women who do not have intercourse and to older women rather than to young ones, for their wombs are lighter. It usually occurs because of the following: when a woman is empty and works harder than in her previous experience, her womb, becoming heated from the hard work, turns because it is empty and light. There is, in fact, empty space for it to turn in because the belly is empty. Now when the womb turns, it hits the liver and they go together and strike against the abdomen – for the womb rushes and goes upward towards the moisture, because it has been dried out by hard work, and the liver is, after all, moist. When the womb hits the liver, it produces sudden suffocation as it occupies the breathing passages around the belly. (Hippoc. *Mul.* 1.7)

If the womb did not return to its proper place spontaneously, the doctor used a form of aroma therapy. Sweet and foul-smelling substances were applied at either end of the body, mouth and cervix, to coax the womb back into place. Plato even goes so far as to describe the womb as a wild animal with a mind of its own. For what it's worth, he similarly characterizes the penis as an unruly creature (Pl. *Tim.* 73c). The cure for this beast is naturally conception and pregnancy, a condition that effectively moisturizes, and therefore weighs down, the light, dry uterus:

> For women have an animal within them eager for conception, which whenever it goes without issue for a long time beyond its proper season, becomes angry and miserable and wanders everywhere around the body, blocks the outlets for air, and prevents respiration, causing extreme helplessness and bringing on all sorts of other diseases until the desire and passion of both the man and the woman bring them together, and as if they were picking fruit from a tree, they sow into the field that is the women living beings that are too small to be seen and formless. (Pl. *Tim.* 90e–91d)

Both of these accounts serve to reinforce a male agenda. A woman who did not engage in regular sexual activity with her husband or maintain a constant state of pregnancy ran the risk of her uterus going rogue. The concept of the wandering womb further justified social ideology. If a woman could not maintain control over her own body, how could she exercise authority over others? The job was best left to men who did not suffer from the vagaries of the female body and its negative impact on the female mind.

5.7 Mothers and Children

> And mothers love their children more than fathers, because they think that the children are more their work; for people estimate work by its difficulty, and in the production of a child the mother suffers more pain. (Arist. *Eth. Eud.* 1241b5–10)

Figure 5.5 A young woman takes a male infant from the lap of his mother; Attic red-figure hydria, attributed to the Circle of Polygnotos, c. 440–430 BCE. Cambridge, Arthur M. Sackler Museum, Harvard University Art Museums, Bequest of David Moore Robinson, 1960.342.

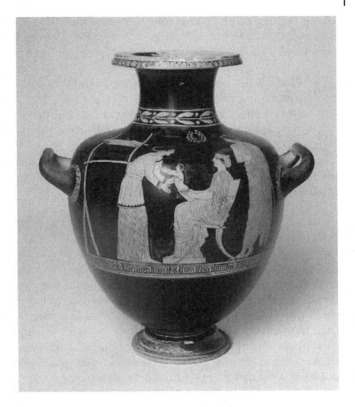

Although it has been argued that parents did not tend to get as attached to their infants as in the modern period because of the high rate of infant mortality, it is clear from literary and visual sources that the Greeks believed that mothers had a particularly close emotional attachment to their children. The philosopher Aristotle repeatedly states that mothers love their children more than fathers do, even in the animal kingdom. At one point, he explains that this is because the mother is more certain that the child is her own (Arist. *Eth. Nic.* 1368a24–25). One Attic vase depicts a mother handing a male infant to a woman, perhaps a nurse, standing to the left and gazing across at a male youth just behind the seated woman (Figure 5.5). The presence of the male baby and youth combined with the standing loom at left express Athenian ideals about marriage and motherhood. Ancient sources idealized maternal love as unconditional, selfless, and stronger than that of a father. Whether she employed a wet nurse or not, she was considered a child's primary caregiver:

> The woman conceives and carries the child, weighed down with pregnancy, risking her life and giving a share of her own food; and, with much labor, having endured to the end and given birth to her child, she rears and cares for it, although she suffers ill-treatment and the baby neither recognizes why he thrives nor can he communicate what he wants from her. Still she divines what is good for him and what he likes and tries to provide these things and tends to him for a long time, working day and night, not knowing what return she will get. (Xen. *Mem.* 2.2.5)

Greek tragedy is full of references to the tender affection felt by mothers for their children. Andromache, the wife of Hector, expresses her love for her baby just before the conquering Greeks kill him:

> O my little son, a mother's dearest armful, o sweet scent of your skin, in vain did my breasts nourish you wrapped in your swaddling clothes. In vain did I labor and wear myself out. Embrace your mother now, and never again, fall upon your mother, wrap your arms around my neck and put your mouth to mine! (Eur. *Tro.* 757–63)

The perceived intensity of the mother–child bond even drives a few female characters in Greek myth to commit unspeakable crimes, as well as explains their involvement in funerary ritual as mourners, as we see in the next two chapters.

5.8 Conclusion

The principal virtue of a Greek wife was self-control, that is, sexual fidelity within marriage. By remaining loyal to her husband, she maintained the integrity of the family line and ensured the continuation of his household. Characters such as Penelope and Alcestis provide mythic models of the virtuous wife. Like Penelope, wives in ancient Greece contributed economically to their husband's households through their industry, mainly in the form of textile production. In Xenophon, this industriousness affords husbands the leisure to engage in politics, attend the theater, or pursue philosophy. In addition, they guarded their households from intrusions by outsiders by remaining faithful. Like Alcestis, good wives put their husbands, and their children first, sacrificing their own happiness for the good of the family. They bore male children, thereby ensuring that the family line would continue into the future. Sexual attractiveness, maintained through the worship of Aphrodite and adornment in the form of clothing, footwear, and makeup, was a key ingredient in reproductive success. Failure to conceive could be addressed by petitioning the gods or by seeking medical assistance. In the latter case, a doctor might prescribe a woman an elaborate regimen to promote fertility. Childbirth itself was a dangerous, and often fatal, event in the lives of women. Once a woman had successfully completed this harrowing transition, it is easy to imagine her gratitude to Artemis and why she would have been eager to dedicate textiles in her honor. It is also understandable that the new mother may well have had stronger feelings for her offspring than her husband. In the next chapter, we look at a few women, both mythic and historical, who depart from this model, mainly through their disregard for sexual norms.

Questions for Review

1 Why was Aphrodite important to married women?

2 What are some of the most desirable qualities in a Greek wife?

3 What protections were in place for citizen women in classical Athens?

4 How did medical theories of the female body justify social ideology?

5 Why might the Greeks have fantasized about male birth?

Further Reading

Primary Sources

Aristophanes, *Lysistrata*
Euripides, *Alcestis*
Hesiod, *Theogony* and *Works and Days*
Hippocrates, *Diseases of Women* and *On Infertility*
Homer, *Odyssey*
Lysias, *Against Eratosthenes*
Xenophon, *Economics*

Secondary Sources

Dean-Jones, Lesley (1994). *Women in Classical Greek Science*. Oxford: Clarendon Press.
  Examines Greek medical ideas about the female body focusing on Aristotle and the Hippocratic corpus.
Demand, Nancy (1994). *Birth, Death, and Motherhood in Classical Greece*. Baltimore, MD: Johns Hopkins University Press.
  Considers social and cultural construction of childbirth in ancient Greece in light of feminist theory and anthropological studies.
King, Helen (1998). *Hippocrates' Woman. Reading the Female Body in Ancient Greece*. London and New York: Routledge.
  A lively account of the influence of Hippocratic ideas about the female body in Western medicine until the Victorian period.
Lacey, Walter Kirkpatrick (1968). *The Family in Classical Greece*. Ithaca, NY: Cornell University Press.
  An accessible and comprehensive account of the development of the Greek family from Homer through the classical period.
Pomeroy, Sarah (1997). *Families in Hellenistic and Classical Greece*. Oxford and New York: Oxford University Press.
  Updates the work of Lacey by providing an authoritative account of the Greek family from a variety of perspectives, literary, inscriptional, archaeological, art historical, and anthropological.
Rosenzweig, Rachel (2004). *Worshipping Aphrodite: Art and Cult in Classical Athens*. Ann Arbor, MI: University of Michigan Press.
  Explores the various meanings of Aphrodite to fifth-century Athens, with a focus on her cults and their visual representations.

6

Adultery and Prostitution in Greece

For she who surpassed all mortals in beauty, Helen, her most noble husband left behind and sailed to Troy, remembering neither her child nor her dear parents, but love lead her astray ....

(Sappho Fr. 16.6–12)

The preceding chapter explored the desirable characteristics of the virtuous wife and the construction of motherhood in the Greek literary and artistic traditions. This chapter focuses on representations of women who violate these social and sexual norms, starting with Helen in the opening epigraph. The ideal wife remained faithful to her husband and offered her body only to him. She brought wealth to his house in the form of a dowry, bore him sons, and managed daily life, supervising the production of textiles and tending to the sick. Her social identity revolved around the family as she linked generations and households. She participated in both domestic and civic religious rituals and had a particularly important role as a mourner. As an Athenian citizen during the classical period, she imparted political rights to her sons. The Greek literary tradition, however, has little interest in such virtuous women but rather gravitates toward female characters who transgress gender ideology. For every Penelope or Alcestis, we find many more notorious females, especially on the tragic stage. Such women dare to venture outside the house to intervene in male affairs, fail to rein in their lust, cheat on their husbands, and act publicly in defiance of male authority. This chapter explores some of the negative representations of women in ancient Greek literature. It shows how many of these images derive from male ambivalence toward female sexuality and fear of women operating outside of male control. We then look at nonwives, the prostitutes and courtesans whose bodies not only provided them with a means of economic support but also defined them as far outside the parameters of citizen wives. Although some enjoyed relative freedom and independence, most had no control over their sexual partners and the sex acts they were forced to perform.

6.1 *Eros* Unbound

In the last chapter, we observed the importance of female sexuality within marriage, a sphere governed by Aphrodite. The goddess is closely associated with another divinity, Eros, the personification of the overwhelming physical desire that attracts individuals to each other. Indeed, the two gods were jointly worshipped at a sanctuary on the north slope of the Athenian

Women in Classical Antiquity: From Birth to Death, First Edition. Laura K. McClure.
© 2020 John Wiley & Sons, Inc. Published 2020 by John Wiley & Sons, Inc.

acropolis and in some accounts he is her son. Eros is so central to human reproduction that he is one of the first gods to be created in the Greek cosmogony:

> First Chaos came into being, then Earth, the broad-breasted, firm seat of all the immortals who hold the peaks of snowy Olympus, and gloomy Tartarus of the broad paths in the interior of the earth, and Eros, the most beautiful of the gods, who unstrings the limbs and conquers the mind and thoughtful counsel in the hearts of all the gods and mortals. (Hes. *Theog.* 117–22)

He weakens the body and obliterates reason, equally afflicting men and women, gods and mortals. In Homer, he is the sexual desire that draws Paris to Helen, Zeus to Hera, and loosens the limbs of Penelope's suitors. Sappho describes him as impossible to resist: "Once again limb-loosening Eros shakes me, a bittersweet, irresistible creature" (Sappho Fr. 130 L–P). In contrast to our modern ideas about sexuality, the ancient Greeks defined eros as a dangerous, unwelcome, and uncontrollable lust that could be satisfied only by sexual intercourse. The god had various cults in ancient Greece and much individual worship. In art Eros often appears alone, carrying a lyre or hare, or in winged form in the company of Aphrodite, sometimes with a bow and arrows. He is a standard figure in wedding scenes.

Because the Greeks believed that women had less ability to control their erotic impulses, they worried constantly about the possibility of sexual promiscuity in their wives. Fidelity and self-control, as we saw in the last chapter, comprised the primary virtue for married women. By ensuring a wife did not stray, a man protected the purity of his family line and the future of his property. This surveillance began with the spatial control of women within the house, restrictions on their movements out of doors, prohibitions against exposing the female body, and the regulation of female speech. Adulterous wives thus posed a primary threat to the male social order by introducing uncertainty into the family's genealogy. Closely allied to this fear was the implicit knowledge that men could not completely control their wives. The story of Pandora exemplifies the problem: she is a creature whom men cannot resist and yet she introduces a myriad of problems into their world.

6.2 Helen: Archetype of Adultery

As early as the Homeric poems, we find the Greeks preoccupied with questions of monogamy, succession, and the management of female sexuality. Penelope, of course, represents the ideal: she has borne and raised a son, remains loyal to her husband, and keeps his house intact for over 20 years, resorting to trickery only to uphold these values. A different standard, however, applied to men: Odysseus cohabits with the goddesses Circe and Calypso for prolonged periods before his return home, delaying his journey by one and seven years respectively. The plot of the *Iliad*, in contrast, revolves around the problems engendered by an unfaithful wife, the notorious Helen, who left her own husband to sail to Troy with her lover, Paris. Despite the fact that Homeric poems do not contain a word for adultery, Helen nonetheless provides a prototype for the much-reviled adulteress:

> Then Helen, shining among women, answered him, saying: "You are both revered, dear father-in-law, and feared, I wish that evil death had pleased me when I followed your son, leaving my bridal chamber and siblings, my only daughter and the lovely girlfriends of my youth. But that was not to be and now I waste away in grief." (Hom. *Il.* 3.171–5)

Figure 6.1 Paris abducts Helen; Attic red-figure skyphos, Makron (painter) and Hieron (potter), c. 500–450 BCE. Boston, Museum of Fine Arts, 13.186.

Helen provides a striking contrast to Penelope: she has left her home and child and forsaken her husband for another man. Instead of "remembering her husband well," she has forgotten both husband and child, as Sappho describes at the beginning of this chapter. Although she will be the subject of much criticism in the later literary tradition, in the *Iliad* she is portrayed as the blameless victim of divine will, as Priam says, "You are not to blame in my view, but it is the gods that are to blame, who incited against me this grievous war of the Achaeans" (Hom. *Il.* 3.164–5). In particular, it is Aphrodite who has driven Helen to Troy and continues to goad her; when Helen later refuses to sleep with the cowardly Paris, the goddess forces her into his bed. In the epigraph, Sappho paints a slightly different picture of Helen. Both passages emphasize not only Helen's abandonment of her husband but also of other family members, particularly her daughter and parents. Sappho, however, praises Helen for her choice to pursue love and beauty over family. In one vase painting (Figure 6.1), Paris leads Helen away by the wrist in a gesture often associated with marriage. Like a bride, she is heavily veiled and wears a crown, and the Eros figure in between the pair suggests their erotic attraction. But contrary to this iconography, their union is illicit and results in the destruction of countless men. Whether a helpless victim of male abduction or a willing partner in an extramarital affair, Helen nonetheless becomes the prototype for the adulterous wife in the Greek literary tradition.

6.3 Adultery and Athenian Law

Moving from the character of Helen as the mythic model of female sexual infidelity, let us consider now attitudes toward female adultery in the classical polis. As we have seen, elite Athenian men went to great lengths to control the sexuality of their daughters and wives, whether through seclusion indoors that restricted contact with unrelated men, the requirement of veiling when outside the house, or the avoidance of naming them in public or in literary texts intended for public use, such as court speeches. These strategies ensured that their daughters had the proper qualifications for marriage and that their children would be their own. The Athenian legal system further protected the integrity of the family through the regulation of the sexual behavior of those outside the house.

A court speech by Lysias, *On the Murder of Eratosthenes*, details a real-life case. We looked at this text in Chapter 2 in connection with domestic space, at the section in which the defendant, Euphiletus, describes moving the women's quarters from upstairs to the first floor to better accommodate the needs of his wife (who is never named) and their new baby. This arrangement actually facilitates the love affair between the woman and her alleged lover, a certain Eratosthenes. According to the speech, Euphiletus found out about the affair, ambushed the couple during one of their nocturnal assignations, and killed Eratosthenes on the spot (he was literally caught with his pants down). The dead man's relatives subsequently prosecuted him for murder. In his defense, Lysias argues that the crime was not premeditated but rather an act of justifiable homicide in accordance with Athenian law. The speech is full of interesting details about daily life in classical Athens. For instance, you might wonder how the wife managed to meet her lover, given the restrictions placed on respectable women. Indeed, we know in this case that the house had a segregated space for women. But the wife uses that to her advantage, swapping rooms on the pretext of nursing the baby and ultimately locking her husband in the women's quarters to meet with Eratosthenes. Further, Lysias tells us that Euphiletus' wife met her lover at, of all places, his mother's funeral! You might also wonder how the pair managed to conduct their affair without the husband's knowledge. They enlisted a female servant as their intermediary. Threatened with being "whipped and sent to work in a mill," the girl later confesses everything to Euphiletus, who reports as follows:

> She accused [Eratosthenes] first of approaching my wife after the funeral, and then described how at last she became their messenger, and how my wife in time was persuaded and by what means she arranged his visits, and how at the Thesmophoria, while I was away in the country, she went to the temple with his mother. (Lys. 1.20)

This passage is remarkable first in reporting the words and actions of a slave. It also gives us a realistic sense of women's lived experience. Religious events such as funerals and festivals – the Thesmophoria was a women-only fertility celebration, to be considered more fully in the next chapter – presented one of the few opportunities for respectable women to leave the house. It shows the extent to which well-born women had to rely on domestic servants to interact with the public sphere and carry out their plans. The women's quarters not only kept women away from other men, it also afforded privacy and fostered friendship, and even complicity, among women. In keeping with Greek stereotypes about adulterers, the oration clearly holds Eratosthenes responsible for the affair: although the woman arranges the visits, he initiates the affair and persuades her to reciprocate.

Terms for adultery appear relatively late in the ancient Greek language. A male adulterer was a ***moichos***, a coarse term of abuse common in invective and comic poetry. There is no word that refers to a woman who commits adultery because she was always considered the object of adultery rather than an agent, as we saw in Lysias' speech. The law held only the male partner responsible, because it considered the woman incapable of controlling her impulses and easily led astray, much like a child. Some scholars have argued that the seducer, by persuading a woman to cheat on her husband, committed a crime as serious, or even more serious, than rape for the Greeks, a view that has met with controversy. As with adultery, the Greeks did not have a dedicated term for rape. They used terms like hybris, discussed previously, to refer to sexual violence against both women and men. Both words are inadequate to describe our modern concept of rape, which focuses on the absence of the victim's sexual consent. As we have seen, ancient authors had very different notions of a woman's ability to grant consent and were often more involved with questions of honor. For instance, in the story of Persephone's abduction, her own mother seems to care more about the disrespect shown to her by the male gods, who arranged the marriage behind her back, than about the abuse of her daughter.

In any case, the man who seduced another man's wife was a particularly reviled figure in ancient Greece, beginning with Helen's lover, Paris/Alexander in Homer's *Iliad*. Such a man corrupted the mind as well as the body of the woman, potentially gaining access to her husband's property and casting doubt on his children's lineage. Adultery represented an offense against natural marital relations because it had the potential to destroy marital love (Xen. *Hier.* 3.3). From the male perspective, adultery was thus an offense against marriage, a violation of the husband's claim of exclusive access to his wife's body, and an assault on the marital bonds of trust. We know little about the apprehension and punishment of adulterers; some men chose to do nothing, as Aristotle speculates, because they were ashamed to expose their wives' sexual transgressions (Arist. *Rhet.* 1373a). Others could derive financial benefit through extortion, as we see in the case of the courtesan, Neaera, toward the end of this chapter.

Draco's law on justifiable homicide established in 621 BCE provides the earliest glimpse of regulations for dealing with sexual misconduct. It permitted a man to kill another man involved in sexual relations with his wife, mother, sister, daughter, or concubine, that is, any of the women under his legal protection. This is the law invoked by Lysias in *On the Murder of Eratosthenes* to argue for the acquittal of his client. The law implicitly recognized the sanctity of the family and governed not just adultery but also rape. Solon later introduced a modification, decreeing that if a man were caught in the act with a woman who practiced prostitution he could not be accused of adultery ([Dem.] 59.67), a policy later adopted by the Romans. This law had the unintended consequence of legalizing and defining prostitution in Athens: any woman who offered sexual favors for profit put herself outside the protective sphere of the household. Another law introduced just after Pericles' citizenship law required a husband to divorce a wife who had cheated on him or risk disenfranchisement. The wife became an outcast from his home, just as she did in ancient Rome and ancient Near Eastern cultures. It further banned the adulteress from entering all public temples. The punishment of a woman caught with a moichos thus entailed public censure: mandatory divorce, expulsion from the oikos, and exclusion from sacred spaces, all the female equivalent of the stripping away of citizen rights.

The moichos is the frequent target of jokes in Greek comedy. In a parody of Draco's law, Aristophanes states that a moichos when caught in the act might be subjected to the humiliating and painful penalty of being "radished," which involved forcing a radish up his anus and singeing off his public hair (Ar. *Nub.* 1083). This penalty paints the moichos as a particularly unmanly and despicable sex offender. Another comic character complains about the impact Euripides' tragedies are having on her sex life. By portraying respectable wives as engaging in adulterous affairs, the tragic poet has made Athenian husbands suspicious of their every move. They scan the house for any hidden lovers as soon as they return from the theater and keep close tabs on their wives: "Because of him, they have now put seals and bars on the women's quarters and guard over us, and then they keep pit bulls to scare off our lovers" (Ar. *Thesm.* 414–17). Another character – actually a man pretending to be a woman – describes a tryst with her lover while her husband sleeps: "I poured some water on the door hinge to make it quiet and then went out to meet my moichos" (Ar. *Thesm.* 481–9). These and other passages portray the moichos as the rival of the husband and as a nocturnal sexual predator who secretly enters another man's house and seduces the women within. As such, adultery for the ancient Greeks represented a violation not only of a female member of a man's household but also an assault on his citizen status and even his property, a fear played out again and again on the stage.

6.4 Desperate Housewives

Although sex outside of marriage for women was considered problematic during all periods of ancient Greek civilization primarily because it threatened male succession, this concern seems to have intensified during the classical period when the status of mothers became determinative of their sons' citizen status. Tragedies frequently reflect male anxieties about the social and sexual control of women during this period through their portrayal of women behaving badly. Given the extensive nature of the evidence, we focus on just four examples of tragic women who fail to control their lust or are accused of this weakness. Clytemnestra in Aeschylus' *Agamemnon* exemplifies a flagrant adulteress, whereas Phaedra in Euripides' *Hippolytus* attempts not to become one. Although Deianira in Sophocles' *Women of Trachis* and Medea in Euripides' same-name play do not commit adultery, their uncontrolled lust results in catastrophe for all concerned.

Produced in 458 BCE, Aeschylus' *Agamemnon* dramatizes the myth of the return home of the Greek general, Agamemnon, after the fall of Troy. As with so many tragedies, his absence has given scope for action to his wife, Clytemnestra, who has had 10 years to plot his demise as a punishment for sacrificing their daughter. The queen commits several transgressions that violate Athenian gender ideology. Instead of remaining faithful and preserving her husband's household in his absence, like Penelope, Clytemnestra has taken her husband's cousin as her lover, who now "lights the fire" on her hearth and shares her bed. She has laid claim to male political power, ruling Argos in her husband's place, like a man, or as the watchman describes her, "a woman in passionate heart and male in strength of purpose" (Aesch. *Ag.* 11). Lastly, she has hatched a plan to avenge the death of their daughter, Iphigenia, and now waits and watches for the first sign of his return to put it into effect. When Agamemnon finally arrives, Clytemnestra persuades him to enter the house by walking on expensive tapestries, symbol of Asiatic arrogance and of her fatal control over him. Instead of using weaving as a feminine stratagem to preserve her husband's oikos, as does Penelope, she uses textiles as an accessory to murder. Once inside the house, she envelops Agamemnon in his bath with a "web" of cloth and then kills him with an ax, along with his concubine, the captive Trojan princess Cassandra (the social status of concubines is examined at the end of this chapter. Later she returns onstage to boast about it to the chorus. In another reversal, the symbol of female caregiving and wifely solicitude – the bath – becomes the site of a brutal murder. Also contrary to custom, Clytemnestra refuses to mourn for her dead husband and to accomplish proper funerary ritual, such as offering libations. She shares with her sister, Helen, a chronic disregard for the standards of female sexual conduct: both women betray their husbands with other men, destroying others in the process. Unlike Penelope, she has allowed a stranger into the marriage bed. She uses women's weaving in the form of the tapestries spread out before the king to entrap and kill her husband rather than to protect and preserve his household.

Euripides explores the consequences of one woman's unsuccessful attempt to contain her passion in two versions of the myth of Hippolytus and his stepmother, Phaedra. As a celibate follower of Artemis, Hippolytus refuses to worship Aphrodite, thereby rejecting marriage and sexual maturity. In the first play (now lost), Phaedra, the wife of the Athenian hero, Theseus, is depicted as a brazen woman who makes direct sexual overtures to her stepson in response to her husband's philandering. Appalled, the pure Hippolytus veils himself out of shame. Such a frank display of illicit female desire apparently shocked the spectators and resulted in a loss at the tragic competition. A second version of the play (428 BCE) exculpated Phaedra by making her the hapless tool of a vengeful Aphrodite. To penalize the youth Hippolytus for dishonoring her, the goddess instills in the wife a desperate love for her stepson that she tries unsuccessfully to resist. As she wastes away from lovesickness, Phaedra's nurse discovers the secret object of her passion, promises to help her with love magic (see Box 6.1), and confesses it to Hippolytus in the hope of uniting the pair. In his response, he angrily condemns the entire race of women:

> And from this it is clear that a wife is a great evil: her father, having begotten and reared her, sends her out of the house with a dowry, so that he can be rid of the evil. And the husband takes the ruinous creature into his house and delights in adding a beautiful ornament to this most evil statue, and the poor wretch expends the wealth of the house in attempting to outfit her in clothes. (Eur. *Hipp.* 627–33)

His words recall the "beautiful evil" of Pandora whose outer beauty and costly apparel conceals a wicked nature. But the main focus of the youth's harangue is the sexual misbehavior of wives and the female servants who abet them. The speech concludes with a savage declaration of hate:

> Not ever will I have my fill of hating women, not even if someone says that I never stop talking about it. For truly they, too, will always be somehow base. Either let someone teach them to be chaste, or let me always trample on them. (Eur. *Hipp.* 664–8)

Despite the pervasive sexism of Athenian society, this outburst must have seemed extreme even to the male spectators. Betrayed, Phaedra contrives to salvage her reputation, and that of her sons, by inscribing a charge of rape against Hippolytus on a tablet before committing suicide. When Theseus returns, he finds the letter attached to her corpse and immediately utters a curse against Hippolytus that brings about his death and the fulfillment of Aphrodite's plan. As in the *Agamemnon*, the lack of male oversight in the oikos allows the wife to act on her sexual impulses to the detriment of men. In contrast to Clytemnestra, however, Phaedra struggles mightily to maintain her self-control but in the end succumbs to the power of Aphrodite, "virtuous she was in deed, although not virtuous" (Eur. *Hipp.* 1035). The paradox of Phaedra suggests that even sexual fantasies about another man amounted to committing adultery and therefore invited public censure.

Other tragedies suggest that respectable wives should not only keep outsiders out of their beds and thoughts, they should also temper their desire for their own husbands. In Sophocles' play, *Women of Trachis* (c. 430 BCE), Deianira loves her husband, Heracles, but too much. When she learns that the captive of war she welcomes into her house is actually his new bedmate, she realizes that the girl may eventually supplant her:

> I have received the girl – or, I suppose, a girl no longer – but already yoked, just as a captain takes on a load, freight that destroys my mind. Now we two wait under one blanket for one man's embrace. This is the reward Heracles has sent me for keeping his house, he whom I called faithful and good. But I do not know how to be angry with him who is often afflicted with this sickness. Then again, what woman could live together with this girl, sharing in the same marriage? I see the flower of her youth is blossoming while mine is fading. The eyes of men love to pluck the flower of youth, but they turn away from the old. (Soph. *Trach.* 540–50)

Like Phaedra, Deainira attempts to do the right thing: she accepts her husband's philandering, welcomes the girl into the house, and professes her love for her husband. But her despair drives her to take extreme measures. She attempts to restore his affection by administering a love potion in the form of an ointment rubbed into a cloak she has woven for her husband. Soon after, she discovers its destructive effect when she sees it dissolve a tuft of wool activated by the sun. But it is too late. Heracles has already put on the corrosive cloak. It clings to his skin and eats away at his flesh, forcing him to beg for death in an attempt to end his pain. Deainira has no choice but to commit suicide out of shame. Although she has desire only for her husband, Deainira's lack of sexual self-control ultimately destroys them both.

Another variation on the theme of sexual jealousy is found in Euripides' *Medea* (431 BCE). Abandoned by her husband for a trophy wife, the foreigner and sorceress determines to get revenge. She describes the experience of marriage for women, highlighting their powerlessness over the process:

> Of all creatures that breathe and think we women are the most wretched. First, we must pay an outrageous price to purchase a husband and master of our bodies. (This evil is more painful than evil.) But the greatest trial is this: whether we get a bad or good man. For divorce is not respectable for women, nor is it possible to refuse to marry. When a

---

Box 6.1 Women and Love Magic

Ancient literary sources abound with examples of magical practices performed predominantly by women, beginning with Homer and ending with early Christian literature. In most cases, their magic attempts to attract and retain the attentions of men. Recall that Aphrodite in the *Iliad* lends Hera her magical breast-band so that she can seduce Zeus, and the nymph Circe in the *Odyssey* uses potions, salves, and a magic wand to perform magical tricks, including turning men into pigs. The stories of Deianira and Phaedra further associate women with love magic in a desperate attempt to restore or awaken a man's affections. The nurse promises to make Hippolytus fall in love with Phaedra through the use of love magic:

> Inside the house are enchanting charms for love; they will end your lovesickness without any shame or damage to your mind – if you do not become cowardly. But we need to get some token from the man you desire, either a lock of hair or a scrap of his clothing and to join one benefit from two. (Eur. *Hipp.* 509–15)

In Theocritus' second *Idyll*, the desperate Simaetha also uses love magic to compel her lover, Delphis, to return to her, repeating the incantation, "Iynx, draw you that man to my house," as she turns the iynx, a magic wheel and source of our English term "jinx."

Magic took several forms in the ancient world: curse tablets, incantations, the use of drugs and poison, dolls pierced with needles or melted in fire, and the destruction of a person's hair, nails, or cloak as a means of harming him. Most of our nonliterary evidence for magic comes from two sources, "binding spells," which consist mainly of inscribed lead tablets and the magical papyri. Curse tablets from the classical period are found around Attica, Sicily, and the Black Sea area, whereas later they are scattered throughout the Greek-speaking Mediterranean. To make a curse, a person inscribed the victim's name on a metal or wax tablet, rolled it up, pierced it with a nail, and then deposited it somewhere underground. The purpose of these spells was to bind or restrain the victim, inhibiting the words, actions, or even the sexual performance of a rival. Those composed by women typically seek to prevent their lovers or husbands from sleeping with others. Another popular form of love magic attempted to force a female victim to make love to the male practitioner. It has been argued that men and women used love magic in different ways in the ancient world. Men tended to use binding rituals to compel women into sexual submission whereas women seem to have used spells less aggressively, to instill and maintain affection in men, rather than to compel them to have sex.

woman comes into new customs and laws, she must guess, since she did not learn it at home, how best to manage her husband. If we skillfully work it out and our husband lives with us not resenting the yoke of marriage, then life is enviable; if not, we might as well be dead. (Eur. *Med.* 231–43)

Even though Jason had earlier been rescued by Medea when he came to her homeland for the golden fleece, now he jilts her for a new marriage to the wealthy young Corinthian princess. When confronted, Jason accuses her of being oversexed:

How was this a bad plan? Not even you would say so if the marriage did not provoke you to jealousy. But you women are so far gone that if all is well in bed you think you have everything, while if some misfortune in marriage occurs, you regard what is more desirable and best as hateful. Mortals ought to beget children from some other source, and there should be no female sex. Then mankind would have no trouble. (Eur. *Med.* 568–76)

Instead of trying to rekindle his affection, like Deainira, Medea brutally contrives the worst possible form of revenge, not his own death but that of everyone he loves. First she uses poison to kill the princess and her father. Rubbing the toxin on a robe and diadem, she has her children deliver the poisoned wedding gifts to the girl. Shortly after contact, the girl's body is consumed with fire and her flesh begins to melt from her bones. Delivering a final blow to Jason, Medea then kills her own children, thereby eradicating any possible future for their own family or the royal line.

6.5 Courtesans and Prostitutes

Although promoting the fidelity and chastity of wives, the sexual double standard of the Greeks permitted men to look outside their marriages for sexual gratification, whether with boys or women. Several kinds of women could meet their needs: household slaves, concubines, female dancers, mimes, musicians, courtesans, and brothel prostitutes, many of whom participated in the symposium. The epitaph that begins Chapter 5 draws a clear distinction between these types of sex partners and citizen wives, "Courtesans we keep for pleasure, concubines for daily attendance upon our person, but wives for the procreation of legitimate children" ([Dem.] 59.122). The main terms for these women are **hetaera** ("courtesan"), **porne** ("whore"), **auletris** ("female flute-player"), and **pallake** ("concubine"). For many years, scholarship on prostitution in ancient Greece has treated the hetaera and porne as occupying opposite ends of the sex-worker spectrum, viewing the hetaera as an independent contractor barely distinguishable from a wife and the porne as a lowly brothel slave. In fact, it is important to keep in mind that these different categories of women are not always distinguishable from one another. Often the same terms are applied interchangeably to the same woman. To further add to the confusion, in visual representations it is often difficult to determine whether a female figure is a respectable woman or hetaera. Take, for example, a red-figure vase (Figure 6.2) that depicts a naked woman at left, spinning in front of a draped seated woman at right. Scholars have interpreted this scene as a madam forcing her porne to work wool during her off hours to earn extra cash. Others have pointed out that the vase was found in a tomb, which may indicate an association with marriage. It has also been noted that female nudes often appear on vases associated with women, such as this water vessel. This ongoing debate illustrates the difficulty of pinning down the social status of representations of women not only in Greek art but in some literary sources as well.

Figure 6.2 Naked woman spinning wool next to a seated woman, Attic red-figure hydria by the Washing Painter, 450–400 BCE. Copenhagen, National Museum, 214971.

Prostitution thrived in ancient Greece from as early as the archaic period, especially in the large port cities of Corinth and Athens where sailors sought to indulge in pleasures while ashore. The practice was so widely accepted that Solon allegedly established state-owned brothels. Because citizen men and women could not sell their bodies or they would lose civic privileges, sex workers tended to be foreigners and slaves from the towns of eastern Greece, near Persia. Prostitutes had to be registered and paid a special tax. At the top of the social scale, in terms of economic success in any case, was the hetaera. The term simply means "female companion" and refers to a woman lavishly maintained by an admirer in exchange for his exclusive sexual access to her. Typically, she did not reside in his home, at least not when other family members were present. Xenophon describes an encounter between Socrates and the courtesan Theodote, a woman "ready to sleep with anyone who pleased her." Upon hearing of her legendary beauty, the philosopher proposes a visit to her house to see for himself:

> Socrates noticed that she was sumptuously dressed and that her mother at her side was also wearing expensive clothes and jewelry; and she had many pretty servant girls, who were also well-cared for, and her house was lavishly furnished. (Xen. *Mem.* 3.4)

As this passage indicates, many courtesans were public celebrities in classical Athens. In contrast to respectable women, a hetaera could and did appear in the male sphere, in the theater or the law court, and could be publicly named. Indeed, she was a public celebrity of sorts. She also participated in the symposium, where she entertained the male participants with her witty banter, her knowledge of poetry, and her ability to engage in philosophical dialog. She took great pains to appear sophisticated, alluring, refined, and outwardly respectable. In Lucian's

Dialogue of the Courtesans (second century CE), a mother instructs her daughter on how to become a successful courtesan by advising her how to act at a symposium:

> In the first place, she dresses attractively and is well behaved. She's vivacious with all the men, without laughing too loudly and readily as you usually do, but she smiles sweetly and seductively. Then she converses cleverly and does not cheat anyone, whether a visitor or escort, and she never makes the first move. If ever she takes payment for going out to dinner, she doesn't drink too much – that's ridiculous and men hate the sort of women who do – nor does she rudely gorge herself with food, but she handles it with her fingertips and eats in silence, not stuffing both cheeks full, and she drinks quietly, without slurping, taking short rests. (Luc. *Dial. Meretr.* 6.3)

A skillful hetaera disguised the crude commercial aspect of her relationship with her partner by acting more or less respectably in public. She expected relative permanence in her liaison with her patron and professed fidelity to him. In this regard, she styled herself almost as a wife: miming self-control and hinting at her sexuality rather than boldly displaying it. Ironically, the more a hetaera resembled a proper citizen wife, the more money she could charge for her services and the more desirable she was to her clients.

The earliest use of the term hetaera in reference to a courtesan is found in a passage from Herodotus' *Histories* (c. 440 BCE), in which he discusses the question of whether the hetaera Rhodopis financed the building of a small pyramid in Egypt. That question aside, we can learn much from his account about the possible career trajectory of such a woman:

> Rhodopis was brought to Egypt to ply her trade by Xanthes of Samos, but upon her arrival was released for a lot of money by Charaxus, son of Scamandronymus and brother of Sappho, the Melic poet. Thus Rhodopis lived as a free woman and remained in Egypt, where, as she was very attractive, she acquired a lot of wealth. Seeing that to this day anyone who likes can calculate what one tenth of her worth was, she cannot be credited with great wealth – enough for a Rhodopis but not enough to fund a pyramid …. Later Rhodopis wanted to leave a memorial of herself in Greece, by having something made which no one else had thought of or dedicated in a temple and presenting this at Delphi to preserve her memory. So she spent one tenth of her wealth on the making of a large number of iron spits, as many as the tenth would pay for, and sent them to Delphi. These lie in a heap to this day, behind the altar set up by the Chians and in front of the shrine itself. The courtesans of Naucratis in Egypt are especially attractive, for the woman of whom this story is told became so famous that every Greek knew the name of Rhodopis, and later on a certain Archidice. (Hdt. 2.134–5)

Like many courtesans, Rhodopis was born a foreigner and came from eastern Greece, in this case from the island of Samos. She started as a slave and yet evolved from the lowest category of sex worker into an independent hetaera. She consorted with famous men, like Charaxus, the brother of Sappho, whose patronage helped buy her freedom from sexual servitude; indeed, he is named in Sappho's newly discovered "Brothers Poem." Her success as a celebrity courtesan enabled her to make an expensive public benefaction in the form of sacrificial skewers placed in the sanctuary at Delphi. These activities made her famous – everyone knew her name and she entered into public and literary discourse.

The oration entitled *Against Neaera* (c. 340 BCE) provides yet another perspective on the life of a hetaera during the classical period. Purchased as a child by the brothel keeper Nicarete, a former slave herself, Neaera grew up under her tutelage. The older woman supposedly had a good eye for "recognizing beauty in small children and she knew how to raise them and train them skillfully, for she made this her profession and got her livelihood from them" ([Dem.] 59.18). (It is shocking to contemplate today an adult woman being permitted to purchase little girls for the sole purpose of profiting off of them in the sex trade.) Neaera probably joined her house around 390 BCE, where she underwent training with six other girls. Nicarete called them "daughters" in order to maximize her profits, because clients would pay more to sleep with a free girl than a slave. These girls attracted important clients, such as the orator, Lysias, and accompanied them to festivals and dined with them at symposia. As a slave who "worked with her body, selling herself to anyone who wanted to get near to her" ([Dem.] 59.20), Neaera probably did not belong to the highest order of courtesans. Or possibly the speaker uses this language to denigrate her.

Once Nicarete had reaped the profits of her youth, she sold the courtesan, probably now in her early 20s, to two of her regular clients, Timanoridas and Eucrates, for the sum of 3000 drachmas, roughly equivalent to the earnings of a skilled worker or a hoplite over an 8- to 10-year period. After they had sown their wild oats and were ready for marriage, they decided to liquidate their asset and offered to let Neaera buy her freedom at a discount – 2000 drachmas – stating that "they did not want to see her, who had been their hetaera, working in Corinth or being under the control of a brothel-keeper" ([Dem.] 59.30). Neaera took them up on their offer, using her own savings and borrowing some from her other former clients. When she fell short, a playboy named Phrynion stepped in and made a hefty donation, then took her with him to Athens. There he mistreated her, having sex with her in public and allowing other men to do the same at orgies. Tired of his debauchery, Neaera left him and moved to Megara, taking both her personal possessions and some of his. There she took up with another man, Stephanus, and subsequently moved back to Athens, bringing along her three children, two boys and a girl named Phano. Neaera pretended to live with Stephanus as his wife and in the process violated Athenian citizenship laws by attempting to pass off her daughter as a citizen and marrying her to a citizen man. On the basis of this offense, Apollodorus brought both Neaera and Stephanus to trial and prosecuted them. Unfortunately we do not know the outcome of the trial or what happened to Neaera after it concluded. The story of Neaera provides a more realistic glimpse of the Greek hetaera and tells us that such a life was not always glamorous. At the same time, it suggests that a courtesan, and her daughter, could not be easily identified as sex workers but could even be mistaken for citizen women.

In contrast, the term porne means "bought woman," from the Greek verb "to sell." As a common whore, she differed from the hetaera in the number and anonymity of her partners, as well as by the fact that she could not choose them. She had to sell herself to anyone who wanted her services and had no control over her earnings. The brothel keeper, almost always male, dictated her movements and her price. The porne charged her customers for each sex act performed. The fee ranged between one obol and one drachma, the latter amount equal to one day's wage for a skilled worker. Whereas the hetaera entertained men in private households, the porne plied her trade on public streets and brothels, scantily clad and garishly made up. Some wore shoes inscribed with erotic messages on their soles, such as "Follow Me," to advertise their availability. A character in a lost comic play describes the availability and easy accessibility of such sex workers:

> In this city, there are very pretty girls in the brothels whom you can see basking in the sun, their breasts unclothed, stripped for action and arrayed for battle. You can choose from these the girl that pleases, thin, plump, compact, tall or withered, young, old, middle-aged, over-ripe, and not set up a ladder and climb in secretly, nor creep in through the chimney below the roof, nor be craftily carried inside under husks. For the women

use force and drag them in, calling those who are old men, "Daddy," and the younger ones, "Little Brother." And you can have any one of these without fear, at little cost, during the day, at evening, and in any sexual position. (Xenarchus, Ath. 569b–c)

This passage contrasts the uncomplicated sex (for men, at least) offered by brothel prostitutes in Athens with the temptations and dangers of adultery, which, according to the passage, involves sneaking around behind the husband's back and the risk of getting caught, both experienced by Eratosthenes in Lysias' speech. Unfortunately, no concrete evidence of a purpose-built brothel survives intact from classical Athens, as it does from Roman Pompeii, considered in Chapter 14. One building located in the Athenian cemetery, so-called building Z, may have served as one, based on the presence of a series of small cubicles clustered around a central corridor, multiple dining rooms, a local water source, and the presence of objects used by women. But there is considerable disagreement about what happened there. Despite the harsh conditions of the lowly brothel slave, even she could gain her freedom and become an independent contractor and potentially become the hetaera lover of a famous politician or intellectual. But such an achievement must have been quite rare for the average woman.

Closely related to the porne were female entertainers, musicians, dancers, singers, and mimes. The interior of an Attic red-figure drinking cup shows a young dancer entertaining a male youth as he reclines on a couch, holding an aulos (Figure 6.3). These women not only provided musical, acrobatic, and theatrical entertainment for the male symposiasts, they also engaged in sexual activities with them. The female entertainer most commonly represented in

Figure 6.3 A young hetaera dances before a male youth; tondo of an Attic red-figure kylix by the Brygos painter, c. 490–480 BCE. London, British Museum, GR 1848.6-19.7 (Cat. Vases E 68).

art and literature is the auletris (see Figure 2.4 in Chapter 2). She played a double-reed instrument closer to a modern-day oboe than a flute and performed regularly at the symposium. Although famous female flute players such as Lamia and Nanno are also often called hetaeras, most hailed from the brothel where they worked as common prostitutes for hire. A passage from the historian Xenophon describes these performers at a drinking party:

> When the tables had been removed and the guests had poured libations and sung a hymn, a man from Syracuse entered to entertain them. He brought an accomplished flute-player, a dancing girl – one able to do amazing moves – and a very handsome boy who was skilled at playing the lyre and dancing. The man earned money by displaying their performances as a spectacle. The flute-girl played for them, and the boy played the lyre, and both seemed to entertain them especially well. (Xen. *Symp.* 2)

Although this account does not hint at sexual favors, many literary sources equate the flute-player's musical ability with a propensity for fellatio. In Aristophanes' *Wasps*, an old man drags an auletris from the symposium so that he can have her for himself:

> Come up here, my little golden beetle; take this "rope" here in your hand and hold it. Be careful, as the rope is a bit worn out. But even though it's worn, it's not bad. Do you see how cleverly I took you away when you were just about to perform oral sex on the symposiasts? (Ar. *Wasps* 1342–45)

Although the auletris, like the porne, may have been identified with casual sex and brothel slavery, she also could escape her dire conditions and achieve an enduring attachment much like a hetaera.

In contrast to the hetaera, who might feign respectability, comporting herself like a citizen wife, the concubine actually functioned much more like a wife. The term pallake refers to a kept woman engaged in an exclusive relationship with one man over a long period of time. She was probably not a prostitute but a sort of common law wife without citizen status, because she was of foreign birth. She resided within the man's oikos, although only in the absence of a wife, and tended to the physical needs of her male partner much as a servant. Unlike a slave, however, she may have been cherished and protected like a wife and her children might have enjoyed a status similar to legitimate offspring. We are told, for instance, that the law against adultery discussed earlier in this chapter applied both to concubines and wives and possibly reflects early Athenian legal structures that recognized the offspring of concubines as legitimate, although unequal, members of the oikos. The most famous concubine of the classical era was Aspasia, mistress of the great Athenian statesman, Pericles. Little is known of her background other than that she was born in Miletus, a Greek coastal town in Asia Minor, probably to a wealthy family, around 470 BCE, and eventually made her way to Athens. There is some ambiguity about her status: she might have originally been a brothel owner and a hetaera rather than a concubine and she may have lived with Pericles simply as his mistress. Whatever the case, her status as a foreigner entitled her to legal freedoms unavailable to respectable wives, such as the ability to participate in public life. Highly educated, she entertained many important intellectuals in her home, purportedly even instructing the philosopher, Socrates, in rhetoric. When Pericles divorced his wife in 445 BCE, Aspasia lived with him as his consort and bore him a child, Pericles the Younger, who, despite his foreign mother, was made an Athenian citizen by special decree around 430 BCE. Pericles was so enamored of her that he kissed her when he left for work and when he came home each day, apparently quite odd behavior for a married couple in classical Athens. Around 438 BCE, she was prosecuted for impiety, probably for political reasons. Several comedies attack her for her political influence over Pericles, comparing her to notorious mythic figures such as Helen and Deianira.

6.6 Conclusion

Unfaithful wives far outnumber virtuous ones in the Greek literary tradition. Indeed, the foundational narrative of ancient Greek civilization, the Trojan War, revolves around the adultery of Helen. Although the Homeric poems do not attach blame to her actions, the later tradition upholds her as an archetype of female sexual misconduct. Such a woman is unable to control her eros, an overwhelming power to which women are viewed as particularly susceptible. In her desperation, she often resorts to love magic to attract her lover or to restore the affections of her husband. She encounters potential lovers at religious occasions such as funerals and festivals and makes use of female servants as go-betweens. The women's quarters, although it kept women apart from men, also provided the perfect venue for plotting and carrying out adulterous liaisons. Female adultery threatened not only the emotional relationship between husband and wife, it also potentially damaged the husband's estate by casting doubt on the legitimacy of his offspring. At the same time, the wayward wife incurred less blame than her male seducer, because he committed an act that was both premeditated and cowardly. In contrast to their wives, men enjoyed a sexual double standard. They could frequent prostitutes of every stripe, male or female, young or old, slave or free, whenever they wished. The hetaera had relatively high social status and independence: she could choose her own lovers and earn great wealth and fame from her beauty. The porne, on the other hand, worked out of a dirty brothel and had no control over her clientele or her wages. But because we have no first person accounts from any ancient prostitutes, we will never know for certain their lived realities.

Questions for Review

1 Why were the Greeks so preoccupied with female adultery?

2 What motivates women who commit adultery in Greek tragedy?

3 Why might the Greeks associate love magic more commonly with women?

4 Why did the Athenians blame extra-marital affairs on men?

5 What is the different between a hetaera and porne?

Further Reading

Primary Sources

Euripides, *Hippolytus* and *Medea*
Lysias, *On the Murder of Eratosthenes*
Pseudo-Demosthenes 59, *Against Neaera*
Plato, *Menexenus*
Sophocles, *Women of Trachis*

Secondary Sources

Blondell, Ruby (2013). *Helen of Troy: Beauty, Myth, Devastation.* Oxford: Oxford University Press.
Examines the destructive power of the beauty of Helen of Troy in early Greek epic, Sappho, and tragedy and relates it to contemporary ambivalence about beauty, its danger and allure.

Cohen, David (1991). *Law, Sexuality, and Society: the Enforcement of Morals in Classical Athens.* Cambridge: Cambridge University Press.
Chapters five and six provide an extensive discussion of the regulation of adultery in classical Athens and the social control of women.

Davidson, James (1997). *Courtesans and Fishcakes: The Consuming Passions of Classical Athens.* New York: Harper Collins.
A highly readable account of prostitutes and courtesans in ancient Athens and what they reveal about Athenian attitudes toward pleasure and sexuality.

Faraone, Christopher (2001). *Ancient Greek Love Magic.* Cambridge, MA: Harvard University Press.
Discusses the evidence for erotic spells and magical practices in ancient Greece with a view to gender dynamics.

Hamel, Debra (2003). *Trying Neaira: The True Story of a Courtesan's Scandalous Life in Ancient Greece.* New Haven, CT: Yale University Press.
An attempt to reconstruct the woman behind Apollodorus' famous law court speech, *Against Neaera*, with attention to social and political practices.

McClure, Laura (2003). *Courtesans at Table: Gender and Greek Literary Culture in Athenaeus.* New York and London: Routledge.
Explores Athenian views of prostitution from the perspective of the late second-century CE encyclopedist, Athenaeus.

Patterson, Cynthia (1998). *The Family in Greek History.* Cambridge, MA: Harvard University Press.
Chapters four and five discuss adultery laws in classical Athens and its presentation in tragedy and comedy as a way to understand the classical definition of the Greek family.

7

Women, Religion, and Authority in Greece

And in divine matters – for I think this of first importance – we have the greatest part. For at the sanctuary of Phoebus women prophesize Apollo's thought. At the holy seat of Dodona by the sacred oak the female race conveys the thoughts of Zeus to all Greeks who desire it. As for the holy rituals performed for the Fates and the unnamed goddesses, these are not holy in men's hands; but among women they flourish, every one of them. So in divine matters the judgment of women prevails.

(Eur. *Cap. Mel.* Fr. 494 K 12–22)

Over the course of the last four chapters we have looked at mostly male perspectives on women from infancy to marriage and motherhood in ancient Greece. In general, these representations emphasize the characteristics that ancient Greek men found desirable in women and that contributed to a successful marriage, the economic prosperity of the household, and the production of legitimate children. These qualities typically involved obedience, loyalty, and modesty. Women who transgressed these norms – like the adulterous wives of myth and history – posed a threat to the stability and continuity of the family and the larger community. Although we saw that women could and did exert influence and authority within the domestic sphere, their power was confined to the family. This chapter takes a closer look at the possibilities for women's civic engagement and public authority in ancient Greece, including myths of female empowerment, like those of the Amazons (see Box 7.1). In particular, it shows the importance of women as religious agents and how they helped shape their communities through their active role in cult. Such a view complicates and enriches the traditional binary distinction between household and city that has largely dominated classical scholarship on women in ancient Greece over the past half century.

7.1   Older Women

The Greeks believed women reached old age sooner than men because their reproductive lives were shorter. A woman was considered old when she ceased bearing children and therefore lost her procreative power, perhaps around age 50, if she lived that long. Although Greek medical writers worried about menstruation as the precondition for female fertility, they did not much concern themselves with menopause. Once beyond the childbearing years, worries about the legitimacy of her offspring ceased. No longer subjected to the physical fluctuations of their reproductive years, older women were considered more rational and more capable of self-control. Old age gave women authority and afforded them more freedom and autonomy than younger women. They assumed supervisory and advisory roles at home and had more freedom

Women in Classical Antiquity: From Birth to Death, First Edition. Laura K. McClure.
© 2020 John Wiley & Sons, Inc. Published 2020 by John Wiley & Sons, Inc.

to move about unaccompanied in public. They played an important role in Athenian religious activities, as there were a number of priesthoods open only to women past childbearing age. The mythic prototype for this life stage is the goddess Demeter, who assumes the form of "a very old woman cut off from childbearing" in her wanderings as she searches for her lost daughter (*Hom. Hymn Dem.* 104). This freedom of movement allowed older women to help build social networks and forge solidarity across generations of women. One imagines them

---

Box 7.1 Warrior Women

A mythical tribe of fierce warrior women, the Amazons, offers another way of imagining how women could be powerful in ancient Greece. In Greek myth, they were warriors of exotic origins, whose fighting skills matched those of men. They played a part in the legendary Trojan War as well as in the foundation of Athens. Many of the great mythic heroes, like Achilles, Heracles, and Theseus, proved their strength by overcoming these powerful warrior queens and their armies of women. Queen Penthesilea helped Priam, king of Troy, against the Greeks and eventually died at the hands of Achilles, but only after inflicting major damage. Heracles had to steal the belt of the Amazon queen, Hippolyta, as one of his labors. Theseus in turn abducted either her or her sister, Antiope, and took her to Athens, where she bore a son, Hippolytus. In retaliation, the Amazons journeyed to Attica and fought the Athenians on the Areopagus until they came to a truce.

The Amazons lived either in Themiscyra, in what is today central northern Turkey, or in the region of the Caucasus Mountains, an area identified by the Greeks with the Scythians. They were the offspring of the war god Ares and the nymph Harmonia. Defying ancient views of gender and sexuality, they were warriors and nomads, skilled at riding horses and archery. The Greeks believed their name meant "without breasts," explaining that they removed one of each girl child's breasts so that it would not interfere with her use of the bow and arrow or javelin. They honored Artemis, the virgin huntress and the deity least inclined to associate with men. Their female-only culture excluded males. When they wished to bear children, they slept with men from neighboring tribes but reared only their female babies. Herodotus recounts that they rejected the offer of the Scythians to settle down on the basis of their different ideas about gender roles:

> We shoot the bow and throw the javelin and ride, but have never learned women's work; and your women do none of the things we relate, but they remain inside the wagons and do women's work, and do not go out hunting or anywhere else. So we could never get along with them. (Hdt. 4.114)

The Greeks and Romans did not dispute that the Amazons had once existed in the remote past, and many reported similar women inhabiting the region around the Black Sea and beyond. Although it is now generally agreed that the Amazons were wholly mythical, recent excavations of ancient Scythian tombs reveal that genuine warrior women actually lived. Their graves contained the battle-scarred skeletons of women buried with their weapons, horses, and other possessions. Often interpreted as the product of male anxieties about female power, the myths of the Amazons show that the ancient Greeks could at least imagine a form of gender equality, female leadership, and military prowess despite its absence from their own culture. As we see in the next chapter, warrior women in Northern Greece may have influenced the role of women in Macedonian monarchy.

carrying news between households, conversing with young wives stuck at home, and offering advice about matters such as pregnancy, birth, and child-rearing.

In Greek comedy, women at this life stage are often portrayed sympathetically and even heroically. In Aristophanes' *Lysistrata*, the chorus of older women serve as leaders and representatives. They seize and defend the Acropolis, then claim that they have the right to advise the citizens because they have borne sons to the city:

> I owe it to the polis to offer some good advice. Even if I was born a woman, don't hold it against me if I manage to suggest something better than the present situation. I pay my taxes – I contribute in the form of men! (Ar. *Lys.* 648–51)

Legal speeches similarly suggest that older women, particularly widows, actively worked behind the scenes to manage the affairs of their households and that they could command extensive knowledge about its business operations. One speech describes a widow defending the interests of her children against their guardian (her own father) in a family council (Lys. 32.12–18). The mother displays a detailed knowledge of loans, mortgages, and wheat imports. Although she has to make apologies for daring to speak before men, no one questions her right to involve herself in the family's financial matters. Another speech claims one man's mother had such an in-depth understanding of leases that as long as she was alive, he did not attempt to make his illegitimate claim (Dem. 36.14). Whatever the reality, both cases demonstrate that older women's influence over business matters would have been considered plausible and appropriate to an Athenian jury.

In addition to financial acumen, both comedy and oratory attribute political savvy and moral authority to older women. Again in *Lysistrata*, an older woman tells a city official who has come to arrest her that wives are not only fully aware of what's going on in Athenian politics, but some even have the audacity to question their husbands' decisions. In the prosecution of Neaera, discussed in the last chapter, the speaker imagines what the wives of the male jurors will say if they acquit the courtesan:

> And the women, upon hearing this, will say, "Well what did you do?" And you will say, "We acquitted her." Then will not the most well-behaved of the women be angry with you, since you sanctioned her to participate in the city and its rituals the same as them? And those women who lack all sense, you clearly show that they may do whatever they wish, since they have no fear of you or the laws. ([Dem.] 59.111)

This passage similarly implies that Athenian men would have had to account for their bad legal and political decisions upon returning home at night to their wives. Some women must have taken a keen interest in current affairs and probably voiced their opinions at home. As we have seen, their status as citizen wives and the mothers of legitimate children – especially sons – and their role as managers of the household gave them authority within the home and a vested interested in the political matters that might have affected them. They derived further influence in the public sphere from their religious participation in the city, through cult activities, priesthoods, and the performance of rituals. The rest of this chapter sketches some of these activities and their meanings for both family and city. Although priestly offices, festivals, and ritual duties did not always require women to be of advanced age, and in fact the age of the female participants is not always clear, many of these tasks relied on the knowledge and experience of mature women. Their ritual engagement endowed them with respect and allowed them opportunities for influence and action not otherwise available to citizen women.

7.2   Women as Ritual Agents

When we think of public and religious holidays today, we envision only a handful of occasions in which individuals take a break from work, gather with family, and participate in annual rituals, whether secular or religious. The picture was far different in classical Athens, where religion permeated every aspect of the city-state. Daily life was filled with ritual activities, most of which were performed by women, including nuptial preparations, funerals, visiting and tending graves, and the departure of soldiers for war. To put it in perspective, the Athenians observed 170 festival days, that is, days set aside for the worship of a particular deity in the religious calendar, whereas the Assembly convened only 145 days per year. Over 2000 cults existed in Attic territory alone. Religious activities thus occupied a huge part of the average citizen's daily routine. Women participated in around 85% of all religious activities and were in charge of more than 40 major cults, as well as had primary responsibility for domestic rites involved in weddings and funerals. Religion thus put men and women on more or less equal footing in relation to the gods. If the mark of citizenship for the Athenians was participation in the city's rituals, as has been argued, it stands to reason that women had an equal share in civic life as men. Moreover, women's religious engagement enabled their widespread movement throughout the city as they participated in processions and visited shrines, sanctuaries, and cemeteries, suggesting that prevalent literary images of female seclusion did not accurately reflect social reality. Understanding the role of women in Greek religion affords an exciting glimpse of women's agency and authority in the Greek world, but it is nonetheless a challenging process. We have little secure information for the majority of cults and festivals that marked the Athenian calendar year and the sources are often obscure and run the gamut from fragmentary inscriptions to late, Christian texts, which reflect an antipagan bias.

7.3   Priestesses

One of the main ways women gained prestige and exerted influence in ancient Greece was through priestly office. The fragment from Euripides' lost play, *Captive Melanippe* (c. 420 BCE), quoted at the beginning of this chapter, underscores the powerful role of female priestesses in the Greek world. Although the unidentified speaker focuses on female cult personnel at the oracles of Apollo and Zeus, there were many other types of priesthoods available to women. Indeed, we have already examined the kanephoros, the girl who carried the basket containing ritual objects in sacrificial processions. It is important to note that in contrast to the roles of priests in later religions, pagan priests for the most part did not devote their whole lives to religious service but rather performed their duties on an as-needed basis, with the notable exception of the Vestal Virgins at Rome. Nor was there a separate religious community with its own hierarchy and personnel. Rather, both male and female priests, along with other religious officials, had families and managed their own estates when not engaged in their ritual duties.

An early depiction of a female priestess is found in Homer's *Iliad*. The Trojan women approach Theano to request Athena's aid in preventing the Greek army from advancing on their city (Hom. *Il.* 6.297–310). The priestess opens the doors to the temple of the goddess and places a large, beautifully woven robe on the knees of the cult statue and leads the women in a supplication ritual. She then prepares to offer 12 unblemished bulls in sacrifice to Athena. The poem offers an early model for female sacred service. The priestess often, although not always, served a female deity and functioned as a leader in the community of women. She performed a variety of functions related to the worship of the deity. Within the sanctuary, she carried the key to the temple and washed and dressed the cult statue much as a woman managed her own household. She participated in sacred processions, often as a prelude to animal sacrifice. She carried holy implements and once at the sanctuary where the sacrifice was to take place, she led a prayer with arms raised and palms upturned. A libation or liquid offering was poured to reinforce the prayer. Then the priestess performed formal rites of dedication and consecration of the animal, followed by purification. Although long a subject of debate, it is now believed that women probably participated in many aspects of animal sacrifice, from the selection and decoration of the victims to leading them in procession and to the butchering, distribution, and consumption of the meat.

Priestesses enjoyed significant material rewards and great prestige within their communities. Remuneration included hides, meat, wheat, honey, oil, and firewood from the sacrifices where they presided, special access to sacred space, and reserved seats at the theater, a place normally off limits to Athenian women. Some received the privilege of eponymy, a practice by which religious events were dated according to the names and priestly term of the women. Sometimes even historical events were marked according to their names, an honor parallel to that of the male archon, one of the highest political officials at Athens. For example, Thucydides used the 48th year of the priestess Chrysis' service at the sanctuary of Hera in Argos to date the outbreak of the Peloponnesian war. In contrast to most respectable citizen women, the names of priestesses were widely known. They were inscribed on their statue bases and dedications. Some of their names became household words and the fodder of jokes in the theater. The practice of civic and sacred eponymy ensured that their names would never be forgotten.

One of the most famous priesthoods reserved for older women was that of the **Pythia** who relayed the oracles of Apollo at Delphi, an exception to the general rule that women served only goddesses. Originally she was chosen from among unmarried local girls but in time only women over the age of 50 could hold the office, mainly because it required lifelong celibacy. Although advanced in years, she wore the costume of a young girl to commemorate the earlier custom of the virgin priestess. The Pythia could have been married and had children prior to holding office, but once appointed, she was required to live apart from her husband and remain chaste until her death. She performed her duties for just nine months each year because the oracle did not operate during the winter. The Pythia further issued prophecies only on the seventh day after the new moon, which meant she was available for consultation only nine days per year. Her limited availability eventually required the addition of two other priestesses who worked a shift system during the classical period.

To consult the oracle, the petitioner provided his question in advance and then entered the inner part of the temple on the appointed day to receive an answer. Typical inquiries related to war, famine, sickness, and infertility. The priestess pronounced her prophecies while sitting on a tripod placed in the inner sanctum of Apollo's temple. Responses took the form of poetry or prose and were famous for their ambiguity. They were then relayed to petitioners through male functionaries. Oracles that did not come true were attributed to misinterpretation on the part of the inquirer. A recent geological survey has revealed that the sanctum was positioned directly over two faults that cut through a bituminous limestone formation from which gasses, such as ethylene, could have escaped in antiquity. It has been argued that the vapor induced a trance in the priestess, enabling her to pronounce her obscure prophecies. A scene between a male worshipper and the Pythia appears on the interior of a red-figure cup (Figure 7.1). Seated on a tripod, she wears a crown of bay leaf on her head and holds a sprig of bay from the tree sacred to Apollo. Originally only male petitioners were allowed to approach the priestess, but later women could consult her after they had sacrificed an animal. Female concerns are clearly represented in the temple inscriptions, which record that many questions put to the Pythia involved issues of fertility and childbirth.

Figure 7.1 The Pythia, priestess of Apollo, at left sits on the sacred tripod in the inner sanctum of the temple, holding a sprig of laurel; to her right stands a petitioner; tondo of an Attic red-figure kylix by the Codrus Painter, c. 440–430 BCE. Berlin, Staatliche Museen Antikensammlung F2538.

The widespread authority of this priestess is evidenced by the fact that many of the petitions sought her advice about political and community matters, such as the creation of a new constitution or how to address illness or famine.

A prominent priestly office in Athens was that of Athena Polias (Athena of the City). It was one of the oldest female priesthoods in Athens and probably the most important priesthood held by either gender. It was also a hereditary position, open to married women from the Eteoboutad clan who held the position for life. The names of 25 of these priestesses can be identified from inscriptions. The priestess of Athena Polias presided over sacrifices to Athena and cared for her archaic cult statue housed in the Erectheion on the Acropolis. She also supervised the Arrhephoroi, the little girls who set up the warp in the loom for the weaving of Athena's peplos dedicated annually at the festival of the Panathenaea, as discussed in Chapter 4. The political influence of this position is seen in Herodotus' account of the role played by one priestess of Athena Polias in persuading the Athenian citizens to evacuate the city prior to the battle of Salamis in 480 BCE (Hdt. 7.142-4). Among the many priestesses of Athena Polias, one in particular stands out. She is Lysimache, the first identifiable priestess, who held office from 430 to 365 BCE. An inscribed statue base near the south wall of the Acropolis relates that she was the daughter of Drakontides of Bate and that she raised four children. She appears to have died at age 88, having served as priestess for 64 years. The presence of the base further suggests that the city must have sanctioned the erection of the statue probably as the result of an honorary decree. Some scholars think that the character of Lysistrata in Aristophanes' same-name play was based on this historical priestess. Indeed, the date of the play, 411 BCE, falls squarely within the tenure of her office. Moreover, there is a similarity in form and meaning of the two names: Lysistrata means "disbander of armies" whereas Lysimache means "disbander of battle." The identification of Lysistrata with a contemporary priestess helps to explain her characterization as a leader and public figure of authority capable of brokering a treaty between warring male factions within the play.

Another highly prestigious sacred position for women was the priestess of Demeter and Kore at the sanctuary of Demeter at Eleusis. Originating in the Bronze Age, this ancient agrarian cult involved secret rites still not fully understood today because initiates were sworn to secrecy. In brief, the mysteries recalled in some form Hades' abduction of Persephone and involved the revelation of secret objects hidden in a covered chest and basket. Those initiated believed they would achieve immortality and release from suffering. Every September, the priestess of Demeter and Kore – the only cultic official to have the names of both goddesses in her title – would leave the sanctuary at Eleusis and lead a procession 10 miles to Athens, accompanied by other priestesses and young soldiers mounted on horseback. She carried unspecified sacred items to be deposited at the sanctuary of the City Eleusinion, near the Athenian acropolis. This visually impressive journey marked the start of the Eleusinian mysteries and occurred annually for over one thousand years. The sacred items were kept at the shrine for four days, during which time the opening of the Mysteries was announced to the general public. Those about to be initiated then bathed in the sea and washed piglets for the sacrifices that followed. They spent the fourth day sequestered at home and on the fifth processed to Eleusis, led again by the priestess of Demeter and Kore and joined by the priestess of Athena Polias. This priestess officiated at a large number of festivals, including the Eleusinian Mysteries, the Haloa, and the Thesmophoria, a festival examined more fully in the next section. The position entailed significant financial rewards; indeed, inscriptional evidence indicates that it was the most lucrative of all the sacred offices open to Attic women.

7.4 Women-Only Religious Festivals

Although not everyone had the opportunity to hold the distinguished office of priestess, citizen women regularly participated in religious activities central to the community. Given the number of festival days in classical Athens, they would have had ample opportunities for ritual expression. Women-only festivals from which men were strictly excluded comprised an important part of the ritual calendar and provided a special occasion not only for worship but also for female solidarity and leadership. These typically honored Demeter and her daughter Persephone and celebrated motherhood and the power of both agrarian and human fertility. The main festival was the **Thesmophoria** in honor of Demeter Thesmophoros. It was observed in almost every part of the Greek world, but we focus on the most-documented account, that of the festival of the Thesmophoria annually held at Athens. It was the largest and perhaps oldest Athenian festival celebrated by women and was part of the official state religious calendar. It was thus a public rather than private religious occasion. The civic aspect of the festival is evidenced by the fact that there was a special space reserved for it, the shrine of the Thesmophorion, adjacent to the area where the Assembly met. Further, citizen men were expected to pay all expenses for their wives to attend. The main features of the festival were secrecy, pig sacrifice, and rites for promoting agricultural fertility.

The Thesmophoria was held over three days in late September or early October, a period that coincided with the fall planting of winter wheat, barley, and legumes. During the celebration at Athens, married citizen women left their homes and set up temporary quarters near the seat of male government on the Acropolis, rigorously excluding all men. Although the festival was obligatory for married women, virgins could not attend because they had not yet achieved sexual maturity. The festival promoted fertility but paradoxically required women to remain sexually abstinent. They scattered on the ground beneath them special plants believed to suppress sexual desire in order to promote chastity and also chewed garlic to keep their husbands away.

It was preceded in the days before by two other festivals in honor of Demeter. First, citizen wives traveled to neighboring Halimus to celebrate the local version of the Thesmophoria where they danced and offered sacrifice. At the Stenia, a preliminary feast to the Athenian Thesmophoria, they gathered and engaged in risqué conversation, an activity referred to as *aischrologia*, in which they mocked each other and told sexual jokes. Although the purpose of this rite is obscure, the elements of secrecy, the exclusion of men, and obscenity suggest that it promoted agrarian and female fertility. There were thus five festival days during the early fall set aside for women and from which men were barred. It must have been a busy ritual time for female citizens and perhaps a welcome break from domestic responsibilities and the demands of caring for their families. These festivals of Demeter all occurred during the sowing season and all aimed to promote agrarian and human fertility. Women's religious activities at this time reinforced men's labor in the fields by attempting to ensure the growth of the newly sown crops.

Because men did not attend and women performed their rites in secrecy, we do not have a full picture of what went on during the Thesmophoria. The best source, Aristophanes' *Women of the Thesmophoria* (411 BCE), pointedly imparts little information about the actual rites. Instead it comically portrays a male spy infiltrating the women's festival by disguising himself as a woman in order to defend his relative, the tragic poet Euripides, from prosecution by the women for his negative portrayal of them in his plays. Piecing together various sources, the following picture emerges. Preparation for the festival began well in advance. Piglets were sacrificed in midsummer, probably at the Skira, another festival of Demeter largely celebrated by women and about which little is known, and then their remains were placed in caverns along with cakes in the shape of phalluses and snakes. These items were connected with fertility. Pigs were offered in honor of Demeter because of their fecundity as evidenced by their large litters but also because the Greeks associated them with female genitalia. Snakes were associated with Demeter and with the earth more generally. The phalluses represented male fertility, of course. The recovery of the decayed remains played a central role in the Thesmophoria. A select group of women called "Bailers" retrieved the mixture at some point during the festival and then spread it out on altars as a sort of fertilizer to be mixed with seeds before planting to ensure a good harvest. Because this mix of decayed flesh, dough, and pig bones was considered sacred, the Bailers had to observe a state of sexual purity three days before they assumed their duties.

On the first day, *Anodos* ("Way Up"), women assembled and hiked up to the Thesmophorion shrine carrying the implements necessary to perform their rituals and the provisions for their stay. Their departure must have caused a disruption for we are told that on the middle day of the festival neither the law courts nor the Assembly met. The second day, *Nesteia* ("Fast"), consisted of fasting and mourning. It commemorated Demeter's refusal to eat out of grief for the loss of her daughter as represented in the myth of her abduction. On the third day, *Kalligeneia* ("Beautiful Birth"), the women feasted, partaking of the meat of sacrificial pigs, offering cakes in the shape of genitals, and eating pomegranates. After remembering the sorrows of a mother who had lost her only child, the women celebrated the gift of childbirth and children. The fertility of earth at seedtime was closely linked to the bearing of fine children within the Athenian community. The women further engaged in the same ribald banter or aischrologia practiced at the Stenia. In the context of the Thesmophoria, this jesting recalled the crude remarks of the servant Iambe who made the goddess laugh despite her sorrows in the *Homeric Hymn to Demeter*. By encouraging sexual expression, this ritual joking was thought to promote sexuality within marriage and therefore female fertility. Like other women-only festivals in ancient Greece, the Thesmophoria established a female culture in which women were ritually and politically in charge, if only temporarily. The celebration emphasized that the continuity of the polis and its welfare depended upon women's reproductive power. It is noteworthy, however, that women could hold power only in the total absence of men, just like the mythical Amazons.

The **Haloa**, a lesser known, all-women festival, similarly stressed the role of female sexuality in the promotion of fertility. The name derives from the Greek word for "threshing floor," a stone circular area located outside rural Greek villages. The relation of this space to the festival is unknown. It was celebrated in late November or early December and honored Demeter and Dionysus as the gods of female fertility and wine, respectively. The only extant description of the festival states that it was restricted to women and also held at Eleusis. After male officials prepared an elaborate feast, they left and the women took over the proceedings. This Thanksgiving-like banquet may have recognized the gift of agriculture, and therefore of food, that Demeter imparted to the Eleusinians as told in the *Homeric Hymn to Demeter*. The focus soon shifted from food to sex as the women handled clay models of male and female genitals and indulged in the obscene language and abuse characteristic of the aischrologia associated with Demeter in her other ritual contexts. While the wives feasted and drank and no doubt laughed at the verbal and visual obscenities, priestesses sidled up to them and whispered in their ears, allegedly to encourage adultery. The banquet included cakes baked in the shape of genitals, symbols of human procreation, fish, and grains, but no meat. Although this late account sounds more like a male fantasy of what the women were up to at their secret festivals, an enigmatic scene on a red-figure vase, no doubt also fashioned by a man (Figure 7.2), appears to confirm the sexual aspect of female Demetrian worship. A woman leans forward to the left of the vase and sprinkles something from a rectangular box held in her left hand. On the ground stand four phalluses with leaves of barley curling around their bases. These might be the clay models used by the women in the Haloa or the Thesmophoria. The woman has brought them to the field and planted them among the newly sprouted crops. She is sprinkling them with something meant to stimulate their growth in conjunction with the phalluses. Of course, there is no way to know for certain the meaning of this enigmatic scene.

Figure 7.2 A woman sprinkling something from a box over four clay phalluses planted in the ground, possibly a representation of the Haloa; Attic red-figure pelike attributed to the Hasselmann Painter, c. 430 BCE. London, British Museum E 819.

Whatever the correct interpretation of the vase, the festival of the Haloa probably arose from a phallic rite practiced by women to promote the growth of grain. According to Christian authors, it was an all-night orgy of indecency in which the women reveled in their freedom to do and say whatever they wished. Because of its connection with licentious behavior, the Haloa eventually came to be associated with courtesans. Although prostitutes could participate, it is clear that this festival was not exclusively reserved for them. The combination of sex talk and obscene objects was not only thought to encourage fertility but also provided a ritual space that facilitated women's social networks and allowed a moment of temporary license in their otherwise restricted lives.

7.5 Women and Funerary Ritual

In the first part of this chapter we saw how much of women's public ritual engagement revolved around fertility rites. Festivals in honor of Demeter channeled the generative power of women to stimulate both agrarian and human productivity. Let us turn now to the other main ritual duty allocated to ancient Greek women, the care of the dead. Although these two religious roles – promoting life and supervising death – may seem contradictory at first, a certain cultural logic connects the two. For the Greeks, the beginning of life implied its end. We are told, for instance, that the great hero Achilles will suffer "such things as Destiny wove with the strand of his birth that day his mother bore him" (Hom. *Il.* 20.128). In other words, an individual's fate or death comes into being at the same time as her life. And it is the mother who engenders the condition of mortality in her child. The Fates spin the threads of destiny for each mortal at birth, measure out a span, and then cut it off. The length of the thread symbolizes the life span of the individual and cannot be changed. Women's rituals thus marked all of the stages of life, from birth to death. As with other ritual contexts, women's role in death ritual closely paralleled their domestic duties, because they had as their primary responsibility the task of washing and dressing the corpse before interment. At the same time, funerary ritual took them out of the house, into the public sphere, where they tended the graves of their relatives and ensured they were not forgotten.

Death for the ancient Greeks signaled the transition of the individual from the world of the living to the underworld. The rituals that marked this passage gave mourners the chance to strengthen their own identities and that of their clan as they confronted finitude. The process of acknowledging death happened gradually. The deceased remained in a state of flux until the funerary rituals that facilitated the transition to the other world were accomplished. In classical Athens, the funeral was the legal responsibility of the deceased's relatives, particularly sons, and had three parts: the **prothesis** ("lying in state"), the **ekphora** ("procession to the grave"), and interment in the grave. Women were actively involved in the first stage of the funeral. Immediately after a death, they prepared for the prothesis, which took place on the next day. It was held either indoors or in the courtyard. First the eyes and mouth were closed, sometimes using a chip strap to hold the latter in place. The body was washed, anointed, and dressed, usually in white. Antigone in Sophocles' same-name play states that she has performed this ritual for all the members of her family: "For when you died, I washed and dressed you all with my own hands, and poured the libations on your graves" (Soph. *Ant.* 900–3). A deceased unmarried or newly married person might be dressed in wedding attire. The body was wrapped in a shroud (the garment Penelope weaves for her father-in-law in the *Odyssey*) and placed on a bier, with a mattress, pillow, and cover and with the feet placed toward the door or street. Sometimes the body was strewn with wild herbs to ward off evil spirits or to mask the smell. The head was crowned with garlands of laurel and celery. A water jug stood at the door to purify anyone who came into contact with the body before leaving the house. A branch of cypress – a tree associated with cemeteries – was hung on the front door to alert passers-by of the presence of death.

A major focus of the prothesis was mourning by the female members of the household. Women stood around the body and sang ritualized laments, with the chief mourner, usually the mother, at the head. By the classical period, no woman under 60 could participate, unless she was within the range of cousins or closer in relation. The songs belonged to a female poetic tradition handed down over generations that involved conventional themes and phrasing as well as improvisation. The earliest depiction of a scene of lamentation occurs at the end of Homer's *Iliad*. When queen Hecuba learns of the death of her son, Hector, she throws the veil from her head and begins to lament him, joined by king Priam and the rest of the city. Once the body has been brought to the palace, the women, led by his wife, Andromache, who cradles his head in her arms, engage in lamentations with other singers. The captive Briseis similarly throws herself on the corpse of Patroclus in grief when she sees his body:

> And now Briseis in the likeness of golden Aphrodite, when she saw Patroclus mutilated by the sharp bronze, flung herself about him and uttered a shrill cry, and with her hands tore at her breasts and her soft throat and her lovely face. The woman like the goddesses spoke to him through tears: "Patroclus, most pleasing to my heart in its sorrows, I left you here alive when I went away from the shelter, but now I come back, lord of the people, to find you have fallen." (Hom. *Il.* 19.282–9)

Briseis accompanies her cries with ritual gestures of lament, including the laceration of skin, the beating of the breasts and head, and the tearing of hair. Men also participated, although in a less emotional way. They stood at a distance from the corpse, raising their arm in a gesture of farewell. A funerary plaque from the late fifth century BCE (Figure 7.3) depicts this arrangement. The corpse rests on a couch, his head propped up by a pillow. The female mourners – distinguished by their white skin – stand closest to the body. The chief mourner, probably his mother, holds his chin. The other women touch their hair and raise their hands. The men are off to the side and raise their hands in a final, restrained salutation to the deceased.

Before dawn on the third day, the body was brought to the cemetery in a procession called the ekphora, the most public part of the funerary rites. Men walked in front and women behind. As in the prothesis, no woman under 60 could participate unless she was the child of a cousin or closer relation. By the classical period, limitations were also placed on the number of female mourners who could participate. These limitations also prohibited them from wearing more than three cloaks in the procession. Nor were they allowed to lacerate their flesh, sing set dirges, or mourn anyone besides the deceased. Lastly, women were not supposed to carry tomb offerings in baskets larger than one cubit, the length of a forearm. The purpose of this legislation has been variously interpreted. It may have been intended to check women's disorderly conduct in public or extravagant displays of wealth. A large cortège of hired female mourners sumptuously costumed advertised the status and prosperity of Athenian elite at a time when a more democratic social agenda prevailed. Whatever the rationale, these restrictions had the effect of muting the one form of public verbal expression permitted to women in classical Athens.

Once at the tomb, the body was either interred or cremated. Libations were poured and possibly an animal sacrificed. If cremated, the remains of the body were collected and put in an urn, which was then buried. Offerings were placed on and around the grave, typically ribbons and funerary lekythoi, which held oil to be poured as an offering for the dead. Many of these

Figure 7.3 Mourners at a prothesis; archaic black-figure terracotta funerary plaque, c. 510–520 BCE. New York, Metropolitan Museum of Art, Rogers fund, 1954, 54.11.5.

vases self-referentially depict women bringing these offerings to the grave. One beautiful example (Figure 7.4) shows two women preparing to visit a tomb. They hold broad, flat funerary baskets filled with offerings of ribbons and lekythoi. The relatives then returned to the house for a banquet that reunited the surviving relatives. Observance of tomb cult was so important in classical Athens that neglect of these duties could affect a legal dispute and a childless man might adopt a son to perform them. Commemorative rites took place at the grave on the third, ninth, and thirtieth days, and then annually, after burial. The Athenians also celebrated an annual civic festival called the Genesia, during which they frequented the graves of family members. Visits could also be made at other times. Tomb visitations affirmed that the deceased had not been forgotten and that the women of the family had taken proper care of their loved ones. Both the ribbons and the vases left at the grave represent a sort of promise that mourners, particularly women, would not forget the dead but would continue to visit them. Conversely, the neglect of the grave diminished the status of the deceased and served as a particular reproach to the female members of his household. In Aeschylus' *Libation Bearers*, king Agamemnon's grave has been all but forgotten by the members of his household. Clytemnestra expresses her hatred for her husband by refusing to mourn him or make offerings at his tomb. The task of remembering belongs to Electra who pours libations for her father as the play opens.

Women's role in funerary ritual is paramount in Sophocles' *Antigone* (c. 441 BCE), a play discussed in connection with heroic virgins in Chapter 4. King Creon has decreed Antigone's brother, Polyneices, an enemy of the state for bringing an army against his native city in an attempt to reclaim his rightful place on the throne. The king prohibits his burial while lavishing all the honors of a full military funeral on his dead brother, Eteocles. Polyneices' naked body has been cast outside the city walls, unburied and unlamented, a feast for dogs and birds. This state

Figure 7.4 Two women preparing to visit the grave; white-ground lekythos attributed to Near the Timokrates Painter, c. 460 BCE. Madison, Wisconsin, Chazen Museum of Art, Edna G. Dyar Fund and Fairchild Foundation Fund purchase.

so distresses Antigone that she secretly visits the corpse and performs the customary rites in violation of the king's command. The guard who discovers her describes her actions as follows:

> She wailed aloud with the shrill cry of a grieving bird as when inside its empty nest its sees the bed bereft of its young. So, too, when she saw the naked corpse, she burst out in a cry of lamentation, calling terrible curses on those that had done the deed. Immediately she took thirsty dust with her hands and from a bronze-beaten pitcher, she crowned the corpse with trice-poured libations. (Soph. *Ant.* 423–31)

Antigone performs a makeshift prothesis and interment together. First she mourns over her brother's body. Because of its high pitch, the sound of female mourning is often compared to the cry of birds in Greek poetry. She then sprinkles the corpse with dust in lieu of actual burial and pours the customary libations over his head instead of decking him with a crown. When brought before Creon, Antigone defends her actions in a famous speech in which she privileges divine over human law:

> It was not Zeus that made this decree, nor did Justice who dwells with those below establish these laws for men. I did not believe your decrees had such power that you, a mere mortal, could override the unwritten and unerring customs of the gods. They are not of

today or yesterday, but they are eternal. No one knows when first they arose. I did not intend to be punished by the gods for ignoring these out of fear of one man's arrogance. (Soph. *Ant.* 450–9)

Antigone argues that the divine imperative to mourn and bury the dead surpasses any human decree. She does not fear the consequences of violating Creon's edict because she knows that in doing so she honors the gods and follows tradition. This powerful play suggests that women in their capacity as ritual agents provided their families and communities with a moral compass. Their ritual duties invested them with agency and gave them the authority to intervene in male affairs when men went astray.

Euripides' *Suppliant Women* (423 BCE) similarly affirms the importance of women in steering the men toward the path of right action, again through their involvement in death ritual. The play in fact tells the story of the war between the two brothers that resulted in Antigone's disobedience. Just as he had refused to bury to Polyneices, Creon now refuses either to bury the bodies of the enemies fallen in battle or to release them to their aged mothers, who long to perform the rituals of prothesis and interment for them. When their petition fails, the mothers of the heroes approach Athens for help in recovering the bodies. Theseus, the Athenian leader, wages a military campaign against Thebes, retrieves the bodies, and brings them back to Athens for the performance of funerary rites. A pivotal role is played by Theseus' mother, Aethra, as a figure of moral authority who urges her son to honor ancestral laws regarding burial and supplication. Her age and maternal status combined with the religious imperative of the mourning mothers allow her to act as moral agent who persuades a reluctant male to obey ancestral laws. Euripides' *Suppliant Women*, like Sophocles' *Antigone*, demonstrates that religion offered a chance for women to take action on behalf of their families and communities, investing them with authority and influence, even over powerful men.

7.6 Conclusion

Once past childbearing years, women in ancient Greece seem to have enjoyed more freedom and exerted more influence on their families and communities than their younger counterparts. In Athenian drama, they reinforce traditional values, persuading men to act in accordance with religious precedents. In oratory, they play an important role behind the scenes, advising their male relatives as to the proper course of action. Although some priestly positions were open only to older women, others afforded opportunities for younger women to guide and influence their communities, not only in religious matters, but sometimes in politics as well. Famous priesthoods, such as that of the Pythia at Delphi, Athena Polias at Athens, and Demeter and Kore at Eleusis, brought great wealth and prestige to a select few. They enjoyed special privileges such as front-row seats in the theater and dedications in the form of statues. Although not every woman could aim for such a high office, all could participate in other aspects of religious life, such as the women-only fertility festivals. The mandatory participation of Athenian wives in the festival of the Thesmophoria not only promoted the prosperity of the city, it also provided an opportunity for female leadership and community. At home, women were responsible for a wide variety of rituals, especially those surrounding weddings and funerals. They completed an individual's circle of life by caring for the body of the deceased, gave form to disordered grief through their ritual songs, and ensured that the loved one would be remembered long after death.

Questions for Review

1   Why did older women enjoy more freedom than their younger counterparts?

2   What duties did priestesses perform?

3   What is the Thesmophoria and why was it important?

4   What role did women play in funerals?

5   Why were women involved primarily in rituals surrounding fertility and death?

Further Reading

Primary Sources

Aristophanes' *Women of the Thesmophoria*
Euripides' *Suppliant Women*
Sophocles' *Antigone*

Secondary Sources

Alexiou, Margaret (2002). *The Ritual Lament in the Greek Tradition*, 2e. Lanham, MD: Rowman and Littlefield.
  Explores the genre of the lament in cultural context from classical antiquity to modern Greece.
Connelly, Joan (2007). *Portrait of a Priestess: Women and Ritual in Ancient Greece*. Princeton, NJ: Princeton University Press.
  A fascinating analysis of female priestesses in ancient Greece, with attention to their duties, clothing, privileges, and commemoration. Emphasizes throughout the forms of agency and influence ritual participation gave women.
Dillon, Matthew (2003). *Women and Girls in Classical Greek Religion*. London and New York: Routledge.
  Offers a comprehensive account of the ritual lives of women from childhood to adulthood through a detailed discussion of primary evidence. Chapter 4 deals with women-only festivals and chapter 5 with women and death ritual.
Kaltsas, Nikolaos and Shapiro, Alan (2008). *Worshipping Women: Ritual and Reality in Classical Athens*. New York: Onassis Foundation.
  An exhibition catalog of images and artifacts related to women's religious practice accompanied by essays on goddesses and heroines, women and ritual, and the female life cycle.
Mayor, Adrienne (2014). *The Amazons: Lives and Legends of Warrior Women Across the Ancient World*. Princeton, NJ: Princeton University Press.
  Explores the ancient evidence for the existence of warrior women as reflected in their myths, from Italy to China.
Oakley, John (2007). *Picturing Death in Classical Athens*. Cambridge: Cambridge University Press.
  An examination of representations of death on Attic white-ground lekythoi, many of which feature women engaged in various aspects of funerary ritual.
Parke, Herbert (1977). *Festivals of the Athenians*. Ithaca, NY: Cornell University Press.
  Provides a chronological account of the major festivals on the Athenian religious calendar.

Interlude

Women in the Hellenistic World

8

Women in the Hellenistic World

> For everything, whatever is and happens anywhere, is in Egypt: wealth, wrestling schools, power, prosperity, reputation, sights, philosophers, gold, young men, the temple of the Sibling Gods, the good king, the Museion, wine, all the good things that a man could want, women, as many, by Persephone, as there are stars in the sky …
>
> (Herod. 1.26–33)

In this chapter, we move away from the narrow confines of the Greek polis and beyond the classical period to the vast world of Hellenistic kingdoms and global migrations. How did women experience and shape this new world? Which ideas about gender remained constant and which changed? We turn to the urban landscape of Alexandria in Egypt, center of the Hellenistic Greek world, as the opening epigraph indicates, until it became a Roman province under the rule of Augustus. This chapter departs from the previous format in that it focuses more on the historical role of women during this period rather than on the female life cycle. It considers first how the conquests of Alexander the Great reshaped the cultural landscape and their impact on representations of women in literature and art. A large part of the chapter focuses on the place of royal women in Hellenistic history: Olympias, the mother of Alexander III/the Great, and two Ptolemaic queens, Arsinoe II and Berenice II. Royal women navigated a complex familial and political landscape at court. Polygamy, intrigue, betrayal, murder, and even sibling marriage helped them to acquire and consolidate their power and that of their children. Despite continual interfamilial strife, they enjoyed a degree of influence, prestige, and freedom unimaginable to their classical Athenian counterparts. This new type of woman culminates in one of the most fascinating female figures in all of classical antiquity, Cleopatra VII, ruler of Egypt and lover of the Roman leaders, Julius Caesar and Mark Antony. She was descended from the powerful dynasty of the Ptolemies as seen in Chart 8.1. We consider the major changes in the Greek world brought about by the conquests of Alexander that paved the way for her rule. Although the main focus is on Hellenistic queens and how they influenced their families and communities, we consider the emergence of a female perspective in Hellenistic poetry and the lives of nonroyal women as found in some remarkable documents, letters written by women and marriage contracts between their husbands and fathers. Because this period of history links the Greek and Roman worlds, it is particularly critical for understanding Roman views of women and gender.

Women in Classical Antiquity: From Birth to Death, First Edition. Laura K. McClure.
© 2020 John Wiley & Sons, Inc. Published 2020 by John Wiley & Sons, Inc.

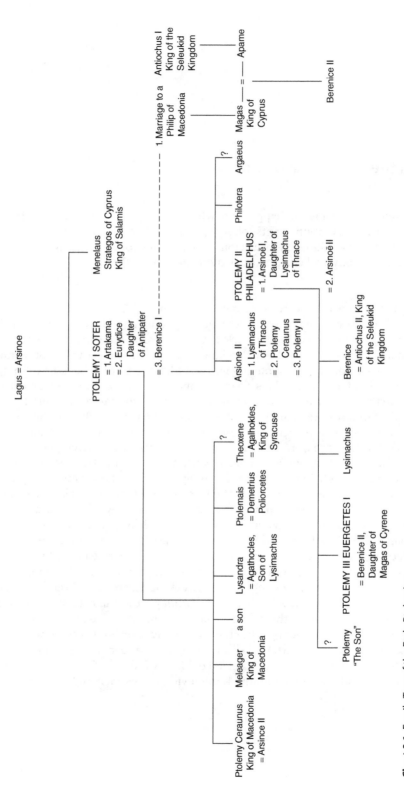

Chart 8.1 Family Tree of the Early Ptolemies.

8.1   The Rise of Macedon and Alexander the Great

The Hellenistic period encompasses the time span from the death of Alexander in 323 BCE to the suicide of Cleopatra in 30 BCE, marking the transition from the small, contained world of the Greek polis to large urban centers such as Alexandria, Pergamon, and Antioch. During this time, Hellenic values and ideals were imparted to a diverse population until they were eventually overcome by Rome. This story begins in Macedon, a remote cultural backwater in Northern Greece prior to the fourth century BCE (see Map 1). Its customs and political institutions differed in important ways from other city-states. Some have characterized Macedonian society as "Homeric" because it perpetuated a warrior culture that revolved around clans. Men were expected to be violently competitive in every aspect of life, but especially in hunting, war, and politics. Those who had not yet killed an enemy in battle were publicly shamed by a particular style of dress (Arist. *Pol.* 1324b). In one of the tombs found at Vergina, a Macedonian necropolis or "city of the dead," the presence of military equipment to mark a female burial suggests that martial prowess was also valued in women. In contrast to democratic Athens, Macedonia was a nonurban, kinship-based monarchy. One clan, the Argeads, to which Alexander and his father, Philip II, belonged, dominated the often violent and chaotic political environment. Also distinctive was their custom of polygamy. Marriage to multiple women maximized the number of potential heirs and thereby ensured succession. However, because the Macedonians did not establish any clear principles for succession, rival wives were forced to compete against one another in a constant struggle for status and legitimacy. These rivalries had the effect of strengthening ties between full siblings and their mothers because of their shared political interests while fostering distrust of the father. As difficult as this situation must have been for the women, it nonetheless facilitated the exercise of female power at court.

The reigns of Philip II and his son Alexander provide a glimpse into the impact of polygamy on women in the Macedonian dynasty and the possibilities for influence and authority it engendered. Philip II ascended to the throne after his brother and thousands of other Macedonians were slaughtered in a battle against a neighboring tribe, the Illyrians. His first order of business was to defeat them in turn, incorporating the states of upper Macedonian into his kingdom. With his newly expanded army, he acquired Athenian colonies on the Aegean coast, annexed Thessaly, and finally defeated Athens at the battle of Chaeronea in 338 BCE. These military victories enabled Philip to unite Greece under his rule while making Macedon into a more urban, wealthier, and Hellenized realm. Critical to his success was polygamy, and indeed, this pattern was followed by his successors, including the Ptolemies in Egypt. Although earlier Argead kings probably practiced it, Philip did so to an unprecedented degree. His liaisons with at least seven different women – some courtesans, some legitimate wives – forged alliances with conquered city-states, established internal stability, and extended Macedonia's reach. They also increased the possibility of male heirs, although in the end he had just two, Alexander and his half-brother, Philip III Arrhidaeus (hereafter "Arrhidaeus"), who seems to have mentally impaired.

Philip married as many as five brides within a two-year period, culminating with his marriage to Olympias, future mother of Alexander. These marriages mainly served a political purpose. They helped to stabilize his kingdom and secure its borders, because most of the women were not Macedonian but came from regions critical to Philip's military agenda. For instance, his first marriage to Audata, the daughter of an Illyrian chieftain, secured peace between Macedon and Illyria, whereas his marriage to Olympias helped him to acquire the kingdom of Molossia. Philip II's polygamy combined with his numerous love affairs with both men and women caused continual unrest within his household. Without a hierarchy of wives or clear system of succession, each woman was left to her own devices to plot the ascent of her son and secure the king's favor.

The success of royal women thus resided in their ability to influence the monarch, advocate for their children, scheme ruthlessly against rivals, and build alliances. It also united mother and son in the common goal of succession, because they alone could trust one another. For this reason, women at court had more power during the reign of their sons rather than that of their husbands. To protect their interests, royal women, especially mothers, informed themselves about political matters, especially if they wanted to ensure their sons succeeded to the throne. In this regard, they did not experience the sexual and political dichotomies of their Athenian counterparts. Because monarchy is the rule of the family, it involves women as well as men and opens up the possibility that women could act autonomously and exert power over others, particularly in the absence of men. For example, Philip II's mother, Eurydice, saw to it that all three of her sons ascended to the throne in a time of great political upheaval through her internal and international connections. She further consolidated their power by eliminating their half-brothers from a rival wife, Gygaea, none of whose sons ever reached the throne. Eurydice and her patronage helped to establish and strengthen the rule of her sons. Macedonian royal women also controlled their own wealth and could choose how to expend it, in contrast to Athenian women. Often they used their money to finance lavish dedications to gods and sanctuaries as a means of public display, serving as benefactors in their communities, a practice later adopted by prominent Roman women.

8.2   Olympias: Mother of Alexander

Olympias, the fifth wife of Philip, the mother of Alexander the Great and grandmother of Alexander IV, operated in much the same way as Eurydice, shrewdly advocating for her descendants during all three reigns. After Philip II's death, she tirelessly promoted the political careers of her son and grandson, viewing any check on their power or position as a threat. Olympias was a Molossian princess whose family claimed descent from Neoptolemus, son of Achilles. According to Plutarch (c. 50–120 CE), she was a jealous and angry woman who may have been responsible for the mental condition of Alexander's half-brother and competitor for the throne, Arrhidaeus, giving him drugs "which injured his body and ruined his mind" (Plut. *Alex.* 77). Here it should be noted that ancient accounts of Olympias and other royal women are notoriously unreliable because they draw heavily on stereotypes and literary tropes rather than actual fact. Then as today, female ambition is often depicted as something monstrous and terrifying rather than admirable. Olympias stressed her heroic lineage and encouraged her son to view himself as the embodiment of Achilles; indeed, he is said to have slept with a copy of Homer's *Iliad* under his pillow. As we saw in Chapter 2, such a model involved striving to "always be the best," to be preeminent among all others. But in contrast to the Homeric emphasis on paternal lineage, Alexander seems to have identified more closely, at least initially, with his mother's side of the family. Although her ancestry distinguished her from Philip's other wives from the beginning, Olympias did not establish her dominant position over them until the 16-year-old Alexander was appointed co-ruler in 340 BCE.

Once Alexander took the throne, Olympias exercised much more influence as the mother of a king than the wife of one. Determined to preserve her son's power, she was calculating and ambitious, unforgiving to her enemies and loyal to her friends. She took part in the purges that secured Alexander's rule, eliminating Philip's seventh wife, allegedly butchering her daughter in her lap before forcing the mother to hang herself. The fact that Alexander was slow to marry, and possibly more inclined toward men, further strengthened Olympias' position in Macedon, despite his long absence from court. After the death of his father, Alexander swiftly brought the central Greek city-states under Macedonian control and then set off to conquer Persia. His military campaigns over the next 11 years covered a vast territory, extending from Persia to Egypt, Afghanistan, and even as far away as India. Part of his success derived from his policy of tolerance toward conquered territories. He left their financial and administrative system intact and installed Greek administrators to collect tributes and taxes. Little changed therefore in the everyday operating systems of ancient cities under Hellenistic monarchy. Olympias frequently corresponded with her son during his campaigns, advising him on political matters and upholding his interests in Macedon. She also engaged in international diplomacy through religious benefactions. She may have even inspired Alexander's conviction that he was the son of a god, which set a pattern for later Hellenistic dynasts eager to exploit their newly acquired royal status.

Alexander died suddenly in Babylon at the age of 32, possibly of a combination of illness and heavy drinking. Although polygamous like his father, he had left behind no heir, until his first wife, Roxane, a noblewoman from central Asia, gave birth to a son, Alexander IV, after his death. The only other possible contender for the throne was his disabled half-brother, Arrhidaeus. Alexander's death sparked two decades of power struggles among his relatives and generals in Macedon. Olympias worked to maintain her position and influence in a rapidly changing and chaotic political situation. When Arrhidaeus subsequently became king, Olympias with the help of the Macedonian army had him and his wife captured and executed, along with a hundred of his partisans. The next man to take the throne ordered her to be taken into custody and killed. The soldiers refused on the grounds that she was the mother of Alexander. In the end, the families of the victims she had executed stoned her to death. Olympias died as she lived, trying to acquire power for herself and preserve the rule of her descendants. Her example shows just how much could be achieved by a well-born woman of ambition and intelligence early in the Hellenistic period. But it also shows the limitations of being female. Her failure was ultimately military. Without the ability to amass and command an army, she could not hope to maintain her dominance.

8.3 The Spread of Hellenism

Alexander's conquests established monarchy as the primary political institution, one largely unfamiliar to the Greek world, and established kingship as the model for subsequent generations. By the end of the third century, the Macedonian dynasty had disappeared and the Successors, Alexander's rival generals, had assumed royal titles in an attempt to become sole ruler. Instead they established individual monarchies. From 275 BCE on, three kingdoms dominated the Eastern Mediterranean until the Roman conquests and were often at war with one another (see Map 2). The first and most powerful was that of Ptolemy I Soter (hereafter "Soter"), a Macedonian nobleman and a member of Alexander's entourage, in Egypt, which lasted until the defeat of Cleopatra VII by Octavian. Seleucus I captured Babylon in 312 BCE, the largest of the three empires at its height. It extended from Western Turkey to Afghanistan, with Syria at its center. After a long struggle, the Antigonids controlled Macedonia from 276 BCE onward. Within two generations, all of the rulers of these kingdoms were related, much like many of the royal families in Western Europe today, and many shared the same names. The Successors did not attempt to expand the boundaries of their rule and enjoyed relative stability for almost a century, until around 200 BCE, when a power that had largely been ignored, Rome, began the annexation of the eastern Mediterranean with the goal of world dominion. Egypt would become its greatest prize.

Alexander's conquests not only united disparate nations and diverse cultures, they also disseminated Hellenic culture across thousands of miles of the ancient Near East and even to

India. Alexander founded numerous cities on his campaigns, naming many after himself. The most famous was Alexandria in Egypt, built on the harbor along the eastern stretch of the North African coast. The Seleucids created over 60 new settlements from Western Turkey to Iran. All of these cities were Greek. Both the rulers and governing classes were Greek and spoke a simplified or "common" form of ancient Greek as their official language. Greek literary forms, modes of thought, political and social institutions, and art and architecture predominated. The emergence of the Hellenistic kingdoms (Map 2), with their huge populations, signaled the decline of the small, independent Greek polis. The cumbersome democratic process was replaced by efficient autocracy. Cities relied on a system of patronage and public honors in which women also took part, much like Roman women centuries later.

8.4   Women and Hellenistic Literature

Under the patronage of the Ptolemies, Alexandria (Map 2) rapidly emerged as the cosmopolitan and literary center of the Hellenistic world, although nothing of the city remains today. Thanks to revenues from the cultivation and export of grain and papyrus, the city soon became famous for its opulence. Its location on the Mediterranean encouraged international commerce and its liberal immigration policy led to a diverse population that included Greeks, native Egyptians, and a large Jewish community. Soter's love of learning influenced the dynasty and attracted numerous foreign poets, scholars, and artists. Through the establishment of the Mouseion, the world's first research institute, and a library, he claimed Hellenic heritage as his own intellectual property. The library housed approximately half a million scrolls; thousands more were stored in a second library nearby. This was an age of literary preservation and imitation rather than innovation. A new class of professional scholars toiled among these book rolls, standardizing the texts of earlier Greek poets and composing commentaries on them, not unlike like classical scholars today. Indeed, we owe the bulk of our modern copies of ancient Greek texts to these efforts.

In addition to the preservation and transmission of archaic and classical texts, the library at Alexandria fostered a new literary culture represented by a group of third-century poets called the Alexandrians, and including Theocritus, Herodas, Callimachus (fl. 285–246 BCE), and Apollonius of Rhodes, all foreigners. These scholar-poets flourished at the court of Soter in the middle of the third century BCE and produced court poetry that was extremely learned, intended for an erudite audience and flattering to their patrons. They combined continuity with innovation, adapting and imitating earlier models yet introducing new themes and situations. Popular new genres such as the idyll, mime, and epigram reflect a newfound interest in personal feelings and realistic settings, and often focus on previously marginalized figures such as women, children, and non-Greeks. For instance, Theocritus' *Idyll* 15 follows the course of two immigrant Greek housewives as they move from their private household to the streets of Alexandria and then to the royal palace to attend a festival of Aphrodite and Adonis organized by Queen Arsinoe II, considered more fully at the end of this chapter. The dialog conveys a female perspective as the women complain about their husbands, their servants, the price of clothing, and other matters central to their lives:

GORGO:	Is Praxinoa in?
PRAXINOA:	Gorgo dear, how long it's been. Yes, I'm in. I'm amazed you've come at last. See that she has a chair, Eunoa; put a cushion on it.
GORGO:	Thank you.
PRAXINOA:	Sit down.

GORGO:	I'm so incompetent. I barely got here in one piece, Praxinoa, there was such a crowd, so many chariots, everywhere boots, everywhere men wearing cloaks. And the road is endless. Every time you move further away.
PRAXINOA:	It's my crazy husband. He brings me here to the boonies, and gets me a shack, not a house, so that we can't be neighbors, out of spite, envious brute. Some people never change.
GORGO:	Don't talk about your husband that way, dear, when your little boy's around. You see, Praxinoa, how he's looking at you? Don't worry Zopyrion, sweet baby. She isn't talking about daddy.
PRAXINOA:	The child understands, by the great goddess.
GORGO:	Nice daddy! (Theoc. *Id.* 15.44–50)

Theocritus uses Homeric language and motifs to describe a distinctly nonepic situation. The poem portrays an almost exclusively female world: the two main characters are wives, they attend a festival in honor of a female goddess sponsored by a woman ruler where they are entertained by a female singer. The emergence of a female perspective in Hellenistic poetry may indicate that many of its readers were women. It also reflects the influence of powerful female patrons, such as queen Arsinoe II, whose favor poets cultivated with their poems.

Herodas' mimes show a similar interest in women, offering humorous and often coarse sketches of everyday life. In Mime 1, an old woman seeks to persuade a younger woman to take on a lover while her current partner, possibly her husband, is away in Egypt. In Mime 6, a woman called Metro visits a friend to enquire where she got her new dildo so that she can buy one for herself:

METRO:	Dear Coritto, who was it who stitched the scarlet dildo for you?
CORITTO:	And where, Metro, did you see it?
METRO:	Nossis, daughter of Erinna, had it two days ago. Great gift!
CORITTO:	Nossis?! Where'd she get it?
METRO:	Will you be mad if I tell you?
CORITTO:	By your sweet eyes, Metro, nothing you say will escape from my mouth.
METRO:	Eubule, Bitas' wife, gave it to her and told her not to tell anyone.
CORITTO:	Women! That woman will destroy me yet. She begged me and I took pity on her and gave it to her, Metro, before I had a chance to try it myself. But she, as if winning the lottery, gives it to people she should not. A fond farewell to a friend like that; let her look on someone else as her friend instead of me. To think she lent my property to Nossis! (If I speak more strongly than is right, forgive me, Nemesis). Even if I had a thousand, I would not give her even one rotten one. (Herod. 6.19–36)

The characters, language, and subject matter of this scene are reminiscent of the sex-striking wives of Aristophanes' *Lysistrata* but they are recast into a contemporary urban setting in which average women are permitted to move about the city freely, purchase sex toys, and congregate together. The derogatory references to the female poets, Nossis and Erinna, also point to a literary culture that included female writers in addition to female readers and patrons.

Women are vividly represented in another popular form, epigram, the literary equivalent of the inscription. Those about women are often funerary, such as this one, by the female poet Anyte (fl. early third century BCE), which commemorates a girl who died before marriage:

> Instead of a bridal chamber and wedding hymns, your mother, Thersis, placed on this marble tomb the statue of a maiden, with your shape and beauty, so we may address you even though you are dead. (Anyte, *Anth. Gr.* 7.649)

Love epigrams deal explicitly with sexual longing and erotic encounters and feature sexually available women of indeterminate social status; they could be hetaeras or prostitutes or unmarried foreign women living independently. Asclepiades (fl. 270 BCE), a contemporary of Theocritus and Callimachus and one of the earliest erotic epigrammatists, frequently details his amatory exploits in his epigrams:

> Lamp, Heracleia swore three times in your presence that she would come. But she hasn't come. So lamp, if you're a god, get back at that lying girl. Whenever she has a lover inside and is messing around, go out, give no more light. (Asclepiades, *Anth. Gr.* 5.7)

As we shall see, the women of Hellenistic epigram serve as a prototype for the poet's girlfriend or mistress in Latin love elegy. The emphasis on romantic love and erotic attraction is also found in Apollonius' epic poem, *Voyage of the Argo*, which combines aspects of Homeric epic and Greek tragedy, specifically Euripides' *Medea*. Instead of focusing on Jason's betrayal of Medea and her revenge, however, the poem chronicles the beginning of their affair, sympathetically portraying the destructive passion of the barbarian girl:

> Then Eros crouched down small at Jason's feet, fitted the notch to the middle of the bowstring, pulled it straight apart with both hands and shot at Medea. A stunned silence seized her heart. Then he darted out of the high-roofed hall, laughing as he went. And the arrow burned deep in the heart of the girl, like a flame. Again and again she cast longing glances at Jason, and in her torment common sense fluttered from her breast. She forgot everything, for her heart was filled with sweet suffering. As when a woman scatters bits of twigs on a burning log – a hired woman, whose job it is to attend to the spinning – to provide light under the roof at night as she sits near, and from the small log the flame destroys all the twigs as it rises, ineffable; such was the destructive love that wrapped around her heart and burned in secret. (Ap. Rhod. 281–98)

Apollonius' depiction of the infatuated girl reflects the Hellenistic fascination with the individual and the psychopathology of erotic love. It also points to a contemporary concern with women's power and privilege in a changing world.

Outside of Alexandria, female poets flourished. Moero of Byzantium (fl. late fourth-early third century BCE) composed epic poetry, as did her son, but only 10 verses from her poem, *Mnemosyne*, and two epigrams survive. Anyte (third century BCE), author of one of the epigrams quoted previously, hailed from the region of Arcadia in Greece and followed in the tradition of the earlier Peloponnesian female poets, Telesilla (fifth century BCE) and Praxilla (fl. 451 BCE). She seems to have had a special interest in women, children, and nature and was famous for her funerary laments for animals. Nossis (c. 300 BCE) was from Locri in Southern Italy, a region inhabited by Greeks, and author of a dozen extant epigrams in the *Anthology*, mostly inscriptions for votive offerings and works of art dedicated by women in a temple of Aphrodite. In one epigram, she even boldly equates herself to Sappho:

> Stranger, if you sail to Mytilene, city of the lovely choruses, which sparked Sappho, flower of the Graces, say that the land of Locri gave birth to one dear to the Muses and her equal, and that her name is Nossis. Go! (Nossis, *Anth. Gr.* 7.718)

Erinna (fl. 350 BCE) possibly lived on the Greek island of Telos near Rhodes. According to an epigram by Asclepiades, she died unmarried at age 19. Three epigrams in the *Anthology* are attributed to her, although she is more famous for her longer poem titled *Distaff*, considered in Chapter 3. As we saw, the largest surviving fragments lament her friend Baucis, who died shortly after marriage, and recalls the tortoise game they used to play.

I lament you, poor Baucis, wailing deeply over you. These traces of you still lie warm in my heart, dear girl. All that we once enjoyed is embers now. We clung to our dolls in our rooms as little girls, like newly married women free from worries…. (Erinna, *Distaff* 5–9)

Although a small detail, it is striking that Erinna refers to the girls playing with their dolls, a topic rarely mentioned by male authors, despite their ubiquity in the ancient world, and a topic that is further discussed in Chapter 10. These female perspectives on childhood, friendship, love, and loss reflect the Hellenistic emphasis on the emotional lives of individuals and attest to the increasing visibility of women in a changing world.

8.5   Aphrodite and the Female Nude

Today we are so inundated with images of female nudity in art museums, movies, television, video games, and the Internet that it is hard to believe the opposite held true for the Greeks of the archaic and classical periods. Now feminist film directors, writers, and television producers often choose to depict men without clothes as a radical statement about how the female body is usually objectified by our cameras. Around 350 BCE, the Athenian sculptor, Praxiteles, forever changed the course of Western art with his revolutionary new image of the goddess Aphrodite, called the Cnidian Aphrodite (Figure 8.1). This was the first monumental, three-dimensional female nude in the history of Greek sculpture. Almost 7 ft. tall and housed on a cliff high above the Mediterranean, the statue stood at the Greek seaport of Cnidos for almost 800 years, serving as the sailor's goddess. Although nudity had been commonplace in renderings of her Near Eastern counterpart Ishtar/Astarte, it was previously associated only with hetaeras and prostitutes in Greece. Praxiteles combined both traditions in his Aphrodite, purportedly modeling the goddess after his mistress, the hetaera Phryne. She was made famous by a shocking moment in court. Put on trial for impiety, she was defended by the orator Hypereides. Afraid that he was about to lose the case, the orator dramatically stripped off her robe and bared her breasts to the jurors, instantly winning her acquittal.

The teasing half-smile and languorous gaze of the Cnidian are directed off to the left as if looking at someone, perhaps at her lover, the war-god Ares. According to one epigram, the statue was so realistic that when goddess herself viewed it, she asked, "Where did Praxiteles see me naked?!" (Plato, *Anth. Gr.* 16.160). According to another anecdote, the sculpture so aroused a male viewer that he tried to have sex with it:

> The little temple in which the statue is placed is open on all sides, so that the likeness of the goddess can be seen in the round, an arrangement favored by the goddess herself, it is generally believed. Indeed, from whatever point it is viewed, it is equally to be admired. They say that a certain individual, seized by desire for this statue, hid himself in the temple at night and then had sex with the image, and the mark of this lust still stains the marble. (Plin. *NH* 36.4)

The Cnidian's nakedness signifies not vulnerability but rather divine autonomy and the power of sexual choice, becoming the prototype for many subsequent sculptural representations of the goddess. The emergence of Aphrodite as a popular subject in the arts reflects the growing importance of her cult in the Hellenistic age and marks a cultural shift in the prestige and power of women. Another sign of the enhanced status of women during this period is the presence of female portraits on coinage (see Box 8.1).

Figure 8.1 Cnidian Aphrodite, Roman copy of a bronze original from 350 BCE by Praxiteles. Rome, Musei Vaticani. Harcourt Gomez/Alamy Stock photo.

Box 8.1 Ancient Faces

In the age of the selfie, it is difficult to imagine a time when realistic likenesses of individuals did not exist. The static kore statues discussed in Chapter 4 could be broadly understood as portraits in the sense that they embody the idealized qualities of the girls whose names they bear. But they conform to an ideal type and do not contain differentiating features. Beginning with Alexander, artists for the first time attempted to render a realistic likeness of the individual by incorporating specific attributes. Alexander was no Achilles. He did not conform to the heroic visual ideal: he was short, beardless, and covered with battle scars. He had a crooked neck, weak gaze, and unruly cowlick. Instead of eliminating these imperfections, portraitists used them to communicate aspects of his inner character and stature. The popularity of portraiture resulted in the visual representation of new categories of individuals, from public figures such as orators, poets, and philosophers to ordinary people, including women. These images were realistic in that they incorporated idiosyncratic features specific to the individual, his or her status and life stage.

Another intriguing form of portraiture is found on gold and silver coins. Coinage presented the perfect venue for broadcasting political ideas because they were handled daily by everyone in the city, although of course it is impossible to gauge how much attention people paid to them. Classical and archaic Greek coins are impersonal in that they depict only deities, heroes, and their attributes. Not until the fourth century BCE do coin portraits of living rulers appear. Hellenistic monarchs exploited the potential of coinage to promote their policies and successes. Portrait coins minted under the Ptolemies are particularly fine because of the dynasty's enormous wealth. The largest group are those in the name of Arsinoe II, minted after her death in 268 BCE. The obverse of a beautiful gold octadrachm (Figure 8.2) shows the queen as an elegant young woman, with her hair arranged in the "melon" style, beneath a diadem and veil. On the reverse is a double cornucopia filled with fruit, symbol of abundance and fertility. Despite the realism of some Hellenistic portraits, these ancient faces are in a sense "role portraits" rather than the ancient equivalent of the selfie. They represent not the actual physical qualities of their subjects but rather their role or status in life and the image they wished to project to others.

Figure 8.2 Gold Octadrachm, with portrait of Arsinoe II on the obverse and a double cornucopia on the reverse, inscribed with the words in Greek, "Arsinoe Philadelpha," c. 271 BCE. Bologna, Italy, Palagi Collection, Archaeological Museum of Bologna, inv. 21233.

8.6   Traces of Women in Hellenistic Egypt

In addition to the emphasis on the female perspective in literature and art, papyrus documents in the form of marriage contracts and letters reinforce the picture of the growing independence and legal capacity of women in Hellenistic Egypt. Written in Greek between 300 BCE and 600 CE, the marriage contracts represent legally binding agreements between spouses, much like a modern prenuptial agreement. The earliest document, dated from 311/10 BCE, comes from Elephantine, located far from Alexandria on the border between Egypt and Nubia, and contains the contract of the couple Heraclides and Demetria (*Papyrus Elephantis* I). It stipulates that Demetria will bring to the household as her dowry 1000 drachmas in clothing and jewelry. Heraclides in turn promises to provide for her physical welfare, although he will choose where they live in consultation with her father. It further regulates the sexual conduct of the partners: Demetria is not to commit adultery or otherwise bring dishonor to her husband, whereas Heraclides is prohibited from introducing another woman into their house or begetting children with someone else. In the case of wrongdoing, the injured party will air his or her grievances before a mutually agreed upon judge. These contracts were made between men, usually the father and the husband, but sometimes we find mothers giving away their daughters, and even, in one case, a bride making these arrangements herself! Their involvement points to the expanded legal authority of Greek women during the Hellenistic period and prefigures in some respects the status of Roman women.

Letters written by women in Greek and Egyptian, between 300 BCE and 800 CE, are a fascinating and particularly valuable resource for understanding women in Hellenistic Egypt, because they allow us access to a much broader sector of society than the literary texts. More than three hundred survive, probably written by professional scribes rather than in the women's own hand. Judging by the content, the women who wrote these letters predominantly belonged to upper- and upper-middle class families. This genre allowed them to express themselves on their own behalf, without male intervention. The letters are practical rather than personal: they address family, business, or work concerns; convey news; request items; or accompany the sending of gifts and supplies. Most of these letters belong to the Roman period and follow Roman epistolary conventions. They are written on papyrus, a relatively inexpensive medium. Many papyri refer directly to landed property belonging to the writer and her family, including valuable assets such as olive groves, vineyards, farmland with irrigation equipment, and cattle.

The letters contain a wealth of information about the daily activities and concerns of the women who wrote them. Nearly a dozen refer to pregnancy and childbirth. Many discuss the welfare of children and their care. At least 50 contain greetings to and from children and inquiries about their health. When mentioned in the main body of the letter, the concerns revolve around education, suggesting that women participated equally in arranging their studies. Many letters show that women were actively involved in managing the family's estates and businesses. Some women were property owners in their own right and may have represented one fifth of the landowners in Roman Egypt. Approximately 40 letters refer to women traveling, usually to manage property. And yet not a single letter mentions a woman traveling by herself. These letters attest to the increased mobility and financial independence of women in Hellenistic Egypt.

8.7 Ptolemaic Queens: Arsinoe II

The political shift toward monarchy in the Hellenistic period had another unprecedented impact on women, the creation of powerful queens often identified with the goddess Aphrodite. This section and the following one discuss two early Ptolemaic queens, Arsinoe II and Berenice II. The two women lived a generation apart and were related by blood (see Chart 8.1). Arsinoe II (c. 316–268 BCE) led a tumultuous and traumatic life that culminated in marriage to her full brother, Ptolemy II Philadelphus (hereafter "Philadelphus") and international fame. She controlled great wealth and exercised political influence but suffered extreme domestic strife for most of her life. She participated in the courts of four kings, married three times – twice to her brothers! – witnessed the brutal murder of her young sons, fled two kingdoms because of danger, and ended her days in great wealth and security. She was the daughter of the founder of the Ptolemaic dynasty, Soter. He kept many wives and mistresses at court, a pattern followed by his successors. Many of his marriages served political ends, but his last, to Berenice I, was probably for love (see Chart 8.1). She was purportedly the most powerful and intelligent of Soter's wives (Plut. *Pyrrh.* 4). With her he had four children, including a son, whom he named Ptolemy after himself, rather than following the custom of naming sons after grandfathers, and two daughters, Arsinoe II and Philotera. He had an elder son by another wife, also called Ptolemy. By using a single name for his sons, he symbolically replicated himself, and his dynasty, over several generations, perpetuating the illusion of immortality. The two Ptolemy sons, later differentiated by their epithets Ceraunus ("Thunderbolt") and Philadelphus ("Sibling-loving"), were sworn enemies from birth. As the younger wife, Berenice I and her offspring probably at first lived in the shadow of the other women and children at court. But eventually she supplanted her rivals in achieving the favor of Soter, resulting in the appointment of the younger Ptolemy, Philadelphus, as his co-ruler in 285 BCE. From her brother, Arsinoe must have learned at an early age the tactics necessary for survival at court. Personal qualities such as boldness and a willingness to take risks led to her most important successes and failures. Like Olympias, she aggressively pursued honor for herself, her children, and her dynasty.

Little is known about Arsinoe's childhood. She may have received some education alongside her brother given Soter's habit of inviting famous intellectuals to tutor his sons at court. At the age of 15, she was married to a man old enough to be her grandfather, 60-year-old Lysimachus, a former member of Alexander's entourage who had received Thrace as his province. He also controlled parts of Asia Minor and, with the help of his young bride, soon took over Macedon. The marriage produced three sons in rapid succession, the eldest also called Ptolemy, followed by Lysimachus and Philip. Like the other Macedonian kings, Lysimachus was polygamous and already had children from other wives, including an heir apparent.

Although her position within her husband's household remained insecure, two international events brought her great prestige. Her brother, Philadelphus, became king of Egypt and her mother, Berenice I, won an Olympic victory in the four-horse chariot race. The latter might seem like a minor achievement to the modern reader, but female Olympic victors were extremely unusual in the ancient world. Because of the expense, only kings could afford to participate in horse racing. They did not physically compete but rather hired others to train and drive their teams. This practice of patronage opened the games to women who would have otherwise been barred from the festival. The earliest female victor was Cynisca of Sparta, who won the prize in the chariot races at the beginning of the fourth century. Berenice's daring athletic victory would in turn serve as a model for subsequent Ptolemaic queens, putting them almost on equal footing with men. In an epigram, Philadelphus asserts, "I do not set up the glory of my father as great, but this is the great thing, that my mother, a woman, took the victory in the chariot race" (Poseid. 88.5–6 Austin and Bastianini).

After Lysimachus' death and a brief marriage to her half-brother, Ceraunus, Arsinoe returned to Egypt around 276 BCE. There she shocked the world by marrying her full brother Philadelphus: "This Ptolemy fell in love with Arsinoe, his sister on both sides, and married her, contrary to the customs of the Macedonians, but in line with the Egyptians, over whom they ruled" (Pausanias 1.7.1). This was the first full sibling marriage of the Ptolemaic dynasty and one of the world's first "power couples." It was to become the precedent for virtually all subsequent Ptolemaic marriages. The reasons for the union have been much debated. It may have been inspired by the Pharaonic custom of brother–sister marriage in imitation of the sibling gods, Isis and Osiris. The Greek parallel is the brother–sister couple, Hera and Zeus. From a political perspective, perhaps they felt as full siblings from the same mother in a polygamous system that they could trust only each other. It also avoided the problem of marriage to outsiders and their competing bids for succession. In this respect, it strengthened the claims of Philadelphus' immediate family group as the only legitimate descendants of Soter. An important consequence was that it elevated the status of the royal wife almost to that of co-ruler. It also made succession matrilineal, through princesses and queens, because only marriage to a female family member could produce legitimate offspring.

Just as the use of the single male name of Ptolemy for successive generations of rulers implied the continual rebirth of the king, so, too, brother–sister marriage allowed the royal couple to reincarnate earlier pairs on the divine scale. Philadelphus and Arsinoe reinforced this idea through the establishment of a dynastic cult, the Sibling Gods. The epithet stressed their blood relationship and both justified and promoted the concept of royal sibling marriage. Theocritus glorifies their union as follows:

> He and his fair wife – indeed, no one better than her embraces in her arms a bridegroom at home, loving with her heart her brother and husband. In this way even the sacred marriage of the immortals was accomplished, whom queen Rhea bore to be rulers of Olympus. And Iris, still a virgin, after washing her hands with myrrh, made up one bed for Zeus and Hera to sleep. (Theoc. *Id.* 17.128–34)

By directly comparing the marriage of Philadelphus and Arsinoe to that of Zeus and Hera, the poet sanitizes it for a Greek audience and legitimates it as divinely sanctioned. Because the couple had no children together, Philadelphus appointed his son by Arsinoe I, Ptolemy III Euergetes (hereafter "Euergetes"), as co-regent. He was to be the husband of Berenice II, discussed in the next section.

Exceptionally for a woman, Arsinoe appears to been engaged in military affairs as well as foreign policy. Like her mother, she won chariot races at the Olympian games in 272 BCE. She also controlled great wealth, having received from her first husband entire cities as gifts. These holdings expanded the reach of Egypt when she married Philadelphus. They also enabled her to finance a major architectural dedication – again, unusual for a woman in the ancient world – the rotunda on Samothrace, the largest round building in the Greek world. In addition to her deification through the cult of the Sibling Gods, she also received her own cult. She had her own priestess, a kanephoros, and became the first Ptolemaic ruler to enter the Egyptian temples as a "temple-sharing goddess." Just as her mother, Berenice I, had earlier been associated with Aphrodite in her capacity as goddess of married love, so Arsinoe had a temple dedicated to her as the embodiment of Aphrodite at Zephyrium near Alexandria. Her deified image appears on coins, both alone and with her brother (Figure 8.2), and on mass-produced wine pitchers used in her cult, depicting her with her emblem, the double cornucopia, and a libation bowl (Figure 8.3). Such vases held offerings of wine used as part of ruler cult festivals. They illustrate the influence of ruler worship in Egypt and rituals involved in their cults.

8.8 Ptolemaic Queens: Berenice II

Although virtually unknown today, queen Berenice II (c. 226–221 BCE) similarly exerted great influence at the court of Alexandria and abroad, not only as a celebrated wife and mother but also as an ambitious ruler in her own right. Much of her legacy survives in the form of a poem composed by Callimachus, titled "Lock of Berenice." She may also have served as the model for Medea in Apollonius of Rhodes' epic, *Voyage of the Argo*. Although she carefully crafted a public image of traditional female virtue, in actuality, she possessed enormous territorial resources – much like Arsinoe II before her – which she used to put herself on almost equal footing with kings. Berenice's birthdate is unknown, although it must have occurred prior to 264 BCE. She was born in Cyrene, a wealthy Greek city on the coast of North Africa in what is now Libya. Her parents were Macedonian aristocrats who belonged to the circle of Alexander. Her father, Magas, was the son of an unknown Philip and Berenice I, who later became one of the wives of Soter. Her mother, Apama, was the daughter of Seleucus I. She was their only child. Soter put Magas in charge of Cyrene in the mad scramble for territories precipitated by Alexander's death. When Philadelphus succeeded his father, Magas declared himself king of Cyrene and attempted to invade Egypt. Although he failed, the stepbrothers reconciled and

Figure 8.3 Faience oenochoe from a grave in Canosa (Southern Italy), Arsinoe II, Alexandria, c. 270–240 BCE. London, British Museum, 1873,0820.389.

Magas betrothed his only child, his daughter Berenice II, to Euergetes, the son and successor of Philadelphus and Arsinoe II (see Chart 8.1).

Unfortunately Magas died before seeing his daughter safely married and the queen of a vast and wealthy kingdom. But Apama had other plans. Like other successor queens, she continued to act on behalf of her natal family even after marriage. She broke off the engagement with Euergetes and married Berenice II instead to Demetrius the Fair, half-brother of the king of Macedon, in an attempt to remove Cyrene from the control of the Ptolemies. Demetrius indeed lived up to his epithet "the fair," for Apama found him so irresistible that she began a love affair with him at once. When Berenice learned of the situation, she dispatched assassins to kill him. She then fulfilled her father's wishes, traveling to Alexandria to marry Euergetes, who had recently become king of Egypt, and bringing with her as part of her dowry the province of Cyrene. Berenice gave birth to six children in the first seven years of their marriage and then abruptly stopped. In contrast to his forebears, Euergetes had no other wife nor mistresses and had all of his known children with Berenice, leaving no doubt as to the identity of the successor, their firstborn son, Ptolemy IV Philopator (hereafter "Philopator").

As a familiar figure at court, the poet Callimachus probably interacted directly with Berenice II. The fact that he was also born and raised in Cyrene may have strengthened their bond. Whatever the reality, she loomed large in his literary work, serving as the subject of his famous poem, "Lock of Berenice." Although only fragments of the original poem survive in Greek, thanks to the Roman poet, Catullus, who is introduced in more detail in Chapter 13, we have a Latin translation of the "Lock of Berenice" in the form of his poem 66. Told from the perspective of a snippet of Berenice's hair, the poem addresses the astronomer, Conon, who first noticed him, the Lock, as a constellation shining brightly in the sky. He then goes on to narrate how he ended up there. When her newly wedded husband left for war, Berenice in her sorrow vowed she would dedicate a strand of her hair in the temple of Arsinoe for his safe return. The Lock consoles the weeping bride by reminding her of her former adolescent courage:

> But certainly I knew you to be bold from the time you were a small girl. Or have you forgotten the noble crime by which you acquired a royal marriage, which no stronger person dared? (Catull. 66.25–8)

The Lock refers here to her part in the murder of Demetrius the Fair after catching him in her mother's bed. Euergetes soon returns, the dedication is made and the rest of the poem chronicles the Lock's traumatic separation from Berenice's head and his subsequent translation to the sky. The poem concludes with an exhortation to newly married brides to give gifts to the Lock out of reverence for chaste wedlock. Although the poem alludes to Berenice's former crime, it portrays her as a tearful young wife devoted to her husband and the incarnation of Aphrodite's nuptial power.

Like the Ptolemaic queens before her, Berenice II derived international prestige from her victories in the four-horse chariot races in the Greek games and even surpassed them in the number of her success. Callimachus celebrates her win at Nemea in his poem, "Victoria Berenice." He takes a traditional form devoted to male athletic success, the victory ode, and refashions it to praise a female subject. The fact that such poems were normally composed on commission further reflects her great wealth and importance. Other victories are commemorated in the more modest form of the epigram, such as this one by Poseidippus:

> The maiden queen with her chariot, yes, Berenice, wins all the crowns for chariot races in the games, at your festival, Nemean Zeus. By the speed of her horses the chariot left behind the many drivers … the horses with slack reins reached the Argive judges first. (Poseid. Fr. 79 Austin and Bastianini)

Through these athletic competitions and their commemoration in poetry, Berenice advertised her wealth and power and that of her family. Their importance for future generations is evident in the foundation of a cult in her honor by her son Philopator, in which she was worshipped under the title "prize bearer," just like Arsinoe's kanephoros. It suggests that the priestess bearing this title participated in ritual processions carrying sacred objects, probably an athletic prize such as a wreath of olive.

Like Philadelphus and Arsinoe II before them, Euergetes and Berenice II received worship in the form of their own cult, the Benefactor Gods. And like Arsinoe, Berenice II was also depicted on mass-produced wine jugs used in ruler cult similar to Figure 8.3. Her wild-eyed portrait on a floor mosaic at Thmuis in Lower Egypt (Figure 8.4) presents another facet of her deification, as a guardian of the sea. Dressed in military clothing, she wears a ship's prow on her head and holds a mast in her hand. Unfortunately, Berenice II's long and prosperous life came to an abrupt and violent end. Her son Philopator systematically set about eliminating possible rivals, including his uncle and his younger brother, whom he scalded to death in his bath, in order to secure the throne. His third victim was his mother, Berenice II, either because she favored his brother or because of her potential for retaliation. Matricide thus brought to an end the golden age of Greek Alexandria, when the Ptolemaic empire was at its peak. Berenice II's contribution to this epoch is difficult to assess. By killing an unwanted suitor, she secured her marriage to Euergetes. She inspired and possibly patronized important Hellenistic poets, such as

Figure 8.4 Berenice II, floor mosaic from Thmuis (Tell Timai), third century BCE. Alexandria, Egypt, Graeco-Roman Art Museum, inv. No 21739 and 21736.

Callimachus and Apollonius of Rhodes. As the mother of six children, Berenice II used her fertility it to consolidate her royal power. She won international fame through her victories in the four-horse chariot races in the Greek games. Perhaps the root of her downfall lay in these very successes. Her reputation for daring and her enormous influence at court in the end may have posed too great a challenge for Philopator. Her consolation was poetic immortality, in the form of the "Lock of Berenice," which inspired a generation of Roman poets.

8.9 Conclusion

This chapter has shown the ways in which the lives of queens and ordinary women in Macedon and Egypt differed dramatically from those of elite women in the classical polis. Monarchy as a political institution collapsed the distinction between household and family that characterized classical Athens, allowing royal women more scope for action and influence. The practice of polygamy further contributed to their power by forcing mothers to strategize, form alliances and court political influence in order to secure their own positions and those of their children. The ambition, daring, and cruelty of Olympias, the mother of Alexander the Great, exemplify the qualities and tactics necessary not only for her own survival but for the political future of her son. Through her efforts, Alexander rose to power and expanded the borders of Greece beyond what could have ever been imagined, thereby spreading Hellenic culture and values throughout the ancient world. At its center was Alexandria, where scholars, poets, artists, and thinkers flourished under the patronage of the Ptolemies, combining earlier traditions with new forms and subject matter, often from a female perspective. Against this backdrop, queens such as Arsinoe II and Berenice II came to power, who represented themselves as incarnations of Aphrodite and used their enormous wealth and influence to help create the golden age of Ptolemaic Egypt, almost as the equal of their husband-kings. Their public presence in turn served as a model for female civic engagement as benefactors and priestesses in the Roman world.

Questions for Review

1   What impact did the practice of polygamy have on royal women?

2   How did Alexander's conquests change the ancient world?

3   How does Hellenistic poetry convey a female perspective?

4   Why was Aphrodite such an influential goddess during this period?

5   Why did the Ptolemies introduce sibling marriage and how did it affect women?

Reference

Carney, Elizabeth (2014). Arsinoe of Egypt and Macedon: A Royal Life. Oxford: Oxford University Press.

Further Reading

Primary Sources

Apollonius of Rhodes, *Voyage of the Argo*
Catullus, Poem 66
Herodas, *Mimes* 1, 6
Menander, *Samia*
Plutarch, *Life of Alexander*
Theocritus, *Idyll* 1

Secondary Sources

Bagnall, Roger Shaler and Cribiore, Raffaella (2015). *Women's Letters from Ancient Egypt: 300 BC–AD 800*. Ann Arbor: The University of Michigan Press.
    A collection of letters written by women in Greek and Egyptian, translated into English, with chapters on their form, content, and history.

Burn, Lucilla (2004). *Hellenistic Art: From Alexander the Great to Augustus*. London: British Museum Press.

A recent and concise study of Hellenistic art that traces the development of Hellenistic culture as shaped by artists who spread innovations throughout the Mediterranean and monarchs who commissioned their works.

Carney, Elizabeth (2013). *Arsinoe of Egypt and Macedon: A Royal Life*. Oxford: Oxford University Press.

The first book-length biography of Arsinoe II to be published in Engish. Surveys the archeological and literary evidence to reconstruct an accessible portrait of her life.

Carney, Elizabeth (2006). *Olympias: Mother of Alexander the Great*. London and New York: Routledge.

The first book-length study of Olympias and her role in Alexander's reign from the perspective of Macedonian social and political practices.

Carney, Elizabeth (2000). *Women and Monarchy in Macedonia*. Norman, OK: University of Oklahoma Press.

Examines the role of royal women in the Macedonian dynasty from the sixth century to 168 BCE. Demonstrates that royal women played important roles in Macedonian public life and occasionally shaped national events.

Clayman, Dee (2013). *Berenice II and the Golden Age of Ptolemaic Egypt*. Oxford: Oxford University Press.

First book-length study of the Ptolemaic queen, Berenice II, published in English. Reconstructs a portrait of a powerful woman virtually unknown today who had a significant impact on Hellenistic culture at its zenith.

Green, Peter (2008). *The Hellenistic Age*. New York: Modern Library, Reprint Edition.

A highly readable account of the rise of Alexander the Great, his conquests, and the subsequent dynastic successions of the Hellenistic kingdoms.

Pollitt, Jerome J (1986). *Art in the Hellenistic Age*. Cambridge: Cambridge University Press.

A comprehensive account of Hellenistic art, organized around five central themes: fortune, theater, individualism, cosmopolitanism, and scholarship.

Pomeroy, Sarah (1984). *Women in Hellenistic Egypt: From Alexander to Cleopatra*. New York: Shocken Books.

Studies the lives of women from various social classes in Hellenistic Egypt, from Ptolemaic queens to Jewish slaves.

Rome

9

An Introduction to Ancient Rome

> Who is so ignorant or lazy not to want to know how and by what system of government the Romans in less than 53 years managed to subject almost the whole inhabited world to one rule, a thing which had not ever happened before?
>
> (Polyb. 1.1.5)

Who were the Romans? How did they differ from the Greeks? A look at their origins, history, and customs offers an important context for understanding the role of women and gender within their society. One striking contrast between the two cultures is the degree of openness to outsiders. As we saw in Chapter 2, the Greek city-state can be characterized as a fundamentally closed society, with little interest in the incorporation and assimilation of outsiders. Myths of autochthony, in which the earth spawns progeny to populate the new city-state, epitomize this type of thinking. Athenian law further mandated that only the child of an Athenian mother and father could become a citizen, thereby discouraging intermarriage. It was therefore difficult to become a full-fledged member of the Greek city-state if you were not already born into it. Rome, in contrast, can be broadly characterized as an open society, whose success relied on a willingness to offer asylum to foreigners and, within certain parameters, incorporate them into the state. Perhaps because of this openness, Roman women had more independence and public visibility than their Greek counterparts. Nonetheless, many attitudes toward gender and women persisted, in part because the Greeks profoundly influenced the ancient Romans, and in part because these two premodern, agrarian Mediterranean societies organized themselves in similar ways. Although Roman history spans a period of over a thousand years, this chapter focuses principally on the late Republic and the early empire, before the spread of Christianity. We further focus mainly on upper-class individuals, defined as the members of the senatorial and equestrian classes, who were eligible to participate in political offices, as distinguished from freed people, because we have the most information about their lives.

Rome originated as a small town on the Tiber River and eventually came to rule a broad empire, starting with a diverse group of settlements scattered across the Italian peninsula (see Map 3). The region is bordered by the Alps in the north and divided in the middle by the Apennines, a chain of mountains that runs almost the length of Italy. Whereas the Greeks shared the same language, practices, and gods, despite inhabiting independent city-states, the earliest residents of Italy were diverse both in language and customs. Before Rome united the peninsula, there were about forty separate languages or dialects spoken by several distinct peoples, including foreigners like Greek settlers. Those who settled in what later became the city of Rome spoke an early form of Latin whereas their enemies, the Samnites, spoke a related language called Oscan. Celtic was spoken by the Cisalpine Gauls, who lived on the Italian side

Women in Classical Antiquity: From Birth to Death, First Edition. Laura K. McClure.
© 2020 John Wiley & Sons, Inc. Published 2020 by John Wiley & Sons, Inc.

of the Alps. (The Latin word *cis* means "on this side," as opposed to *trans*, "across"; the modern term *cisgender* refers to those whose gender identity conforms to their biological sex.) Ancient Greek was the language of the Greek colonies in Apulia and around the bay of Naples in Southern Italy.

The most important indigenous group of pre-Roman Italians were the Etruscans, who developed a powerful state system that exerted a lasting influence on later Roman civilization. Their society also seems to have been more egalitarian in its treatment of women than that of the Greeks (see Box 9.1). Although their origins have been much debated, current opinion holds that they descended from Villanovan iron-age culture. They spoke a unique non-Indo-European language not related to any well-known language. After contact with Greek traders in the seventh century BCE, they adopted a variation of the Greek alphabet for their script, which in turn became the source of the Latin alphabet. They established polis-communities between the

---

Box 9.1 Etruscan Women

The nineteenth-century antiquarian who posited Minoan matriarchy, Johann Bachofen, advanced a similar theory about female power in Etruscan society in his essay, "The Myth of Tanaquil." Colorful Roman myths about Etruscan women emphasize their independence, audacity, and political ambition. Take the story of Tanaquil. The daughter of a powerful Etruscan family in Tarquinia, she married the lowly son of a Greek immigrant, Lucius Tarquinius Priscus. Seeking to increase their status and power, she persuaded him to move to Rome, "where all nobility is a thing of recent growth" (Livy 1.34.8). Near the city, an eagle swooped down, lifted Priscus' cap, and then put it back on his head. Tanaquil interpreted it as an omen that her husband would achieve the highest form of honor. Indeed, through hard work and generosity he became king of Rome. After his assassination, Tanaquil again intervened, tricking citizens into thinking her husband had survived and urging them to obey her son-in-law, Servius Tullus, thereby assuring his acquisition of the kingship. In the next generation, the fiercely ambitious Tullia convinced the last of the Etruscan kings, Lucius Tarquinius Superbus, to murder her husband and sister, to marry her, and to seize power by killing her own father. As Livy (59 BCE–17 CE) describes, "evil was drawn to evil, but the woman took the lead" (Livy 1.46.7). Tullia then boldly appeared in public to proclaim Tarquin king, defiantly driving her carriage over her father's corpse and bringing an end to just and legitimate monarchy at Rome.

Archeological evidence suggests that Etruscan women did indeed enjoy more public visibility and prestige than other women in the ancient Mediterranean. They used their own names, as evidenced by this funerary inscription, "Arnthi Metli was the wife of Larth Spitu. (She) lived 64 years. Having brought forth three sons, (she) raised (them)" (*TLE* 888). Arnthi is the woman's given name, like Tanaquil. Metli, her family name, differs from that of her husband. Matronymics – the identification of a woman by her mother's name, rather than her father's – are also found. Although this practice does not prove the existence of a matriarchal society, it suggests that Etruscan women had independent identities, not just those derived from men. Many were literate. They could leave the house and participate in activities normally associated with men. One fresco from the necropolis at Tarquinia shows male and female spectators sitting together on wooden stands, watching a chariot race. Widespread are images of women enjoying banquets as equals of their husbands, a practice that shocked the Greeks, who associated it with promiscuity. The vivid fresco in the Tomb of the Leopards (Figure 9.1) depicts pairs of elegantly dressed men and women, conversing on Greek-style couches placed outdoors, perhaps at the funerary banquet of the deceased. Following Greek convention, the women are depicted as white skinned and are therefore difficult to detect against the light backdrop.

Figure 9.1 Tomb of the Leopards, showing an Etruscan banquet scene with men and women dining together, c. 480–470 BCE. Tarquinia, Italy.

modern cities of Rome and Florence, eventually expanding as far south as the bay of Naples and north to the Alps. When Rome was but a cluster of simple huts dotting the hills above the Tiber, the Etruscans constructed elaborate houses and religious sanctuaries, inscribed texts, and laid out vast necropoleis. These "cities of the dead" consisted of blocks of large family tombs, lavishly decorated and filled with luxury goods, including a number of vases imported from the best Athenian workshops. Some, like the tombs of Tarquinia, were adorned with vivid, naturalistic wall paintings of banquets, games, and hunts (Figure 9.1). The Etruscans worked in bronze, produced their own type of pottery glazed black to resemble metal, and crafted exquisite gold jewelry influenced by Near Eastern and Greek motifs. According to Roman tradition, the Etruscans transformed Rome into a city, constructing the first sewer, the Cloaca Maxima, and erecting its most important building, the Temple of Jupiter Optimus Maximus on the Capitoline Hill (see Map 4). Despite these achievements, Etruscan civilization began to decline in the fifth century BCE as the Romans advanced into Etruria and Umbria. Nonetheless, many of their customs and innovations – like the alphabet, haruspicy (divination from animal entrails), gladiatorial combat, and the triumph – were formative to the development of Roman culture.

Roman legend put the city's foundation at 753 BCE. According to the archeological record, however, it was occupied as early as the tenth century BCE, when inhabitants settled in a marshy area on a bend of the Tiber River as it flows from the Apennines to the sea. This location served as the stopping point for ships as they made their way upriver from the sea and as a crossroads for people traveling by foot along the west coast of Italy. These first settlers spoke an early form of Latin, cultivated crops, and raised livestock. They were dominated by a few small clans of wealthy nobles who sought to enhance their status through warfare and public display, not unlike the Homeric warlords discussed in Chapter 2. By the early seventh century, small reed huts began to appear on the Palatine hill, an area that would later become the most exclusive address in Rome. By the late sixth century, this collection of houses had become a small urban center of some 20 000 residents, with public buildings, temples, and a public space between the Capitoline and Palatine hills, later known as the Roman Forum, that had been drained and artificially raised to keep it from flooding (see Map 4 for the layout).

The question asked by Polybius (c. 200–118 BCE) in the epigraph at the start of this chapter has been continually debated since antiquity: how *did* such a sleepy backwater come to dominate the ancient world, a vast expanse stretching from modern Scotland to Syria? To answer this question, it is necessary to examine ancient Roman civilization more closely, including the early origins of the city, the transition from monarchy to the Republic, the conquest of the Italian peninsula, and finally its development into a global superpower under a military dictatorship (see Timeline). This survey focuses on elite Romans – the senators, equestrians, and emperors that comprised the top half percent of society – to understand Roman constructions of masculinity and how they contributed to the formation and success of the Roman state. Although male self-control certainly remained a philosophical goal, as in Greece, traits such as violence, self-interest, deception, and manipulation were important in the struggle for status and power according to Roman historiographers. At the same time, the Romans exhibited a surprising degree of tolerance toward those they subjugated, in contrast to the relatively closed society of the Greek city-state. Eventually, anyone could become a Roman citizen and even those of low birth could rise to the highest levels of society. This openness is also reflected in the position of women in Roman society, who, relative to their Greek counterparts, had more freedom and independence, even the ability to inherit and own property and run large-scale businesses.

The Romans have left us an immense amount of literary and material culture in the form of poetry, letters, orations, histories, inscriptions, graffiti, monuments, villas, tenements, and even entire city blocks. Roman writers and some of the Greeks living under their rule shared a fascination with their past and chronicled their history in great detail, although not always reliably in the modern sense. Indeed, much of Roman historiography consists more of fiction than of fact, with a flair for the sensationalizing detail or lurid plot twist. Central to this enterprise was the practice of exemplarity: the retelling of stories of influential figures and events, both mythical and historical, to serve as **exempla** ("role models") for future generations. Their feats of conquest, resistance, and self-sacrifice in turn encouraged young men, and women, to strive for their own tales of glory. This chapter focuses on some of the exemplary men who shaped events in the Roman Republic and empire, the problems they confronted, and the characteristics and values that underpinned their success.

9.1 Roman Foundation Myth

The Romans had a clearly defined mythology regarding their origins that borrowed from both Greek and native Italian traditions and that diverged sharply at points from historical reality. These stories survive for us because they are recorded in Livy's *History of Rome* and Vergil's epic poem, *Aeneid*. These texts were composed hundreds of years after Rome's foundation, during the reign of Augustus. They thus reflect Augustan perspectives on Roman values, politics, and identity and are intended to provide models for the upper classes. Combining foundation and revolution with rape, bride theft, intermarriage, and even death, these fictive narratives also speak volumes about Roman attitudes toward women and gender. Both writers attribute the foundation of Rome to the Trojan hero, Aeneas. He is mentioned in Homer's *Iliad* as one of the one of the few Trojans to survive the fall of Troy (Hom. *Il*. 20.302–5). By attaching the origins of their city to the Greek mythic tradition, Roman authors attempted to forge a continuity between their own culture and that of the Greeks. After escaping from the burning city with his father and young son, Aeneas sails to Italy, forms an alliance with the native Latins, and marries Lavinia, the daughter of their king. The main event of the poem – the civil war for control of Italy – prefigures the legacy of civil conflict that would plague Rome from its inception. Vergil portrays this process of foundation as predestined and divinely determined in order to justify the Roman quest for world dominion. Aeneas' status as a foreigner underscores the fact Romans were all originally "foreigners," always from somewhere else.

To connect Aeneas' flight from Troy in the twelfth century BCE to Rome's foundation over five hundred years later, Vergil relies on a mythological variant circulated by the Julian clan. This version makes Aeneas' son, Iulus, the founder and first king of a city near Rome and the progenitor of the Julian clan, including Romulus. Moving from Vergil to Livy and skipping forward several generations, Romulus and his twin brother Remus are born of a political rivalry between their grandfather, Numitor, and their great-uncle, Amulius. When Amulius takes the throne, he forces Numitor's daughter, Rhea Silvia, to serve as a Vestal Virgin, a powerful female priesthood that required virginity, as we see in Chapter 14, in order to prevent the birth of children who would supplant him. Raped by Mars, the god of war, Rhea Silvia becomes pregnant and gives birth to the twins Romulus and Remus. Amulius ordered the babies drowned in the Tiber. His servants balk at the task and instead leave the babies in a basket on the river's banks. Before being washed away to their death, they are rescued by a nurturing she-wolf. Because the Latin word for wolf, ***lupa***, also means "prostitute," Livy speculates that a local prostitute rather than a wild beast took in the infants.

The youths eventually decide to found a new city but quarrel over its location: Remus chooses the Aventine hill, and Romulus begins building on the Palatine. In the escalating conflict, Romulus kills Remus and names the new city after himself. As the products of war and rape, Romulus and Remus are orphans abandoned by their family and literally "raised by wolves." Their lack of personal attachments even leads to fratricide. These mythic figures embody many of the characteristics celebrated by Roman males: ferocity, ruthlessness, devaluation of personal ties in favor of the state, the ability to withstand hardship, and the willingness to endure and perpetuate violence. Along with the hero Aeneas, Romulus and Remus function as powerful, albeit problematic, symbols of Rome's domination of the Mediterranean and the masculine characteristics necessary for its success. The widespread popularity of the myth of Romulus and Remus across Rome's history and geographical expanse can be seen as far north as England, in a floor mosaic from the fourth century CE that depicts a cheerful mother wolf protecting her two human babies (Figure 9.2).

The second part of the foundation story explains another key ingredient of Roman success in consolidating and expanding their power. Although Romulus had become sole ruler by an act of fratricide, he nonetheless governs an empty city:

> Next, so that his city would not be empty, using an old plan for increasing the population borrowed from the founders of cities, who gather together an obscure and humble crowd but pretend they are born from the earth, Romulus opened a refuge in the place that is now surrounded by two groves as you go up the Capitoline hill. There a mob from neighboring towns, both slave and free without distinction, took refuge, eager for new things, and that was the first addition of strength to the fledgling greatness of the city. (Livy 1.8.4–6)

Livy here pointedly rejects the idea of autochthony associated with the Greek city-state. Rather, the concepts of asylum and assimilation are central to this narrative: outsiders, even of lowly status, are welcome to become Romans. This cultural tolerance was integral to the growth of

Figure 9.2 Roman mosaic depicting Romulus and Remus suckled by the she-wolf, c. 300–400 CE. Aldborough, England, Leeds City Museum, LEEDM.D.1968.0046.

the empire as Rome expanded its boundaries and linked together diverse cultures under one government. In contrast to Greece, membership in the Roman community did not depend entirely on place, birth, or biological ties.

The same principle applied to women, as illustrated in the next part of Romulus' story. Although many men emigrated to the newly founded city, they brought no women. Without them, it could not continue beyond a generation. When their neighbors, the Sabines, refuse to allow them to marry their daughters, the Romans retaliate with an act of sexual violence. Inviting them to the city on the pretext of a religious festival, Romulus and his men proceed to abduct the Sabine women, leading to a war between the two communities. As the fighting progresses, the women intervene:

> Then the Sabine women, whose unjust treatment had given rise to the war, with disheveled hair and torn garments, their feminine fear overcome by their troubles, dared to go into the middle of the flying missiles. Rushing in from the side to separate the hostile forces and dissolve their anger, pleading with their fathers and their husbands on each side not to stain themselves with the impious bloodshed of father- or son-in-law, nor pollute future generations with parricide, grandsons to one side, sons to the other. "If this tie between you, this marriage, troubles you, then turn your anger against us. For we are the cause of war, we are the cause of the wounds and slaughter of our husbands and fathers. Better for us to perish rather than live without one or the other of you, as widows and orphans." (Livy 1.13.1–3)

This collective and courageous female action symbolically underscores how affective family ties created and maintained by women anchored the Roman state. It further reveals yet again the necessity of assimilation, here in the form of intermarriage, to Roman foundation myth. The women act not simply as passive vessels for the transmission of male citizenship but rather actively assist in the creation of the Roman state. As mythic examples of female virtue, they embody self-sacrifice, loyalty to their husbands, and even a willingness to die for the state. Their selfless example counteracts the legacy of violence and murder perpetuated by Roman men.

According to Livy, Rome was under the control of kings until the end of the sixth century, although modern scholars have challenged this view. In actuality, these were probably warlords or chiefs from diverse backgrounds: Numa, the successor of Romulus, was a Sabine, whereas Lucius Tarquinius Priscus, the husband of Tanaquil; Servius Tullius; and Lucius Tarquinius Superbus, husband of Tullia, were all Etruscans. A critical moment in regime change comes during the increasingly tyrannical rule of the latter. His autocratic behavior, and that of his family, leads to a revolution that would end the monarchy, establishing the Roman Republic. Its creation follows a similar pattern of sexual violence found in the stories of Rhea Silvia and the Sabines. While away on campaign, a group of Roman soldiers drunkenly debate about their wives' virtue. To settle the matter, a man named Collatinus, eager to show off his own wife, Lucretia, proposes that they return home immediately to check on the women. As expected, they find her dutifully working wool late into the night while the other wives, all Etruscans, partake of a luxurious banquet. Her virtue and beauty so arouse the lust of Tarquinius Superbus that he later returns in secret to try to seduce her. Slipping into her bedroom with a sword, he vows to kill her if she refuses him. Only when he threatens to disgrace her by killing her and laying the naked corpse of a male slave by her side does she relent. When her father and husband return from campaign, she confesses her "crime," resolving to commit suicide:

> "You will decide," she said, "what that man deserves. Although I acquit myself of the crime, I am not free from punishment. No unchaste woman shall live in the future through the example of Lucretia." Then taking a knife she had hidden under her dress, she drove it into her heart, and sinking forward over the wound, she died as she fell. (Livy 1.58.10–12)

Lucretia's fatal gesture not only proves her innocence, it provides an example of female heroism for future women. In dying to protect her reputation, she reaffirms the significance of female sexual virtue, designated by the term ***pudicitia,*** for both the family and the state. The outrage provoked by her violation and death in turn prompts a political revolution leading to the expulsion of Tarquinius Superbus and the establishment of the Roman Republic. These three stories of Roman foundation point to the values that facilitated Roman domination of the Italian peninsula and later much of the ancient world: openness to other cultures and recognition of their importance for the survival of the Roman state; a legacy of violence and an inclination toward warfare and brutality; and the need to win honor through heroic deeds, for both men and women, that could serve as a lesson for others. Although these stories on one level legitimize violence against women as a necessary component of state formation, they also show how women as loyal wives and mothers contributed to this project and perhaps even spurred men on to justice.

9.2 The Early Republic

Although these sensationalizing stories depict the transition from monarchy to the Republic as a sudden break – a sexual crime that sparked regime change – in reality the process occurred much more slowly, over a period of decades, if not centuries. The primary religious and political institutions remained intact, continuing to protect the interests of a powerful closed caste of ancient clans, known as the ***patricians***, to the detriment of the ordinary people, called ***plebeians***. Instead of kings, now at the head were two new officials drawn from the patrician class, the consuls, who presided over politics at home and military campaigns abroad with input from the senate. The members of the senate also came from the patrician class and returned to their ranks at the end of their political terms. The consuls held office together as a pair only for a single year. This form of shared governance mitigated the potential for a single man to take absolute control as the earlier kings had.

Religion was one tool that the patricians used to strengthen their political position. From the start, religion and politics were deeply intertwined in the Roman state. The Romans expressed their reverence for the gods through the performance of religious rituals and expected in return that the gods would favor their city. Roman religious practice thus reinforced the political structure and military goals of the state and justified its conquest of the Italian peninsula and beyond. Roman gods were adapted versions of the Greek gods combined with native deities, many of which were Etruscan (see Chart 2.1). Jupiter Optimus Maximus, whose temple was one of the oldest buildings in the Forum, was central to the military achievements of the Roman state. His wife, Juno, a leading Italian deity, was associated with women and presided over childbirth in the form of Lucina. Mars was an old Italian god concerned with warfare. Ceres, as the goddess of growth, was important to the poor and became identified with the Greek Demeter. The Italian goddess Minerva governed crafts and later became identified with Athena. Lesser deities encompassed a divine aspect of some social, natural, or agricultural function, such as Cloacina, goddess of the main sewer in Rome.

The aristocracy monopolized the priesthoods, controlled access to records, dictated religious observance, and approved new cults. The most powerful priestly college was that of the pontiffs, a term applied today to the pope of the Roman Catholic Church. This group oversaw the calendar and supervised private family matters such as adoptions, wills, and inheritance. At the head was the Pontifex Maximus, the most powerful religious official in the Republic, an office that eventually fell to the emperor during the principate. The college included priests called ***flamines***, who were associated with individual gods, particularly the ones most important to the state, such as Jupiter and Mars. Under its auspices were also the Vestal Virgins, priestesses who tended the flame on the city's sacred hearth, discussed more fully in Chapter 14.

The first two centuries of the Republic were marked by a series of violent social clashes, called the "Conflict of the Orders" (from Latin *ordo* or "social rank") between the patricians and the plebeians. Gradually, the plebeians won more political rights from the patricians but not without a series of revolts. A strike staged by the plebeians shortly after the founding of the Republic led to several concessions that gradually eroded the differences between the classes and effectively revised the political structure of the city. First, the plebeians received official representation in the form of two tribunes of the people, positions similar to the consuls, followed by the creation of a special assembly for the people only, whose decisions were given the binding force of law over all Roman citizens by the beginning of the third century BCE. But the senate was still the body exercising real and legal power. Other reforms included the opening up of major offices, such as the consulships and some priesthoods and the abolishment of debt enslavement.

One of the earliest social conflicts in the early Republic centered on the creation of the first written law code, the Twelve Tables (c. 450 BCE). These instructions covered marriage, property, assault, debt and debt bondage, and legal procedures. The last two areas were of special concern to the plebeians. According to Livy, what precipitated revolt was a toxic mix of aristocratic privilege and male predation. Although the patrician lawmakers added a clause that banned intermarriage between the classes, they nevertheless felt entitled to help themselves to plebeian women. Once again, sexual assault, in this case attempted, plays a pivotal role in bringing about regime change. As Livy tells it, the lawmaker Appius Claudius lusts after a young plebeian woman named Verginia ("virgin"), who was already engaged to a tribune. When she rejects his advances, Appius convinces a friend to allege that she was his slave, stolen from him by her father. Because the judge in the case is Appius himself, he finds in favor of his friend and goes to claim Verginia. In the subsequent fight, Lucius Verginius, Verginia's father, picks up a knife and kills the girl on the spot, proclaiming, "I am making you free, my child, in the only way I can" (Livy 3.48.5). In this disturbing story, a daughter's brutal death at the hands of her father saves her from sexual violence, ensuring that her body will remain "free." Like the story of Lucretia, the threat of violating the female body spurs a political revolution, demonstrating just how profoundly Roman conceptions of gender informed political discourse.

9.3 Expansion of Roman Rule

As the Romans struggled with social unrest at home, they nonetheless increasingly sought to bring the other Italian states under their control. Although Roman expansion in hindsight might seem inevitable, in reality, there was initially no coherent plan for conquest. First they turned to the area around Rome, defeating their neighbors and then cities further afield during the fourth century BCE. By around 270 BCE, the Romans had brought about a major transformation of Italy that could not be reversed (see Map 3). Although they proved to be more resilient and persistent than their neighbors, their success did not arise from military strength alone. A constructive and flexible approach to dealing with defeated cities forged strong alliances with Rome and contributed to the establishment of a stable, centralized government. Some became part of the Roman state as self-governing communities with full citizenship; others were granted a lesser form of citizenship that carried some of the privileges and obligations of citizenship, such as supplying troops, but without voting rights. This practice was a radical development unimaginable to the ancient Greeks, for whom the polis represented the most fundamental aspect of their identity. By offering citizenship to people with no direct geographic ties to their city, the Romans reconfigured the link between citizenship and territory. Another result was dual citizenship: a man could become a Roman citizen while also retaining citizen status at home. These arrangements represented a crucial step in Roman expansion and were to serve as a template for the next several hundred years.

By the third century BCE, military distinction achieved through the acquisition of commands, military victories, and plunder had become critical to advancing the political careers of elite Roman men. It also illustrates the typical career trajectory of aspiring Roman politicians open only to men of senatorial rank. This path consisted of a sequential series of elected offices, both military and political. It began with 10 years of military service and ended with a consulship. The epitaph of Cornelius Lucius Scipio Barbatus ("the Bearded"), ancestor of an illustrious line of Romans, recounts the military and political successes that defined his career:

> Cornelius Lucius Scipio Barbatus, descended from Gnaeus, his father, a man strong and wise, whose appearance was a match for his virtue (*virtus*). He was consul and censor and aedile among you. He captured Taurasia and Cisauna from Samnium. He subdued all of Lucania and took hostages. (*CIL* VI 1285)

Inscribed on a huge family tomb, the epitaph establishes Barbatus as a role model for future generations. He was first elected consul and censor, the latter an official responsible for enrolling citizens and assessing their wealth. Outside of Rome, he won two military campaigns, underscoring the importance of military victories to the public image of prominent Roman men. The term ***virtus*** ("virtue" or "excellence") mentioned in the epitaph comes from the Latin term for man, *vir*, and thus equates "manliness" with martial valor, involving "contempt for death and contempt for pain" (Cic. *Tusc.* 2.43).

9.4   Roman Spectacles

Two Roman institutions that arose during this period reinforced this culture of masculine militarism: the triumph and gladiatorial combats. In the triumph, a Roman general who had won a major victory was allowed to enter the city (normally he could not do so without surrendering his command) and parade through the streets with his troops, displaying his spoils and prisoners to the cheering crowd. Although the origins of the triumph are unknown, evidence suggests that the Etruscans practiced a similar ritual. The triumph was typically awarded when a general had won a war against a declared enemy, in which at least 5000 had been killed, while serving as a magistrate in his own province. Later only an emperor and members of the Imperial family could be granted a triumph, with the actual commander reduced to receiving "triumphal ornaments." The spectacle of the triumph reinforced the supremacy of the Roman people over their subjects, displaying the vastness of their empire, while also portraying the conqueror as a kind of deity. He entered through a special gateway, dressed in the costume of the early kings, with his face painted red like the statue of Jupiter, and stood in a chariot drawn by four horses. He traveled to the heart of the city by a special road, to the temple of Capitoline Jupiter where he laid down a laurel wreath on the statue's lap. His name was then inscribed in the triumphal record. This was the supreme ambition of Roman manhood: to become, in a sense, god for a day and have his name go down in history. A panel from the Arch of Titus commemorating the Roman victory over Judaea (Figure 9.3) depicts the spoils taken from the

Figure 9.3 South panel from the Arch of Titus, depicting a triumph in honor of Roman victory over Judea, c. 82 CE. Rome. Werner Forman/Getty Images.

Temple of Jerusalem. The primary focus is a menorah carved in deep relief and displayed in the triumph, along with other objects.

Gladiatorial competitions also glorified warfare by graphically enacting the violence and cruelty of the battlefield within the confines of the city. The Etruscans first held gladiatorial combats at the funerals of their dead warriors. They were introduced to Rome in 264 BCE when three pairs fought to commemorate the death of Junius Brutus Pera. Although at first intended to honor a deceased male relative, gladiatorial fights became an increasingly important tool of politicians for garnering popular support. The contests took place in the Roman Forum until the construction of the Flavian amphitheater, better known as the Colosseum, in 80 CE (Figure 9.4). Professional gladiators were either slaves, purchased and trained for the purpose, or volunteers who signed a contract giving up their protection under the law and allowing themselves to "be burned, chained, beaten or killed" by their owners. There is also some evidence for female gladiators. Distinct from these were the criminals who did not compete for sport but were executed in the amphitheater. An inscription from Pompeii advertises both types of entertainment: "Twenty pairings of gladiators and their back-ups will fight at Cumae on October 5th and 6th. There will also be crucifixions and a wild beast hunt" (*CIL* IV 9983a). Some members of the senatorial order were attracted to gladiatorial sport because of its allure of danger, sex appeal, and fame. Augustus later introduced legislation to prevent the upper classes from participating in this disreputable profession. The fact that later emperors, like

Figure 9.4 Interior view of the Colosseum, showing the infrastructure below the floor and seating at the sides, c. 80 CE. Rome. Fotosearch/Getty Images.

Caligula (see Chart 10.1 for his family tree), trained and fought with gladiators or actually entered the arena to fight, like Commodus, probably struck the Roman audience as extraordinary, even degenerate, given the stigma attached to gladiators.

Roman spectators also enjoyed blood sport in the form of animal combats, either fights between animals only, or between beast and man, whether gladiators or convicted criminals. The hunt became a major spectacle at Rome starting in 186 BCE, fueled by the conquest of territories beyond Italy. It offered sponsors a chance to display their generosity to the people while showing off the reach of Rome and its power over nature in the form of exotic species such as crocodiles, rhinoceroses, panthers, and bears. The emperors offered exceptionally lavish displays: during the dedication of the Colosseum, for instance, approximately 9000 animals were killed. The gladiatorial combats and the beast hunts brought into the city the shocking violence and cruelty of warfare, legitimating the terrible cost of conquest before the very eyes of the spectators. In a sense it normalized these values as necessary components of Roman life, cultivating male aggression to bolster an increasingly ambitious military agenda. They also diffused social conflicts by pacifying the masses with entertainment.

Once the Italian peninsula had been secured, Rome faced another challenge, the state of Carthage, located near the modern city of Tunis (see Map 3). The three Punic wars (264–146 BCE) – from the Latin word for Phoenician (*Poenus*) – marked the first Roman military campaigns outside of Italy. This long series of conflicts resulted in the defeat of Carthage and the emergence of Rome as a Mediterranean superpower. The First Punic War (264–241 BCE) started as a minor scuffle but soon escalated into a full-scale war driven in part by Roman greed and fears over Carthaginian advances in North Africa and Spain. Although the Romans were not well equipped for success at sea, they ultimately prevailed when they managed to construct a powerful fleet using a captured Carthaginian ship as a model.

Two decades later, Carthage initiated the Second Punic War (218–201 BCE). The skilled Carthaginian general Hannibal invaded Rome from the north, crossing the Alps with a large infantry, cavalry, and his famous string of elephants. Despite several successes, the army lacked sufficient manpower and attempted to recruit Rome's allies, most of which remained loyal. Under the command of Publius Cornelius Scipio, great-grandson of the exemplary Barbatus, the Romans defeated Hannibal in Africa, conferring upon Scipio the honorific agnomen (fourth name) "Africanus." The end of the Second Punic War established Rome as the most powerful state in the Mediterranean, inciting further hostilities throughout the region. In swift succession, Rome destroyed Macedon, decisively defeated Carthage in the brief Third Punic War (149–146 BCE), and crushed the Greek city of Corinth, annexing a vast stretch of the ancient world beyond Italy.

The conquest of Greece had a major impact on Roman culture. As Horace (65–8 BCE) writes, "Captive Greece captured her savage conqueror and instilled her arts in rustic Latium" (Hor. *Ep.* 2.2.156–7). He meant that even as the Romans subjugated Greece, they nonetheless assimilated many of its institutions and ideas, from banqueting to philosophy. The steady flow of resources from the Greek east into Rome profoundly affected the development of Roman literary and visual culture. Prior to this period, the Romans had used writing mainly for non-literary purposes, to inscribe rules and regulations like the Twelve Tables, public notices, and contracts. Exposure to Greek literature, particularly drama, sparked the beginnings of Latin literature. The earliest known work of Latin poetry is a translation of Homer's *Odyssey* by Livius Andronicus (c. 284–205 BCE), of which only a handful of lines exist. The popular Roman comedies of Plautus (c. 254–184 BCE) and Terence (c. 190–59 BCE) were based on Greek New Comedy and featured Greek settings and characters. Latin literature produced thereafter engaged heavily with Greek models, appropriating the earlier tradition to express a distinctly Roman outlook.

9.5   The Collapse of the Republic

Just as Rome began to bring large territories abroad under its control, it confronted insurmountable problems at home, which ultimately led to the collapse of the Republic. What follows is an attempt to summarize a complex sequence of events and multiple historical figures, all men. The attentive reader may find many similarities between Roman politics of this period and contemporary political debates in the United States and United Kingdom. For instance, one factor in the demise was the greed of the aristocracy, who kept the spoils of war for themselves and ignored the needs of the poor. As consensus among the elite broke down, a series of individuals dominated Roman politics either through military might or the exploitation of popular support, or both. In a reprise of the earlier conflict between the orders, two groups vied for control: the **optimates**, aristocrats and other men of property invested in protecting the status quo, and the **populares**, who sought popular support by advocating measures that benefitted the people, the ancient equivalent of populist movements today. The latter group might consist of aristocratic citizens who used the popular platform to advance their own political careers, not necessarily to help the poor. Tiberius Gracchus (c. 165–133 BCE) was one such politician. Elected tribune for 133 BCE, he came from an illustrious family. His exemplary mother, Cornelia, whom we meet again in Chapter 12, was the daughter of Scipio Africanus. Tiberius sought to address the shortage of land for small farmers. In particular, he blamed wealthy landholders for stealing the property of soldiers away on campaign. Backed by impoverished supporters, he introduced a bill aimed at preventing any individual from holding a large share of public land. While standing for election a second time, he and hundreds of his supporters were bludgeoned to death by a band of senators and their followers and their bodies were thrown into the Tiber.

Tiberius' brother, Gaius (154–121 BCE), was elected tribune a few years later. He sought to address another pressing social issue, the second-class status of the Italian allies. He introduced a reform proposing to grant full citizenship to all Italians. Like those of his brother, these measures did not please the senate. He, too, was killed, along with 3000 supporters. The actions of the Gracchi exerted much influence on later politics. Although the senate had won in both instances, the actions of the brothers demonstrated the enormous potential of the tribunes to effect social change and raised questions about popular sovereignty. In later Roman rhetoric, their murders are portrayed as a turning point in Roman politics and the start of a decline in morality and political integrity that eventually led to civil war.

Thanks to the Gracchi, subsequent politicians increasingly mobilized popular support in their quest for power. The influential general, Gaius Marius (157–86 BCE), added a new twist to this model by combining a populist message with military achievements. Despite his nonaristocratic background, he was able to rise to the level of consul through distinguished military service and the backing of key senators. His strategic change in military policy – the recruitment of volunteers into the army without the usual property qualification – meant that a charismatic general could turn his army into a personal entourage, with allegiance not to the state but to himself alone. This was to set a dangerous precedent.

Meanwhile, the Italian communities, still without citizenship, declared war on Rome in the so-called Social War (91–88 BCE, from the word *socii*, "allies"). This war forced Rome to concede citizenship to all those Italian cities that had not revolted. Against this backdrop, another ambitious statesman came to power, Lucius Cornelius Sulla (138–78 BCE). An optimas from a patrician family, Sulla was elected consul for 88 BCE and given the governorship of Asia. When ordered to relinquish his post, he refused and instead marched against Rome with his own army. For the first time in Roman history, a politician had used his army for personal ends, a pattern that would soon be repeated. Sulla was the first dictator to exercise unchecked power.

Julius Caesar would be the second. With guaranteed immunity from prosecution, he set about introducing a series of conservative policies and organized the first purge of political enemies in Roman history. Lists, called **proscriptions**, were published with the names of targeted individuals, and a bounty offered to those who killed anyone on the list. His example demonstrates how ruthlessness, disregard for law, and a tendency toward autocracy became requisite weapons in the arsenal of ambitious politicians by the end of the Republic.

9.6 Julius Caesar

Julius Caesar (100–44 BCE), nephew of Marius and another rising star in the political scene, profoundly shaped the course of Rome's future. He was born into the prestigious Julian clan, which claimed descent from the goddess Venus. He followed the usual progression of a Roman political career, beginning with the governorship of Spain and finally achieving consul in 59 BCE. To win that election, however, he needed the support of two key individuals: Pompey the Great (106–48 BCE) and Crassus (115–53 BCE), both generals who had served under Sulla. These three formed an alliance, known as the first triumvirate, to circumvent the senate and promote their political agenda. All three enlisted popular support to further their interests, Caesar through his efforts to distribute public land in Italy to a large number of impoverished citizens, including Pompey's veterans. Increasingly, political success depended on military support, the consulship, and the tribunes of the plebeians, not on the senate. Caesar's blatant disregard for the senate and unconstitutional manipulation of the political process unwittingly paved the way for a new regime.

Following his consulship, Caesar was appointed to govern Gaul, where he remained for eight years, adding the territories of modern France and Belgium to the Roman empire. His vast wealth backed by his powerful and loyal army put him almost beyond the reach of the government. When tensions between him and Pompey increased after the death of Crassus in 53 BCE, Caesar continued to recruit soldiers and ingratiate himself with the people. Wary of his growing power, the senate began to agitate for his dismissal from his military command. With the majority against him and the law on his enemies' side, Caesar entered a state of open rebellion once he crossed the Rubicon river with his army from Cisalpine Gaul for Italy without laying down arms. In the ensuing civil war, he quickly conquered Italy, defeated Pompey's officers in Spain and then crossed into Greece where he won a decisive battle at Pharsalia. Pompey fled to Egypt and was beheaded when he landed in 48 BCE. Caesar followed him there and soon became involved with Cleopatra VII, with whom he had a son, Caesarion, before campaigning in Syria. (More will be said about this fascinating queen in Chapter 14.) Celebrating four successive triumphs in 46 BCE, Julius Caesar was now the undisputed master of the Roman world.

The civil war did not end with the death of Pompey but continued to fester throughout the Mediterranean. After years of giving orders and expecting obedience, Caesar failed to perceive how much his autocratic style offended the senate. Or perhaps they lured him into accepting honors in order to justify his murder. Like Sulla, he announced decisions without debate. But whereas Sulla renounced the position of dictator after the civil war, Caesar refused to do so. Indeed, he expanded the office to 10 years in 46 BCE and then 2 years later, into perpetuity. He also held the consulship two times in the intervening years. To the senators, this conduct challenged the democratic values upon which the senate and the Roman Republic were founded. Indeed, the honors granted him just before his assassination likened him to a god. He had a cult with his own priest, adorned his house with a temple-style pediment, and displayed his likeness in formal processions of the images of gods. He was also the first living person to have his head featured on a coin minted in Rome, an act associated with divinized Eastern

Figure 9.5 A Roman silver denarius coin with the wreathed Julius Caesar (at left) and the goddess Venus on the back, struck in 44 BCE. Appleton, Wisconsin, Ottilia Buerger Collection of Ancient and Byzantine Coins, Wriston Art Gallery, Lawrence University, inv. 90.106.

monarchs (Figure 9.5). Struck in 44 BCE, either before or after his death, the coin shows Caesar's wreathed head on the front and Venus, ancestor of the Julian clan, on the back, holding the figure of Victory in her hand. For some Romans, Caesar's self-deification was just too much. On the morning of the Ides of March (March 15) 44 BCE, Caesar was stabbed to death by a crowd of senators, led by Marcus Junius Brutus, at a meeting of the senate convened in the theater that Pompey had built.

9.7 The Transition to Empire

The assassination of Julius Caesar plunged Rome into political chaos. First, the followers of Caesar took revenge on his murderers and then turned against each other, splitting into different factions according to their view of another important Roman political figure, Mark Antony (83–30 BCE). Antony, who had served under Caesar in Gaul and had earlier defended his interests as tribune, now in his capacity as consul sought a compromise between the assassins and allies. But an unexpected rival suddenly entered the political arena: Gaius Octavius (63 BCE–14 CE), Caesar's 19-year-old great-nephew who was adopted posthumously in Caesar's will. His unconventional rise to power bypassed the normal cursus honorum. Octavius eagerly sought to take advantage of Caesar's death, working to acquire money, allies, and the loyalty of Caesar's soldiers in a bid for power. By changing his name to Gaius Julius Caesar Octavianus, or Octavian, he sought to lay claim to Caesar's legacy. Many at first underestimated the young man. But in 43 BCE, in a demonstration of shrewdness and ambition, Octavian marched on Rome to seize the consulship, initially supported by the senate and Cicero (106–43 BCE). A key player in Roman politics for decades, Cicero rose to fame as a gifted orator and writer with a flair for invective. As a politician, however, he had failed to offer any substantial solution to pressing economic and social concerns and may have attempted to redeem himself by aiding Octavian. Among his many writings, his letters, almost 90 of which have survived, offer extensive insight into his personal life, particularly his relationships with his wife, Terentia, and daughter, Tullia, that inform subsequent chapters. Cicero negotiated with the senate on Octavian's behalf, offering the use of the latter's private army against Antony in exchange for an exemption from the age requirement of 41 for consulship. Octavian thus became the youngest man ever to serve as consul. What he learned from this experience – that the constitutional basis of the Republic had ceased to function – influenced his rebuilding of it once he became emperor. Traditionalism in some areas and innovation in others became the hallmark of his new regime.

After the violent years between 43 and 30 BCE, Octavian was the only leader left standing. The path to power, however, was never preordained. At several points, the outcome could have been different. So what were the factors in Octavian's success? First, he had the capacity for great cruelty, as exemplified by his mutilation and decapitation of Brutus' corpse, one of Caesar's assassins. His military prowess soon earned him a victory celebration just a notch below a triumph. He had the ability to earn and keep the respect of his troops. Most importantly, Octavian had a knack for thinking ahead and turning events to his advantage, capitalizing on his opponent's errors. Once he had achieved his aim of gaining legal standing as consul, he entered into an alliance with Antony and Lepidus (c. 89–12 BCE), formerly a former ally of Caesar, called the second triumvirate. This was, in effect, a triple dictatorship. A wave of proscriptions followed. Cicero himself was a victim, hacked to death on the grounds of his villa, his head and hands cut off and sent back to Rome, where they were displayed on the speaker's platform in the Forum.

This group proceeded to divide the empire, with Antony taking the eastern provinces and Gaul, Octavian the west and Lepidus Africa. Amid escalating tensions, Octavian removed Lepidus from power and a new agreement was brokered with Antony, cemented by his marriage to Octavian's sister, Octavia. Now the empire was effectively divided between two men. In need of resources, Antony took up with Cleopatra VII, who had earlier been Julius Caesar's lover. Together they had three children, including the twins Alexander Helios (Sun) and Cleopatra Selene (Moon). Now the real trouble began between the two men as they battled to publicly discredit and demonize each other. Whereas Antony portrayed his rival as a low-born coward, womanizer, and monster of cruelty, Octavian in turn played off Antony as a drunkard and a slave to a foreign queen. When someone leaked Antony's will, in which he requested to be buried next to Cleopatra and their children declared his heirs, that was the last straw. His consulship was revoked and his property confiscated. The hostilities culminated at Actium, where Antony's fleet was defeated. Antony and Cleopatra committed suicide as Octavian entered Alexandria in 30 BCE, marking the end of civil war and the demise of the Republic.

9.8 Augustus and Imperial Rome

Octavian triumphantly returned to Rome in 29 BCE and set about systematizing the innovations and changes he had introduced in the 30s. Chief among these was the continuation of the Republic and its unwritten constitution, mechanisms, and offices. These were not abolished but rather absorbed into the new constitutional structure with him at the helm. His title was not king or dictator but rather ***princeps***, that is, "first citizen." (The term *principate* refers to the new system of government under the leadership of the princeps.) This hybrid was a republic headed by a monarch, or in the view of some, a more perfect form of the Republic. For many Romans who had suffered through the years of civil war, with its proscriptions, high taxation, and constant turmoil, the new regime represented a return to law and order. Gone was the young, murderous killer, replaced by a merciful and moderate ruler. Not wanting to style himself as a king, he refused the senate's repeated offers of supreme power. Instead, Octavian worked within the Republican framework to accomplish his goals. In 27 BCE the senate conferred on him the name of "Augustus" ("favored by the gods"). The name evoked an association with sacred and creative power and recalled the posthumous deification of Julius Caesar in 42 BCE. All later Roman emperors adopted this title. Although Augustus maintained control over all things political and institutional, he accompanied this new supremacy not with ostentation but rather with reserve. Hailed as "the father of the country," he styled himself as a caring father figure who also wielded power over his family. And like a Roman father, he did not act as an autocrat but consulted with his friends and family, especially his wife, Livia, whom we examine more fully in subsequent chapters.

Augustus dominated the Roman landscape for more than fifty years. He was the longest reigning emperor in Roman history. His decisions determined the layout of Roman territory, the administration of the provinces and legions, the organization of time, and even the shape of future European geography. By eliminating the prospect of civil war that had plagued Rome for so many decades, Augustus' regime ushered in a new era of unprecedented political stability called the **Pax Romana** ("Roman Peace"). Vergil celebrates the beginning of this peace, which lasted for over two hundred years, in his *Aeneid*:

> Then the harsh ages will grow mild, with wars abandoned, white haired Faith and Vesta, and Quirinus with his brother Remus will make laws. The gates of war, grim with iron and narrowed by bars, will be closed.... (Verg. *Aen.* 1.291–96)

The passage alludes to the Roman practice of closing the doors of the Temple of Janus in the Roman Forum during times of peace. The Roman concept of peace, however, did not imply the absence of war but rather the subjugation of all enemies and the elimination of all possibility of revolt, as Augustus himself states, "When victories had secured peace by land and sea throughout the whole empire of the Roman people" (Aug. RG 13). The Altar of Peace, dedicated in 9 BCE to commemorate Augustus' return from Spain and Gaul, encapsulates this paradox. The surrounding frieze depicts the Imperial family in procession as the benefactors of the peaceful rebirth of Italy brought about by Roman conquest. The space that the monument occupied, the Field of Mars, where the army gathered and trained, reinforced the militaristic nature of this peace. We return to this monument in more detail in subsequent chapters.

Augustus died at Nola in 14 CE just short of his 76th birthday. Much of his career had been preoccupied with the problem of succession. His massive tomb, completed in 28 BCE, seemed to announce his ambition to found a dynasty. His political reforms that promoted marriage and children combined with the idealized public display of the Imperial family members further reinforced the importance of hereditary rule in the new regime. And yet Augustus faced a chronic problem of succession throughout his life because he had no direct male heirs, and the heirs he adopted all died young, as we see in the next chapter. Augustus had a monumental impact on his world. He restored order in Rome after civil wars, introducing a new era of peace and prosperity after decades of senseless bloodshed. At his death, the Roman Empire was far more powerful than any of the areas that surrounded it. The population was exponentially larger, around 7 million in Italy and 45.5 million across the entire empire (see Map 5). Augustus' greatest achievement, however, was the stable foundation he constructed for Roman rule in the form of the principate for almost 200 years. Internal peace allowed for significant development, including the creation of new roads, aqueducts, administrative systems, and architecture.

Fourteen emperors reigned after the death of Augustus until the time of Commodus, a period of 180 years. These included some of the most famous names in Roman history: the deranged Caligula, notorious for incest with his sisters and his desire to appoint his horse consul; his uncle, Claudius, the reluctant ruler and shrewd political observer; Nero, known for killing family members, "fiddling while Rome burned," and persecuting Christians; Marcus Aurelius, the philosopher and author of *Meditations*; and Commodus, the emperor depicted in the movie *Gladiator*. Despite all the tales of mad emperors, personal intrigues, sexual perversions, and material excess, the structure of Roman rule remained relatively stable during this period. All followed Augustan precedent in their ascent to power, advertising their generosity to the people and displaying their military might. After the murder of Commodus, however, the Augustan model collapsed, and more then seventy emperors claimed the rule over the next century. It was not fully stabilized until Diocletian and the introduction of the Tetrarchy, in which four emperors ruled the empire together. This arrangement ultimately led to civil war that was finally ended by Constantine, who became single ruler. He shifted the capital east to Byzantium, which was then named Constantinople, and converted to Christianity, which later became the state religion. After his death, the empire never recovered and was further eroded by civil wars, corruption, barbarian migrations and incursions, and economic problems. The deposition of Rome's last emperor, Romulus Augustulus, by Odacer in 476 marked the end of the empire in the west.

9.9 Conclusion

This chapter established a framework for understanding Roman views of women and gender, starting with the Etruscans, the regal period and the transition to the Republic, the gradual conquest of the Italian peninsula and beyond, and concluding with Augustus' new order. In contrast to the Greeks, the Romans exhibited a tolerance toward other cultures, embracing asylum and assimilation as a model for expansion. By the second century CE, any free adult male in the empire could enjoy the benefits of citizenship. Attention to Roman political and social institutions and exemplary historical figures, such as Scipio Barbatus, Julius Caesar, and Octavian/Augustus, sheds light on Roman conceptions of manhood. To be an elite Roman man meant vying with one's peers for political offices, with the ultimate goal of winning a consulship. Political success required above all demonstrated military success through the acquisition of commands. It was also important to be able to manipulate public image and cultivate popular support. By the end of the Republic, career advancement could involve a willingness to resort to cruelty, disregard for the law, and violence, as we saw with Augustus. Although these traits were key to regime change, Augustus set them aside in order to cultivate his image as the first citizen and father of his country, who brought unprecedented stability to the empire. In what follows, we seek to understand what it meant to be female in this world and how it differed from the Greek experience. Upper-class Roman women in general had much greater independence than their Greek counterparts. They were often educated and enjoyed high social status and relative legal independence. They regularly interacted with men in a variety of contexts and could in fact exert substantial power both within the family and in the public sphere. And because so many accounts of both exemplary and notorious historical women survive from ancient Rome – such as Cornelia, Clodia, Cleopatra, and Livia – we consider their stories in greater detail in subsequent chapters.

Questions for Review

1 Who were the Etruscans and why were they important to Roman civilization?

2 What role does violence against women, or its threat, play in Roman foundation myth?

3 What would have been a typical career trajectory for a Roman man during the Republic?

4   How was Rome able to grow from a small city-state into a world power?

5   What are some similarities between Greek and Roman ideas of manhood?

Further Reading

Primary Sources

Livy, *History of Rome*, Book 1
Vergil, *Aeneid*

Secondary Sources

Beard, Mary (2015). *SPQR: A History of Ancient Rome*. New York, NY: Liveright Publishing
   Corporation.
   A sweeping, revisionist account of Roman history that seeks to address the question of how
   Rome grew from a relatively insignificant town to a vast empire and the ways in which it still
   shapes our world today.
Beard, Mary (2009). *The Roman Triumph*. Cambridge, MA: Harvard University Press.
   A comprehensive account of the ancient ceremony of the Roman triumph that attempts to
   recreate its form and reexamines its function in ancient Roman culture.
Campbell, Brian (2011). *The Romans and Their World: A Short Introduction*. New Haven, CT:
   Yale University Press.
   An engaging history of ancient Rome for the general reader that begins with the early years of
   the Republic and continues until 476 BCE when the last Roman emperor was deposed.
Fagan, Garrett (2011). *The Lure of the Arena: Social Psychology and the Crowd at the Roman
   Games*. Cambridge: Cambridge University Press.
   Explores the cultural meaning of spectacles of bloodshed and violence in the Roman
   amphitheater, drawing on contemporary theories of crowd behavior.
Galinksy, Karl (2012). *Augustus: Introduction to the Life of the Emperor*. Cambridge: Cambridge
   University Press.
   A concise overview of Rome's first emperor that covers Augustus' life from childhood to
   deification and seeks to elicit the characteristics and circumstances that lead to his vast
   achievements.
Knapp, Robert (2011). *Invisible Romans*. Cambridge, MA: Harvard University Press.
   Focuses on ordinary, nonelite individuals who tend to be overlooked in standard histories,
   bringing to life the slaves, freedmen, soldiers, female prostitutes, gladiators, bandits, and pirates
   that populated the Roman world.
Potter, David (2014). *Ancient Rome: A New History*, 2e. New York and London: Thames & Hudson.
   Lavishly illustrated with helpful maps, battle plans, coins, and art, this accessible textbook
   introduces students to the key periods of Roman history and attempts to show how Roman
   historians evaluate a broad array of evidence.

10

The Roman Family and Household

> Although she had not yet reached the age of 14, she had the intelligence of an old woman, the dignity of a matron (*matrona*), the sweetness of a girl (*puella*) together with the modesty of a maiden (*virgo*). How she used to hang from her father's neck! How affectionately and modestly she used to embrace us who were her father's friends! Her nurses, her minders and teachers, how she respected each of them according to their duty! With what care and intelligence she used to read. How sparingly and with what restraint she played.
>
> (Plin. *Ep.* 5.16)

What was it like to grow up female in ancient Rome? How did this experience compare to that of girls in ancient Greece? Pliny's letter describes one Roman girl, Minicia Marcella, who died in 105 CE, at age 12 years, 11 months, and 7 days. We know that because, remarkably, her actual funerary inscription survives. Pliny the Younger (c. 61–113 CE) wrote this letter to a friend, informing him of the death of the daughter of their mutual friend and urging him to offer his condolences to the grieving father. He lavishly praises Minicia as an exemplar of Roman girlhood, singling out her affectionate nature, her gravity, her studiousness, and her strong physical and intellectual resemblance to her father. Her life cut terribly short, Minicia nonetheless exemplifies all of the virtues associated with Roman women according to each life stage: *puella* ("young girl"); *virgo* ("maiden"); *matrona* ("wife and mother"); and old woman. Girls, we are told, are supposed to be sweet, maidens modest, matrons serious, and old women wise. These also happen to be the ages around which the following chapters are organized.

The letter further elicits some fundamental departures in Roman attitudes toward women and gender. Minicia inhabited a world in which women, even girls, seem not to have been segregated from men. She is an object of concern not only to her father but also to his friends. Her father's profound grief at her death indicates that daughters could be emotionally valued as much as sons. It is further noteworthy that the primary relationship here is between father and daughter. There is no mention of her mother, who may, perhaps, have been deceased. We also learn that she was engaged at the time of her death, underscoring that elite Roman girls often married very young, sometimes even before puberty. Truly exceptional from a Greek standpoint, however, is the emphasis on literacy and education. Minicia knew how to read, probably read Greek, and learned other subjects. The reference to specialized teachers indicates that Roman wealthy families were willing to invest considerable resources in educating their daughters. Lastly, the letter focuses primarily on Minicia's character and moral qualities, in keeping with the Roman custom of fashioning individuals into exemplary models for future generations, especially after death. But note that neither her education nor her virtues are intended to

Women in Classical Antiquity: From Birth to Death, First Edition. Laura K. McClure.
© 2020 John Wiley & Sons, Inc. Published 2020 by John Wiley & Sons, Inc.

prepare her for a career in politics or public life. Just as in Greece, the lives of Roman girls and women largely revolved around the family and household, despite some substantial divergences regarding education, domestic space, mixed-gender interactions, spatial mobility, and religious roles.

This chapter examines the structure of the family, the organization of domestic space, female education, and private rituals to understand Roman conceptions of girlhood. It focuses primarily on the elite Roman household, because it commands the greatest amount of attention in the ancient sources. We consider two phases: birth to age 7 and then the period just before the onset of puberty. The age terms applied to Minicia reveal the difficulty of clearly delineating phases of childhood for Roman girls. Because she is called a puella, she is clearly a girl, but she stood at the threshold of adolescence, about to become a virgo, on the point of sexual maturity and marriage. As in Greece, girls were of little interest to Roman male authors. They were regarded as doubly unimportant not only because they were young without fully formed social identities, but also because they were female and considered inferior to men. Almost invisible in the literary sources, Roman girls become more visible in the material record, through their sarcophagi and funerary inscriptions, artifacts, sculpture, and wall paintings. For example, dolls were popular playthings for girls of all ages (see Box 10.1) and yet they are rarely mentioned in the male-authored literary sources. Such a small and common everyday object probably went largely unnoticed by Roman men, but they were the cherished and constant companions for the girls, and women, who owned them.

10.1 *Familia* **and** *Domus*

The Roman family defies easy definition. It was an amorphous, undifferentiated entity composed not only of parents and children, slaves, and other property but also larger networks of kin members. Although our English word, "family," comes from the Latin *familia*, the term did not refer to the nuclear family in the modern sense. Rather, it technically denoted the group of slaves connected to a husband and wife. By extension, it could mean a business as the product of specialist slaves within the household and beyond. It could also refer to the family estate. Another way to understand the term is as a set of power dynamics constituted around the *paterfamilias* ("father or master of the household"). He exercised *potestas* ("absolute power") over his wife, his children even when adult, grandchildren, and slaves. Legal adulthood did not exist for any member of the family but him. He owned all property and had authority to make decisions on behalf of the family. A Roman man normally became a paterfamilias after the death of his own father, as the oldest living male in the direct line of male ascent. The paterfamilias had the right to discipline all family members, especially children and slaves, including the power of life and death. In the story of Verginia, we saw that her father exercises this authority by killing her in order to protect her from sexual assault. The term, however, is a bit misleading, because it often means "estate owner," without reference to family relations. It suggests how property ownership and family relations were conjoined in Roman society, particularly in the transmission of patrimony through a will. The moral responsibility of the paterfamilias was thus economic: to manage the patrimony for future generations. Until then, his children were in his power and could not independently own property until he died. His wife, in contrast, held no legal rights or potestas over the family.

An important factor in determining the structure of a Roman family was whether the marriage had occurred with or without *manus* ("the hand"). This determined whether a woman fell under the legal power of her father or her husband. Originally, all Roman marriages were with the hand, that is, the bride passed from the control of her father to that of her husband, much like in ancient Greece. She belonged both legally and ritually to her husband's family and could no longer inherit from her father's estate. Her own property transferred to the ownership of her husband upon marriage, and as a consequence, she had no legal access to it until widowed. In this form of marriage, the wife almost functioned in the legal capacity of a daughter to her husband. In return, she earned the name of **materfamilias** ("mother of the family"), a term that referred to a wife in a manus marriage only during the Republic but was used interchangeably with the more general term matrona ("legally married woman") by the first century BCE. In a marriage without manus, a woman did not fall under the legal authority of her husband but rather remained legally attached to her father and her natal family, even after she had physically moved away. After her father's death, she became legally independent and could inherit a portion of his estate. Her husband, in contrast, might not have the right to make decisions or own property because his father was still alive. A wife in a non-manus marriage might therefore control significantly more assets than her husband. This form of marriage became increasingly common in the late Republic onward, probably as a means to protect assets and ensure that property remained within the family.

To describe the nuclear family, including a wife not under manus marriage, the Romans generally used **domus** ("house"). The word signifies both the physical house and the community that it sheltered as a broader set of kin relations, including husband and wife, their children (whether their own, adopted, or from a previous marriage), slaves, and freed slaves, and sometimes other relatives. Among elite families, the domus served as a central symbol of wealth and honor. It could encompass hundreds of people, such as administrative assistants, cleaners, cooks, entertainers, hairdressers and barbers, teachers, nurses, and gardeners. The domus had a wide range of functions. It was both the basis for economic production and the mechanism for the preservation and redistribution of property through marriage and inheritance. It ensured the transmission of social status and the perpetuation of family cult. It also socialized children into their proper adult roles, whether preparing a boy for a senatorial career or arranging a socially advantageous marriage for a daughter. But the Romans also viewed their families as a source of emotional support between members and a refuge from the other cares of life much as we do today.

Both rich and poor Roman families tended to be small, consisting of two to three children, at most. Lead poisoning, inadequate medical care, female independence, poverty, and biological weaknesses have been adduced to explain low birthrates. Whatever the cause, marriage and children seem increasingly not to have been a priority of the Roman upper classes by the end of the Republic. In response, the emperor Augustus introduced a set of reforms aimed at regulating the sexual behavior of Roman citizens and encouraging the birth of children, collectively called the **Julian Laws**. This legislation formed the cornerstone of his "moral revolution," which sought a return to and renewal of the ancient domestic virtues on which the Roman state had been founded. The marriage statute of 18 BCE encouraged marriage and rewarded parents, and the later law of 9 CE supplemented the first, promoting the bearing of children and eliminating loopholes. They mandated marriage as a duty incumbent on all Roman citizen men between ages 25 and 60 and citizen women between ages 20 and 50. Those widowed and divorced within these age limits were expected to remarry. They further penalized marriage between social classes, prohibiting members of the senatorial order from marrying freed people, actors or actresses, prostitutes, pimps, procuresses, and persons condemned for adultery or caught in the act of adultery, a category encompassed by the term **infamis** (disreputable), discussed more fully in Chapter 13. The offspring of such unions were considered illegitimate, could not inherit, and were not even entered into the public record as legal persons. In contrast, by marrying respectably, a man made himself eligible to be nominated for office, and the fatherhood of three children gave him priority over his peers. But by staying celibate he would exempt himself from office and from receiving legacies from friends or inheritances from any but the closest relatives, a substantial component of any elite man's income. Women who gave birth to three children, even if the babies did not live beyond infancy, were rewarded with legal and financial independence from guardianship. Those who failed to produce children were penalized by restrictions placed on their ability to inherit: the unmarried and childless received nothing and those with at least some children could inherit according to a complex set of rules. Another statute introduced just a few months after the first marriage law in 18 BCE made adultery a criminal offense for the first time in Roman history, a point to which we return in Chapter 13. These laws highlight Augustus' concern that marriages occur only between proper social groups and that property remain within families. Not surprisingly, they were very unpopular with the Roman upper classes, leading to public protests that forced Augustus to modify them. Although the laws remained in effect for three centuries, they seem to have had little effect in promoting marital fidelity and improving birth rates. A hundred years later it was a commonplace of Roman society that the upper-class avoided having children. We look more closely at the impact of these laws on Roman women in Chapter 12.

The Roman family was far more fluid in its structure than its Greek equivalent, in large part because of greater tolerance for using tools such as adoption and divorce to create and dissolve political alliances for its benefit. Further, the growing prevalence of non-manus marriages by the end of the Republic meant that daughters were always at play in the arena of marriage. A paterfamilias could compel his daughter to divorce and remarry if it suited his purposes, even if she was pregnant. High divorce rates combined with early parental death meant that many Roman children grew up in blended families and were raised by stepparents or more distant relatives. Most children had one or two living siblings, but age gaps tended to be large because of premature death and paternal absence. For example, Cicero's daughter Tullia was 11–14 years older than her brother, suggesting that few Roman families had siblings close enough in age to develop an intimate bond. Similarly, the chance of a marriage ending in death before the end of a couple's childbearing years was high.

10.2   The Family of Augustus

Although a childless couple could easily rescue an abandoned baby, legal adoption became a way for Roman elite to ensure the transmission of property and the continuation of the family name in the absence of male heirs. Those adopted tended not to be infants, as today, but rather male teenagers or young adults from distinguished families who had survived the perilous years of childhood. Adoption not only solved the problem of inheritance, it also strengthened political ties between families, much like marriage. As we have seen, Julius Caesar and his successors in the Julio-Claudian dynasty, along with other aristocratic families, used adoption to demarcate an heir among the wider family group. As an example of how adoption and divorce affected the structure of the Roman family, let us look more closely at the life of Augustus. (See Chart 10.1 for a version of his family tree and the rest of the Julio-Claudians.) Born Gaius Octavius, he was raised by his maternal grandmother, Julia, who happened to be the sister of Julius Caesar, after the death of his father when he was just four years old. Having no legitimate children of his own, Julius Caesar named the 19-year-old Octavius in his will as his adopted son and heir. At this point, he assumed the name Gaius Julius Caesar Octavianus. The name Octavianus indicates that he had originally been an Octavius before joining the Julian clan. While married to his first wife, Scribonia, he fell madly in love with Livia, then the wife of Tiberius Claudius Nero and pregnant with their second child. Octavian scandalously divorced Scribonia the day that she gave birth to their daughter, Julia the Elder, and in turn compelled

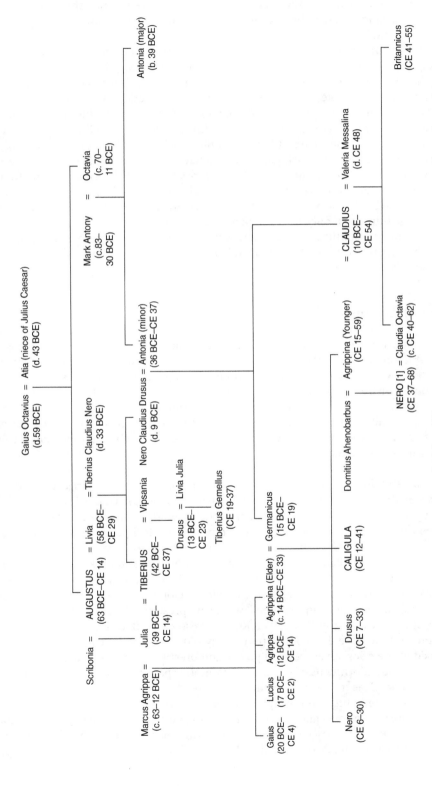

Chart 10.1 Family Tree of the Julio-Claudians. Source: Kamm (2006), p. 157.

Tiberius Claudius Nero to divorce Livia. Octavian and Livia were married three days after she gave birth to her second son, with her ex-husband acting as her paterfamilias, giving her away "just as a father would."

This pattern of divorce and adoption continued into the next generation. When his marriage to Livia failed to produce children, the new emperor planned to acquire an heir through Julia by marrying her off to her cousin Marcellus, but he died young. Augustus then married her to Marcus Agrippa, an ally and key commander in the Battle of Actium, and more than 20 years her senior. Their union resulted in five children, including two sons, Gaius and Lucius. After Agrippa's death, Augustus married Julia to Tiberius, Livia's elder son. Their marriage produced only one child, who did not survive childhood. Looping back to Julia's first marriage, Augustus adopted the two sons of Julia and Agrippa, Gaius and Lucius. Both subsequently died, one of an illness at 19 and the other from a battle wound two years later. The only remaining solution was to adopt one of Livia's two sons, Tiberius, who eventually succeeded him as emperor in 14 CE. From this brief sketch, we can see how high the stakes were in aristocratic Roman families, particularly for the Imperial family, in producing or adopting a suitable heir. Within this system, women helped to forge political alliances between men and ensured the perpetuation of the family name through the bearing of children. When either of these options failed, elite Roman males could and did turn to adoption.

10.3   Roman Domestic Space

> Now we must determine the situation of the private rooms for the paterfamilias, and those which are for general use, and those for the guests. Into those which are private, no one enters, except invited; such are bedrooms, dining-rooms, baths and so on. The common rooms, on the contrary, are entered by anyone, even unasked. Such are the entrance hall, inner court, the peristyle, and those which are for similar uses. Hence for the person of average wealth, magnificent entrance halls are not necessary, nor offices nor atria, because such persons are those who pay their respects to others rather than receiving their own clients. (Vitr. 6.5.1)

Just as membership in the family was constantly changing because of marriage and divorce, so, too, the residents of the physical house also fluctuated. Most upper-class Romans held their wealth in property and were continually buying, selling, and moving house. Senators often owned several properties, including a house in Rome for political purposes and several other residences throughout Italy. A variety of Roman domestic spaces have been excavated, from cramped tenements where the poorest members of society lived and took their meals in local bars to palatial villas, featuring cavernous entry halls, bath complexes, and large gardens with elaborate water features. Most examples of these villas are found in two small Roman towns on the bay of Naples, Herculaneum and Pompeii, which are preserved in amazing detail thanks to the eruption of Mt. Vesuvius in 79 CE. For Roman aristocrats, it was critical to have a fine house, for, unlike their Athenian counterparts, they did much of their business at home. A crowd amassed at the door advertised the power and prestige of the paterfamilias, as did the size, architecture, and adornment of his house. Domestic space therefore mingled public and private, business and pleasure, men, women, children, and slaves.

Although not an elite home, the floor plan of the house of the Vettii, one of the most well-preserved structures in Pompeii and famous for its wall paintings, provides a good example of the organization of Roman domestic space. Located on a back street across from a bar, the house originally consisted of 30 rooms and had recently been remodeled before the eruption.

Although it was customary even for sumptuous villas to have shops at the front, the house of the Vettii was unique in being closed to the street. Guests first entered the house through a front door and narrow corridor leading to an *atrium*, a large reception hall adapted from the Etruscans. Open to the sky, it was designed to impress, with elaborate wall paintings, mosaic floors, sculpture, and beautiful views to the garden at the back of the house. A four-sided roof sloped inward toward a center rectangle in the atrium, admitting light and rainwater, which was collected in a large rectangular pool below. There the paterfamilias received visits from his clients as part of the morning salutations before heading off to the Forum or other business outside the home. The atrium was surrounded by a series of smaller rooms, called *cubicula*, which were used as bedrooms or storage areas. Another standard feature of the Roman villa was the *triclinium* or dining room. Like the House of the Vettii, many Roman villas featured an interior garden with a peristyle with Greek columns and formal plantings. Servants' quarters would have been located upstairs. The location of the rooms marked a progression from public to increasingly private space, and the Roman custom of keeping the door open during the day kept it continually connected to the street and the world beyond.

In addition to its function as a space for conducting business, the atrium was the center of family life. After the master of the house left for the day, children played there and women went about their work. Looms were kept there according to ancient custom. Indeed, Lucretia is portrayed as assiduously working at her wool late into the night in this space. The room also displayed the history of the family through allusions to and representations of ancestors, a practice that seems to have been confined to only the most politically prestigious families. Ancestral masks, called *imagines*, were stored in wooden cupboards and displayed during family celebrations. Family trees, featuring painted portraits joined by lines, sometimes adorned the walls and helped explain the place of each relative within the group (Plin. *NH* 35.6). These depicted not only men but also women and children.

The atrium was also essential to domestic cult, because it usually contained the hearth. On named days of each month and special family occasions, it was adorned with garlands and offerings of food and wine. Also located in the atrium was the shrine of the family gods, called the *Lararium*, which contained the *Lares* and the *genius* worshipped by the entire family. A Lararium located in the second, smaller atrium in the house of the Vettii depicts two Lares holding drinking cups and dancing on either side of the genius, dressed in a toga (Figure 10.1). Beneath is a serpent that represents the guardian spirit of the family. As the defenders of the boundaries between households, the Lares protected the family. Often identified or confused with the Lares were the *Penates*, the keepers of the household's provisions. The genius symbolized the procreative life force of the master of the house and received offerings annually on his birthday. There is some evidence for a female equivalent, the *juno*, who was honored on a woman's birthday.

Rituals marking the life stages also occurred in the atrium. After the birth of a child, a fire was kindled on the hearth and kept alight for the first few days. The naming ceremony was also held there, as well as various other rites aimed at ensuring the survival of the child. In adolescence, the child marked his or her transition to adulthood in this space. Sons dedicated the first shavings of their beards to the Lares before donning the all-white toga of manhood. On the day before marriage, daughters offered their toys, dolls, and other symbols of childhood at the shrine of the gods. Finally, both wedding and funerary rituals took place in the atrium.

The most important gender-related difference between Greek and Roman domestic architecture relates to the organization of space. Roman houses did not contain a women's quarters, which meant that women frequently came into contact with men outside of the family. Women were also free to leave the house to visit friends or conduct business. In fact, the Romans found Greek customs particularly mystifying in this regard:

What Roman would be ashamed to take his wife to a banquet? What materfamilias does not frequent the front rooms of her house and display herself to the crowd? But it is very different in Greece. For there a woman is not admitted to the banquet, unless relatives only are present, and she occupies the interior part of the house called "the women's quarters," to which no man has access unless he is a close relative. (Nep. 6–8)

In another anecdote, the absence of women from the dinner table is so shocking to the Roman guests that they demand that the Greek host summon his daughter (Cic. *Verr*. 2.1.66). When he refuses, saying that respectable Greek women do not dine with men, a fight breaks out. The host is scalded by boiling water and another man dies before the dispute is resolved. In contrast to her Athenian counterpart, a Roman matron was expected to display herself to male guests within her house, to host banquets at home, and to accompany her husband at dinner parties outside the house.

10.4 *Lanificium*: Women's Work

Although Roman women were not confined to a dedicated female space, they nonetheless engaged in gendered activities within the house. As in Greece, the primary responsibilities of Roman women of all classes involved managing the household, including the provision of clothing and the production of textiles. The Latin term ***lanificium*** refers to all stages of this task, from spinning wool to weaving it into finished fabric. The final line of the epitaph for Claudia that begins this book praises her in just these terms, "She looked after the house, she worked in wool" (*Domum servavit, lanam fecit*). Skill at textile production was so closely allied with Roman conceptions of female virtue that the phrase *lanam fecit* could serve as shorthand for "she was virtuous," as we find in another epitaph: "Here lies Amymone, wife of Marcus, the best and most beautiful, worker in wool, pious, chaste, thrifty, faithful, a homebody" (*CIL* VI 11602). These epitaphs mark the culmination of a life spent working wool that began in childhood, under the tutelage of Minerva, the Roman equivalent of Athena:

> When once they have placated Pallas, let girls learn to card wool and to unwind the full distaff. She also teaches how to traverse the upright warp with the shuttle, and she packs close the loose threads with the comb. (Ov. *Fast*. 3.817–20)

In Roman weddings, the bride wore a special homespun woolen tunic and was accompanied on her journey to the groom's house by a servant carrying a decorated distaff and spindle with thread. She thus entered her new life as a wife accompanied by symbols of wool working. The pervasive equation of women, and the female life cycle, with weaving during the Roman period is evident in one interpretation of a common dream: "A woman dreamed she had finished her weaving. She died the next day. Since she no longer had work, she no longer had reason to live" (Artemidorus, *Dreams* 4.40).

Wool working serves as a byword for female virtue in Roman moral discourse of the Imperial period, as exemplified by the diligent Lucretia. For Juvenal (55–117 CE), it evokes a golden age of frugality, industry, and not coincidentally, the total subordination of women:

> In the old days, their lowly position kept women pure. Work, little sleep, and hands chaffed and hardened by Tuscan wool prevented their small houses from being contaminated by vice, and Hannibal close to Rome, and their husbands standing on the Colline tower. (Juv. 6.287–91)

According to the agricultural writer, Columella (fl. 50 CE), a wife's disdain for weaving and homespun clothing represents a moral failing:

> Now, however, when most women are so wasted away by luxury and idleness that they do not think it worth their time to undertake even the supervision of wool working and there is an aversion to home-made garments and by means of their perverse desire they are pleased only by clothing purchased for large sums and almost the whole of their husband's income…. (Columella, *On Agriculture* 12.9)

Despite the importance of wool working to moral discourse on women, the Roman literary tradition on the whole pays far less attention to this form of female labor than the Greek, for several reasons. First, textile production was not exclusively the province of women in the Roman world. Moreover, spinning was considered to be the most menial form of labor within the family and accordingly relegated to slaves. By the end of the Republic, it is unlikely that wealthy Roman women were tasked with providing the clothing for their families or even supervising its production, given the growth of the commercial textile industry. So when Augustus' claims that he compelled his daughter and granddaughters to learn how to spin and weave and that he wore only homespun clothing, he draws on the symbolic value of wool working to advertise Roman traditional values of modesty and frugality. In reality, silk rather than wool had become the fabric of choice for wealthy women at this time. In a poem by Propertius (c. 50–15 BCE), a wife, after measuring her soldier-husband's absence by the number of homespun cloaks she has woven for him (four!), awaits him in beautiful silks and sparkling rings:

> Every love is great, but greater when one's spouse is absent. Venus herself fans this flame, that it may live. Why now would purple clothes shine on me and watery crystal adorn my hands? (Prop. 4.3.49–52)

By the time of the principate, it would seem that the physically demanding job of weaving garments at home had been outsourced and elite Roman women only dabbled in the textile arts as a symbol of their sexual and domestic virtue.

10.5 Growing Up Female in the Roman Family

> "Please give Attica a kiss from me for being such a happy little girl. It is what one likes to see in children." (Cic. *Att.* 16.11.8)

Although the Latin language contains many words for children, it has no specific word for "baby." The Latin term for infant refers to both male and female babies from birth to 7 years, underscoring the relative lack of gender differentiation in the early years. As babies advance to adulthood, they start to assume gendered terminology and characteristics. The Latin term for boy, *puer*, refers to prepubertal boys not yet capable of reproduction or military service; in the plural it can refer to both male and female children. The word puella denotes both young girls from age 7 to 12 as well as young women between puberty and motherhood. As in Greece, childbirth took place at home under the supervision of a midwife and attended by a network of female relatives and servants. A wide array of spirits and divinities were worshiped in connection with every aspect of reproduction, from conception to birth and infancy. Juno Lucina and Diana Lucifera assisted in bringing the baby into the light of day, as their epithets suggest, because both contain the word for light, whereas Cunina watched over the cradle. Another group of gods dealt with the early stages of infant development: from breastfeeding to the first solid food, the prevention of nightmares, and first steps.

The socialization of the infant into the family and adult gender roles began immediately after delivery, when the midwife laid the child on the ground and inspected it for any physical deformities. The paterfamilias then determined whether to rear the child in a ritual that involved lifting the child from the ground in a gesture of acceptance. The child was given its first bath and then wrapped in swaddling bands. The Romans believed swaddling helped control the child and properly shape its physical development. In the case of girls, the breasts were bound tightly and the hips loosely on the grounds that "in women this form is more becoming" (Sor. *Gyn.* 2.15 [84]). A laurel wreath was hung on the front door to announce the birth. Fires were lit on the altars to thank the gods, both at home and at those of friends and parents. A party followed, in which men gathered and congratulated the new father and discussed the child's future.

Within eight days for girls and nine for boys, the infant underwent the ***lustratio***, a private feast at which it was given a name. With this ceremony, the family confirmed that it accepted the child as one of its members. At this time, patrician males received a round gold pendant, called a ***bulla***, worn around the neck until adulthood to protect them from harm as well as to communicate their status as members of the patrician class. It remains unclear whether girls also wore this charm. Some representations show girls wearing a crescent-shaped pendant. A portion of the south frieze of the Altar of Peace (Figure 10.2) shows a small boy, probably Gaius, at lower left wearing the bulla over his toga. To his right, his older sister smiles down at him, dressed in the toga praetexta, discussed more fully later, and wearing a necklace with a crescent moon. The ceremony concluded with the naming of the child. If a girl, she likely received only one name, that of her father, but with a feminine ending. If she had any sisters, they more than likely shared the same name. In that case, she might be distinguished by *maior* ("elder") or *minor* ("younger"), or by a number, *prima*, ("first"), *secunda* ("second") and so on. In public, women were identified more formally by the name of their father or husband, e.g. Clodia Metelli, "Clodia, wife of Metellus." In the Imperial period, many women assumed a second name. Although daughters could not pass on their family names to their offspring, they retained their own family name for life.

Whereas a daughter might have but one name, derived from her father, aristocratic Roman males could possess as many as four names, articulating a more nuanced familial and social identity. A Roman man had a first name or ***praenomen***, derived from a short list of under twenty and usually abbreviated in inscriptions, as in Q. for Quintus. Then followed the hereditary name or ***nomen*** of his ***gens*** ("clan") and the name of the branch to which the man belonged, or ***cognomen***, and sometimes a fourth name that called attention to a special achievement or characteristic called the ***agnomen***. For example: Publius (praenomen) Cornelius (nomen) Scipio (cognomen) Africanus (agnomen). Here the cognomen Scipio identifies his family line within the gens whereas the fourth name, the agnomen, celebrates his victory over Hannibal in North Africa. The baby's name and date of birth were then entered into an official public register and an official declaration made at the Temple of Saturn. Although a Roman father hoped for a son and heir, he also delighted in the birth of a daughter, and their relationship might be particularly close, as was the case with Cicero and Tullia.

In elite families, a wet nurse would care for the newborn. Greek women were considered the best at this job because they spoke Greek and were considered more civilized. Such women enjoyed professional standing and could become cherished members of the family. This specialized health care for childbirth and early childhood reflects Roman priorities and fears about the early years of childhood. The annual celebration of personal birthdays further underscores anxieties about survival. The Romans on their birthdays gave thanks for the past year and prayed for divine protection in the coming year. They celebrated with a fire on the domestic hearth, incense, ritual cakes, garlands, flowers, and white robes. Adult males honored the genius or life spark, often represented as a serpent with the Lares above the family altar, as we saw in Figure 10.1, and women invoked the juno, the female equivalent.

As in Greece, infant mortality rates were high, especially in the years from infancy to age 5. Thirty percent of babies died within their first year, and half did not make it to their tenth birthday. Life expectancy overall was around twenty-five to thirty years. Out of 12 live births, Cornelia, the mother of the Gracchi, saw only three children live to adulthood. But the birth of at least three children who had survived until the naming ceremony cannot have been that unusual or it would not have been a requirement of Augustan family legislation. A particularly poignant source for information about Roman children comes from funerary epitaphs and sarcophagi. Boys under the age of 10 are more likely to be commemorated than girls, and mothers are more frequently mentioned as the dedicators. In a rare example, a mother mourns her young daughter: "To the departed spirits, Silvina lived six years and sixteen days. Her mother Sperata set this up for her sweet daughter" (*CIL* VI 26597). Unwanted babies could be killed, sold, or exposed, possibly more likely with girls than with boys. In a letter composed around 1 BCE from Roman Egypt, a husband instructs his pregnant wife what to do with their baby if it is a girl:

> I ask and I entreat you to take care of the child, and if I receive my pay soon, I will send it to you. Above all, if you bear a child and it is male, let it be; but if it is female, cast it out. (P. *Oxy.* 744 G)

Figure 10.1 Lararium from the house of the Vettii in Pompeii, first century BCE. Italy/Bridgeman Images.

Figure 10.2 A little boy and girl, detail, south panel of the Altar of Peace, 13–9 BCE. Rome, Museo dell' Ara Pacis. ZUMA Press Inc/Alamy Stock Photo.

Upper-class families may have been averse to abandoning their infants because the practice was not socially acceptable and in fact was legally banned in 374 CE. Conversely, about a third of Roman children lost their father before puberty and two-thirds had no father by the age of 25. A mother could continue to care for her orphaned children but as she did not possess the legal rights and powers of the paterfamilias, she required a guardian or ***tutor*** who stood as a surrogate for the father.

Romans of all classes and genders wore the ***tunica*** ("tunic"), which on girls reached to their feet. Some authors indicate that girls also wore the woolen ***toga praetexta***, the toga bordered by a purple stripe, just like their freeborn brothers, and is shown on the little girl in the Altar of Peace frieze (Figure 10.2). This protective border marked their wearers as citizens and thus protected them from profanity and sexual contact when they ventured outside the house. Girls also wore a linen garment beneath the tunic and a band to restrict the growth of their breasts, in keeping with the fashion of a slim upper body. Some had simple hairstyles, others more elaborate coiffures. Young girls wore their hair combed and bound with woolen ribbons called ***vittae***. When attached to altars and animals, these ribbons denoted religious purity and divine protection. They were probably white, a color associated with rites in honor of the gods. Visual sources sometimes depict young girls with a "melon hairstyle," twisted back from the crown in sections and wound into a bun at the back of the head. Unlike in Greece, Roman girls did not wear a veil.

Box 10.1 Roman Dolls

Although rarely mentioned in literature, dolls were popular companions of Roman girls. Nearly five hundred objects have been identified as dolls – not all of which were playthings – with over a dozen found in tombs. Fashioned from ivory, bone, or clay, most Roman dolls resemble elegant adult women. Perhaps the most famous comes from the sarcophagus of Crepereia Tryphaena, who died between the ages of 14 and 17 (Figure 10.3). She was buried adorned with gold jewelry and a brooch and with several items that suggest her imminent marriage. She was crowned with a wreath of leaves and flowers in the manner of a bride. A signet ring inscribed with a male name, Filetus, placed on her finger may also point to a wedding unfulfilled. Pride of place, however, was given to her doll, which rested next to the girl's head. Fashioned out of ivory now darkened with age, the doll measures around nine inches in height. The limbs are jointed at the shoulders, elbows, hips, and knees, such that the girl could pose her and simulate movement. Her slim body, small breasts, and full hips reflect the Roman ideal of female beauty, as does her contemporary hairstyle, which resembles that of the elder Empress Faustina. Wavy locks frame the face beneath a central part with the sides braided and coiled above in a large bun. The mature face represents

Figure 10.3 Ivory doll from the sarcophagus of Crepereia Tryphaena, mid-second century CE. Rome, Antiquarium Comunale. DEA/V. PIROZZI/ Getty Images.

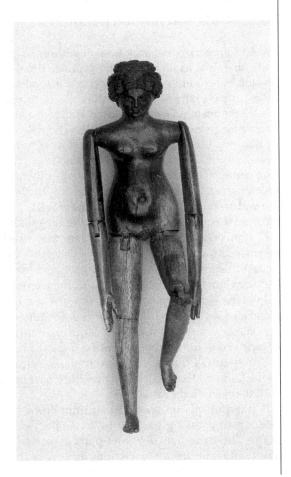

an idealized form of beauty, communicating restraint and serenity. From a golden ring placed on the doll's left thumb dangles the key to a small ivory box, also placed in the tomb, and containing small cosmetic accessories such as tiny combs, a silver mirror, gold bracelets, and earrings. No doubt she once possessed an elegant wardrobe as well.

The large quantity of gifts placed in the grave, the emphasis on grooming, and the expensive material of the doll suggest that she belonged to an aristocratic girl. She embodies the feminine characteristics valued most by the Romans, including neatness, adornment, good grooming, and refinement, all encompassed by the term *cultus*. Dolls thus assisted in the socialization process of young girls, preparing them for their future as wives and mothers of upper-class Roman men. The jewelry and accessories found in the tomb suggest that girls were expected to learn how to adorn themselves in the manner of their dolls. Once they had learned this art from practicing on their dolls, they relinquished them on the eve of marriage. Dolls placed in the tombs of unmarried teenagers like Crepereia and even elderly women, such as the Vestal Virgin, Cossinia (Palazzo Massimo alle Terme 262725), may perhaps symbolize their inability to make the transition to adulthood as a wife and mother.

10.6 Girls and Roman Religion

We find little discussion by Roman authors of the role of children, especially girls, in religion and ritual. Just as men were the primary ritual agents in public religion, so the paterfamilias presided over family cult and in fact was legally required to do so. He performed sacrifices on behalf of the entire family and other minor private rituals, such as daily offerings to the family gods. Important religious duties related to the honoring of the dead also fell to him, and funeral processions were always led by men, who delivered the eulogies and celebrated the sacrifices. In this ritual landscape, girls play a limited role, unless they had been selected to serve as a Vestal Virgin. They probably participated with their brothers in funerary processions, which in elite families comprised a large entourage that progressed from the atrium to the Forum. Actors accompanied these parades, carrying the family's imagines and imitating the deceased "in stature and carriage" (Polyb. 6. 53.6). This practice created a vivid tableau of Roman history and the individual family's place within it, with the children advertising its continuity.

Certain public rites performed for the preservation of the whole community sometimes were entrusted to children, usually as participants in choruses. For example, Augustus commissioned the poet Horace to compose a hymn for one such choral performance in honor of the Secular Games in 17 BCE, featuring a mixed group of 27 boys and 27 girls. Boys and girls also helped the Vestal Virgins sprinkle the area of the temple of Vesta with water. Prepubescent girls could also act as an assistant to priests and other acolytes carrying out rituals, usually sacrifice, at home or at public ceremonies. More often this job fell to boys, but we do have visual evidence of girls acting in this capacity, often depicted holding an incense box. Daughters also assisted in family cult. Tibullus (c. 55–19 BCE) describes a man's little daughter bringing a honeycomb to his Lares (1.10.23–4). They may have also brought some of their family's ancestral images with them when they married.

A handful of Roman wall paintings from private residences from the first century CE offer an enigmatic glimpse into the neglected role of girls in Roman religion. Several landscapes show mother–daughter pairs approaching, or standing in front of, a statue and altar or a temple, performing religious duties. In contrast, boys are never depicted in these contexts. Some scenes may represent women participating in the Feralia, a holiday that featured ceremonies that honored the dead, such as offerings at the grave. Others indicate that mothers and daughters cared for gardens outside the city, where Priapus reigned as the god of health and fertility. These landscape paintings suggest that girls regularly participated in religious rituals outside the house as they accompanied their mothers in sacred groves and rural temples.

10.7   Educating Girls

Elite Roman girls received an education similar to that of their brothers, at least in the early stages. The purpose of this education, however, was to prepare them for their future lives as wives and mothers, not for political advancement. We know from Cicero that Attica, the little girl mentioned in the epigraph cited previously and the only daughter of his friend, Atticus, had a broad knowledge of literature. From the late Republic onward, most, if not all, upper-class girls were educated to have at least basic literacy. Some girls went on to the next stage, instruction by a grammarian, either attending school or learning at home until puberty. Although it is impossible to gauge how many girls received both a primary and secondary education, the idea does not appear to have been considered extraordinary. The Roman philosopher Musonius Rufus (first century CE) argues that females have the same intellectual capabilities as males and that "daughters should have the same education as sons." A broad liberal education was necessary for both sexes among the Roman elite because of its importance to Roman cultural life in which women actively participated. There are many images of women reading and writing in Roman art. A first-century CE wall painting from Pompeii depicts a young girl writing (Figure 10.4). She holds a two-board book, or diptych, in her left hand and holds a pen thoughtfully to her lip in her right.

Roman mothers are credited with guiding the educational and career choices of their children. They supervised the moral and intellectual education of both sexes when young, but focused on that of their daughters thereafter. In a letter to his grieving mother, Seneca (c. 4 BCE–65 CE) urges her to act as a maternal surrogate to his motherless niece, not only as a source of comfort but also to help guide her moral education:

Figure 10.4 Two girls, one holding a stylus and tablet, first century CE, Pompeii. Naples, Museo Archeologico, inv. 9074.

Take this opportunity to form and shape her character; principles that are learned at a tender age sink in more deeply. Let her become accustomed to hearing your discourses; let her character be molded according to your judgment; you will give her much even if you give her nothing but your example. This recurring duty will be a remedy in itself; for only philosophy or a respected occupation can turn from anxiety a heart that sorrows from affection. (Sen. *Helv.* 18.8)

Fathers took a strong interest in the education of their sons, sometimes even providing instruction. One of the most important aspects of the curriculum for both girls and boys was learning to speak and read ancient Greek. Pompey's daughter, Pompeia, received a thorough education in Greek and Latin literature from a private tutor. According to Plutarch, at the age of 9 she recited aloud a passage from Homer to her father upon his return from conquests in the Greek east in 62/61 BCE: "The tutor of his daughter arranged a demonstration of her progress: after a book was brought, he gave the child the following line to start from: 'You came back from the war; I wish you had died there'" (Plut. *Mor.* 9.1.3). The passage seems a poor choice given that it alludes to a line from the *Iliad* in which Helen rebukes Paris for his cowardice. Elite girls would have had access to large private libraries, such as that found in the Villa of the Papyri in Herculaneum, a town near Pompeii also destroyed by the eruption of Mt. Vesuvius in 79 CE. The interplay between public and private space in the Roman villa further supports the idea that girls would have come into contact with resident scholars, visiting poets and intellectuals, poetry readings, and other cultural events at home. Nonetheless, they did not advance to the third and final stage of Roman education, rhetorical training, which prepared their brothers for political careers.

Because girls married in their early or mid-teens, when their brothers were only about half-way finished with the second stage of their education, the grammar course, they could not complete their education before marriage. On her wedding day, a girl was likely only half as educated as her much older husband. If she married older, around age eighteen, she might have been able to finish her education in grammar. Sadly, Minicia Marcella, with whom this chapter started, probably had not advanced very far in the grammatical curriculum, given that she died at age 12. But she is an example of the kind of education an elite Roman girl might have received. Her father, Minicius Fundanus, was interested in philosophy and the liberal arts. Having no sons, he took pains to educate both Minicia and her elder sister. They probably learned not only the grammatical curriculum but possibly also philosophy and math. Minicius Fundanus engaged private tutors for them for their elementary education and specialized instructors for their advanced studies. They had access to books, possibly from their father's library, and they may have been present at conversations between him and Pliny. Although he praises her intelligence and studiousness, he pays far more attention to her moral qualities, particularly her affectionate nature, modesty, and self-restraint, the main virtues of a Roman matron. Instead of producing philosophers, poets, and politicians, a female education aimed to transform the Roman girl into a dignified matron, a chaste and agreeable wife, a competent household manager, and a good mother capable of guiding her children and grandchildren through her example.

10.8 Conclusion

Romans began to socialize children into their adult gender roles at birth. A baby girl first had to survive the critical first days after birth to become a member of the family at the naming ceremony. She received only one or two names, the primary one derived from that of her father, and so became less individuated than her brothers. Whereas he wore the bulla symbolizing his status as a free Roman, she probably did not. Her family would have consisted of only one or two siblings, possibly far apart in age, and assorted half- and stepsiblings. In his capacity as paterfamilias, her father controlled all property and made all of the decisions related to the family, including whether to rear a newborn. At home, a Roman girl learned to spin and weave, following the ancient custom, but did not expect to make an economic contribution to the family through this craft. By the early empire, the task of spinning and weaving for elite Roman women seems to have become largely symbolic and less an economic necessity. She also learned how to read and write and might even have received a broad liberal education that included the study of ancient Greek, mathematics, and philosophy. She could attend school in town or be tutored at home, at first learning the same curriculum as her brother. Once she approached puberty, however, she set aside formal education and prepared for marriage. The example of Minicia Marcella demonstrates that despite her intelligence and seriousness about her studies, the main goal of her education was the cultivation of the moral characteristics appropriate for life as an aristocratic Roman matron. We also saw how the literary and historical records diverge in the example of dolls. Although girls are often absent in literary texts, we get a glimpse of them through the contents of their sarcophagi, in Roman wall paintings and funerary epitaphs, which, although generic in content, often contain small details about their lived reality such as their age at death. Lastly, this chapter noted two other major differences between Greek and Roman cultures. One is the organization of Roman domestic space, which did not seclude women in a private quarter. Rather all family members, including slaves, mingled in the public spaces of the household, particularly in the atrium. Another is the frequency of divorce and adoption, leading to a more fluid family structure and a weaker attachment to the physical space of the house.

Questions for Review

1   What are some of the characteristics the Romans valued in girls?

2   What is a manus marriage and how did it affect the structure of the Roman family?

3   What were the main rooms in a Roman house and how were they used?

4   What are some of the ways the Romans shaped gender identity in early childhood?

5   What kind of education did Roman girls receive?

Reference

Kamm, Anthony (2006). *Julius Caesar: A Life*. London and New York: Routlege.

Further Reading

Primary Sources

Cicero, *Letters to Atticus* 13.12–13, 15, 17–19, 21, 27, 44, 49, 51; 15, 16.11
Pliny the Younger, *Letters* 5.16

Secondary Sources

3D Animation Reconstructs an Upper-Class House of Pompeii Before the Vesuvius Disaster. http://www.realmofhistory.com/2016/10/05/3d-animation-reconstructs-pompeii-house (accessed 14 October 2018).

Dixon, Suzanne (1992). *The Roman Family*. Baltimore, Maryland: The Johns Hopkins University Press. A broad overview of the Roman family that begins with problems of evidence, then explores what the concept of the "family" really meant and how it functioned. Other topics include the legal status of the family, marriage, children, aging, and death.

Gardner, Jane and Thomas Wiedemann (1991). *The Roman Household: A Sourcebook*. London and New York: Routledge. Short primary sources translated into English that deal with the economics of the family, the life course, inheritance, and emotions. The authors provide informative introductions to each passage.

Laes, Christian (2011). *Children in the Roman Empire: Outsiders Within*. Cambridge: Cambridge University Press. Traces the invisible children in the Roman empire from a wide variety of sources, including literature and inscriptions, archeology, and iconography.

Rawson, Beryl (2003). *Children and Childhood in Roman Italy*. Oxford: Oxford University Press. A comprehensive analysis of sources on children in ancient Rome, including a strong chapter on education.

Wallace-Hadrill, Andrew (1994). *Houses and Society in Pompeii and Herculaneum*. Princeton, NJ: Princeton University Press. Provides valuable insights into Roman social life through an exploration of houses preserved by the eruption of Mt. Vesuvius, showing the interconnectedness of public and private, work and leisure, family and outsiders.

11

Female Adolescence in Rome

Now with manly courage (*virtus*) held in such esteem, women too were moved to seek public honors. The maiden (*virgo*) Cloelia, one of the hostages, deceived the guards and, leading a band of maidens (*virginum*), swam across the Tiber amid a shower of enemy spears, since the Etruscan camp was located not far from the bank of the Tiber. She restored all the girls, unhurt, to their families in Rome. When this news was brought to the Etruscan king, he was at first consumed with anger; he sent messengers to Rome to demand the hostage Cloelia – the other girls were of no significance to him. Later, having changed to admiration of her courage, he said that her deed was greater than those of Horatius and Mucius.

(Livy 2.13.6–8)

This snippet of a much longer myth introduces Cloelia, an unmarried teenage girl, as a defender not only of Rome but also of virginity. Her story belongs to the period of struggle just after the foundation of the Roman Republic, when Lars Porsena, an ally of Tarquinius Superbus, allegedly attempted to help the Etruscans regain the throne by laying siege to the city. According to Livy, the bravery of the Romans so impressed Porsena that he decided to make a truce. In exchange, he asked for young girls and boys of the leading Roman families to be sent as hostages. Inspired by examples of male courage, Cloelia imitates their heroism by eluding the enemy and rescuing her female companions from the threat of sexual violence. Given a second opportunity to rescue some of the remaining hostages, she chooses the others most vulnerable to sexual assault, the young boys. Styled as a "manly maiden" in the literary tradition, which stresses her masculine courage, her patriotism, her leadership, and her public commemoration, Cloelia recalls the heroic virgins of Greek myth like Antigone and Iphigenia. But this story differs in its distinct emphasis on virginity: Cloelia not only preserves her own chastity, she protects that of the other elite children, defending the principle of physical inviolability for all free Romans. Like those of Lucretia and Verginia, this historical fiction links the threat of sexual assault, particularly against women, to a moment of political upheaval and civic danger. This discourse about exemplary Roman women whose actions contributed to the foundation of Rome and its stability had an ideological function as well, reinforcing Roman values and encouraging proper conduct through imitation. The myth of Cloelia helps to understand how the Romans constructed female adolescence. As a legendary example, she demonstrates the importance of virginity and its protection from ruin at all costs for upper-class Roman girls. Praised as a virgo who shows virtus, "a virgin greater than men," Cloelia's masculine courage does not conflict with but rather facilitates her transition to Roman womanhood. This chapter explores Roman conceptions of female adolescence, particularly how expectations about virginity, the female body, and education prepared them for marriage and motherhood, culminating with a discussion of a Roman wedding.

Women in Classical Antiquity: From Birth to Death, First Edition. Laura K. McClure.

Let us consider first the Latin terminology for unmarried females, because the terms puella, the primary term for "girl" and the subject of the last chapter, and virgo, literally "virgin," are often used interchangeably in Roman texts. This lack of sharp distinction points to the virtual absence of adolescence as a life stage for Roman girls, because physical maturation and first menarche often coincided with, or in some cases even followed, marriage. We may remember that Minicia Marcella, the subject of Pliny's letter to Fundanus that introduced the last chapter, was about to be married when she died just before reaching her thirteenth birthday. The letter, however, emphasizes her status as a puella and daughter still dependent upon her father. In poem 61 of Catullus, a wedding song discussed more fully at the end of this chapter, the young bride, Junia, is interchangeably called a puella and virgo. Livy similarly refers to the plebeian maiden Verginia with both terms, although he places more emphasis on her status as a virgo, "now in the bloom of her youth and beauty" (Livy 3.44). This description suggests a degree of physical maturity that signals a girl's marriageability, sexual attractiveness, and reproductive capacity. In Latin love elegy, the term puella has sexual overtones, because it refers to a female who takes on multiple love affairs instead of marriage and whose beauty and literary sophistication are irresistible to the male poet. We meet a few of these women in Chapter 13. The association of female adolescence with physical development, sexual attractiveness, and sexual desire posed a challenge to the preservation of virginity, especially given that Romans girls were not confined to the house, did not veil themselves, and frequently came into contact with men to whom they were not related. Roman elites responded to this problem in a number of ways, including punishment for premarital sex, dietary restrictions and exercise to regulate desire, and bringing adolescence to a swift end through early marriage.

11.1 *Pudicitia*: Protecting Purity

Because the only career open to a Roman girl was marriage, her primary task, and that of her parents, was to preserve her chastity. Her lost virginity not only threatened her chances for marriage, it also damaged the reputation of her family. Because she could leave the house and wore her hair uncovered, a Roman girl was especially vulnerable to unwanted male attention. To prevent sexual harassment, she was expected to dress modestly, perhaps in special clothing that clearly signified her status as a marriageable, freeborn maiden. Such girls could be easily recognized and were visually distinct from women of other social classes:

> If someone accosted virgins, but they were dressed like slave girls, his offense seems lessened, and it is much less if women were not dressed as matrons but as prostitutes. So if a woman was not wearing the clothes of a respectable married woman and someone accosted her or lured her escort away, he is liable for damages. (Ulpian 47.10.15)

Here the writer recommends reducing the punishment of a rapist if there is any ambiguity about the girl's social status based on her clothing. In addition to modest dress, respectable girls were accompanied by a male chaperone who could ward off any unsolicited male attention when they left the house. Elite girls and young women, however, usually spent most their time in the company of other women, from whom they learned the qualities of decorum, modesty, and affection most likely to attract a good husband. A lovely fragment of a Roman fresco (Figure 11.1) depicts two graceful women, sitting close together and wearing elegant jewelry, their loose coiffures bound by a coil of hair. One could imagine they are a mother–daughter pair, with the older woman at right sitting close to the maiden at left, both wearing the garments of wealthy and respectable women. Her delicate dress calls attention to her beauty and desirability and her downcast gaze displays her modesty.

Figure 11.1 A fragment of a Roman fresco showing two elegant women, c. 1–75 CE. Malibu, California, Getty Museum, gift of Barbara and Lawrence Fleischman.

These external measures were reinforced internally for both girls and married women by the cultivation of sexual virtue of pudicitia to ensure that their purity remained uncorrupted. In a letter to his mother, Seneca calls this quality "The loveliest form of beauty… the greatest adornment." The term always refers to sexual behavior, whether applied to men or women. This concept shared similarities with the Greek aidos, although it differed in that it was a personal quality of married women that needed to be displayed and seen by others. Through her appearance and conduct, an elite Roman girl or wife protected her good name and reputation. In turn, she received public acknowledgment of her virtue, as we can see in this funerary inscription commissioned by a husband for his young wife:

> To the spirits of the dead, [Fannia] Sebotis, daughter of Publius. Quintus Minucius Marcellus, son of Quintus, of the Palatine tribe, to his most dear, most dutiful, most chaste wife, who never wanted to go out in public or to a bath or to any place at all without me, whom I led in marriage as a virgin of fourteen years, from whom I have a daughter, with whom I saw a sweet time of life, who made me happy, but I would prefer that you were alive. She was my happiness. If only I had left you surviving. She lived 21 years, 2 months, and 21 days. (*AE* 1987.179)

Married at 14, Fannia is identified first by her father and then by her husband. She is remembered for her sweetness, her devotion, and her chastity, which she vigilantly protected by never walking leaving the house without her husband, even though she could have (see Box 13.1). In fact, her premarital virginity was so important to her husband that he thought it worth mentioning on her gravestone. It's hard to imagine such a thing today! Possession of these virtues could in some cases make up for the lack of a dowry, whereas any hint of promiscuity turned potential suitors away. As the singular virtue of women, pudicitia is the female equivalent of the male virtus. Both required a sense of honor, fear of shame, and concern for reputation, as modeled by the figure of Lucretia. Their display met with public approbation and commemoration.

As discussed in the last chapter, the Roman state under Augustus attempted to regulate teenage sexuality. The emperor's law against adultery passed in 18 BCE not only penalized extramarital sex but also punished men who sexually assaulted, threatened, or harassed young girls and other vulnerable free persons. This crime falls under the general category of **stuprum**, a broad term applied to sexual misconduct, and considered damaging not only to the victim but also to her paterfamilias, who had the right to punish the violator, even if the girl had consented. Moreover, his power of life and death over family members meant that, in theory at least, the father could also commit violence against a daughter who had failed to maintain her virginity. Indeed, a father's response could be harsh. Recall the mythical Verginius' preemptive murder of his daughter, Verginia, to ensure she would not suffer shaming sexual assault at the hands of Appius Claudius. Valerius Maximus (early first century CE), in his discussion of pudicitia, describes fathers as the "strict guardians" of their daughters' virtue, citing as an example a knight who murdered both his daughter and a slave who had procured her for a seducer named Fannius Saturninus:

> No less strong-minded was Pontius Aufidianus, a Roman knight. Learning that his daughter's virginity had been betrayed to Fannius Saturninus by her tutor, he was not content to punish the rascally slave, he also killed the girl herself. Rather than celebrate a disgraceful marriage, he gave her an untimely funeral. (Val. Max. 6.1.3)

As in the case of Verginia, the paterfamilias rescues daughter and family alike from disgrace by a terrible act of domestic violence. It is very unlikely, however, that elite Roman fathers would have reacted in this way. A fictional legal case depicts a more sympathetic father who defends his reluctance to prosecute his daughter's rapist out of concern for her suffering:

> I am licking my wounds, rebuilding my household, lamenting the attack on my house, consoling my daughter for the loss of her virginity, guarding her when she threatens to take her own life. (Sen. *Controv.* 3.5)

Preserving the virginity of daughters was of utmost importance to Roman families, so important that commemoration of this virtue might follow a woman to her grave. But it must have been quite a challenge, given how many contexts in which girls could have encountered predatory males, whether walking to school or attending large public events outside the house, or at home, where they mingled freely with their father's friends and other men.

11.2 Medical Views of Female Adolescence

Early marriage was one popular strategy among upper-class Romans for ensuring a girl preserved her chastity until her wedding day. Some Imperial medical writers, however, had misgivings about this practice, citing the health risks to both mother and baby. Soranus (first-second century CE) and Rufus of Ephesus (c. late first century CE) took a special interest in female maturation and its health consequences, focusing, like their Greek antecedents, on reproduction. To review, the Hippocratic authors thought that the female body produced an excess of blood in the transition to adolescence, which needed to be expelled in order to avoid debilitating problems or even death. The "cure" was sexual intercourse and pregnancy. By the time of the Roman empire, the Hippocratic corpus formed the core of ancient medical knowledge. But contemporary doctors diverged from the earlier tradition in the matter of the wandering womb. Thanks to the new scientific practice of dissection, it was now widely recognized that the womb was anchored to the body by ligaments and did not roam about freely.

Despite this anatomical discovery, Rufus in his *Regimen for Young Girls* follows tradition in viewing menstruation as harmful to the body, leading to sexual and maternal urges that may be remedied only by marriage:

> For the quicker she puts on weight, the quicker she becomes nubile, and the quicker her desire to have sexual relations and to produce children is aroused. It is because of this, more or less, that the law prescribes marrying young girls to older men. (Rufus, *CMG* 6.2.2)

Here medical doctrine rationalizes the social practices – early marriage for girls and the advanced age of their husbands – much like the prescriptions for pregnancy in the Hippocratic corpus. In contrast, Soranus in his *Gynecology* rejects the Hippocratic model of female adolescence, arguing that reproduction does not contribute to female health either at puberty or later. In his view, menarche is no more dangerous than any other life stage as the female body is considered capable of maintaining equilibrium on its own. He concludes,

> Virgins not yet menstruating would necessarily be less healthy [if menstruation were healthful]; if they enjoy perfect health, then menstruation does not contribute to being healthy, but is useful for childbearing only, for without menstruation, pregnancy does not happen. (Sor. *Gyn.* 1.29)

According to this theory, menstruation depletes the body whereas sexual intercourse and pregnancy prematurely age it. Permanent virginity, he argues, would put the least amount of stress on the female body, but he does not go so far as to recommend celibacy as the healthiest choice for women.

Rufus further recommends a change of diet for adolescent girls in preparation for marriage and motherhood:

> When they are older and growth has all but stopped, and [girls] out of modesty do not play childhood games anymore, then one must pay more attention to their regimen. Their consumption of food should be regulated and measured, and they should not touch any sort of meat or other very rich foods. (Rufus, *CMG* 6.2.2, 4.107 Raeder)

Although young girls are allowed wine, it is not recommended for the teenage girl in order to regulate her body and encourage self-control, as drinking wine is believed to encourage licentiousness. Rufus also prescribes low-impact exercise to guard against laziness:

> At this age, it is necessary to prescribe for girls long walks, and if there is no impediment, also to run and to exercise by rolling in the dust. It seems that the activities of the chorus were invented not only to honor the gods, but also with a view to health. There is double exercise in the chorus: one in the dancing and one in the singing. If girls play ball, this exercise is not insignificant nor unpleasant. In a word, we must find all kinds of exercises that are fitting for girls, and to think that idleness is the worst thing for them. For it is

advantageous to do exercises to put heat in the movement and to reheat the body, but in a way that it should remain feminine and not assume a masculine appearance. (Rufus, *CMG* 6.2.2)

Presumably it was common for Roman girls to engage not only in choral performances, like their Greek counterparts, but also in a number of physical activities that took place outside the house, as long as they were not too vigorous and did not masculinize their bodies. Why any girl would want to roll around in the dust is another question. Gentle exercise was also advised to facilitate menstruation prior to first intercourse:

Therefore her walk should be easy and deliberate, passive exercise prolonged, gymnastics not forced, much fat applied in the massage, a bath taken daily, and the mind diverted in every possible way. (Sor. *Gyn.* 1.5.25)

According to this view, being sedentary is considered unhealthy not only for girls but also for pregnant women, wet nurses, and those with uterine problems. The popularity of games and sports for adolescent girls is shown in a late Roman floor mosaic from Sicily. A detail (Figure 11.2) shows two girls playing ball in bikini-like outfits.

These prescriptions for female health potentially conflicted with social norms related to the age at first marriage for girls. Soranus implies that girls should marry at age 13 or 14, typically the age of menarche, and regards the childbearing years as extending from age 15 to 40. In contrast, Rufus argues, consonant with modern views, that "puberty is not a favorable time for childbearing, either for the child, or for its mother. The former is sure to be weak while the latter, distressed before her time, comes to grief and exhibits a damaged womb" (Rufus, *CMG*

Figure 11.2 Girls playing ball, detail from the Mosaic of the Ten Maidens, fourth century ce. Piazza Armerina, Sicily, Villa Romana del Casale.

6.2.2). He rejects the Hippocratic notion that intercourse and pregnancy facilitate female maturation. For this reason, he recommends that women marry in the fifth year after beginning to menstruate, that is, around the age of 18.

11.3 Age at First Marriage

Although these doctors argue that it is best for girls not to marry earlier than age 14, and preferably a few years older, upper-class Roman parents typically did not follow this advice. Marriages for girls could be arranged at a very early age as a means of forging alliances aimed at advancing male political careers and promoting the overall status of the family. Based on literary evidence, which mostly focuses on elite social practices, it has long been held that Roman girls married around the age of twelve. However, recent analyses of funerary inscriptions has challenged this view, suggesting that many girls married much later, possibly as late as their early twenties. Many wealthy Roman parents preferred to find a partner for their daughters as children, arranging for the marriage to take place before they reached the minimum legal age for marriage at 12. Cicero betrothed his "dear little Tullia" to her first husband when she was just 11 and married her off at age 15. His friend Atticus considered future husbands for his daughter when she was only 6 and then married her at age 14 to Marcus Agrippa, a man old enough to be her father. During the principate, Octavia, the daughter of the emperor Claudius, was married at the age of 11 (see Chart 10.1 for her family tree). Agrippina the Younger, Nero's mother, was 11 or 12. Minicia Marcella died on the eve of her wedding just before her thirteenth birthday. There are countless other examples that indicate marriage in the early teens regularly occurred for girls at the highest levels of Roman society. In contrast, their husbands were at least a decade older at first marriage, in their mid-to-late twenties, and some were much older. When Cicero married his second wife, the teenager Publilia, he was 60, old enough to be her grandfather. Pliny and Calpurnia were 40 and 14, respectively, when they wed. There was a material benefit to marrying a rich young wife. For Cicero, it was a means of getting out of debt: "You took as your second wife a virgin, though you were an old man, so that you could pay your debts out of her property" (Dio 46.18.3). Although common, such December-May marriages were frowned upon. And the disparity in age must have weakened the authority and independence of the young wife within the household.

The Romans seem to have been aware that early marriage in an age without reliable contraception posed considerable health risks for women. Pliny the Younger, for instance, attributed his wife Calpurnia's near-fatal miscarriage when she was just 14 to her youth and inexperience, as he explains in a letter to her grandfather:

> Your wish that we give you a great-grandchild cannot be greater than your sorrow will be to hear that she has had a miscarriage. She is young and inexperienced and did not realize that she was pregnant, so did not take proper care of herself, and even did some things she should not have done at all. She has learned a severe lesson and nearly paid for her mistake with her life. (Plin. *Ep.* 8.10; see also 8.11)

Funerary inscriptions further attest to the toll of pregnancy on the teenage body. Herennia Cervilla had already given birth to three children when she died at age 18:

> To the shades below. I, Herennia Cervilla, daughter of Lucius, wife, lived for eighteen years and thirty days. With three children left behind, I ended life in pain. My dear husband, while alive, set this up as a memorial to me, so that acquiring such an epitaph

would be beneficial in my funeral rites. Gaius Carrenas Verecundas to his peerless wife, who deserves it well. (*AE* 1985.355)

This epitaph raises the very real possibility that Herennia had borne her first child as early as age 12 or 13 and died in the process of giving birth to a fourth. A second-century CE epitaph on the sarcophagus of a 27-year-old woman states that she married at age 11:

> Here I lie, a married woman, Veturia is my name and descent, wife of Fortunatus, daughter of Veturius. I lived for three times nine years, wretched me, and I was married for twice eight. I slept with one man, I was married to one man. After having given birth to six children, with one surviving, I died. Titus Iulius Fortunatus, centurion of the second legion Adiutrix Pia Fidelis, erected this for his wife, who showed unequalled and extraordinary devotion to him. (*CIL* III 3572)

By her mid-twenties, Veturia had spent more than half her life as a wife and mother, residing with her husband for more years than her natal family. Within that time, she gave birth to six children and yet, sadly, saw only one survive. Given her near constant state of pregnancy and successive loss of babies, it is no wonder that she maintained complete sexual fidelity to her husband. She would have had little time and energy for other men. This lethal combination of teenage pregnancy and high fertility no doubt contributed in the end to her untimely death. From a modern perspective, we might consider the ancient Roman practice of early marriage to be a form of sexual exploitation or even child labor. This pattern of early marriage, high fertility, and high mortality reflects what must have been a common experience for Roman girls and provides a social context in which to understand many of the medical views and recommendations of Soranus and Rufus.

11.4 Adolescent Girls in Roman Religion

Although Roman girls played little role in state religion, the concept of virginity was enshrined and indeed worshipped through the priestly office of the Vestal Virgins. Although more attention is given to them in Chapter 14, it is relevant to the present discussion to note that they began their careers before puberty and maintained their virginity through their 30 years of service. At any given time, therefore, at least a third of the Vestals were teenage girls. Moreover, their pledge of celibacy effectively meant that they remained virgins for all but the last stage of the female life cycle. Another public task performed by virgins was the weaving of a ritual clothing worn by the *Flaminica*, the wife of the *Flamen Dialis*, the high priest of Jupiter, recalling the civic weaving of the arrhephori at Athens (see Chapter 3). The Flaminica served as a model for wifely virtue and is discussed more fully in Chapter 14. Roman girls also took part in choral performances both for exercise and on various religious occasions, together with boys and in segregated groups. During the Second Punic War, Livy states that 10 boys and 10 girls, all with both parents alive, were called upon to perform prayers for the state (Livy 37.3). On another occasion, after a series of terrible prodigies, including an intersex infant born "the size of a four-year old," the pontiffs ordered 27 virgins to sing a hymn composed by Livius Andronicus. While they were rehearsing, the temple of Juno was struck by lightning. After the soothsayers determined this last portent pertained to matrons, it was decided that a select group should contribute part of their dowries to appease the goddess of marriage (Livy 27.37.1–12). The use of maidens to respond to portents of monstrous birth makes a certain kind of religious sense. On the brink of marriage, their purity and latent sexuality counteracts a portent of aberrant fertility by ensuring the proper guidance of human reproduction by the goddess.

11.5 Virgo Docta

The first part of this chapter looked at several different constructions of female adolescence at Rome: the manly and mythical maiden who risks her life to preserve her own virginity and that of her companions; the modest, well-born girl who exhibits sexual self-control in the form of pudicitia, carefully defending herself from unwanted sexual advances through her dress and comportment; and the medical writer's teenager, who regulates sexual desire through diet and exercise. Another important face of female adolescence in Roman culture is the educated young woman or *virgo docta*. As we have seen, elite girls achieved at least basic literacy, and many learned much more, mastering the ancient Greek language and gaining extensive knowledge not only of the poetic tradition but also of philosophy and mathematics. This curriculum, however, stuck to safe subjects appropriate to girls. To be avoided in particular: erotic poetry. According to Martial (38–101 CE), only "easy" girls read his sexually explicit poetry. "Good" girls prefer the sanitized verse of his poetic rival:

> You write all your epigrams in chaste language, there is no cock in your poems. I admire, I commend. You are the purest of the pure. Whereas no page of mine lacks excess. These then let bad boys read and easy girls, and old men too, but one with a girlfriend to plague him. But *your* language, Cosconius, so respectable and pure, should be read by boys and maidens. (Mart. 3.69)

More appropriate for the "grown girl" (*grandis virgo*) were the genres of tragedy and epic. Acquaintance with such texts reflected refinement and literary appreciation. Such pursuits typically came to an abrupt end when a girl married, although some may have continued to be tutored by their husbands. Refusal to set aside these studies could tarnish the character of a well-born young woman either by associating her with actresses and courtesans, women known for their literary sophistication and easy virtue, or by branding her as arrogant and masculine.

A few young women, however, cast aside convention and read erotic poetry, and even composed their own verse. In doing so, they walked a fine line between reproof and approbation. In one of his poems written in exile, Ovid (43 BCE–17 CE) addresses a young female poet, whom he calls Perilla. Although some have speculated that the name is a pseudonym for his stepdaughter, Nerulla, we know nothing concrete about this girl. Throughout the poem, he is careful to portray her not as an independent and sexually desiring female, a convention of love elegy as we see in Chapter 14, but rather as a chaste, beautiful, marriageable virgo sitting at the side of her sweet mother:

> Are you too still devoted to our common pursuit of singing learned verse, though not in your father's way? For as well as beauty nature has given you modest (*pudicos*) ways and a rare dowry of talent. This I was the first to guide to the stream of Pegasus so that the course of fertile water would not unhappily be lost. I was the first to see this in the tender years of your maidenhood *(virginis)* when, as a father to his daughter, I was your guide and companion. So if the same fire still resides in your breast, only Sappho will surpass your work. (Ov. *Trist.* 3.7.12–18)

By speaking of Perilla's poetic talent as a "rare dowry," the poet likens her to a bride and assimilates her poetic pursuit to marriage. Ovid further situates this shared poetic enterprise within the father–daughter dynamic in which he seeks to protect her modesty, whether alluding to himself as the metaphorical father of her poetry or as her actual father. He contrasts his erotic poetry with her own virtuous verse and further cautions her against following his example,

Figure 11.3 Portrait of a young woman holding a stylus and tablet, Pompeii, c. 55–69 CE. Naples, Museo Archeologico Nazionale, 9084.

"Only let no woman or any man learn from your writings how to love" (Ov. *Trist.* 3.7.29–30). Despite her gender, Perilla's considerable poetic talent engages one of the most important poetic minds of the time without compromising her modesty. The so-called Sappho portrait from Pompeii (Figure 11.3) provides a visual analog for these aspiring female poets. A wealthy young Pompeiian woman, as indicated by a rare golden hairnet, large gold earrings, and prominent ring on her left ring finger, touches a stylus pensively to her mouth and holds wax tablets in her left hand.

Whereas we know nothing certain about "Perilla" nor has any of her work survived, if indeed it ever existed, we do have the slender remains of the only female writer of Latin poetry whose work is, at least partly, preserved. Six short elegies of Sulpicia (late first century BCE), amounting to all of 40 lines, have come down to us as part of the corpus of the poet Tibullus. Although dismissed for years as the product of an unskilled amateur, her work has become more fully appreciated in recent years. As depicted in the elegies, Sulpicia is an unmarried teenage girl from a very distinguished and highly educated senatorial family. She has been identified as the daughter of Servius Sulpicius Rufus who lived during the reign of Augustus. Her father was an accomplished orator who wrote love poetry in his free time and her maternal uncle, Messalla Corvinus, who may have later served as her – rather unreliable – guardian, was a literary patron of Tibullus and casual writer of erotic poetry. This lineage may explain the survival of her six poems, which explore Sulpicia's passion for a man whom she calls "Cerinthus," a pseudonym in keeping with the conventions of love elegy. What is striking is her frank acknowledgment of passion and willing participation in an illicit affair, despite being a teenage girl from an illustrious family:

> At last the love I've waited for has come. (No shame to say so: more so to cover up). My Muse called on her in prayer, and Cytherea brought him to my heart. Venus kept her promise: now she can tell my tale of joy to those who don't believe. I hardly want to give

this letter up so no one else sees it before he does. I'm glad I broke the rules and slept with him – for I hate to wear a mask of respectability, as if he wasn't good enough for me! (Tib. 3.13)

This poem no doubt would have shocked the original readers given the value the Romans placed on virginity for elite girls, especially the last couple of lines in which Sulpicia boldly proclaims to the world that she has consummated her affair with Cerinthus. Another poem takes her lover to task for consorting with a prostitute, reminding him that he has exchanged the high-class Sulpicia, "daughter of Servius," for a common whore. Purported to be written by a respectable virgo on the cusp of marriage, the elegies of Sulpicia unite the two conflicting aspects of female adolescence: the respected, literate, and literary aristocratic maiden and the promiscuous, educated girlfriend/muse of love elegy, discussed in more detail in Chapter 13. The sexual nature of this poetry led to the view that Sulpicia is not actually the author of these erotic poems but rather the recipient. According to this interpretation, they function as a sort of epithalamium composed on the occasion of Sulpicia's wedding imitating the ribaldry of the songs that accompanied the ceremony.

11.6   The Roman Wedding

"Let me be read by a girl (*virgo*) who warms to her betrothed." (Ov. *Am.* 2.1.5)

With this line, Ovid offers to instruct an engaged, sexually inexperienced young woman in the art of love. This tension between the purity and sexuality of the virgo is a common motif in love elegy, as we saw previously, and also a staple of epithalamia or wedding songs explored in this section. The process of socially constructing the sexuality of the bride and future wife began with betrothal. As in Greece, a legal marriage was necessary to ensure the legitimacy of offspring. It required the man and woman to be Roman citizens, to have reached puberty, and to not be closely related by blood. Once these requirements had been met, both fathers and the future bride and groom had to give their consent. All parties were required to be old enough to understand the meaning of consent, which the Roman legal writers set at age seven. The wedding itself, however, could not take place until the bride reached 12, the minimum legal age of marriage. After completing these negotiations, the man offered his **sponsa** ("fiancée") a ring. Many examples of these rings have been excavated from sites around the Roman empire, some featuring clasped hands, a symbol of marriage, or bearing the name of the fiancé, such as "Filetus," the name inscribed on Crepereia's ring (see Box 10.1). The girl's father might host a party to celebrate the engagement, using it as an opportunity to advertise the new alliance.

Although it was the legal responsibility of the paterfamilias to find a suitable husband for his daughter, in reality the search involved an extended network of family members and friends, with women playing an active role. For example, when Cicero had to leave Rome for a provincial appointment in 51 BCE, he allowed his wife, Terentia, and daughter, Tullia, to select a new husband for her. Because it took three months for a letter to get to Rome and back from his post in Cilicia, the final decision rested with the women, who in the end picked none of his top choices. His remark that Tullia might reject one of the prospective candidates further underscores that she had a say in the matter. Of course, she was by then 27 years old and about to marry her third husband. Similarly, Aemilia, the wife of Scipio Africanus, upbraided her husband for not consulting her about the betrothal of their daughter, Cornelia, to Tiberius Gracchus. Social status and wealth were the main factors in selecting a husband, along with character, good health, and looks, "as a sort of just return for a bride's virginity"(Plin. *Ep.* 1.14).

An ambitious father would hope to use his daughter's marriage to gain for himself powerful allies. The right son-in-law might even bring him a consulship.

Roman marriage did not involve the state nor did it require a ceremony or a specific set of rituals. As in Greece, the main event was the transfer of the girl from her father's house to that of her husband. The groom did not even need to be present when she arrived; indeed, he might be away on military campaign or hold an official position abroad, as was often the case. Because consent comprised the legal basis for a Roman marriage, the wedding ceremony largely fulfilled a social purpose. Whereas males marked their transition to adulthood by removing the bulla and exchanging the toga praetexta for the white toga of the Roman citizen, females did not have a distinct and consistent ritual apart from marriage. The wedding, therefore, allowed for the public recognition of a girl's transformation from child to adult.

Like many aspects of female life, the Roman wedding and its rituals are not well documented in either literary or visual evidence, a fact that in part reflects the male bias of the sources. However, it is possible to reconstruct the basic framework of the Roman wedding by consulting works as diverse as literary epithalamia, writings by historians and antiquarians, and Roman art. Like her brother, a girl signaled her transition from virgo to matrona by a change of garments. She may have relinquished the toga praetexta before her wedding and bound her hair with a special type of woolen band. She also put aside her toys and childhood clothing. Various sources describe the dedication of dolls to Venus, "little togas" to the goddess Fortuna, and other objects, such as soft balls, hairnets, and breast bands, to the family gods. Roman girls about to marry thus engaged in dedicatory rituals similar to their Greek counterparts to mark the end of childhood and the transition to adulthood.

At the wedding, the focus was on the bride and her female attendants, who helped dress her and assisted with the various rituals. Then as now, special clothing advertised the young woman's transitional social and sexual status. The night before her wedding, she put on a simple, white woolen garment called the ***tunica recta*** and a yellow hairnet that she had woven herself on an upright loom as proof of her domestic skills. The Romans traced this practice back to the Etruscan queen, Tanaquil, who was thought to have been the first woman to weave this type of garment. A belt tied in a complicated knot, to be undone by her husband on the wedding night, may have cinched the tunic. This knot both symbolized the well-guarded virginity of the bride as well as hinted at her as yet unrealized sexuality. On the wedding day, the hairnet was dedicated to the Lares and replaced by a veil. The bride wore a special hairstyle, called the ***sex crines*** ("six tresses"). Parted with a spear, the hair was divided into six locks or braids and then bound by woolen ribbons. Ancient authors like Plutarch connected the spear to the practice of bride capture and the myth of the Sabine women. This custom seems to have been adopted from the Vestal Virgins, who also wore this archaic hairstyle. On top rested a crown of flowers that the girl had picked herself. The primary signifier of the Roman wedding, however, was the ***flammeum***, or bridal veil. It is the most consistently mentioned item of bridal adornment for Roman women over the centuries. It was probably constructed of a thin, transparent fabric and had a distinctive color, which has been much debated. Whether the color was pink, red, or a deep saffron, its hue, texture, and large size set it apart from everyday head coverings of the matron. Based on visual evidence, the top edge of the flammeum was pulled down over the bride's head to cover her eyes, and the side and back trailed down to her feet, covering most of her body.

On a symbolic level, the bride's adornment both affirmed her virginity as the most precious gift she could give her new husband as well as connected her with important Roman institutions and values. The flammeum and the sex crines alluded to the two most visible female priestly offices in the city of Rome, the Vestal Virgins and the Flaminica, wife of the priest of Jupiter. The woven tunic pointed to her industry and domestic skills. The complicated knot of the belt and the crown of flowers denoted fertility. Her special hairstyle, the woolen ribbons that tied it, and the belt advertised her purity, and the veil evoked maidenly modesty. In contrast to Greek ideas about the bride, many of these symbols reinforced a unique sense of Roman identity related to the Italian soil and Etruscan and Sabine legend. These symbols provided proof of the sheltered upbringing that successfully protected her virginity until marriage and confirmed her readiness to fulfill the legal objective of marriage, the birth of legitimate children and future citizens of the Roman state.

The wedding procession started at the house of the bride, which was decorated with garlands and wreaths, as was that of the groom. The man and woman were brought together and their hands joined by a woman called the ***pronuba***. This woman may have had multiple functions, such as leading the bride to the groom, helping the bride over the threshold of her new house, and carrying torches. The earliest example of a pronuba in Roman literature is Cleustrata in Plautus' *Casina*, who advises the "bride" – in reality a male slave disguised by a head-to-toe flammeum – how to get control over her new husband:

> Raise your feet above the threshold gently, my new bride. Begin this journey safely, so that you will always stand above your husband and so that your power will be greater and you will have the upper hand over your husband and be victorious, and so that your voice and your command will be stronger. Your husband shall clothe you, you shall plunder him. By night and by day you shall trick your husband; remember that, I beg you. (Plaut. *Cas.* 815–24)

Here the pronuba instructs the "bride" in the wedding rituals and acts as an experienced female advisor.

The next stage involved the leading of the bride to her new home. This was a formal, public recognition of the marriage. The trajectory of the wedding connected it to other public processions, such as the Roman funeral and the triumph. These occasions provided an opportunity to showcase the wealth and status of the individual and the family. An epithalamium by Catullus, poem 61, offers the most comprehensive account of the procession of Roman bride to her husband's home in its celebration of the marriage of Junia and Manlius. Junia is the center of attention, but before she appears, the god of marriage, Hymen, is asked to come forth in the costume of a bride, wreathing his head with marjoram, veiling himself, and wearing dainty yellow slippers on snow-white feet. Like Junia, the figure of Hymen combines maidenly innocence with sexuality because he oversees the consummation of the marriage. Functioning more as a kidnapper than guide, he snatches the girl away from her family, "You gave the flower of a little girl from the embrace of her mother into the hands of a passionate youth" (Catull. 61.56–9).

As the bride weeps at the door of her parents' house, the poet invites her to join the procession: "She weeps that she must go; don't cry…come forth, new bride, if it is now your will, and listen to our words" (Catull. 61.80–94). Junia's reluctance confirms her pure and sheltered life among women. He then praises her beauty and virginity, comparing her to a hyacinth, the flower Persephone plucks from the ground when Hades abducts her, and states that her husband will be faithful to her because of her exceptional beauty. After seeing the flammeum approach, the poet calls for torches, songs to the marriage god, lewd jokes, and the distribution of nuts. The reference to humor refers to a ritual form of scurrilous verse perhaps meant to embarrass the bride with its sexual content. Elsewhere we are told that the crowd of guests cried out "Fortuna" or "Talassio!" during the procession. The latter commemorated the abduction of the Sabines as well as possibly promised the bride's skill at wool working.

Once arrived at her husband's house, the bride anointed the doorframe with oil and woolen ribbons and was lifted over the threshold by her attendants. "Lift across the threshold with a good omen your golden feet, and enter within the polished door" (Catull. 61.159–60).

The groom offered her fire and water, two elements fundamental to life and the Roman house and denied to those in exile. Acceptance of these elements effects the transformation of the girl from bride to wife (Ov. *Fast.* 785–92). Plutarch speculates as to the meaning of this custom:

> Is it that of these two, being reckoned as elements or first principles, fire is masculine and water feminine, and fire supplies the beginnings of motion and water the function of the subsistent element or the material? Or is it because fire purifies and water cleanses, and a married woman must remain pure and clean? Or is it that, just as fire without moisture is unsustaining and arid, and water without heat is unproductive and inactive, so also male and female apart from each other are inert, but their union in marriage produces the perfection of their life together? Or is it that they must not desert each other, but must share together every sort of fortune, even if they are destined to have nothing other than fire and water to share with each other? (Plut. *Quaest. Rom.* 1)

Clearly, Plutarch thought that even the Romans themselves did not fully grasp the meaning and origins of this obscure nuptial rite. A nuptial couch, probably for symbolic purposes only, was set up on the atrium and the couple retired to a cubiculum where the marriage was consummated. Martial crudely speculates about the challenges of the wedding night for a groom more interested in sex with men than women. He advises him to practice with a female prostitute to prepare for his new wife:

> Practice feminine embraces, Victor, do, and let your cock learn a trade unknown to it. The veils are being woven for your fiancée, the girl is already being dressed, soon the newlywed will be cropping your boys. She will let her eager spouse sodomize her once, while she fears the first wound of the new lance, but her nurse and her mother will forbid its happening often and say: "She's your wife, not your boy." Ah what embarrassments, what ordeals you will suffer if a vagina is something foreign to you! Therefore hand yourself over as a novice to an instructress in Subura. She will make a man of you. A virgin is a poor teacher. (Mart. 11.78)

The epigram underscores the sexual double standard for men and women: the groom is expected to be sexually experienced before marriage, so that he can teach his sheltered, virginal wife. At the same time, it underscores that certain sexual practices, such as oral and anal sex, were off limits with respectable women and could be monitored by intimates of the bride. A pair of wall paintings from the Villa Farnesina (see Box 11.1), constructed for Agrippa and Julia, daughter of Augustus, in 21 BCE, appear to depict the wedding night of a newly married couple. In the left-hand panel (Figure 11.4), a fully dressed young woman, probably the bride, sits to the right of her unclad, and possibly much older, husband as he pulls her to him on the bed. Her downcast gaze expresses modesty and even reluctance at what is to unfold. The adjacent panel (Figure 13.1) seems to reveal what happens next, as we see in Chapter 13.

Catullus 62 takes us from the procession into the groom's house to examine in more detail the bride's fear as she confronts the prospect of her wedding night. Such a response is understandable given the emphasis on protecting virginity for elite Roman girls and their young age at first marriage. From a broader perspective, the poem addresses the challenge of reconciling the demand for female purity with the necessity of female desire. The first few stanzas celebrate the conclusion of a wedding feast and the arrival of a bride. A chorus of maidens enters and rebukes the evening star for removing daughters from their mothers' arms and handing them over to young men. This image of abduction underscores the passivity of the bride. The maidens liken themselves to flowers about to be picked, but they worry that losing their virginity will

Figure 11.4 A young married couple on a bed attended by a servant, Rome, Villa Farnesina, cubiculum D, c. 19 BCE. Rome, Palazzo Massimo alle Terme, inv. 1188. Photo Deutsches Archäologisches Institut, Rome, inst. Neg. 77–1295.

Box 11.1 Roman Wall Painting

Just as painted pottery is an important source for the study of women in ancient Greece, so, too, Roman wall paintings offer countless images of women and private life. Roman interiors were lavishly painted and stuccoed in a process that involved applying pigments to a coating of damp plaster. Once dried, the colors were permanently fixed, transforming the walls into brightly colored panels. Subjects include portraits, architectural features, gardens and animals, scenes from myth, and erotic encounters. Some rooms even contained 360° panoramas that transported the viewer from the confines of the room into an imaginary world. The painted garden fresco from the Villa of Livia, for example, depicts in lush detail numerous plant species and a variety of birds, even capturing the movement of the wind through the trees. Our richest evidence comes from cities such as Pompeii and Herculaeneum and suburban villas in Campania destroyed by the eruption of Mt. Vesuvius. The paintings have been classified according to four styles. The First Style (c. 200–60 BCE) mostly simulated costly building materials such as marble and masonry, gradually adding the figures of gods, mortals, and heroes. The Second Style emerged in the early first century BCE and attempted to replicate elaborate architectural forms in two dimensions by the skillful use of shading and perspective. Accomplished painters aimed to trick the eye, producing illusionist architecture and portraying objects like metal and glass vases in such a way as to seem real. The Third Style (27 BCE–20 CE) coincided with the reign of Augustus and rejected illusion in favor of greater ornamentation. Wall paintings from this period tend to consist of a single monochromatic background with elaborate vegetal and architectural elements framing a central panel of small figural and landscape scenes. The Fourth Style (20–79 CE) returns to monumental narrative painting, although still retaining the architectural details of the earlier style.

A lovely fragment of a panel from Campania (Figure 11.5) is a good example of the insight into lived female reality that can be gleaned from the frescos. One of four found in the palaestra of the Forum Baths at Herculaneum, it depicts in stunning detail three women at their toilette. A wealthy matron with upswept hair watches from the left side, with her right arm around the shoulders of a young girl. She touches her delicate bordered veil with her left hand and wears golden sandals on her crossed feet. A servant arranges the hair of an elegantly dressed young woman, whose nearly transparent tunic with elaborate border at the hem and golden buttons down her arms resembles descriptions of expensive Coan silk garments. On the right is a wooden tripod table beneath which stands a tall glass spouted jug, illustrating the artistic interest in rendering glassware.

Figure 11.5 Roman fresco depicting three women at their toilette, assisted by a servant at right, first century CE, Herculaneum. Naples, Museo Archeologico Nazionale. © Samuel Magal, Sites & Photos Ltd./ Bridgeman Images.

make them undesirable: "When she has lost her pure flower and her body has been polluted, she is not pleasing to boys or dear to girls" (Catull. 62.43–7). The male youths, in contrast, praise marriage as an arrangement between husbands and parents that strengthens ties between families. According to them, a girl owns only one-third of her virginity, whereas the other two-thirds belong to her parents. Both Catullus 61 and 62 explore the tension between female resistance to and desire for marriage, offering a female perspective as imagined by a male poet on the compulsory nature of marriage and sex.

11.7   Conclusion

Adolescence for Roman girls was brief, and in some cases, nonexistent. In contrast to their mothers, the lives of teenage girls were carefully regulated in order to protect their virginity. The priestly office of the Vestal Virgins and the exemplary stories of Cloelia and Verginia in Roman legend symbolically reinforced the requirement of female sexual purity. Virginity thus did not belong to the girl but rather to her parents, her future husband, and even to Rome itself. Loss of virginity could meet with a violent response from a girl's father and invariably harmed her chances for an advantageous match. Mechanisms to safeguard sexual innocence included modesty in conduct and appearance, regimens for diet and exercise, a carefully edited educational curriculum, and early marriage. Although contemporary medical writers warned against the dangers of teenage marriage and pregnancy, many elite Romans persisted in marrying their daughters off at a young age, some even before menarche, to men often decades older. This practice frequently resulted in early death for women with its toxic combination of teenage pregnancy and high fertility, as Roman funerary inscriptions attest. The figures of the young, unmarried female poet and the adolescent bride illustrate the tension between the competing demands for sexual purity and eroticism in the *virgo*. Despite these restrictions, there are glimmers that a girl might have had some say in her marriage partner, could express herself in poetry as the equal of men, and refuse sex acts she found degrading. In the next chapter, we turn to the formidable figure of the Roman matron, who in contrast to the *virgo*, could exercise quite a bit of power within the family and even affect politics outside of it.

Questions for Review

1   How did Roman parents go about guarding the chastity of their daughters?

2   What recommendations did doctors make to ensure the health of adolescent girls?

3   How did marrying a much older man affect a young bride in her first marriage?

4   Why was education considered dangerous for teenage girls?

5   How does the Roman wedding ceremony compare to that of the Greeks?

Further Reading

Primary Sources

Catullus, Poems 61 and 62
Ovid, *Tristia* 3.7, *Amores* 1.4
Rufus, *Regimen for Young Girls*
Sulpicia, *Love Elegies*

Secondary Sources

Caldwell, Lauren (2015). *Roman Girlhood and the Fashioning of Femininity*. Cambridge: Cambridge University Press.
     The only book-length scholarly study of girlhood in the early Roman empire that illuminates the restrictions placed on them as girls as evidenced by literary, epigraphic, medical, and legal sources.

Greene, Ellen (2005). *Women Poets in Greece and Rome.* Norman, OK: University of Oklahoma Press.
A collection of essays that explores the female literary tradition in classical antiquity, beginning with Sappho and including two chapters on the poetry of Sulpicia.

Harlow, Mary and Laurence, Ray (2002). *Growing Up and Growing Old in Ancient Rome: A Life Course Approach.* London and New York: Routledge.
Examines the impact of age in determining behavior across the Roman lifespan, starting with infancy and childhood and including a chapter on female adolescence and the transition to adulthood.

Hemelrijk, Emily (2004). *Matrona Docta: Educated Women in the Roman Élite from Cornelia to Julia Domna.* London and New York: Routledge.
A study of the education of upper-class Roman women from 200 BCE to 235 CE, with attention to women as literary patrons, female education and literary endeavors.

Hersch, Karen (2010). *The Roman Wedding: Ritual and Meaning in Antiquity.* Cambridge: Cambridge University Press.
A comprehensive and detailed account of the rituals that accompanied the Roman wedding ceremony and marked the female transition to adulthood, with special attention to how they reflect Roman ideals and values.

Laurence, Ray. "Four Sisters in Ancient Rome." YouTube: https://www.youtube.com/watch?v=RQMgLxVxsrw.
A short, animated film that imagines how Roman girls spent their days through a fictional family of sisters all named Domitia.

12

Roman Marriage and Motherhood

> Cornelia took charge of the children and the household, and showed herself so virtuous, so affectionate a mother, and so generous, that Tiberius was thought to have reasoned well when he elected to die instead of such a woman. For when Ptolemy the king offered to share his throne with her and sought her hand in marriage, she refused him. As a widow, she lost many of her children, but three survived; one daughter, who married Scipio the Younger, and two sons, Tiberius and Gaius, about whom I now write. Cornelia raised these sons with such ambition that although surely no other Romans were so well formed by nature, they were thought to owe their excellence more to education than to nature.
>
> (Plut. *Tib. Gracch.* 1.4)

The Romans glorified motherhood but not for the reasons one might expect. Cornelia, the mother of the Gracchi brothers, the plebeian political reformers discussed in Chapter 10, was considered the model of the devoted mother for centuries. Born around 190 BCE, she came from a distinguished patrician family as the daughter of the illustrious general, Scipio Africanus the Elder, who defeated Hannibal during the Second Punic War. She married the much older Tiberius Sempronius Gracchus, a member of an important plebeian family, sometime after her father's death in 183 BCE, and purportedly bore 12 children, but only three, two sons, Tiberius and Gaius, and a daughter, Sempronia – survived beyond childhood. After the death of her husband, she devoted herself to the education of her sons, surrounding herself with leading intellectuals of the day, many of them Greek, in her villa at Misenum on the bay of Naples.

Although it is impossible to know the historical Cornelia, the idealized, mythic version of our sources is nonetheless instructive. She brought to her marriage the tremendous prestige of the Scipio line and an enormous dowry. She was a loving wife so devoted to her husband that she never remarried after his death – even refusing a royal offer. Instead, she remained faithful to his memory, earning the coveted title of ***univira*** ("one-man woman"), because she had honored the bed in which her virginity had been lost, even after her husband's death. She was extraordinarily fertile, having given birth to numerous children. Despite her immense wealth, she preferred a simple life, eschewing elaborate display and costly adornment. In response to a woman who kept flaunting her jewelry, Cornelia is said to have pointed to her children and exclaimed, "These are *my* jewels!" (Val. Max. 4.4). Her famous sons were her greatest accomplishment and the source of her prestige. As a cultured Hellenist and accomplished prose stylist, Cornelia secured the best possible teachers of philosophy and oratory for them, rearing them "not so much in her lap as in her speech" (Cic. *Brut.* 211). Although controversial in her own time because of her sons' radical politics and her tendency to meddle, she was to become one of Rome's most celebrated mothers not only because of their fame but also because of her skill at shaping their characters and careers.

Women in Classical Antiquity: From Birth to Death, First Edition. Laura K. McClure.
© 2020 John Wiley & Sons, Inc. Published 2020 by John Wiley & Sons, Inc.

A century after her death, Augustus placed a bronze statue of Cornelia inscribed with the words, "Cornelia, mother of the Gracchi," in the colonnade he built for his sister, Octavia, as a reminder for upper-class Roman women. The rare commemoration of a woman in the form of a public statue attests to the significance of motherhood in the cultivation of citizen sons under the new regime. It also reflects the emperor's new laws on marriage and adultery that attempted to encourage the rearing of children and harshly penalized the childless, the unmarried, and the sexually profligate. Horace explicitly links this legislation to motherhood in the choral poem commissioned by Augustus for the Secular Games in 17 BCE: "Goddess of childbirth, bring forth offspring, and grant success to the Senate's edicts on the yoking together of men and women and on the marriage law for raising a new crop of children" (Hor. *Carm. saec.* 13–17). The statue of Cornelia reinforced this agenda, as did the public representations of women on the Altar of Peace, the Augustan monument to which we have returned several times.

The altar's reliefs are dominated by images of fertility and family, including depictions of women and children, which are extremely rare in Roman art. Livia, the wife of Augustus, appears dressed in a garland and veil on the south wall of the altar (Figure 12.1), her hand resting on the head of a small child, probably one of her two sons. She is the only other mortal besides Augustus on the monument's reliefs to be dressed in such a way, compelling the viewer to connect her visually to her husband. Combining familial, religious, and civic roles, Livia embodies a new form of motherhood. On the east side of the altar screen, a central, seated

Figure 12.1 Detail of the south frieze the Altar of Peace, with Livia veiled and garlanded at right. 9 CE. Rome, Museo dell'Ara Pacis. Roger Viollet/Getty Images.

female figure holds two male infants in her lap as if to suckle them, surrounded by lush vegetation. Whether the personification of Peace, Italy, or a representation of Venus, the figure symbolizes female fertility and abundance and its importance to the continuity and stability of the principate. Augustus elevated the status of Livia by adopting her into the Julian clan and granting her the title of Augusta in an attempt to give her a formal public role. The senate responded by voting that she be given the title of "mother of the country," the equivalent of the honorific title "father of the country" previously granted to Cicero, Julius Caesar, and, of course, Augustus himself. This astonishing move illustrates how central motherhood had become to the Roman conception of the state during the principate.

Almost 50 years after the dedication of the Altar of Peace, we find another extended portrayal of an exemplary Roman mother one of Seneca's letters to his mother, Helvia, written to comfort her during his exile from Rome. They are the only literary texts addressed by an ancient author to his own mother. Seneca praises her for her simplicity, her pride in her children, and her disdain for cosmetics and lavish adornment, all of which reflect the virtue of matronly pudicitia:

> Nor has the greatest evil of our age, immodesty (*impudicitia*), classed you with the majority of women. Neither gems nor pearls have moved you. Wealth to you does not shine as the greatest good for humans. The imitation of inferior women, dangerous even to the upright, has not diverted you, raised as you were in an old-fashioned and strict household. You have never been embarrassed by your fertility, as if it were a reproach to your youth. You never tried to conceal your swelling womb – as if an obscene burden – like other women, who derive their self-worth from their beauty alone. Nor have you ever torn out the expected child in your womb. You have not defiled your face with paints or cosmetics. Never did you like clothes that that showed your body as plainly as though it were naked. Your sole ornament, a consummate and timeless loveliness, your greatest glory has been your modesty (*pudicitia*). (Sen. *Helv.* 11.16.3–5)

Like Cornelia, Helvia rejects showy displays of wealth in favor of traditional Roman values of simplicity and frugality. Indeed, in the next section Seneca admonishes his mother to model her conduct after the women whose virtus ranks with that of the greatest men. He begs her to show self-control, following the example of Cornelia, who did not grieve excessively despite her numerous losses.

The examples of Cornelia, Livia, and Helvia introduce some core Roman ideas about motherhood that shape this chapter. As a respectable, married Roman citizen, the matrona or materfamilias was expected to show restraint both in her appearance and in her dress. She was to remain loyal to her husband, even after his death, and give birth to numerous children, breastfeeding them herself rather than handing them over to a wet nurse. She should be intelligent and well educated, able to read and write both Latin and Greek, allowing her to play an active role in the education and political careers of her sons. The birth of children enhanced her own social standing, particularly when her sons ascended to the highest ranks of Roman society. A Roman matron could control vast amounts of wealth in the form of property that she inherited or brought to the marriage as dowry. This economic independence was further reinforced by the frequent absences of husbands, which compelled wives to step in and make important business and domestic decisions on their own. As a result, the matrona could exert a formidable influence over her family and even politics. But although motherhood facilitated female agency and social recognition, it also was a source of male control of female bodies and lives. To understand this paradox, it is necessary first to examine the economic implications of marriage and the legal status of Roman wives before considering more general issues such as adornment, domestic responsibilities, pregnancy, and childbirth. We conclude with a discussion of the relationship between mothers and children, with attention to the role of Imperial mothers at court as exemplified by Agrippina, in order to explore the possibilities and limits of maternal authority.

12.1 Marriage and Property

A woman's authority over her husband and children was determined from the start by the kind of marriage into which she entered and whether she brought a dowry and its size. In the early period, as we saw in Chapter 10, a woman normally passed legally from the control of her father into the "hand" of her husband, known as a manus marriage. By the late Republic, the alternative form, non-manus marriage, had become more common, coinciding with economic changes and the increased property holdings of elite women. After the death of her father, a woman in a non-manus marriage could own property in her own right, buy and sell, inherit, or make a will and manumit slaves. A wife could thus potentially bring two types of property to her husband's house: the dowry, which became the husband's for the duration of the marriage but had to be returned in the event of divorce, and private property, often worth a great deal, and over which she retained exclusive control. In the case of her husband's death, such a woman might possess a substantial amount of assets. Marriage without manus thus increased the social and economic power of women.

The dowry obligated the husband to maintain his wife according to her accustomed lifestyle. Cicero's first wife, Terentia, brought considerable property to her marriage in the form of rural estates, public and developed land, and an urban apartment block in Rome that yielded valuable rental income. When a husband fell short financially, a wife could subsidize him, albeit indirectly. Terentia's profits, for instance, helped pay for her son's education and living expenses as well as provided dowry payments to her daughter's third husband when Cicero fell short. Her estates advanced her independence and allowed her, when she needed, to circumvent her husband. Dowry payments could be spread out over a long period of time – sometimes as long as 20 years – much like a mortgage today. In some cases, they could form part of a maternal inheritance. Dowries not only provided leverage over husbands, but could strengthen ties between a mother and her daughters.

In Plautus' comedy, *The Pot of Gold*, composed during a period in which many women still entered into manus marriage, the economic power of a woman with a substantial dowry is portrayed as threatening to men. The character Megadorus rails against wives with immense dowries because it allows them to control their husbands: "These and many other disadvantages, together with unbearable expenses, lie in large dowries: a wife without is in her husband's power; those with a dowry afflict their husbands with misery and loss" (Plaut. *Aul.* 530–5). Such a dowry potentially inverted gender roles by putting the wife in charge of the household, as another Plautine character comments: "They're always like that, those women who expect their husbands to act as their slaves, relying on their dowries and generally savage" (Plaut. *Men.* 765–7). As we saw in the story of Cornelia's jewels, female economic power is set in opposition to the core feminine virtue of pudicitia, which encompasses not only sexual self-control but also traditional Roman values including frugality. Wives are encouraged to reject materialism and vanity in favor of moral characteristics conducive to family life:

> **Alcmene:** I don't consider that to be my dowry which is called a dowry, but chastity and modesty, tempered desire, fear of the gods, love for my parents, friendship with relatives, obedience to you, generosity to the good and help for the honorable.
>
> **Sosia:** (*to Amphitruo*) Well, if she's telling the truth, she's a model of excellence.
>
> (Plaut. *Amph.* 839–43)

At the same time, a wife's personal wealth could be essential to protecting and preserving the family. An epitaph for a woman named Murdia from the first century BCE commissioned by her son suggests how a real wife's economic clout could be wielded within the family. In addition to the standard virtues of modesty, decorum, chastity, obedience, wool working, industry, and loyalty so familiar from funerary convention, she is praised for financially supporting her children and husband:

> She made all her sons heirs in equal proportion and gave her daughter a share in the property. Her maternal love was expressed by concern for her children and the equal distribution to each child. She left a fixed sum to her husband so that her dowry, to which he was entitled, would be augmented by her good opinion of him. Recalling my father's memory, in consideration of that and by her own sense of fairness, she bequeathed certain property to me, not to show preference to me and slight my brothers, but because, remembering my father's generosity, she decided she ought to return to me what she had received from my patrimony, by her husband's wishes, so that after preserving it as part of her income, she might restore to my ownership. (*CIL* VI 10230)

This passage illustrates the ability of Roman women to inherit and transmit property. Murdia bequeathed the greatest part to her eldest son out of a sense of obligation to her first husband, from whom she derived much of her money, and divided the rest between her current husband and their children.

Despite financial independence, a woman could not represent herself in certain legal transactions. Instead, she was required to rely on a legal guardian or tutor, whether father, husband, or appointed guardian, because of her inherent "weakness in judgment" (Cic. *Mur.* 27) and "fickle and changeable" nature (Verg. *Aen.* 4.569–70). According to early Roman law, all women except the Vestal Virgins had to be under male guardianship for life. This restriction, however, did not seem to have interfered much with women's activities. When Terentia is described as selling houses to raise funds for the exiled Cicero or collecting rents from her estates, there is no mention of a guardian. It seems that permission from a guardian was often just a formality. To get around a tutor, a matrona could work the legal system, either by pressuring a male relative to do her bidding or by appealing to the appropriate public official. Eventually, Augustan legislation aimed at promoting marital fidelity and encouraging the birth of legitimate children awarded Roman women various social, political, and economic rights and freedoms. Motherhood was now legally endorsed as a formal source of social and legal power for women and childbirth tantamount to a national duty. Women who had given birth to three children did not require guardianship under the new laws and thus became legally independent. But because the institution of guardianship did not previously severely restrict women's sphere of operation, this right probably functioned more as an honorific, a mark of prestige that reinforced traditional Roman discourse about motherhood as the supreme accomplishment of women.

12.2 Divorce, Roman Style

If Roman writers are to be believed, the divorce rates among the Roman elite surpassed those of today. Although Augustus and Livia's union lasted exceptionally long (52 years), it was the product of a double divorce. By the late Republic, divorce was a legal option for both husbands and wives and neither incurred a social stigma for initiating it. The widespread availability of divorce and the ability of both husband and wife to divorce unilaterally affected Roman ideas about marriage. It has been argued that one out of six elite marriages probably ended in divorce within the first decade and the same number by the death of either spouse. A substantial majority remarried, either once or multiple times. A few, like Clodia Metelli, examined more closely in the next chapter, became independent widows or divorcées after their first marriage. The practices of divorce and adoption taken to their extreme potentially undermined traditional ties forged by marriage and blood. They represented two legal strategies aimed at regulating the circulation of women and wealth, the formation of alliances between families and individuals and the definition of legitimacy in the context of political power. In a sense, divorce functioned as an extension of marriage, making a new marriage possible. Men and women could divorce several times without penalty.

Just as marriage involved the consent of both parties, so divorce entailed the withdrawal of consent by either party. Men had the right to divorce wives who were unable to bear children or who had committed adultery. To divorce a wife of long standing who had given birth to children, however, usually met with disapproval. Cicero, for instance, is criticized for "cast[ing] out the wife with whom he had grown old" (Plut. *Cic.* 41.4). A Roman wife did not expect her husband to be faithful and his sexual infidelity was not grounds for divorce. Indeed, there were considerable incentives for a woman not to initiate divorce, namely, the loss of her children. If she separated from her husband, the children remained in his custody and in his house while she returned, along with her dowry, to her father. A husband could even retain most of the dowry. When Paullus divorced Papiria Masonis, the mother of his four children, in 183 BCE, apparently for no particular reason, he left her destitute until her son restored her former wealth. Conversely, a husband might choose to remain with his wife even in the face of infertility, as in the case of Turia, as we see later in this chapter.

12.3   *Cultus*: The Art of Self-Fashioning

A married woman indicated her social standing and morality by her dress. Ovid cautions modestly dressed women, that is, those who wear long garments and bind their hair with woolen ribbons, to avoid his sexually explicit poems (Ov. *Ars* 1.312). The typical matrona wore a long undertunic fashioned from a wide rectangle of cloth, cinched with a cord under the bust. The length of the garment indicated that she did not engage in manual labor. A sliplike garment with a deep V-shaped neckline, called the **stola**, was layered over the top of the tunic and also secured under the breast. The stola indicated that the wearer was legally married, distinguishing her from disreputable women and therefore protecting her from verbal and sexual harassment when outside the house. In fact, the stola was synonymous with matronly status in the Roman mind. When outdoors, a matrona covered herself with a wrap called a **palla** constructed out of a large rectangle of cloth. One end was draped over the left shoulder, brought around the back and either styled over the right shoulder or under the right arm. The upper edge could be brought over the head as a sort of veil, as a marker of social status and sexual modesty that emphasized the privacy of the matron when in public. Her head was bound by a woolen ribbon or vitta, distinct from that worn by maidens, typically white or purple in color, to indicate her virtue. A special hairstyle, the **tutulus**, probably Etruscan in origin, was also characteristic of the matrona. After dividing the hair into sections, it was gathered into a high bun at the back of the head and bound with ribbons to create a conical shape. The requirement of well-groomed hair and ribbons is evident from a comic passage in which one man advises another to pass off a prostitute as his wife by neatly arranging her hair and binding it with ribbons "after the fashion of matrons" (Plaut. *Mil.* 790–1). (For more on the importance of hairdressing to the Romans, see Box 12.1.)

Box 12.1 Hair and the Matrona

You may find this surprising, but the topic of Roman women's hair has received pages and pages of scholarly attention. This interest reflects the abundant and often humorous references to hair in Latin poetry and the complex and varied female coiffures of Roman portrait sculpture. A woman's hairstyle changed over the course of her life. As a young girl, she wore her hair loose, without a veil. As a bride, she wore six-braided locks arranged in a special fashion. The matrona had a distinct updo bound by ribbons; she wore her hair down when in mourning. As a symbol of cultus, hair was considered intrinsically erotic. Ovid advises women attempting to attract a lover to pay particular attention to their hair:

> Let not your hair be disorderly; the application of the hands can give beauty or negate it. There is no single type of hairstyle: let every woman choose the one that suits her best after consulting her mirror. (Ov. *Ars* 3.133–52)

Official portraits of Imperial women often feature distinctive, complicated hairstyles that changed radically within the span of the first century CE. Busts of Livia, for example, show an elaborate hairstyle in which a large lock folds over the brow in a sort of pad, forming a braid that meets the bun at the back. Two locks on the sides curl loosely over the temples and are twisted back toward the bun, as shown in Figure 12.2. Every elite Roman household included a hairdresser or **ornatrix**, who would style the waist-length hair of the women using combs, curling irons, and hairpins. In order to anchor the creation, she may have also stitched the hair in place with coarse thread. Hairnets, along with oils and waxes, also helped stabilize it. Matrons could be quite demanding about their hair. After one lengthy styling session, Ovid describes one displeased mistress scratching her hairdresser's face and stabbing her arm with a hairpin. Women also dyed their hair, whether out of preference for a different color or to hide the grey. The harsh substances used for dye unhappily left some women bald, as a consequence of overuse: "How many times did I tell you – 'Stop dyeing your hair!' Now there's nothing left to color!" (Ov. *Am.* 1.14). Some women resorted to wigs and artificial locks made of human hair instead, especially as increasingly more complex hairstyles became popular.

Figure 12.2 Portrait bust of Livia Drusilla, second wife of Augustus, marble copy from 4 CE. of an original produced between 27 and 23 BCE. Copenhagen, Carlsberg Glyptothek.

Although Latin literary sources repeatedly rail against the use of cosmetics as immoral, dishonest, and disfiguring, Roman women, as in most other cultures, seem to have largely ignored this advice. An unblemished, pale face and rosy cheeks are most often cited as the beauty ideal. To achieve this effect, white lead shavings were dissolved in vinegar, then dried and ground into a powder and applied to the face. Another formulation has been preserved in a round metal canister unearthed at the site of a Roman Temple in Britain. A mix of animal fat, starch, and tin dioxide, it was probably also used as a foundation. The second most commonly mentioned type of cosmetic is rouge, formulated from toxic substances such as red mercuric sulfide. Although less often discussed, kohl and other pigments could be used to outline the eyelids and brows. Because of poor lighting and a lack of proper mirrors, the effect of cosmetics might have been quite garish and not at all natural in contrast to the modern beauty aesthetic.

By attending to her clothing, hair, and cosmetics, the matrona aimed to project cultus, a noun derived from the verb "to cultivate" (colere) and referring to a quality of refinement achieved through the care of the body, adornment, and clothing. Ovid discusses the importance of cultus at length in Book Three of his *Art of Love*, in which he advises women how to attract and retain a male lover. Sounding at times like a *Cosmopolitan* article, he instructs his female audience in basic grooming, such as teeth brushing, facial cleansing, and deodorant, and then imparts advice about the most flattering hairstyles and colors and how to hide physical defects. Here are some of his makeup tips:

> You know how to make your skin pale with a layer of powder: she who doesn't blush by blood, indeed, blushes by art. You enhance the naked edges of your eyebrows and hide your natural cheeks with little patches. It's no shame to outline your eyes with thinned ashes, or saffron grown by your banks, bright Cydnus. I have a book, a small work, but great in the pains it cost me, wherein I reveal the paints that will make you beautiful; from it too seek means to improve your imperfect beauty: my art is not lazy on your behalf. (Ov. *Ars* 3.199–208)

Here Ovid uses the opportunity to plug his other book, *The Art of Beauty*, which contains five facial recipes in about one hundred surviving lines. He goes on to advise his female readers how to talk, walk, and laugh, encouraging them to learn to play the lyre and read poetry, especially his! *The Art of Love* concludes with a few pointers on how to act in bed, even encouraging women to "fake it" when not in the mood:

> You too whom nature denies sexual feelings, pretend sweet pleasure with your voice. Unhappy girl, for whom that sluggish place is numb, which man and woman equally should enjoy. Only beware when you fake it, in case it shows: act like you mean it in your movements and your eyes. (Ov. *Ars* 3.797–804)

12.4 Managing the Household

> And now she swept the propped up homestead, now she set the eggs to be warmed by the feathers of their mother, or she collected green mallows or white mushrooms. Or she warms the humble hearth with a pleasing fire and in the same way she keeps her arms busy with constant loom work and prepares defenses against the threat of winter. (Ov. *Fast*. 4.695–700)

This cozy picture of peasant life, although a far cry from the well-to-do Republican household, points to the traditional duties of the matrona as the guardian of her husband's property: housework, management of food, weaving, and tending the hearth. If this list sounds familiar, that is because it derives from Xenophon's *Household Economy*, which influenced many Roman discourses about the ideal wife. Cicero translated the text into Latin and later authors quoted it. However, a young bride learned how to manage the house not from a book but from her female relatives, her mother-in-law, and household servants, some of whom she brought with her to her new home. Although respectable Roman women could freely leave the house in contrast to their Greek counterparts, the matrona was nonetheless expected to devote herself to her family and to prefer staying at home and spinning wool. At home, women sat in gardens, received visitors in the atrium, walked the extensive grounds of their villas, and read books. If a matrona left the house, she dressed modestly and took care that either servants or a chaperone accompanied her and that she had a specific and respectable purpose. Although the paterfamilias presided over domestic ritual, the wife assisted in various ritual tasks. At the hearth, she worshipped the household gods of her husband's family, beginning on her wedding day when she placed a coin for the Lares there and offered prayers to its genius. A wife of a consul or praetor also might host the winter festival of the Bona Dea (Good Goddess) at her home, discussed in more detail in Chapter 14.

In addition to managing the house, women from Rome's top echelon spent much of their time socializing and helping to advance their husbands' careers. A wife visited her female friends and attended public events such as sacrifices and games. She kept in touch with her own family, particularly with her mother, and visited their country estates without her husband. Within the house, she served as hostess at his banquets, to which she invited the wives of her husband's friends, avoiding disreputable women such as actresses and courtesans. Indeed, a respectable man dared not invite women to his party unless he had a hostess, usually his wife or daughter. In order to be a good hostess, a matrona had to be able to engage in literary table talk. Her girlhood education, particularly the cultivation of elegant speech, prepared her for this task. Cicero valued in women elegant diction acquired from being raised in a cultured home. Neither he nor his peers would have tolerated an uneducated wife. At least once he wrote in Greek to Terentia, suggesting her mastery of the language.

A wife also took a keen interest in her husband's political interests, acting as an intermediary and advocate at Rome. From Cicero's letters, it is clear that wives were expected to be well informed about politics and to be able to make their own judgments about how contemporary political events might affect their fortunes. A junior senator's wife might approach the wife of a consul rather than the man himself for a favor. As go-betweens, wives engaged in direct negotiations with men. When a husband was exiled, a wife managed the estate, overseeing the administration of revenues and the upkeep of buildings. She might petition friends for aid, intercede with politicians, and relay thanks. An unusually long funeral inscription composed for a woman named Turia by her husband of 40 years, Quintus Lucretius Vespillo, consul in 19 BCE, provides a fascinating glimpse into how a wife could successfully intervene to save her husband and his career during the turbulent period of the late Roman Republic. When Vespillo was proscribed, Turia found him a safe hiding place and sent provisions. Upon receiving the news that Octavian had restored citizenship to her husband, she appealed to Lepidus, the third triumvir, to consent as well. Despite being "dragged away and carried off brutally like a slave" and forced to "listen to insulting words and suffer cruel wounds," Turia nonetheless persisted, continuing to advocate for her husband and in the end prevailed. Although scholars have debated the accuracy of this description, it nonetheless challenges some of our assumptions about the well-behaved Roman wife. Turia is praised for canonical female virtues such as loyalty, obedience, affection, wool working, and modesty in appearance and yet she is credited with "firmness of mind" and even masculine *virtus*. Some women ambitiously pushed beyond the bounds of simple intercession on behalf of their husbands, seeking outright power for themselves, like Fulvia, the wife of Mark Antony:

> She was a woman who gave no thought to spinning or housekeeping, nor did she consider it worthwhile to dominate a man not in public life. She wished to rule a ruler and command a commander. (Plut. *Ant.* 10.3)

But even Fulvia had to work through men rather than directly enter the political arena.

12.5 Roman Views of Contraception and Abortion

Pregnancy and live births among upper-class Romans do not seem to have been frequent. The expenses of a senatorial career and a daughter's dowry could be prohibitive and a reason to limit family size. Many families were unable to produce many children and rear them to adulthood. Cicero and his brother produced a total of only three children. His son, Quintus died unmarried at age 43, and his daughter Tullia died around age 32, leaving only one, short-lived child after three marriages and as many miscarriages. Neither Augustus nor Livia met the requirement for the rewards of his legislation, the birth of three children, and they never had a child together. Literary sources portray elite women as disinclined to bear and rear children, and Augustus' moral legislation may in fact have been a response to this. As in Greece, women could avail themselves of a variety of contraceptive substances and methods of varying availability and dubious efficacy. Because ancient medical writers believed that a woman was at her most fertile just after menstruation, most methods failed. Some were preposterous, like rubbing juniper over the male genitalia before intercourse or wearing the worms found in the head of a type of hairy spider wrapped in a strip of deer hide (we are told by Pliny the Elder it protected the wearer for an entire year!). Somewhat more effective were barrier methods that involved inserting various ointments into the vagina. Contraceptives were sometimes confused with abortifacients, and if all else failed, an unwanted baby could be exposed.

Although abortion was technically legal in Rome both during the Republic and Empire, the sources differ in their views of it. However, because a wife had no legal power over the family she married into and helped to create, including her own offspring, she could not determine whether her child lived or died. By this logic, she had no right to use contraception or seek an abortion. A child conceived out of wedlock, however, was fair game, because it was not in the *potestas* of any father. The Stoic philosophers believed that the fetus resembled a plant and became an animal only when it took its first breath after birth. Roman legal writers did not consider it separate from the mother's body. Literary texts depict abortion as common during the early empire, although many condemn the practice, particularly if it denied legitimate heirs for frivolous reasons, such as to avoid ruining her figure or facilitating an adulterous affair. Pliny viewed it as an unfortunate reminder that women controlled their reproductive capacity and the potential offspring of her husband. Note that Seneca in the letter discussed at the beginning of this chapter praises his mother, Helvia, for not seeking to terminate her pregnancies, an odd concern for an adult son by modern standards, but understandable within a Roman rhetorical framework that valorized Cornelia. In refusing to bring to term a pregnancy, and its corollary, to nurse her own children, a woman threatened traditional Roman values.

The motif of the unmaternal matrona who will do anything to avoid childbirth, including undergo abortion, repeatedly crops up in Latin poetry and is often paired with a refusal to breastfeed. Juvenal in Satire 6, addressed to Postumus ostensibly to warn him against marriage, portrays such women as monsters, unconstrained in their pursuit of pleasure and utterly without maternal instinct:

> But at least these women undergo the danger of childbirth and endure all the work of nursing that their position compelled by their position. In contrast, hardly any woman lies in labor on a golden bed. So powerful are the skills and drugs of the woman who fashions sterility and undertakes the killing of men inside the belly. Rejoice, wretched man, and you yourself offer to drink whatever she has. For if she were willing to stretch and aggravate her womb with jumping baby boys, you would perhaps end up being the father of an Ethiopian. (Juv. 2.6.592–600)

The poet draws a class distinction between peasant women willing to give birth and suckle their babies and noble women who contrive to deprive their husbands of heirs by contraception, abortion, and adultery. Just as well, Juvenal implies, because if your wife did carry a fetus to term, it probably would not be yours! Ovid more sensitively describes the near-fatal self-induced abortion of his mistress, Corinna, blaming himself for their predicament:

> Rashly destroying the load of her heavy belly, Corinna languishes, her life at risk. Surely she deserves my anger for attempting something so dangerous in secret. But anger yields to fear. And yet, she became pregnant by me – or so I believe; what could be is often considered a fact by me. (Ov. *Am.* 2.13.1–5)

He calls, somewhat paradoxically, on the healing and maternal deity, Isis, and on the goddess of childbirth, Ilithyia, the Roman equivalent of Greek Eileithyia, to restore her health. Yet in a paired poem, he rails against abortion, comparing it to military combat:

> What good does it do for girls to be exempt from combat, freed from all the dangers that our soldiers face, if they will suffer self-inflicted wounds far from the front lines, and blindly brandish arms against their own bodies? The woman who first took aim at her helpless fetus should have died by her own javelin. Could it be possible that, simply to avoid a few stretch marks you'd make your womb a bloody battleground? (Ov. *Am.* 2.14.1–7)

The subject matter and imagery seem particularly out of context for love poetry, and yet they call attention to the acute dangers of an adulterous affair so celebrated by the genre.

12.6   Childbirth and Nursing

The main purpose of both Greek and Roman marriage was the production of legitimate children. If both parents were citizens, the children automatically inherited Roman citizen status. Childbirth, however, represented the greatest threat to young adult women at Rome, from the wives of senators to slaves. Thousands of such deaths have been recorded, from Pompey's wife, Julia, to Cicero's daughter, Tullia, and countless ordinary women across the empire, who were commemorated on funerary monuments by their grieving husbands and families. One inscription from North Africa records that a wife "lived for thirty-six years and forty days. It was her tenth delivery. On the third day, she died" (*AE* 1995, 1793). Another from what is now Croatia, records a nightmarish scenario in which the wife "was tortured in her attempt to give birth for four days, and did not give birth, and so died" (*CIL* III 2267). Statistics suggest that at least 1 in 50 women were likely to die in childbirth, with a higher risk for teenage girls. Ovid in his *Metamorphoses* gives voice to this female experience through the character of Alcmene, mother of Heracules, who undergoes a grueling, 10-day labor:

> May the gods be favorable to you and give you a quick delivery when, in childbirth, you call on Ilithyia, goddess of mothers frightened in their labor, who thanks to Juno made things hard for me. When the time for Hercules' difficult birth came, and Capricorn, the tenth sign, was hidden by the sun, the weight of the child stretched my womb – what I carried was so great that you could tell Jove was the father of the unborn child. Nor could I bear my labor pangs much longer. Even now as I speak, cold horror grips my limbs and part of me remembers it with pain. Tortured for seven nights and as many days, worn out with agony, stretching my arms to the sky, with a great cry, I called out to Lucina and her companion deities of birth. Lucina came, indeed, but pledged in advance to surrender my life to cruel Juno. She sat on the altar before the door and listened to my groans. With her right knee crossed over her left and with her fingers interlocked, she stopped the birth. She also uttered spells in a low voice and the spells charms prevented my delivery. I labored on and, mad with pain, screamed in vain against ungrateful Jove. I longed to die, and my cries would have moved the emotionless rocks. (Ov. *Met.* 9.273–301)

Although a goddess of childbirth herself, Juno punishes Alcmene for bearing Jupiter's son by protracting her labor with the help of Lucina, also a birth deity, who crosses her legs to prevent delivery. The fear of a painful, protracted, and potentially fatal labor like that of Alcmene drove Roman women to turn to deities such as Juno Lucina for assistance.

Because Roman medical thought and practice largely followed the Greek tradition, with the exception of folk medicine chiefly found in the work of the natural historian, Pliny the Elder, this section does not look in detail at Roman ideas about the female body. Instead, we consider briefly the role of midwives in labor and delivery, following the account of the Greek physician, Soranus. In his training manual, *Gynecology*, he instructs midwives how to prepare for and facilitate a successful delivery, as well as gives advice for postnatal care of mother and baby. Labor and delivery took place at home and required at least three exclusively female attendants, usually the woman's mother, a female servant, and a midwife. After describing the desirable characteristics to look for in the latter, including good health, competence, and literacy, Soranus instructs her how to prepare for the birth:

> For normal labor one must prepare beforehand: olive oil, warm water, warm compresses, soft sea sponges, pieces of wool, bandages, a pillow, things to smell, a midwife's stool or chair, two beds and a proper room. Oil for injection and lubrication, warm water in order that the parts may be cleansed, warm compresses for alleviating pains, sea sponges for sponging off, pieces of wool in order that the woman's parts be covered, bandages with which to swaddle the newborn, a pillow on which to place the infant below the

parturient woman until the afterbirth has also been taken care of, and things to smell (such as pennyroyal, a clod of earth, barley, as well as an apple and a quince and, if the season permits, a lemon, a melon and a cucumber, everything similar to these) to revive the laboring woman. (Sor. *Gyn.* 1.67–9)

Pain relief was provided by warm compresses and odor therapy, a popular form of treatment in the ancient world, as noted in Chapter 5. To facilitate delivery, the Romans used a birthing stool, with arms at the sides for the laboring woman to grasp, and a crescent-shaped hole in the seat through which the baby was delivered. A relief that perhaps marked the tomb of a midwife (Figure 12.3) shows her kneeling at lower right as she assists a seated woman giving birth, supported from behind by another female. The midwife advised the woman on how to breathe and bear downward with contractions. She then stretched the cervix to help pull the baby from the birth canal, delivering the placenta shortly thereafter. The midwife signaled whether the child was male or female and then placed the baby on the ground to assess whether it was worth rearing. She decided when to cut the umbilical cord, cleaned the baby, and swaddled it tightly in blankets before putting him or her to bed. Midwives enjoyed a high professional standing in both Greece and Rome as practitioners of the liberal profession of medicine.

Because pregnant divorcées were commonplace in Rome, in contrast to Greece, a noteworthy feature of legal discourse on childbirth was advice about how to make sure there was no doubt about paternity. The woman was required to notify her ex-husband of her pregnancy within 30 days of divorce. He in turn had the option to reject the child, accept it after the birth, or do nothing. There were also complex rules for the supervision of a widow's labor to avoid potential inheritance disputes. One edict lays out in detail the legal procedures. First, the woman was required to give birth at the home of a reputable woman. Thirty days before the birth she was required to notify all interested parties, allowing them to send witnesses to the

Figure 12.3 A Roman midwife attends to a seated woman giving birth, at left, c. 100–300 CE. Ostia, Italy, Museo Ostiense. Scala/Art Resource, NY.

event. Prior to giving birth, she was confined to a room with one entrance only and guarded at all times by a minimum of six people. Whenever the woman left, the room could be searched. Even the women attending the birth were inspected to ensure they were not pregnant with a child that could be substituted for the woman's own!

Roman discourse on childbirth is also peculiarly obsessed with the topic of wet nurses and breastfeeding. This debate in some ways resembles discussions in modern Western societies about the advantages of nursing over bottle feeding. Most Roman infants from wealthy families spent the first year of life under the care of a wet nurse, a slave, or freedwoman. She played an important role in the development of the child because of her constant presence. Many scholars think that Roman mothers, whatever their class, did not usually breastfeed their babies. This view, however, is probably not accurate. Given the lack of safe infant formula and the convenience and cost-effectiveness of maternal nursing, it is hard to imagine that many women avoided it. Certainly wealthy women could afford to hire wet nurses, but most Roman mothers could not. Contracts for wet-nursing in Roman Egypt mostly refer to the rearing of slave children, who were, in most cases, abandoned babies pick up from rubbish heaps. In one letter, two women attempt to convince a third to nurse a freeborn baby by emphasizing its nonservile status (*Papyrus Michigan* 3.202). In another, a grandmother insists that she does not want her daughter to nurse her newborn and asks her son-in-law to hire a wet nurse (*Papyrus London* 3.951 verso). Philosophers frequently condemned the use of wet nurses by elite women. Favorinus (80–160 CE) mansplains about the importance of maternal nursing to a young matrona still in her childbed:

> After embracing and congratulating the father as soon as he entered, the philosopher sat down. And when he had asked how long the labor had been and how difficult, and had learned that the girl, worn out by fatigue and wakefulness, was sleeping, he began to talk at more length and said, "I have no doubt she will breastfeed her son herself." But when the girl's mother said to him that she wanted to spare her daughter and provide nurses for the boy, so that she would not suffer in addition to the pains of childbirth the hard and difficult task of nursing, he said: "I beg you, woman, let her be wholly and completely the mother of her own child. For what kind of unnatural, imperfect and half-baked kind of mother is it who bears a child and then immediately sends it away? To have nourished in her womb with her own blood something which she could not see, and not to feed with her own milk what she sees, now living, now a human, now calling for a mother's care? Or do you too perhaps think," said he, "that nature gave women nipples as a kind of beautiful birth-mark, not for the purpose of feeding their children, but as a way of enhancing their breasts?" (Aul. Gell. 12.1.1–5)

The philosopher predictably equates maternal neglect with female vanity in order to valorize childbearing and breastfeeding as the ultimate female virtue. Such a mundane activity is so important that it is commemorated after death, as seen on a funerary inscription of a freed woman, "To Graxia Alexandria, an outstanding example of womanly virtue, who actually reared her children with her own breasts" (*CIL* VI 19128). A charming wall painting from Pompeii reflects the idealization of maternal breastfeeding in its depiction of the hero Perseus and his mother, Danaë. Rather than emphasizing his miraculous conception, imprisonment, or heroic exploits as Greek art does, it portrays instead Danaë tenderly suckling her son at her right breast as she looks apprehensively at the chest into which they will be cast, as a punishment for engaging in premarital sex (Figure 12.4).

Figure 12.4 Pompeiian fresco depicting Danaë nursing the infant Perseus, first century CE. Naples, Museo Archeologico Nazionale, inv. 111212.

12.7 Mothers and Children

In modern Western societies, a mother is expected to be closely involved in caring for her children in the earliest stages of their development and to be affectionate, supportive, and self-sacrificing. In many circles, putting a baby or young child under someone else's care is frowned upon. In contrast, an upper-class Roman mother probably did not participate very much in the physical care of her children. Beginning with the wet nurse, a much wider range of people was involved in the various stages of a child's life than today, including slaves, foster parents, step-parents, and teachers. Mothers might also be separated from their biological children whether because of divorce or the death of a husband, when the children passed into the guardianship of other adult males. After a divorce, her children may not have lived formally with her for years. Males also could establish their own households while teenagers as they sought professional instruction. It has been argued that a Roman mother's relationship with her children probably developed much later than today. As they reached adulthood, married, and embarked on political careers or became mothers themselves, her influence over them probably increased.

Although characteristics such as patience, affection, and sympathy are encouraged in mothers today, discipline and moral purpose were the most admired qualities in a Roman mother. Her job was to model character and to inspire and foster ambition while at the same time curbing excess through the exercise of strict maternal discipline. Tacitus (c. 56–120 CE) attributes this virtue to the mothers of the greatest Roman leaders:

> So we have heard how Cornelia, mother of the Gracchi, Aurelia, mother of Caesar, and Atia, mother of Augustus, took charge of their sons' education and produced leaders. The object of this strict discipline was that the natural disposition of every child, while still sound and pure at the core, not yet warped by any depravity, might at once with heart and soul grasp the respected pursuits. Whether it leaned toward the military or the law, or to the study of eloquence, might make that its sole aim and its all-consuming interest. (Tac. *Dial.* 28)

It was also important for a mother to be cultivated in order to supervise the education of her children and facilitate their social and political advancement. She was considered an early, although not formative, influence in the cultivation of speech necessary for a career in oratory, as we saw with Cornelia. A mother also interacted with children's tutors, visiting intellectuals, and literary guests. The Roman mother clearly had a strong intellectual and moral influence on her children, particularly sons, as she shaped them for their future lives.

Although a mother did not have potestas over her children as her husband did, she could exert considerable influence in other important ways. In addition to guiding her children's intellectual and moral development, she took the lead in choosing her daughter's marriage partner. She also administered her children's finances after the death of her husband. In such a case, a husband could bequeath his entire estate to his wife who in turn managed it while she lived and then passed it on to her children. Daughters received this inheritance, in the form of dowry, at an earlier stage in life, often partly financed by the mother. She could also subsidize her son's political career. The prestige of a woman's ancestry further enhanced her children's status and could advantage them in marriage and politics. Indeed, the difficulty of producing male heirs within Imperial families eventually led to an emphasis on descent through the female line. An illustrious mother enhanced the status of her sons and might help them exert influence at court. Many upper-class Roman mothers thus brought to bear a significant amount of influence over their adult children for an extended period of time.

Imperial mothers, in particular, walked a fine line between ambition and overreach. Abuses of maternal political power were met with harsh criticism and even death. Seneca derides mothers "who exploit their children's influence with female irresponsibility, who fulfill their ambitions through those sons because women cannot hold office" (Sen. *Helv.* 14.2). Livia, for example, intruded into politics early in the reign of her son, Tiberius. Averse to the intervention of women in male affairs, he issued an injunction against Livia involving herself in "serious matters unsuited to a woman." Nonetheless, he seems to have tolerated the proliferation of honors, divine and otherwise, heaped upon her after Augustus' death. Other Imperial mothers were notorious for their powerful and corrupting influence at court and are often depicted by sensationalizing historians as ruthless schemers and manipulative seducers. Agrippina the Younger, the mother of the emperor Nero, is a prime example of maternal overreaching (see Chart 10.1). When she married the emperor Claudius in 49 CE, she lobbied for him to adopt Nero, her son from a previous marriage, so that he would gain precedence over Claudius' younger son. Nero subsequently married Claudius' daughter Octavia. On his accession to the throne in 54 CE, he honored his mother by placing her portrait on a series of coins. Their relationship soon deteriorated. Although Nero continued to honor his mother publicly, conflicts arose over her meddling in politics. He particularly disliked his mother's inolvement in his affair with a freedwoman named Claudia Acte, discussed more fully in the next chapter. Abandoning maternal restraint, Agrippina became increasingly violent and erratic. She was soon banned from the palace and finally murdered three years later, on a charge of plotting against Nero:

> If he had come to commit murder, she would not believe it of her son: parent murder was not their command. But the assassins surrounded her couch and the captain began by striking her on the head with a club. Just as the centurion was drawing his sword to make an end, she held out her belly, crying "Strike my womb!" and with many wounds was killed. (Tac. *Ann.* 14.8)

As a sign of his depravity, Nero did not hesitate to commit matricide, even gazing at her mutilated corpse with approval. Although Agrippina's ambition for her son recalls the exemplary traits of Roman mothers, she took things too far, arrogantly interfering in her son's sex life and asserting herself in politics. Skillful political manipulation required tact and discretion on the part of the mother rather than an outright power grab. The almost parodic portrait of Agrippina can be viewed as a version of Livia taken to its extreme. Her "unnatural" domination over her mad emperor-son stood on its head the model of civic Imperial motherhood encompassed by Livia, "the mother of the country."

Because Roman authors turn most of their attention to sons, we have very little evidence for the relationship between mothers and daughters. In fact, this relationship is the least documented in the Roman family. The interests and responsibilities of mothers and daughters seem to have been closely aligned. Their relationship appears to have been characterized by mutual affection, shared activities, and social networks. A mother trained her daughter for married life, supervised her education, and took a lead role in arranging for her marriage. She was more involved in finding a husband for her daughter than wives for her sons because the age at first marriage was much younger for girls, whose social life was relatively restricted. A girl's dependency on her mother was reinforced, rather than weakened, at marriage because of her need for guidance as a new wife. At this stage, the mother provided companionship, gave marital advice, attended her childbed, and aided in financial emergencies. She helped her daughter negotiate the social landscape and supervised her conduct. For example, Scribonia, Augustus' first wife, escorted their daughter Julia to her exile in Pandateria in 2 BCE, even though they had not formally resided together since Augustus divorced her 36 years earlier. A daughter might even return to her mother's house for a short period when her husband assumed a provincial post. Roman mothers and daughters thus shared a strong bond of mutual interest that did not dissipate after marriage.

12.8 Conclusion

The goal of the exemplary Roman mother was to bear important sons who would make a mark on Roman politics and society. She welcomed pregnancy and childbirth and even willingly breastfed her own babies. Highly educated and from a cultured and prestigious family, she took the leading role in overseeing the early years of her children's education. Prized for her frugality and austerity, she provided a moral compass for her children and instilled discipline and morality, preventing them from straying off the proper path. Her lineage and personal wealth not only enhanced her children's status and improved their social and political prospects, they also strengthened her control over them. She remained loyal to a single husband, even after his death. Although she dressed modestly, the matrona cultivated refinement and elegance in appearance as an outward sign of her wealth and status. Moral discourse in turn conversely chastises upper-class women for their reluctance to bear children, their reliance on contraception and abortion to engage in extramarital affairs and preserve their good looks, and their refusal to breastfeed. Within the family, economic independence afforded by a non-manus marriage arrangement, a hefty dowry, and/or a family inheritance gave women considerable leverage over both their husbands and children. Even the requirement of guardianship seemed to have had little effect in curbing women's legal and economic activities. Some women exhibited shrewd business skills, managing the estates of their husbands in their absence or administering inheritances after their death. The relationship of mothers and their children, although often distant in the early stages of childhood, grew closer during adolescence and into adulthood. Mothers were actively involved in finding marriage partners for their children, acted as allies and advocates in advancing their sons' political careers, assisted their daughters in negotiating the social scene, and provided marital advice. Imperial mothers channeled their ambition into their sons, sometimes playing a formidable role in court politics and paying a steep price if they overstepped their proper role.

Questions for Review

1 Why was Cornelia a model for Roman motherhood?

2 What is cultus and why was it important?

3 How do ideas about motherhood change in the Roman empire?

4 Describe some of the ways in which Roman mothers exerted power within the family.

5 How do Roman views of motherhood differ from today?

Further Reading

Primary Sources

Aulus Gellius, *Attic Nights*, 12.1.1-5
Epitaph for Turia
Epitaph for Murdia
Ovid, *Amores* 2.13 and 2.14; *Art of Love*, Book 3
Plautus, *Casina*
Seneca, *On the Consolation to Helvia*
Tacitus, *Annals* 12-13

Secondary Sources

Barrett, Anthony (2002). *Livia*. New Haven, CT: Yale University Press.
   A comprehensive account of the second wife of Augustus Caesar and mother of the Emperor Tiberius that rejects the traditional image of her as a manipulative and cunning schemer to reveal a complex figure whose political influence continued to shape the Roman government well after her death.

Dixon, Suzanne (2007). *Cornelia: Mother of the Gracchi*. London and New York: Routledge.
   An in-depth analysis of Cornelia, mother of two of Rome's most famous political figures, as the embodiment of the ideal of the matrona during the turbulent context of Rome in the second century BCE.

McAuley, Mairéad (2016). *Reproducing Rome: Motherhood in Vergil, Ovid, Seneca, and Statius*. Oxford: Oxford University Press.
   A study of maternity in Roman literature of the first century CE, with an emphasis on the political, aesthetic, and moral meanings of motherhood through a series of close readings.

Olson, Kelly (2008). *Dress and the Roman Woman*. London and New York: Routledge.
   An engaging account of how Roman women dressed, including girls, and its meaning for Roman society through an examination of literary and visual evidence.

Rawson, Beryl (ed.) (2000). *Marriage, Divorce, and Children in Ancient Rome*. Oxford: Clarendon Press.
   A collection of essays that examines aspects of the composition and inner workings of the Roman family, with special attention to issues of divorce, high mortality rates, and social status.

Treggiari, Susan (2007). *Terentia, Tullia and Pubilia*. London and New York: Routledge.
   Reconstructs the lives of the three most important women in Cicero's household, including his strong-willed first wife Terentia, his daughter Tullia, and his second wife, the teenaged Publilia.

13

Adultery and Female Prostitution in Rome

> If a woman without a husband opens her house to the lust of all men and publicly leads the life of a prostitute, if she frequents dinner parties with perfect strangers, if she does this in the city, in her garden, amid the crowds of Baiae, and finally if she behaves in such a way that not only her bearing, her apparel and her circle of friends make her seem to be not just a prostitute, but a lascivious and lewd prostitute, not to mention the ardor of her gaze, the unconstrained nature of her gossip, even her embraces and kisses and activities, her water parties and her dinner parties. But if a young man was with this woman, Lucius Herennius, would he be an adulterer or a lover? Would it seem that he wanted to assault her chastity or to satisfy her lust?
>
> (Cic. *Cael.* 49)

If you read this passage without any context, you might assume that the woman in question was a prostitute. A woman "common to all," living a public life of pleasure and extravagance, has all the markings of commercial sex in the ancient world. But you would be wrong. This portion of a defense speech by Cicero recounts the activities of a wealthy aristocratic widow, Clodia Metelli. The orator seeks to damage her reputation by portraying her as a woman of shameless promiscuity and reckless extravagance, sexually insatiable and even predatory toward young men. Her alleged sexual misconduct violates the ideology of pudicitia, the sexual fidelity expected of upper-class Roman wives and publicly displayed through their refined appearance and self-restraint. Clodia, in contrast, has sex with numerous men, pursues pleasure instead of virtue, wields a vast fortune seemingly without the constraint of a male guardian, and brazenly flaunts her disregard for sexual and social norms. By comporting herself in this way, Cicero argues that she has forfeited her position as an upper-class matrona and instead resembles a prostitute.

Cicero's Clodia is a largely fictional construct intended to serve a male legal agenda, just as the Greek courtesan Neaera before her. In portraying her, the orator draws on contemporary moral discourse about women and sexuality in the tumultuous period of the late Republic. A shift away from manus marriage among the Roman elite combined with the considerable wealth amassed by many upper-class women may have empowered them to act more independently while fueling male anxieties about their inability to control them. Powerful, financially independent women such as Clodia attracted criticism, usually in the form of allegations of sexual misconduct. The concern about female licentiousness further intensified during the empire. The poet Juvenal in Satire 6, a portion of which we examined in the last chapter, describes a state of moral chaos entailed by a failure of chastity, focusing in particular on the sexual promiscuity of elite wives. In one passage, he describes them desecrating the altar of the goddess Pudicitia at night by urinating on her image and having sex with each other in her sanctuary:

> Now, go ask yourself, why Tullia grimaces as she sniffs the air, what notorious Maura's foster-sister says to her when Maura passes the ancient altar of Pudicitia. It is here that they set down their litters at night, it is here that they urinate and cover the image of the goddess with their powerful streams, and take turns riding each other and thrash around with no man present. Then they go back home. When the light returns, you walk in your wife's urine on the way to see important friends. (Juv. 2.6.306–13)

Here the nocturnal escapades of Roman wives not only violate a sacred space but also trample on sexual and social protocol dictated by pudicitia, while their husbands unwittingly step in the traces of their debauchery on their way to the Forum the next morning. Elsewhere in the poem, Juvenal recounts the sordid sexual adventures of Messalina, wife of the emperor Claudius:

> When his wife perceived her husband was asleep, the Imperial whore would leave, with no more than a single maid as her companion. Preferring a mat to her bedroom in the palace, she dared to put on a night hood. With a blonde wig concealing her black hair, she entered a brothel warmed by old rags to an empty cubicle – her very own. Then she stood there, naked, her nipples gilded, assuming the name Lycisca ("She-Wolf"), and displayed the belly where you came from, noble Britannicus. She fawned over her customers as they came in and asked for their money. Lying there without interruption she absorbed the blows of all. Later, when the pimp was already dismissing his girls, she left in sorrow, waiting until the last possible moment to close her cubicle. She was still burning with her clitoris inflamed and stiff. Tired by the men and not yet satisfied, she left, her face dirty and bruised, sooty with lamp smoke, and she brought back to her marriage bed the stench of the brothel. (Juv. 2.6.116–32)

As "empress whore," Messalina abandons the conjugal bed while her husband sleeps, slipping out of the house in disguise. She makes her way to a common brothel, where she impersonates the lowest form of whore, but for lust instead of money. When the pimp closes shop for the night, Messalina lingers, reluctant to leave. Filthy from her work, she brings the soot and stink of the brothel back to the emperor's bed without his knowing. These narratives about the non-marital sexual pursuits of elite Roman women fuse two distinct moral categories, that of matron and prostitute. None of these women were in fact prostitutes, nor did they actually behave like them. Rather, these accounts reflect the political motives of their authors and their love of moralizing sensationalism. They also underscore how Roman social convention equated female independence, whether economic, sexual, or political, with promiscuity and even prostitution. Although moral discourse exaggerates the sexual misconduct of elite Roman woman, it nonetheless suggests that adultery was an issue of great popular concern in Roman society.

A particular challenge of this chapter, therefore, is distinguishing wives behaving badly from mistresses, courtesans, concubines, and prostitutes not subject to the same moral code. Because respectable matrons were expected to enjoy and actively participate in conjugal sex, they are sometimes difficult to distinguish from sexually available women outside their class. For example, erotic frescos are found both in brothels and in the bedrooms of

Figure 13.1 Male–female couple on a bed attended by two servants, Rome, Villa Farnesina, cubiculum D, ca. 19 BCE. Rome, Palazzo Massimo alle Terme, inv. 1188. Photo Deutsches Archaeologisches Institut, Rome, inst. 77-1295.

private households, whether in the villas of the elite or the lowly freedman. According to Ovid, it was the norm for aristocrats to collect and display small paintings that showed couples engaged in various sex acts. Images found in the Villa Farnesina in Rome, which belonged to Julia, the daughter of Augustus, and her much older husband, Agrippa, feature six scenes of lovemaking located in three adjoining bedrooms. Although less explicit than other erotic paintings, they depict sexually active female partners kissing or embracing male lovers on luxurious couches and beds. Figure 13.1 is the second of a pair of paintings first discussed in Chapter 11. Whereas the left-hand panel (Figure 11.5) shows a reluctant, fully clothed bride with downcast eyes, the one at right (13.1) depicts a woman dressed in a voluminous gown uncovered to the waist reaching her arm around her male partner's neck to pull his head toward her, gazing directly at him. Does this image represent a prostitute and her customer? Or does it narrate the initiation of the modest bride into the pleasures of sex, as she leaves behind her virginity to become a passionate, loyal wife? It is probably the latter, a vignette of the wedding night, narrating the transition from modest bride to immodest wife. The ambiguous sexual status of many female figures in Roman literature and art, whether adulterous wife, courtesan, girlfriend, or whore, allowed the Romans to express a wide range of attitudes – sometimes conflicting – about female sexuality. This chapter first considers how a variety of sources, particularly love elegy, represent elite women engaging in illicit sex and in the process demonstrate the fluidity of moral categories related to this activity. It then looks at Roman attitudes toward adultery, including the laws that regulated it. It concludes with a discussion of Roman prostitution, the women involved in this profession, their clientele, and the spaces in which they worked.

13.1   Clodia Metelli: A Woman of Pleasure

> Let us live, my Lesbia, and love, and value not at all the talk of cranky old men. Suns may set and rise again. When once the short light has set, there remains one unbroken night to be slept by us. Give me a thousand kisses, then a hundred, then another thousand, then a second hundred, then yet another thousand, then a hundred. Then, when we have made up many thousands, we will confuse our counting, so that we may not know the amount, nor arouse the envy of any malicious man, when he knows that our kisses are so many. (Catull. 5)

Latin love poetry of the late Republic and the early empire, like this poem by Catullus, celebrates nonmarital sexual relations in many forms, including adultery, homoerotic desire, and prostitution. This interest may reflect a general perception of marriage as a necessary evil and mainly for the procreation of children rather than for pleasure. The emergence during the mid-Republic of numerous cults to promote female chastity indicates that female sexual misbehavior was a growing concern. Aristocratic women became increasingly known for their divorces, adulteries, and reluctance to bear children. Graphic descriptions of the sexual exploits of elite women from distinguished families such as Sempronia, the mistress of Catiline; Servilia, the rumored lover of Caesar and mother of Brutus; and Clodia Metelli, the woman identified as Lesbia above, all attest to a new moral laxity during the late Republic. The poems of Catullus and the love elegists chronicle a new lifestyle that prized leisure, learning, and desire over ambition. These sophisticated, urban young men and their pleasure-seeking female companions rejected the traditional morality of their parents. In this section, we examine the narratives surrounding one historical woman notorious for her promiscuity and disregard for social convention, Clodia Metelli, in order to understand Roman attitudes toward female adultery.

Clodia (a variant of Claudia) Metelli was born in 95 BCE into the illustrious patrician consular family of the Claudians. Because she was one of three daughters, it is not always possible to securely identify her in the sources. At the age of 15, she married her first cousin, Quintus Caecilius Metellus Celer, and gave birth to a daughter, Metella. Her husband, her oldest brother, and two brothers-in-law were all consuls. Another brother, Publius Claudius Pulcher, was one of Cicero's bitterest enemies and notorious for trespassing at a women-only religious festival called the Bona Dea in 62 BCE, as we see in the next chapter. Metellus died in his early forties in 59 BCE, after two decades of marriage, from poison administered by his wife, if we are to believe Cicero. The marriage could not have been all that bad, given that it lasted 20 years despite the absence of a male heir. During that same year, Clodia began an affair with the poet Catullus. A little while later, she took up with Caelius Rufus, a dissolute party boy active in Roman politics. After her husband's death, she continued to reside in their house on the Palatine, held the title to a well-known garden villa along the Tiber, and possibly owned a property at Baiae, the summer playground of the ultrarich on the bay of Naples. In terms of her property, Clodia was regarded as completely independent, able to negotiate on her own behalf, and to make financial decisions without consulting others. When Cicero discusses his interest in buying her pleasure grounds, a guardian is not mentioned. Technically an univira as a widow who never remarried, Clodia does not appear to have actively embraced its duties and sentiments by honoring her husband's memory and devoting herself to her child, as custom dictated, but rather entertained frequently both at Rome and Baiae. She was strongly attached to her brother Publius and openly supported his political agenda.

What we know of Clodia comes from two polemical sources, Cicero's *In Defense of Caelius* and a series of poems by Catullus. Given the difficulty of dating the latter, it is impossible to know whether Cicero's depiction influenced the poet or vice versa. Clodia's reputation for promiscuity is largely the product of these two sources. Cicero sought revenge on Clodia's brother for his role in the orator's exile in 58 BCE by defending her former lover, Caelius Rufus, on several charges, including attempted murder. Clodia was the key witness for the prosecution, testifying that she had financed the murder plot with gold she had loaned to Caelius, who in turn had tried to poison her. In the first lines of his speech, Cicero immediately begins his character assassination, alleging that "the resources of a prostitute" are being brought against his client. He then goes on to claim that Clodia had invented the story to avenge herself on the defendant for jilting her. His detailed account of her debauchery paints her as a prostitute in all but name:

> A woman who made herself common to all, who openly always hadsome devoted lover, into whose gardens, house and place at Baiae the lusts ofall passed freely, who even supported young men, and augmented their fathers'stinginess at her own expense; if a widow were living without restraint, ashameless widow living impudently, a rich widow living extravagantly, a lustfulwidow living like a prostitute, should I regard any man guilty of adultery ifhe had been somewhat free in his attentions to her? (Cic. Cael. 16 [36])

As a highly visible society woman, Clodia participated in an array of sophisticated social networks. Like other women of her station, she hosted many visitors at her house, frequented dinner parties, took trips to Baiae, and offered financial support to her favorites. Cicero, however, puts a sinister spin on these activities. He equates profligacy with prostitution, suggesting that Clodia not only indiscriminately offered her own body for sex but also attempted to buy the sexual services of young men. Her public presence in male spaces, flagrant display of sexuality, and financial control of men underscores her deviation from Roman social norms as an independent woman not under the control of a husband or father. Cicero further likens her to a cheap whore, of the type that patronizes the baths of foreign men, trading sex for admission (see Box 13.1). He argues that in acting like a prostitute, she has forfeited the privileges and protections of the revered Roman matrona. Cicero's hyperbolic account of Clodia's sexual misconduct is an example of a traditional forensic strategy deployed against both male and female opponents. By focusing on Clodia's promiscuity, the orator deflects attention away from his client and his behavior, undermines her credibility as a witness, and ultimately damages the reputation of her brother, Publius Clodius Pulcher. The entire defense speech invites an obvious question: if Clodia had truly acted as immorally as Cicero argues, why would the prosecution have called on her as a witness in the first place?

The other source for Clodia is a series of poems by Catullus, a poet profoundly influenced by the Alexandrians as discussed in Chapter 8. He similarly focuses on her sexual behavior. Catullus was born into a distinguished, propertied family of Verona but spent most of his life at Rome. Although only marginally involved in politics, he participated in the radical social change that marked the end of the Republic. Like the other "new poets," he rejected traditional moral values in favor of Hellenistic Greek culture, which influenced not only his poetic practice but also his lifestyle. In over 20 poems, Catullus chronicles his affair with an aristocratic married woman called "Lesbia," who has been identified as Clodia Metelli. As a poetic convention, the use of a Greek pseudonym was designed not only to disguise the mistress's true identity but also to evoke the Greek tradition of erotic poetry and female poets. The choice of "Lesbia" recalls the amorous verse of Sappho that overtly celebrates female–female desire. Catullus depicts the liaison as clearly adulterous. In one poem, Lesbia berates the poet in front of her husband. In another, Catullus draws a contrast between a legitimate bride, "led by her father's hand" and their illicit affair: "For she did not come to me led by her father's right hand into a house fragrant with Assyrian perfume, but she gave me stolen gifts taken from the very lap of her husband" (Catull. 69.143–6).

The poet depicts his mistress as self-assured, beautiful, and cultured, indeed, as his muse and the ideal reader of his verse. In the first poem, Lesbia appears as a tender yet passionate puella, who sexually arouses the poet as he watches her caressing her pet bird, "Sparrow, darling of my girl, with whom she is accustomed to play … I wish that I might play with you as she does!" (Catull. 2). But as the poet realizes she has been unfaithful, he denounces her, much like Cicero, as an insatiable whore:

> Whatever the will of the gods shall bring, just announce to my girl a few not very nice words: let her live and be happy with her lovers, whom she holds in a single embrace, three hundred at a time, loving none truly, but over and over busting the balls on them all; let her not look to my love as before, for thanks to her it has fallen like a flower at the meadow's edge, after it's been nicked by the passing plough. (Catull. 11.15–20)

Lesbia's rapacious sexuality disrupts the gender hierarchy; she alone chooses her partners, preferring indiscriminate sex to a single love affair. By acting like a man, she emasculates her poet lover, who is likened to a fragile, feminine flower. The dynamic of the male poet debased by his dominant mistress is a motif that recurs through Latin love elegy, as we see in the next section.

13.2 Women in Latin Love Elegy

Through the last two decades of the first century BCE, the elegiac poets Gallus (c. 70–26 BCE), Tibullus, Propertius, and Ovid published collections of love poems on the model of Catullus. The poems of Sulpicia, discussed in Chapter 11, also belong to this period and genre. Autobiographical in form, love elegy focuses on the tempestuous relationship between the poet-lover and the woman he desires, who is beautiful, sophisticated, and sexually available, but not always to him. The poet describes his erotic trials metaphorically as a form of sexual servitude or military campaign. He rejects the duties of citizen and soldier, and his mistress operates outside of the conventional roles of wife and mother. The elegiac preoccupation with this female figure, alternately called puella, *amica* ("girlfriend"), and *domina* ("mistress"), offers insight into the erotic and emotional landscape of the Roman elite in the Augustan era. All of the elegiac poets, including Sulpicia herself, portray their female subjects as demanding and domineering, uninterested in marriage, children, and the traditional female virtues of chastity and fidelity. The poets place these women outside of a strictly Roman context by referring to them with Greek names, such as Lycoris, Delia, Cynthia, and Corinna, a practice borrowed from Catullus. Because they are called by pseudonyms, the status and identity of these women are mostly unknown. Various attempts have been made to link them to historical women, like Catullus' Clodia, without success. They may have been adulterous wives or foreign courtesans, as in the case of Volumnia Cytheris. More likely, they are conventional poetic types that do not directly reflect social reality yet are also not complete fictions. These "poeticized girlfriends" offer a complex and nuanced perspective on female personal relationships with men in the age of Augustus.

Soldier, statesman, and first elegiac poet, Cornelius Gallus wrote four books of love poems addressed to his mistress Cytheris, whom he calls Lycoris. She is the only elegiac woman who can be linked to a historical figure based on external evidence. Cytheris was born a slave, possibly around 70 BCE, and was probably of foreign origin. Cytheris, an epithet for Aphrodite, was her stage name. It may also indicate her status as a courtesan or prostitute. Her master was a Roman man of equestrian rank, Publius Volumnius Eutrapelus. At some point, he freed her, perhaps in order to make her attractive to influential men, who would not have consorted with a slave. As freedwoman of Volumnius Eutrapelus, she received the legal name of Volumnia upon her manumission. Rather than helping us understand her true identity, her three names – that of a slave, Cytheris, of a freedwoman, Volumnia, and her poetic pseudonym, Lycoris – actually conspire to obscure it. All we know is that Cytheris was a ***mima***, an actress-dancer who specialized in the art of mime, a form of theatrical improvisation, featuring obscene jokes, gestures and public nudity. Much like the Greek *auletris*, the mima was practically a synonym for prostitute. Indeed, both prostitutes and actresses were tainted by the stigma of the label *infamis*, a form of legal and social discrimination. Mime performances also occurred at the Floralia, a spring festival associated with prostitutes. Volumnius Eutrapelus profited by offering her services to friends and allies, initially functioning as her male relative. She in turn used her connections to establish important relationships for herself, later becoming mistress both to Brutus and Mark Antony, sleeping both with Caesar's assassin and his biggest supporter.

Beyond love poetry, our knowledge of Cytheris derives in large part from Cicero, just like Clodia. In an invective against Mark Antony, the orator recalls an incident in which the politician appeared in an official capacity accompanied by Cytheris and several pimps, insultingly placing his mother behind them:

> Although a tribune of the plebs, [Antony] was riding in a luxurious wagon. In front of him walked laurel-bearing lictors, and between them was conveyed in an open litter a mime actress. Prominent citizens from the towns obliged to go out and meet them greeted her not by her well-known stage name [Cytheris] but by the name of Volumnia. Another vehicle followed with the pimps, the most worthless of companions. His mother, relegated to the rear, followed her filthy son's girlfriend, as if she were her daughter-in-law. (Cic. *Phil.* 2.58)

Cicero portrays Antony as illegally employing public officials, passing off his mime-actress girlfriend as his wife and surrounding himself with men of the lowest social order. Although taking on an actress as a lover was permissible, treating her like a legitimate wife crossed the line by humiliating the respectable women in his family. In this defamatory picture, Cicero employs a familiar rhetorical technique. Just as we saw with Clodia, Cicero uses a woman of questionable morality to cast aspersions on an enemy, targeting not the woman herself but the man with whom she consorted. Caesar forced Antony to end his relationship with his "mime-wife" in 47 BCE, a break that Cicero defined as a divorce, using the legal formula "to take away her keys" (Cic. *Phil.* 2.28.69). The last traces of Volumnia Cytheris are found in a poem by Vergil. He relates Gallus' sorrow after being abandoned by Lycoris to follow her new lover, a soldier, across the Alps to Gaul (Verg. *Ec.* 10.43–49).

Tibullus, the second love elegist, rejects military service as a means of financial support despite his diminished resources, preferring instead to remain on his country estate, where he can enjoy the love of his *domina*, pseudonymously called Delia. His poems narrate his love for his mistress and his despair at her infidelity. She is represented not as a wife but as a kept woman who participates in midnight trysts. The love elegies of a near contemporary, Propertius, focus on a beloved called Cynthia, recording the various phases of this single affair. In poem

2.7, the poet represents his mistress as overjoyed at the elimination of an Augustan law requiring at least one of them to marry, which would have compelled them to end their relationship:

> Never will wife or mistress separate us, you will always be my mistress and you will always be my wife. Surely you rejoiced, Cynthia, at the repeal of that law. We wept for a long time at the thought it might divide us still, not even Jupiter himself can part two lovers against their will. "But Caesar is mighty." Yes, but mighty in warfare. In love conquered nations are worth nothing. (Prop. 2.7.1–6)

Here the poet-lover overtly challenges the authority of Augustus, asserting that personal love triumphs over war and politics. He further protests that marriage would be a fate worse than death, comparing it to decapitation. Even the most deeply held Roman value is rejected, the perpetuation of the family and the state through the birth of sons, "How should I provide sons for our country's triumphs? No soldier shall ever be born of my blood!" (Prop. 2.7.13–14). The message of this poem is, in effect, "make love, not war." The campaign of love is the real military service and the pursuit of pleasure more important than a political career. No doubt this rebellious message appealed to many elite members of Roman society, male and female alike, as a way to protest the new constraints placed on sexual and reproductive behavior.

Ovid elaborates on the settings and motifs of his predecessors in his collection of love poems called *Amores*, which include the two on abortion discussed in the last chapter. These relate the most comprehensive account of a love affair in extant elegy. The first book introduces the poet's mistress, Corinna, utilizing stock scenes and standard characters. The second focuses on threats to the liaison in the form of erotic rivals and separations brought about by travel and illness. In the final book, the poet-lover elaborates the demise of their affair, graphically portraying an episode of impotence as a sign of his diminished interest in Corinna:

> Not that I think the girl isn't beautiful, or not attractively groomed, not that I haven't often wished for her in my dreams! And yet when I held her in my arms, I was sadly limp and could not perform, but lay a shameful burden on an idle bed; though I really wanted it, and the girl wanted it too, I could not use the pleasurable part of my exhausted groin. (Ov. *Am.* 3.7.1–6)

Much more so than Tibullus and Propertius, Ovid focuses on his physical desire, frankly discussing the charms of the naked Corinna, his attraction to a variety of women, including her hairdresser, and his prowess in bed.

Apart from Volumnia Cytheris, the identity and social status of the women in love elegy remains an enigma. They may have been unattached women legally ineligible for marriage because they were foreign, as in the case of Cytheris. Or perhaps they were female citizens already convicted of adultery and therefore socially exempt. It is more likely, however, that Delia, Cynthia, and Corinna should be understood as married women engaging in adulterous affairs. Their illicit relationships run counter to traditional Roman family values and even defy Augustan law, as we see in the next section. Like their male lovers, they do not wish to trade in their passionate affairs for a socially sanctioned, legally recognized union and the promise of children. The ambiguous status of the elegiac girlfriend also serves an important poetic function by defining the male poet as unconventional, rejecting marriage and children in favor of love and literary pursuits. Augustan elegy and its women parallel and critique the model of the virtuous wife and mother and of the male soldier citizen promoted by Augustan ideology.

13.3   The Augustan Law Against Adultery

By the reign of Augustus, policing the sexual behavior of the Roman elite had become a prime concern of the Roman state. As discussed in Chapter 10, the emperor passed legislation, known as the Julian laws, in 18 BCE in an effort to establish a new moral ideology centered on marriage and the bearing of children. A second statute criminalizing adultery was introduced a few months later. It was specifically aimed at punishing the extramarital affairs of married women and imposed harsh penalties for such misconduct. Once regarded as a private family matter, adultery now became a criminal offense, to be tried publicly in a special court. The law further allowed husbands and fathers to kill adulterous women, and their lovers, under certain circumstances. At the very least, a husband was expected first to divorce his adulterous wife and then to prosecute her within two months of discovering her crime. If he did not do so, he himself could be prosecuted for acting as a pimp. Once the two-month period had elapsed and neither the father nor husband had brought charges, any member of the community could do so, for up to five years. The new system encouraged spies and informants who received a substantial cut of the confiscated property. Although this legislation must have exposed any member of the elite with enemies to slander and denunciation, surprisingly we hear of very few cases.

The penalties for a convicted wife were exile to a remote island, confiscation of half her dowry and a third of her other property, and loss of inheritance rights. Her male partner suffered exile to a separate island and confiscation of a third of his property. The woman further exchanged her position as a *matrona* for that of an *infamis*, a person "lacking in reputation," a category that applied to anyone engaged in a disreputable profession, such as brothel keepers, prostitutes, actors and actresses, gladiators, and the trainers of gladiators. These individuals were subject to a range of legal disabilities, including disqualification from marriage to Roman citizens. The association with prostitution was further symbolically marked by a change of clothing. The unfaithful wife could no longer don the crucial sartorial markers of the respectable *matrona*, the long, sleeveless tunic known as the *stola*, and the woolen ribbons, the *vittae*, that bound her hair. She was forced instead to wear the toga, the dress of the Roman male citizen and the prostitute. The poet Martial remarks, "You give scarlet- and violet-colored clothing to a notorious adulteress. Do you want to give her just what she deserves? Send her a toga!" (Mart. 2.39). In contrast to the fine Coan silks worn by wealthy Roman women, the toga was not expensive, beautiful, nor feminine and may have suggested the woman belonged to the public sphere.

By penalizing adultery and legitimizing prostitution, Augustus' laws inadvertently created a legal loophole that was famously exploited by an aristocratic woman named Vistilia. Although she conducted numerous extramarital affairs, her husband refused to prosecute her, forcing the emperor Tiberius to step in and bring charges against her. Vistilia cleverly evaded the penalty by publicly registering as a prostitute. In doing so, she received immunity, as the law did not apply to slave women or those classified as *infamis*, such as prostitutes and actresses. According to the historian Suetonius (69–122 CE), many other respectable women allegedly resorted to this maneuver in order to circumvent the legal system. Tiberius subsequently changed the law to prevent this. Vistilia's story points to other important facets of Roman sexual mores. First, her husband's reluctance to prosecute indicates that men commonly tolerated this behavior. Second, it shows how the distinct moral categories of *matrona* and prostitute became increasingly elided during the early empire.

The most notorious offender against Augustus' adultery law was ironically his only biological child, Julia, born to his first wife Scribonia in 39 BCE. Raised in austerity in the house of her father and her stepmother Livia, Julia was taught to spin and weave and strictly chaperoned. But little of this upbringing seems to have rubbed off on her, because she purportedly engaged in numerous extramarital affairs as an adult. Her promiscuity, however, was offset by her many good qualities, particularly her erudition, keen wit, and congeniality:

> Of course her love of literature and considerable learning, as was easy in that household and also her kindness, gentleness and good temper had won her immense popularity, and people who knew about her faults were amazed that she combined them with qualities so much their opposite. (Macr. *Sat.* 2.5.2)

Worried about her choice of friends and extravagant lifestyle, Augustus repeatedly warned Julia to be more moderate. And although he may have suspected her infidelities, her children all bore too close a resemblance to Agrippa for him to press the issue. Indeed, the undisputed paternity of her children produced the punch line for one of her most famous jokes. When a friend expressed amazement that all of her children looked like their father, she quipped, "that's because I take on passengers only when the cargo is already loaded!" That is, she cheated on her husband only while pregnant. Many of her other jokes involve the daughter getting the better of her father. When she appeared before Augustus wearing a seductive outfit, he said nothing, but when she came to him in more appropriate dress the next day, he praised her for her modesty. Julia responded that she was dressing today for her father, but the night before for her husband. These jokes convey a confident and strong-willed woman not afraid to stand up to men, even to an emperor!

In 2 BCE, her third husband, the future emperor Tiberius, somehow discovered that she had been committing multiple adulteries and indulging in public debauchery in the Forum while he was away in Greece. Seneca describes the rumored behavior, characterized as impudicitia or the opposite of pudicitia, that led to the charges:

> The divine Augustus banished his daughter, who was shameless beyond the reproach of shamelessness, and made public the scandals of the Imperial house, that she had made herself available to throngs of lovers, that she had roamed the city in nocturnal escapades, that the very Forum and the rostrum, from which her father had proposed the law against adultery, had been chosen by the daughter for her debaucheries, that on a daily basis she frequented the statue of Marsyas, and there turned from adultery to prostitution, and sought the right to every depravity with even an unknown adulterer. (Sen. *Ben.* 6.32.1)

The passage deploys several rhetorical tropes familiar from Roman descriptions of female adultery: indiscriminate sex with multiple partners, nocturnal forays out of the house, defilement of male public space, and prostitution. The author even throws in for good measure the irony that Julia outrageously defiled the very stage on which her father had proclaimed his law against his adultery. Once the infidelities were discovered, the emperor himself made the indictment, providing a list of her alleged partners in crime and an account of her sexual misconduct. There was no trial and no public confirmation of the charges. Julia was convicted and banished to the remote and windy island of Pandateria, accompanied by her mother Scribonia. There she was not allowed to drink wine – virtually the only beverage available to Romans besides water – nor to eat sumptuous food. No freed man or slave was allowed contact with her without prior permission from Augustus. After five years, she was allowed to return to the mainland, to Rhegium, where she lived under straightened circumstances. But did Julia in fact commit adultery? Although it is not implausible that she may have taken on a lover during the five years of her husband's absence, accusations of adultery were an easy way to dispose of inconvenient aristocratic women. Indeed, adultery charges led to the removal of several prominent individuals from Rome. Debate over whether Julia's crime was actually sexual misconduct or part of a political conspiracy continues to this day.

13.4   Concubines

We have considered thus far several types of women who did not conform to traditional Roman values related to female sexual conduct, including the adulteresses Clodia Metelli and Julia Augusti and the fictive mistresses Cynthia, Delia, Corinna, and Lycoris/Volumnia Cytheris chronicled in love elegy. The latter figure is of special interest because although an actress, she lived with Antony as his "second wife" in a quasi-marital relationship whose termination was characterized as a form of divorce. Was Cytheris a courtesan or concubine, or both? In Roman law, the Latin term ***concubina*** referred to cohabitation between two partners in which one member was ineligible to marry. The man usually did not have a legal wife but rather chose to live with a woman of lower social status, either before marriage or after the death of a wife who had given him enough children already. Concubines were selected precisely because their low status precluded marriage under Augustan law. A Roman governor or emperor might have a number of slaves or freed mistresses in his service. Such women combined aspects of the faithful wife and the sexually available prostitute. This relationship likely gave the man a stable and affectionate sexual relationship with a companion and domestic partner without the complications of property, inheritance, and succession, because the concubine had no claim to his wealth and no expectation that she would bear him children. The woman, in return, received a higher standard of living than if she had married a man of her own station.

Concubines became an increasingly common presence at court during the empire. We have already met Claudia Acte, a freedwoman from Asia Minor and the mistress of the emperor Nero. She may have been a slave of the Emperor Claudius acquired during his campaigns in the east or she could have been purchased later by the Imperial family, adopting their name upon manumission (see Chart 10.1). Nero took up with Acte shortly after he ascended to the throne at age 17 in 54 BCE, just after marrying his cousin, Octavia. The couple remained romantically involved for three years, until his marriage to his second wife, Poppaea Sabina, in 58 BCE. Praised for her loyalty and devotion to Nero, Acte could not escape court politics. Some supported the girl as a way to thwart Agrippina, Nero's mother, who disapproved of the affair, whereas others viewed their relationship as an appropriate safety valve:

> Meanwhile, maternal authority had gradually weakened. For Nero had fallen in love with a freedwoman named Acte … even his older friends showed no reservation that a girl of her station should gratify the emperor's desires without harm to anyone, since he loathed his wife, Octavia, in spite of her high rank and well-known virtue … it was also feared that he might sexually assault respectable women, if he was prevented from that pleasure. (Tac. *Ann.* 13.12)

Acte served as a tool between warring factions, driving a wedge between mother and son and distracting Nero from the sexual pursuit of respectable women, who might well exert real power. Again we find a familiar pattern: the threat posed by a powerful man's preference for a woman of low station over his wife. By loving a freedwoman instead of his legitimate wife, the emperor insulted his mother, potentially diminishing her own status and inverting the social hierarchy. "Agrippina raged like a woman about having a freedwoman for a rival and a handmaid for a daughter-in-law" (Tac. *Ann.* 13.13). Putting up with Nero seems to have been worth it. Thanks to him, Acte ended up with extensive property in North Africa.

Although loyal concubines could influence their powerful partners, they posed less of a threat than Imperial wives and mothers because they did not have the protection of a distinguished family nor did they enter the relationship with economic autonomy. Caenis, a slave and secretary of Antonia the Younger, the mother of the emperor Claudius, gained significant wealth and influence as the concubine of Vespasian (9–79 CE), both before and after his marriage to Flavia Domitilla. After Flavia's death, Caenis became a freedwoman and functioned almost as a wife to the emperor. Another Imperial concubine, Marcia, began first as the mistress of a consul and then after his assassination, took up with the emperor Commodus (161–191 CE). In contrast to other such women, she was not originally a slave in an Imperial woman's household but rather the daughter of the freedwoman Marcus Aurelius Sabinianus. Before her liaison with the emperor, she was the lover of his cousin and subsequently the wife of his servant, Eclectus. Although implicated in a plot to murder Commodus, she managed to escape charges and to become his mistress when he chose not to remarry after the adultery and exile of his wife. She used her position as Imperial concubine to persuade the emperor to become more tolerant of Christians and to commute the sentences of those condemned to the mines of Sardinia. Whereas Roman empresses continued to amass power as public figures of authority who controlled vast wealth, concubines often functioned as traditional wives devoted exclusively to the emperors they served.

Box 13.1 Sex and the Suburban Baths

Whereas bathing is a private activity in many cultures today, for most Romans, it was a communal event. Men, women, and children of all classes frequented the baths, sometimes bathing together. As the Forum was the center of Roman economic and legal activities, the public baths were its social center. More than just a way to stay clean, they offered food and drink, a place to gossip and plot intrigue, and, of course, sex. A line from a funerary inscription by a wife for her husband celebrates the pleasures found there: "Wine, sex, and the baths ruin our bodies, but wine, sex and the baths make our life good!" (*CIL* VI 15258). The association between public bathing and sex is illustrated in the Suburban baths at Pompeii. The complex offered a number of amenities unavailable in other bathing facilities in the town. The rooms were large and had many luxury features. In addition to the usual heated rooms, bathers could enjoy dry heat in one room and even a large heated swimming pool. Nor were the Suburban baths divided into separate sections for men and women. There is only one changing room and it is unknown whether the two sexes bathed at the same time or at different times. The room is noteworthy for a series of explicit images of sex acts located above a shelf where patrons stored their clothes prior to bathing, perhaps functioning as identifying labels. The graphic paintings depict types of sex not usually found in erotic art, such as fellatio, cunnilingus, threesomes, foursomes, female-to-female and male-to-male sex. The series begins with a frontal view of a woman lowering herself onto a man's penis (Figure 13.2). The sexual position of the woman astride shows off her face, breasts, and torso, allowing her to dominate the visual composition and her smaller, supine male partner. How would a female bather have reacted to this painting? She might have viewed it as a display of feminine beauty and power at the expense of the male. Or perhaps she was one of the prostitutes who occupied the rooms above the bath, ready to gratify a male bather, but at a high price. One graffito on the way outside states, "Whoever sits here, read this above all: if you want to fuck, look for Attice. You can have her for sixteen asses" (*CIL* IV 1751). Despite the pleasures they offered, the baths posed a serious health risk. The water was not changed very often, meaning that whatever dirt, grime, bodily fluids, and germs entered it was shared with others. The place even repelled some Romans. "What does bathing look like to you? Oil, sweat, filth, sludgy water, everything disgusting" (Marcus Aurelius, *Meditations* 8.24). No wonder the wealthy desired to incorporate private bathing facilities into their own homes!

Figure 13.2 A male and female couple on a bed, Pompeii, Suburban Baths, apodyterium 7, scene I, c. 62–79 CE. Suburban Baths, Pompeii. Scala Archives AF00033.

13.5 Female Prostitution

Although Roman law and moral discourse assimilate unfaithful wives to prostitutes, actual prostitutes lived radically different lives from those of elite Roman girls and women and even the concubines and actresses. The main Latin term for prostitute is ***meretrix***, which designates a range of sex workers, from courtesans to brothel workers. The terms ***scortum*** ("hide") and ***lupa*** ("wolf-bitch") are more derogatory and indicate the lowest type of prostitute on the social scale. Roman legal texts define a prostitute as "she who makes a living by her body." Although completely legal, prostitution brought disgrace to its practitioners, many of whom were men, branding them with the designation infamis. As a profession, prostitution in Roman towns was involuntary, degrading, and dangerous. Physical abuse was probably common. Judging by graffiti from Pompeii, prostitutes were typically foreigners, purchased as children by freedmen specifically for the sex trade. They worked under the control of a male pimp, less often a madame, either out of a brothel or on the street. A large number, however, were slaves born at home and were prostituted by their owners. Some of these may have received customers in their home, as evidenced by the presence of single rooms, referred to as cribs, with erotic frescos in otherwise private villas in Pompeii. A majority of these women probably sold sex only occasionally, or for limited periods of time, or only under certain circumstances. At Pompeii, the cost of a prostitute's sexual services ranged from 2 asses, the price of a cup of cheap wine or loaf of bread, to 16 asses at the high end, the price given for Attice in the Suburban baths (see Box 13.1). A number of graffiti list fellatio as the service available, but most refer only to a price. Prostitutes were thus readily available and most were fairly cheap. The customers were probably not members of the Roman elite, because they had access to multiple sex partners outside of marriage, starting with their own slaves. Those with resources might keep a concubine, as we have seen. Rather, the main consumers of commercial sex were lower-class men and male slaves.

The Romans did not relegate prostitution to a specific zone or red-light district as in modern Amsterdam. Prostitutes were ubiquitous in ancient Roman towns and could even work out of a room in a private house. Walking down the street of any town, you would have encountered prostitutes hanging around the Forum, standing in a doorway, or approaching you as you left the theater. Respectable women, even Vestal Virgins, would have regularly encountered prostitutes as they went about their business on the street. It has been estimated that 1%, or 100 from a population of 10 000, were prostitutes in Pompeii. The rates were of course much higher among women between the ages of 16 and 29. Perhaps as much as 10–20% of "eligible" females worked at least occasionally as prostitutes. Venues for sex were scattered throughout towns, with more activity around the Forum, temples, and on the narrower streets with few atrium-style houses, and at Rome, the crowded, lower-class area known as the Subura. Cemeteries were also frequent haunts of prostitutes. They trawled the arches, called *fornices*, from which we get the English term "fornication," of large public buildings such as theaters and amphitheaters. Taverns and snack bars were synonymous with prostitution, featuring rooms at the back or upstairs where customers could have sex with bar maids, a type of worker typically identified with sex for pay. The public baths naturally attracted prostitutes because of their large male clientele (see Box 13.1). Often a single lit oil lamp placed in a niche signaled a prostitute within.

The most organized venue for commercial sex was the brothel, called a ***lupanar*** ("wolf house," "whorehouse"). A popular tourist destination today, the Lupanar in Pompeii is the only building to survive from classical antiquity that exclusively functioned as brothel. It is tiny in comparison to many of the town's houses. The Lupanar contained 10 rooms in total, 5 in its upper story and 5 on the ground floor. An exterior wooden staircase led to the upper rooms, which were accessible from a balcony. There was a bell at the entrance and a toilet under the stairs. Inside, a central hall led to a series of dark cramped cells without doors, containing masonry beds and "pillows" (Figure 13.3). There is little space for loitering and scant privacy. Above the entrance to the rooms and on the walls were erotic paintings of various sex acts and positions that patrons might contemplate as they waited their turn. Perhaps the frescos represent the "menu" of sexual services offered by the sex workers. Or perhaps they are a lower-class fantasy of lovemaking. The comfortable and luxurious setting of their soft beds and blankets stand in stark contrast to the dank and cramped booths they were about to enter. Some clients whiled away their time by scrawling graffiti on the walls, recording their names and those of the prostitutes and informative statements such as *hic bene futui*, "I had a good fuck here." In reality, the brothel at Pompeii must have been much like the sordid place Juvenal describes in his account of the "empress-whore" Messalina: filthy, humid, dark, and without ventilation, reeking of sweat and urine. Brothels clearly catered to the poorer, rougher end of the social spectrum, a point reinforced by the graffiti, which contains no names of local elite families but only the names of slaves and freed persons.

Although the Roman legal system basically left prostitutes alone, they were carefully regulated and controlled by their communities. Women who derived their income exclusively from

Figure 13.3 Entrance to a room in the Lupanar at Pompeii. Scala Archives AF00280.

sex work had to register with town officials. A prostitute or her owner also had to pay a tax at the rate of a single sex act per day. A receipt from Upper Egypt indicates that a prostitute might apply for a permit from officials to work the streets on a special holiday:

> Pelaias and Sokraton, tax collectors, to the prostitute Thinabdella, greetings. We give you permission to have sex with whomever you might wish in this place on the day written below. Year 19, the 3rd day of the month Phaophi. [signed] Sokraton, Simon's son. (*WO* 1157)

More likely, the brothel owner paid the tax levied on a prostitute. Even with the tax, prostitution had the potential to produce a good income, paying much better than other occupations open to women, such as weaving and working as a wet nurse. For poor women without male support, prostitution could mean the difference between abject poverty and relative comfort. In Lucian's fictional conversations of courtesans, a mother tries to persuade her daughter of the advantages of prostitution for a family that has lost its male head of household:

CROBYLE: Let me give you the rest of my instructions about what to do and how to behave with the men; for we have no other means of support, daughter, and you must know how badly off we've been in the two years since your blessed father died .... I've scarcely been able to put food on the table, now by weaving, now by drawing down the thread or spinning the warp. I've fed you, daughter, in the expectation .... that being at the age you are now, you would support me, that you would outfit yourself with clothes, that you would be rich, and have purple dresses and maids.

CORINNA: How so? What do you mean, mother?

CROBYLE: By associating with young men, drinking and sleeping with them for money.

CORINNA: Like Daphnis' daughter, Lyra?

CROBYLE: Yes.

CORINNA: But she's a courtesan.

CROBYLE: That's nothing terrible. You will also be rich like her, and have many lovers. Why do you weep, Corinna? Don't you see how many courtesans there are, how much they are in demand, and what money they earn?

(Luc. *Dial. Meretr.* 6)

Although a highly constructed image of the hetaera that draws on earlier Hellenistic models, this passage nonetheless shows how prostitution might mean the difference between survival and destitution for Roman women without husbands and fathers. It also reminds us that a daughter's sexual choices and her control over her own body were quite limited in both the Greek and Roman contexts. Her sexuality, like her virginity, belonged to her family to dispose of however they wished. Female bodies were thus considered an economic resource not only of slave dealers and owners but also of any family network.

Although most prostitutes were slaves who worked in a brothel, tavern, or bath under the control of a pimp, some were freedwomen who must have earned enough to buy their own freedom and even to run their own brothels. A woman named Vibia Chresta erected a funerary monument for herself, her family, and her freedwoman, Vibia Calybe, whom she calls a *lena*, a female brothel manager:

Vibia Chresta, freedwoman of Lucius, set up this monument to herself and her own, and to Gaius Rustius Thalassus, freedman of Gaius, her son, and to Vibia Calybe, her freedwoman and brothel manager. Chresta built the memorial entirely from her profits without defrauding anyone. This grave is not to be used by the heirs! (*CIL* IX 2029)

Vibia Calybe may have formerly worked as a slave prostitute and amassed enough wealth for her manumission. The reference to "brothel keeper" implies that it was a respectable lower-class profession and a path of social mobility for economically disadvantaged women. The inscription also reflects the Roman preference for commemorating those in managerial positions. Another inscription from Casinum, Italy, describes an agreement between four freedwomen to manage a tavern near a shrine of Venus. The fact that their names evoke famous Greek courtesans and that they operate a tavern, a familiar venue for commercial sex, near a shrine of the goddess most associated with sex for pay may indicate that they were once prostitutes:

Flacceia Lais, freedwoman of Aulus, Orbia Lais, freedwoman of Caia, Cominia Philocaris, freedwoman of Marcus, Venturia Thais, freedwoman of Quinus, established an eating-house for Venus, at their own expense; the franchise can be revoked. (*AE* 1975.197)

13.6   Conclusion

It is easy to see how certain aspects of Roman life contributed to a culture of adultery in contrast to the Greeks. The Roman matron frequented public spaces and interacted regularly with men outside of her family. Marriages were arranged with the exclusive purpose of furthering male political careers, without regard to affection. The trend toward non-manus marriage weakened the authority of husbands over their wives and put many elite women in control of large property holdings. Divorces were frequent and incurred little social stigma. The widespread practice of adoption further reduced the need to produce a male descendant to continue the family line and retain its property. A wealthy, upper-class wife thus had the means, the mobility, and the connections to make her own choices and to conduct adulterous affairs if she wished. And yet a matrona who engaged in adultery shamelessly violated the deeply held dictates of pudicitia, threatening the stability not only of the family but also of the Roman state. The need to control the sexual and reproductive behavior of women thus became the centerpiece of Augustan moral legislation. Under the new law against adultery, men and women who engaged in illicit sex incurred penalties much harsher than in any previous generation. A convicted wife lost her husband, social standing, her ability to remarry, and much of her property, becoming an infamis, just like a common prostitute. In oratory, a sexually promiscuous woman could be used as a political tool to damage the reputation of an enemy, as in the case of Clodia Metelli. Charges of adultery could also help to eliminate an inconvenient aristocratic woman, such as Julia Augusti. In contrast, the male elegiac poets celebrated these sexually adventurous and irresistible women with a countercultural discourse that challenged contemporary social and sexual norms. Variously identified as a courtesan, unfaithful wife, or literary fiction, the elegiac mistress defies categorization, rejecting cultural expectations of marriage and motherhood to pursue a life of pleasure and poetry with multiple lovers. Conversely, the concubine maintained a long-term relationship with one man above her social station, functioning much like a wife, but without the rights and privileges conferred by lawful marriage. At the lowest end of the social spectrum were female prostitutes, usually foreign slaves, who worked under the control of a pimp, in squalid brothels, at the public baths, and in graveyards, for low pay with rough clientele.

Questions for Review

1   How are adulterous women characterized in Roman literature?

2   What was the Augustan law against adultery?

3   Why would a Roman husband not want to pursue charges against his adulterous wife?

4   What do the names associated with the mime-actress Cytheris tell us about her life?

5   What is the difference between a meretrix and a matrona?

Further Reading

Primary Sources

Catullus, 'Lesbia' poems, 2, 2b, 3, 5, 7, 8, 11, 36, 37, 51, 58, 68, 70, 72, 75, 76, 79, 83, 85–7, 91–2, 104, 107, 109
Cicero, *In Defense of Caelius*

Lucian, *Dialogues of the Courtesans*
Plautus, *Comedy of Asses*
Propertius 2.7

Secondary Sources

Clarke, John (2001). *Looking at Lovemaking: Constructions of Sexuality in Roman Art, 100* BCE–AD *250*. Berkeley and Los Angeles: University of California Press.
    Explores a wide range of erotic images to understand Roman attitudes towards sex, including those of nonelite women and men. Includes a detailed discussion of the Lupanar in Pompeii.
Edwards, Catherine (1993). *The Politics of Immorality in Ancient Rome*. Cambridge: Cambridge University Press.
    Considers Roman moralizing discourse in a wide range of texts and its articulation of anxieties about gender, social status, and political power, with a chapter on adultery.
Fantham, Elaine (2006). *Julia Augusti, the Emperor's Daughter*. Oxford and New York: Routledge.
    A scholarly biography of the daughter of Augustus that examines each stage of her life in remarkable detail.
James, Sharon (2003). *Learned Girls and Male Persuasion: Gender and Reading in Roman Love Elegy*. Berkeley and Los Angeles: University of California Press.
    A comprehensive reevaluation of Latin love elegy that reads the poems from the perspective of the "learned girls" to whom they are addressed.
Laurence, Ray (2007). *Roman Pompeii: Space and Society*. Oxford and New York: Routledge.
    Looks at the latest archaeological and literary evidence for Pompeii, focusing on the relationship between the geography of the city and its inhabitants, with a chapter on prostitution.
McGinn, Thomas (2003). *Prostitution, Sexuality, and the Law in Ancient Rome*. Oxford: Oxford University Press.
    A comprehensive study of the legal rules regarding the practice of female prostitution at Rome, examining the formation and content of legal norms for the profession and its practitioners, with close attention to their social context.
Skinner, Marilyn (2011). *Clodia Metelli, The Tribune's Sister*. Oxford: Oxford University Press.
    A scholarly biography of an aristocratic woman that seeks to reconstruct an objective account of her life from biased sources and recover the role she played during a turbulent period of Roman politics.
Strong, Anise (2016). *Prostitutes and Matrons in the Roman World*. Cambridge: Cambridge University Press 2016.
    Provides the first substantial account of elite Roman concubines and courtesans, as well as sexually promiscuous and notorious women like Clodia and Messalina, to challenge the traditional binary distinction between respectable wives and prostitutes.

14

Women and Public Life in Rome

> To Campia Severina, chief Vestal Virgin, most holy and most kind. In gratitude for the benefits of equestrian rank and a military post of the second rank that she obtained for him. Aemilius Pardalas, honored at her request with the command of the first cohort "Aquitania," dedicated this.
>
> (*CIL* VI 2132)

In this dedication inscribed on a statue base bearing the image of a Vestal Virgin named Campia Severina and dated around 240 CE, Aemilius Pardalas thanks the priestess for securing his admission to the equestrian class and a military promotion. Another text records that this same woman used her influence over the emperor to obtain a post for another man, Quintus Veturius Callistratus, as the financial supervisor of the Imperial libraries. An enormously powerful woman in her day, Campia Severina participated in a variety of patronage networks on equal footing with men, dispensing favors and receiving public recognition in various forms. In Chapter 7, we considered women's public engagement in classical Athens through a variety of religious activities, such as the festival of the Thesmophoria and priestly office, observing that older women likely had more freedom to participate in the public sphere because they were beyond the age of childbearing. Notably absent from that discussion is their involvement in their city as patrons and business-women. Unable to own or inherit property, Athenian citizen women simply did not have the means to finance major civic monuments, although a successful and celebrated courte-san might. Not until the Hellenistic queens, like Arsinoe II, do we find women in command of large property holdings and therefore able to finance and dedicate important public works, have their images minted on coins, and to enter athletic competitions as sponsors. Wealthy Roman women similarly exhibited a degree of civic engagement unimaginable in classical Athens thanks to the lack of constraints on their movement in public spaces combined with their economic independence. This chapter thus breaks from the life stage approach to consider first the material traces of women's involvement with their communities as benefactors, business owners, and managers, and then turns to the public role of women in Roman religion as cultic personnel and performers of ritual. Many, although not all, of these women were of advanced age – Ummidia Quadratilla was a grandmother when she made many of her benefactions – a time when they had the independence, financial means, and social connections to make an enduring impact on Roman society.

14.1   Benefactors and Businesswomen

To understand women's economic interactions with their communities, let us review briefly the economic standing of upper-class Roman women. They could own land and other types of property in their own names if independent of their fathers and husbands. Indeed, most fathers did not live long enough to have much control over their daughters' lives. The decline in manus marriages also meant that women did not usually come under their husband's legal control by the end of the Republic. They were not, however, completely free to dispose of their property as they wished. Legal guardians had to approve these transactions, even if it was merely a rubber stamp, until Augustan legislation awarded elite women who had given birth to three or more children the right to operate without a guardian. Roman women of all classes thus could engage in business enterprises appropriate to their station. There are even a few examples of extremely wealthy women who appear to acquire, administer, and transmit their own wealth in ways similar to men from the late Republic on. Like their brothers, they inherited their primary wealth from their parents and increased it by investments and subsequent nonfamilial inheritance. These substantial assets typically at their disposal later in life allowed elite women to enter into complex patronage networks that both benefitted their communities and enhanced their own social standing.

Like the Greeks, the Romans looked down on paid labor, including all trades, but especially those that involved the body or catered to pleasure. To conduct business, they relied on extensive networks of friendship and patronage outside of the family. The performance of personal favors created and reinforced the ties between individuals. Many of these took the form of loans issued to the benefactor's own freed slaves as start-up funds for a business, which returned interest and some of the profits to the patron. This civic generosity involved a two-way process. The benefactor provided his community with public buildings, entertainment, and other services, and the beneficiaries expressed their gratitude with an inscription, funerary epitaph, or honorific statue. This dynamic fostered civic unity and contributed to the stability and beauty of civic life.

Women were an important part of this culture of financial favors and exchanges. Within the boundaries of propriety, a woman of means could freely offer financial help and advice to men or use her influence with family friends. But such favors, especially from women to men, were particularly vulnerable to moral attack and distortion, as we saw in the case of Clodia Metelli. The most common benefactions by women were public buildings, particularly temples, and infrastructure such as aqueducts. The following discussion considers the mark four different women made on their communities, from a local to an international level: Ummidia Quadratilla, a patrician woman whose benefactions left a permanent mark the topography of her city; Eumachia, a wealthy patron of the textile guild in Pompeii; her fellow citizen, the innkeeper Julia Felix; and the empress Livia, wife of Augustus.

Ummidia Quadratilla, who died around 100 CE at the age of 80, must have been an interesting woman to know. From a distinguished consular family in Casinum, she lived a life of leisure, surrounding herself with a coterie of mime-actors, probably not for their acting talents alone. Pliny the Younger in one of his letters paints a vivid portrait of the octogenarian just after her death:

> She kept and indulged some pantomimes, more lavishly than proper for a noble woman. But Quadratus, her grandson, never saw their performances, neither in the theatre, or at home; nor did she ask him to. When she entrusted her grandson's studies to me, she said that it was her custom, since habit, as a woman in the leisure of her sex, to entertain herself by playing dice, and to watch her pantomimes performing (Plin. *Ep.* 7.24)

Despite these scandalous hobbies, Ummidia redeemed herself by making several significant gift to her city. From local inscriptions, we know that she built a temple and an amphitheater and that she restored the theater, perhaps giving a public banquet for the townspeople to celebrate its dedication. The letter further indicates that Ummidia herself produced shows in the theaters, sending her mime-actors to perform during public games and festivals. Although she lived at least part of her life at Rome, these lavish benefactions reflect her deep ties to her birthplace. Ummidia must have been a prominent and popular person in her city, because she is described as a female *princeps*, or leading lady. Her high rank and generosity brought her fame among her city's residents not only during her life but even after her death.

Although of humble origins, Eumachia, who lived around the same time, managed to become one of the most distinguished citizens of Pompeii. After inheriting a substantial sum from her father, Lucius Eumachius, who earned his fortune from the manufacture of bricks and amphoras, Eumachia married into one of Pompeii's leading families. Her new social status combined with her wealth allowed her to assume the office of public priestess and become a patron of one of the town's most important guilds, the fullers. Fullers were workers who treated and cleaned wool. Eumachia's main benefaction did not have to do with garments but rather took the form of a large, multipurpose building erected in a publicly prominent spot, on the east side of the Forum in Pompeii. A dedicatory inscription advertises her patronage to passersby:

> Eumachia, Lucius' daughter, public priestess, built at her own expense in her name and in the name of her son Marcus Numistrius Fronto the porch, the covered passage, and colonnade, and she dedicated them to Concordia Augusta and Pietas. (*CIL* X 811)

This text shows a woman acting on behalf of herself and her son to provide her city with a spacious and luxurious building in the heart of Pompeii. It included a front porch with niches for statues, a colonnaded courtyard, and corridors along three sides of the courtyard. Dating to the early first century BCE, the building could have served as a small park, offering relief from the noise and crowds of the Forum, a meeting place for the fuller's guild, or as a venue for informal or formal events. Eumachia's importance was also manifest in a portrait statue set up by the fullers that stood in one of the niches within the porch. A color illustration based on an early nineteenth century drawing captures what the statue might have looked like in its original setting (Figure 14.1). The base is inscribed "to Eumachia, daughter of Lucius, public priestess, [dedicated by] the fullers." Although the cult is unspecified, public priesthoods also incorporated women into patronage networks, requiring them to make benefactions and publicly recognizing their gifts in return. Outside the city walls, Eumachia built for herself and her family one of the largest tomb-complexes at Pompeii.

At the other end of town, Julia Felix owned a capacious house with a beautiful garden, private bathing facilities, and multiple reception and dining rooms. She was not a patron, like Eumachia, but rather a successful businesswoman. At the entrance to her building, a sign advertised the availability of parts of her property for a five-year lease, much like an ancient version of Craigslist:

> To rent, for the period of five years, from the thirteenth day of next August to the thirteenth day of the sixth August thereafter, the Venus bath, outfitted for the best people, shops with living quarters above, and apartments on the second floor, located in the property owned by Julia Felix, daughter of Spurius. (*CIL* IV 1136)

It was not uncommon for Roman women of means to profit from real estate. Sulla's daughter, Cornelia Fausta, purchased Marius' former estate at Baiae and then proceeded to resell it for

Figure 14.1 Color lithograph of the statue of Eumachia in its original niche, by D. Capri after an illustration by V. Mollame. De Agostini Picture Library/G. Dagli Orti/Bridgeman Images.

30 times what she paid for it. Terentia owned an apartment block in Rome that brought in lucrative rents and seems to have managed her rural property holdings with a view to profit. Located near the amphitheater, Julia and her neighbors capitalized on the presence of frequent crowds by converting their gardens into open-air restaurants and bars. The reception and dining areas created a lavish and exotic environment, with a large dining room overlooking the garden and its long, rectangular pool. The "Venus bath" catered to an upscale clientele, with features such as a sauna, sweating room, and open-air swimming pool in the courtyard, all features unusual in private homes. Along the street was a snack bar. These aspects of the property point to a savvy entrepreneur trying to maximize the profits from her investment. What is unusual is that a woman owned and ran this establishment. Like Eumachia, Julia Felix was not born into one of Pompeii's aristocratic families. Rather, she was of low birth, an illegitimate "daughter of Spurius," a name given to a child born out of wedlock and the source of the modern adjective "spurious." Or she may have descended from an imperial freedman, one of the emperor's ex-slaves. We do not know if she managed her business alone or had silent partners, perhaps even the Imperial family, judging by her name and the lavish appointments of her house. All we know is that she must have possessed significant assets in order to be able to purchase the house and repurpose it as a dining hall.

In addition to leasing property, elite women could have extensive business interests that they managed themselves. The brick industry seems to have been particularly attractive to female entrepreneurs. Imperial brick and amphora stamps reveal the extensive involvement of upper-class landowners in the production, sale, and export of commodities such as wine, bricks and amphoras. These large-scale commercial enterprises did not meet with disapproval, like the trades, probably because they were viewed as an extension of agriculture. The stamps on the bricks and amphoras attest to substantial female landholding, viticulture, and brick production. Amphoras were used for storing and transporting wine and other types of consumables. The stamps on the necks of these vessels contain the names of some women. Bricks were also sometimes stamped with the name of the owners of their factories and their managers. These also bear the names of a few female managers and many owners of clay fields and factories, including some Imperial women. It is estimated that out of 149 such landowners with production facilities on the premises, fully one-third were women. Domitia Lucilla the Younger (d. 155–61 CE), the mother of the emperor Marcus Aurelius, was one such woman. She owned huge clay fields inherited from her father, grandfather, and uncle. Her bricks must have been exceptional because they are found in some of the most magnificent buildings in Rome, including Trajan's Market, the Pantheon, and the Colosseum, and were exported throughout the Mediterranean. Lucilla used more than one brickmaker as surviving bricks show. One example (Figure 14.2) bears the symbol of a trident and words indicating that the brick came from the estate of Lucilla, produced by the brickmaker Ulpius Anicetianus, during the consulship of Commodus and Lateranus. The same characters later appear together with her daughter's name, Annia Cornificia Faustina, indicating that she followed in her mother's footsteps after her death.

More often Imperial women made their public mark as benefactors, helping petitioners, promoting religious cults, and making charitable contributions. In Chapter 10, we looked at Livia as the model for the Imperial wife and mother celebrated by the Altar of Peace and then considered in Chapter 12 her testy relationship with her emperor-son, Tiberius, as an example of the limits of maternal ambition and influence at court. As the wife of Augustus, she was expected to be a generous patron and to extend benefactions to individuals from all backgrounds. She took a particular interest in impoverished families. She paid the dowries of impoverished girls and even assumed responsibility for raising the children of respected but indigent parents. Other recipients of her generosity included the future emperors Galba and Otho and the victims of fires in Rome. Her patronage networks even extended beyond Rome to the fringes of the Roman world where she formed close friendships with leading figures. As we have seen, a wealthy and powerful benefactor did not simply aid individuals but also used her private wealth to benefit the community. In fact, women are associated with many of the most prestigious building projects in the Roman empire. Livia beautified Rome through her involvement in the construction or restoration of several important buildings, including the construction of the Portico of Livia and the temple of Concordia and the refurbishment of the Temple of the Bona Dea Subsaxana.

Because patronage was a reciprocal concept, Livia received numerous material and honorific benefits in the form of extensive estates, portrait statues, and monuments with dedicatory

Figure 14.2 Brick from the estate of Domitia Lucilla. Oxford, Ashmolean Museum, AN 1872.1502.

inscriptions scattered across the empire. Her immense popularity was expressed in other ways as well. An official celebration in Rome marked her recovery from a serious illness in 22 BCE. Other communities celebrated festivals in honor of Livia. But the most common means of expressing regard and respect for Livia came in the form of divine honors, revealing the link between patronage and religion. Just as Hellenistic queens had been venerated as goddesses, so, too, Livia achieved divine status in the eastern provinces. In this context, it is ironic that the breaking point in her relationship with Tiberius involved an act of patronage. The emperor balked when Livia advocated for a favorite to serve as a juror, even though he had only recently become a citizen. He approved the appointment but insisted that the announcement contain a postscript stating that he acted under pressure from his mother. This anecdote underscores the power of female patronage and its potential for distortion. Livia's reputation as a generous benefactor was turned against her and used to censure her presumption at court. Another influential figure, Cleopatra VII, the mistress of both Julius Caesar and Mark Antony, also had a profound impact on Roman society, but, as an Egyptian queen, in ways quite different from Livia (see Box 14.1).

Box 14.1 Cleopatra VII

Cleopatra VII (69–30 BCE) was the most powerful woman in Roman history. As the Greek queen of Egypt and the last of the Ptolemies, her romantic liaisons with two of Rome's most powerful men, Julius Caesar and Mark Antony, have largely overshadowed her record as a gifted politician. Propertius calls her the "whore queen" (*meretrix regina*), sexualizing her power, as we have seen with so many other ambitious and independent women of the period. As pharaoh, her goal was to strengthen Egypt and to keep it independent. To that end, she brokered a treaty with Rome, expanded her territory, and managed to protect Egypt from further incursion until 31 BCE. Cleopatra was born in 69 BCE to Ptolemy XII Auletes. After his death, she became queen, ruling first by herself and later with her younger husband-brothers, following the Ptolemaic custom of sibling marriage. A mixture of toughness and intelligence set Cleopatra apart from her brothers. As a teenager, she had accompanied her father on diplomatic missions where she learned first-hand the cost of his subservience to Rome. She was able to converse in seven languages, except Latin (!), and was the first of the Ptolemies to speak Egyptian. Her conversational skills and charisma were said to captivate her listeners:

> For her beauty, as they say, was not in itself unrivaled, nor such as to startle those who saw her; rather living with her held an inescapable spark, and her presence, along with her persuasiveness in dialog, and the character suffusing her conversation was keenly stimulating. (Plut. *Ant.* 27.2)

The affair between Julius Caesar and Cleopatra began after he seized Alexandria in response to Pompey's death in 48 BCE. She strengthened her position by appointing their infant son, Caesarion, born nine months after their first meeting, as her co-ruler. Her visit to Rome the next year caused a major scandal because Caesar was still married to Calpurnia. And it did not help that he erected a golden statue of her in the guise of Isis in his family's temple. Still in Rome after his assassination in 44 BCE, she sided with Antony against Octavian. After a dramatic encounter in Tarsus, in which Cleopatra arrived styled as Venus, Antony spent the year with her at Alexandria, where she gave birth to their twins. A third child, Ptolemy Philadelphus, was born soon after. Octavian's victory in the naval battle of Actium left the couple with no choice but to commit suicide. Upon his return to Rome, Octavian celebrated with a major triumph that included a life-size effigy of the dead Cleopatra reclining on her couch. Although displayed as the spoils of war, the queen exerted a lasting influence on Roman culture, inspiring Egyptomania in everything from wall paintings to hairstyles. Egyptianizing motifs even adorned the walls of Augustus' own villa on the Palatine.

14.2 Female Political Protests

Like the 2017 Women's March on Washington, D.C., which expressed opposition to the policies of President Trump, elite Roman women also banded together on a few occasions to protest male decisions that affected them. They occupied public spaces such as the Forum or the battlefield, sometimes dressed in mourning and accompanied by small children, to resist injustice. Such demonstrations were always nonviolent and almost always successful. A mythic prototype for this type of action is the intervention of the Sabines that put an end to the battle between their fathers and husbands and unified their two communities. In this section, we examine two of the most important collective demonstrations by women in Roman history, the call to repeal the Lex Oppia in 195 BCE and the protest of 1400 of Rome's wealthiest matrons against a special tax imposed on them in 42 BCE.

Before turning to these actions, it is necessary to understand the culture of wealth and status display in which elite women functioned. Whereas Cornelia may have been content to show off her children rather than her jewels, most wealthy Roman women took very seriously the need to indicate status by their appearance. The right to wear elaborate hairstyles, costly garments, and expensive jewels distinguished the wealthiest Roman women from those less fortunate and reflected well on their husbands, just as the bearing of prominent sons further reinforced their place in Roman society. In a sense, female adornment and overall refinement denoted by the concept of cultus comprised a form of compensation for women's lack of public honors:

> No offices, no priesthoods, no triumphs, no insignia, no gifts, no spoils of war can come to them; elegance, adornment, care for appearance (*cultus*) – these are the insignia of women; in these they delight and exult; these our ancestors called "the female world." (Livy 34.7.8)

Valerius, the speaker here, gets one thing wrong, however. Women could and did serve in an official and public capacity in Roman cult, as will be shown later. These outer marks of feminine distinction further ensured that their wearer would be treated with the appropriate respect. One example of female sumptuary display is Aemilia Tertia, wife of Scipio Africanus and mother of Cornelia. Participation in religious processions afforded the opportunity to show off the incredible wealth her husband had amassed, probably from his military conquests during the second Punic War:

> It happened that Aemilia, for this was the name of the appointed woman, had a lavish entourage at the women's processions, since she shared in the property and fortune of Scipio at its height. For apart from the adornment of her own dress and of her carriage, all the baskets, cups, and other utensils for the sacrifice, whether silver or gold, accompanied her on these public occasions, and a large number of male servants and maids in attendance also followed. (Polyb. 31.26.3–6)

This excessive display of wealth, which includes not only elaborate costumes and conveyances but also precious ritual vessels and a large entourage of servants, is the female equivalent of the military triumph, where men like her husband paraded their booty before admiring crowds. In contrast, a woman who had fallen on hard times avoided going out into public because she did not have the array of trappings appropriate to her station. When Aemilia died, her heir transmitted her property to his own mother, a woman named Papiria (we met her in Chapter 12), who until then stayed at home during the major festivals because "she lacked the means to put on a display commensurate with her nobility" (Polyb. 31.26.6). Thanks to this windfall, Papiria was able to attend the next gathering resplendent in Aemilia's regalia, even down to the horses and drivers, which all of the women immediately recognized. It was thus entirely socially acceptable and even in a woman's best interest to display her wealth and rank publicly.

All of that changed in 215 BCE. After a disastrous military defeat, the Romans passed the first of a series of austerity measures called the ***Lex Oppia*** that restricted not only a woman's wealth but also its display. Specifically, it prohibited women from possessing more than a half-ounce of gold, wearing purple garments, or riding in a two-wheeled carriage in, or within a mile of, the city, except on religious occasions:

> Let the women, then, be adorned not with gold nor precious stones, nor with bright-colored and purple clothing, but with modesty, with love of their husbands and children, with obedience, moderation, with the established laws, with our arms, our victories and our trophies. (Zonar. 9.17)

Although the purpose of the law was primarily economic, the speaker, Cato, infuses it with a moral tinge, chastising the desire for luxury and promoting traditional Roman values of modesty, frugality, and obedience for women. The law perhaps represented a response to women's increased wealth during the second Punic War, as illustrated by Aemilia. They showed off this new prosperity in their choice of clothing, jewelry, and vehicles, much like today. Whatever the reality, the women must have experienced the Lex Oppia as an outrageous insult to their position within Roman society.

Roman victory over Carthage in 201 soon brought an infusion of wealth from the conquered territories into Rome's ruling class and financial restrictions were no longer necessary. In 195 BCE, a motion was passed to repeal the Lex Oppia but it was threatened by a veto. This event prompted the largest collective intervention of women in Roman history. Matrons could not be convinced to remain at home "by advice or modesty or their husbands' orders" (Livy 34.1.5). They blocked the streets and the approaches to the Forum, begging the men as they entered to restore their former ornaments. The crowd of women grew larger by the day, drawing reinforcements from the surrounding towns. Livy gives a fictional account of the debate between the consul, Cato, who argues in support of the Lex Oppia, and the tribune, Valerius, who advocates for its repeal. Cato first asserts that the law is necessary to reign in female licentiousness. Without male control, female extravagance would be unrestrained. If the women prevail over the Lex Oppia, what's to stop them from overturning all of the laws that limit them? Valerius, in contrast, points out the injustice of excluding women from the political and economic benefits of the economic recovery enjoyed by men. The next day, an even larger crowd of women appeared and blockaded the houses of the men opposed to the repeal until they withdrew the veto. In another version of events, Valerius invites the women to take part in the assemblies of the people. Rushing in, they denounce the law, effectively repealing it. To celebrate, they immediately put on their jewelry and proceed to dance. Yet another account states that the women protested the law by refusing to bear children, either by keeping their husbands away (Plut. *Quaest. Rom.* 56) or resorting to abortion (Ov. *Fast.* 1.621–6), until the honor of riding in horse-drawn carriages was restored.

Another female act of resistance occurred during a similarly trying time at the end of the Republic. In 42 BCE, the triumvirs Octavian, Antony, and Lepidus tried to raise money to fund the war against Caesar's assassins by proscribing wealthy enemies and confiscating their property. The plan backfired. Because people were reluctant to buy confiscated property, they were unable to raise the requisite funds. They then took the unprecedented step of ordering 1400 of the richest Roman women – most of whom were related to the proscription victims – to assess their property and contribute a fixed amount to the state. When no man dared to challenge this law, the women took matters into their own hands. At first, they went through the proper channels, petitioning the wives of the triumvirs. But after Antony's wife, Fulvia, rudely dismissed them, they forced their way into the Forum. Hortensia, the daughter of the gifted orator, Hortensius, was appointed to speak on their behalf, one of the few rare examples of a female oration to survive from classical antiquity:

> Why should we pay taxes when we have no part in the offices, honors, commands, or governance, about which you fight for such a great amount of evil? "Because this is a time of war," do you say? When have there not been wars, and when have taxes ever been imposed on women, who are exempted by their gender by all men? Our mothers once rose above gender and made contributions when you were in danger of losing the whole empire and the city itself through the conflict with the Carthaginians. But then they contributed voluntarily, not from their land, their estates, their dowries, or their houses, without which life is intolerable for free women, but only from their own jewelry, and even these not according to fixed valuation, not under fear of informers or accusers, not by force and violence, but what they themselves were willing to give. (App. *B Civ.* 4.33)

Hortensia argues that stripping the women not just of their personal jewelry, but also of their property, will reduce them to the level of slaves, thereby abolishing class distinctions. Moreover, requiring women to finance a war, especially a civil war, when they cannot vote or share in military honors and commands is deeply unjust and violates Roman custom. Previous generations of elite women were not required to do so, she states, not even under tyranny, although in one instance they contributed their personal jewelry to the treasury without compulsion. The triumvirs were angry that the women had dared to hold a public meeting and refused to pay the tax while men were at war. When the lictors attempted to remove the women, protests from the crowds forced them to stop. Their intervention persuaded the triumvirs to postpone the matter. And they prevailed on the next day, when the triumvirs reduced the number of women who would be subjected to the tax to 400 and forced some of the richest men to make up the difference.

Collective, independent actions by women appear sporadically throughout Roman history and myth, starting with the Sabines. Although their aims may have been different, they suggest that women could and did have a political voice through peaceful protest. Given the fact these protests were all overwhelmingly successful, we might even speculate that they formed a necessary corrective to male injustices. Or that, at the very least, such collective female actions seemed plausible to a Roman audience. Surely a key ingredient to their success was the rank and power of the women who participated and the respect they commanded as matrons. They also demonstrate that courage was a valued characteristic of the matrona. Roman women clearly had the requisite contacts and skills to stage a large-scale public action. Perhaps some of competence came from their organization of religious ceremonies for women discussed in the next sections.

14.3 Women and Roman Religion

Thus far we have considered the direct impact of women on the public sphere. Female benefactors like Eumachia shaped the topography of their cities and in turn received public commemoration. Businesswomen like Domitia Lucilla left their mark on the bricks that went into constructing temples and porticos throughout the Roman world and on infrastructure such as aqueducts and pipes. Female political interventions, although rare, brought upper-class women out of the house and into the Forum where they successfully challenged male public policy. In the second half of this chapter, we consider how women engaged with their communities through their religious activities. In comparison to Greece, the evidence for women's ritual practice in Roman literary sources is scant, in part because male authors were more interested in military and political events. Epigraphic evidence, however, tells a different story. It reveals a religious landscape full of women with official titles in cult practice. Priesthoods were among the few public offices that Roman women were allowed to hold, nor were they always ancillary to men. Although Vestal Virgins, with whom we begin our discussion, are the most famous example, there were also smaller local priesthoods open to women throughout Italy. Girls and women participated together with men in the expiation of prodigies – recall that a chorus of teenage girls was organized in response to the birth of a hermaphrodite in Chapter 11. Women also participated in collective public prayer during times of crisis brought on by famine or plague. Some had large-scale financial involvement in the restoration and maintenance of temples, as we saw in the case of Livia. The civic ritual calendar also contained numerous events that addressed women and their concerns in the form of matronal cults. Religious practice thus represented a significant venue for the civic engagement of upper-class Roman women during all periods of Roman civilization.

14.4 Priestesses

There was a close link between priesthoods, political office, and patronage in Roman religion, even in the case of women. Eumachia, for instance, was commemorated both as a patron and as a priestess. As a priestess, she was expected to finance religious festivals or bestow other benefactions on the city. Outside Rome, priestesses generally seem to have been wealthy and locally prominent women, selected by a local council. They served an array of female deities mostly connected to agriculture and fertility or in the Imperial cults of empresses like Livia. The most important duties of priestesses were sacrifice and prayer. Although the role of women and sacrifice in the ancient world has been much debated, most scholars now reject the traditional view of women's sacrificial incapacity and assume, in the absence of compelling evidence to the contrary, that priestesses directed and participated in public sacrifices.

We know more about the religious program of the **Vestal Virgins** than any other priesthood at Rome, largely because it was so closely tied to the destiny and prosperity of the city from the earliest period. Although Roman legend attributes the foundation of Roman cult to Numa, it also relates that the mother of Romulus and Remus, Rhea Silvia, was a Vestal in the Latin city of Alba Longa. Vestals were the guardians of the communal hearth in the Temple of Vesta. The eternal flame symbolized the permanence of the city and its empire, and the Romans feared its extinction "above all misfortunes" (Dion. Hal. *Ant. Rom.* 2.67.5), believing that it portended the destruction of the city. Although Vestals had many ceremonial duties, their primary ritual tasks were preparing the mixture of grain and salt used for public sacrifices and the tending of the undying fire of Vesta. The Vestal order belonged to the pontifical college, the largest and one of Rome's most prestigious colleges, which was supervised by the priest of the Roman state, the Pontifex Maximus. In contrast to most priests, who only served part time, the Vestal Virgins were full-time religious professionals. They lived together in the sanctuary of Vesta in the Roman Forum (see Map 4) and devoted themselves exclusively to their ritual practice on a daily basis, observing a busy religious calendar. Selected before puberty, they were obligated to serve the cult for a minimum of 30 years, but most remained Vestals until death. Their positions were demanding and included the performance of extensive ritual activities and the rigorous maintenance of their virginity.

Who was eligible to be a Vestal? There was a strict protocol to determine who could enter the Vestal order. Before choosing a new priestess, the pontifex scrutinized a girl's age, legal status, and physical condition, as well as the legal and social standing of her parents. As ritually pure, virginal daughters of exemplary Roman families, the Vestals represented the symbolic family of the Roman state at the public hearth of Vesta. The girl had to be between the ages of 6 and 10, of sound mind and body, and the legitimate daughter of two living, freeborn citizens not involved in a disreputable profession. Like a sacrificial beast, only a perfect candidate from an ideal family could be consecrated to Vesta. The girl's young age at selection further ensured that the new Vestal entered service well before she reached puberty and so was both sexually pure and not yet committed to anyone as a future bride. Her virginity was integral to her religious identity and agency. Twenty girls were selected from those eligible and a lot was drawn. Once the pontifex had selected a candidate, he "seized her" in a rite known as ***captio*** and pronounced the following words, "I take you, Amata, to be a Vestal priestess, who will carry out sacred rites which it is the law for a Vestal priestess to perform on behalf of the Roman people" (Aul. Gell. 1.12.9). After the ceremony, the pontifex exercised the same power over the girl as her paterfamilias.

This series of rituals brought about a radical shift in the girl's social and legal status, particularly given her age and gender. In contrast to other respectable Roman women and girls, the Vestal was almost completely independent of male authority. Her relationship with her birth family was severed the moment she entered the order. Freed from the power of her father, the Vestal was no longer a daughter. She was also not a wife and as a virgin she could not be a mother. Her anomalous legal status distanced her from the traditional family structure and bound her closely to the Roman state. The loss of the ability to inherit her father's property also indicates that the Vestal belonged to the community as a whole. Yet Vestals were free to manage and dispose of their own property, which could be quite substantial. They also enjoyed a variety of unique privileges, some closely related to their ritual duties. They were permitted to ride in covered carriages within the city on festival days. They were considered sacrosanct and could not be touched. This inviolability also protected them from becoming ritually impure and potentially polluting the fire they guarded. They could also employ a lictor. Under Augustus and Tiberius, they received additional honors, including the right to sit in prominent seats at the theater.

On the streets of ancient Rome, a Vestal would have been easily identifiable by her unique hairstyle, headdress, and clothing. She wore the sex crines, the six braids, of the Roman bride. Roman sculpture depicts this style as hair parted at the center and waved back along the side of the head. On top of the six braids, the Vestal wore a distinctive ritual headdress composed of the ***infula***, a white and scarlet woolen band, wound around the head up to six times, and the vittae, the woolen ribbons of a Roman matron, which were attached to the infula and hung down on either side of the head (Figure 14.3). Whereas the vittae denoted female respectability and modesty, the infula communicated a Vestal's priestly status. A short, white veil completed her head covering. The dress of the Vestals does not seem to have been particularly distinct. She probably wore the stola, the long, sliplike garment with over-the-shoulder straps and a deep V-shaped neckline, worn over a tunic and belted under the breast, just like the matrona.

A Vestal's legal and ritual status was predicated on her virginity, because it was tied to the purity of Vesta and the flame of her hearth. As we have seen in the stories of Lucretia and Verginia, the sexual integrity of the female body was a powerful symbol of political stability for the Romans. Because the Vestals were in constant contact with the goddess, they could not engage in sexual activity, which would pollute her pure fire and jeopardize the welfare of the Roman state. The extinction of the fire in turn was taken as evidence of a Vestal's impurity. Any strange portent or civic misfortune could also be blamed on the sexual transgression of a Vestal.

Figure 14.3 Detail of Frieze B of the Cancelleria Reliefs depicting a Vestal Virgin. Rome, Vatican Museums, inv. 13392.

When a virgin from a prominent family was struck by lightning and instantly killed while traveling, shredding her clothing and exposing her naked body, the state diviners interpreted it as a sign that something was amiss in the temple of Vesta. Three Vestals were convicted of *incestum* and put to death. The term incestum does not imply the modern concept of incest but rather "impious inchastity," that is, a violation of the requirement of chastity leading to ritual impurity. On at least two other occasions, Vestals were found guilty of incestum in the aftermath of serious epidemics that attacked pregnant women and livestock. The loss of Vestal chastity put the whole community at risk.

In response to an allegation of impunity, the accused Vestal was ordered to cease her ritual service in order to prevent further contamination. At the trial, she was permitted to speak in her own defense. If the pontifex condemned her, she was forced to remove her special headdress, signifying her termination. She was then placed on a litter, covered, and bound down with straps to muffle her voice. In silence, the crowd watched the litter as it was carried in a solemn funeral procession through the city, "No other spectacle is more terrifying, nor does any day bring more gloom to the city than this" (Plut. *Num.* 10.6). When the retinue reached a place near one of the city's gates, the Vestal descended into an underground chamber, which contained a bed, a burning lamp, and a few "necessities of life," such as oil, bread, water, and milk. Once she had disappeared from sight, the ladder was pulled up and the entrance covered.

> When the litter arrives at the special place, the attendants undo her chains and the chief priest pronounces prayers and lifts his hands to the gods in prayer because of necessity, and he leads the veiled victim out and brings her to the ladder that carries her down to the room. Then he, along with the other priests, turns away. The ladder is removed from

the entrance and a great quantity of earth is piled to hide the underground chamber, so that the place is on a level with the rest of the mound. That is how those who abandon their sacred virginity are punished. (Plut. *Num.* 10.5)

Another important female priesthood in Rome was connected to the worship of Jupiter, the principal deity of the Roman state. This was a joint priesthood shared by a married couple, the Flamen Dialis and his wife, the Flaminica Dialis. They entered cultic service together and continued only until one or the other died. Strict rules bound both husband and wife. The prospective priestess was required to be a univira, a woman in her first marriage, placed under her husband's manus by means of a special wedding ceremony. She was not allowed to divorce and continuously wore the flammeum, the brightly colored bridal veil. Her husband wore a special ritual garment woven by her as symbol of their marriage. The Flaminica enabled the Flamen to perform his religious role; in fact, there were many ceremonies that he could not perform without her. Taken together, the priest and priestess of Jupiter embodied the traditional ideal of marriage necessary for the survival and prosperity of the Roman state.

14.5 Matronal Cults

In addition to priesthoods, Roman women engaged in a variety of other religious activities, many organized around so-called "matronal" cults that had a specific focus on marriage, childbirth, and fertility and typically involved married women of the senatorial class. The one for which we have the most evidence is the **Bona Dea** ("Good Goddess"). The title "Bona Dea" is not her name but rather a euphemism designed to protect the identity of a goddess "whose name it is not right for men to know" (Cic. *Har. resp.* 37). The origins and history of her cult are obscure. As an Italian agrarian deity, some aspects of her worship resemble the festival of the Thesmophoria at Athens. Although classified as "matronal," the cult permitted men in the Imperial period, though women still predominated. Virtually all of the priests and all religious functionaries were female but the cult was not part of the public pantheon. Her worship involved two main events. In the spring, a sacrifice was offered to the goddess in her temple at the foot of the Aventine. Little is known about the rites except that myrtle and wine, both associated with sex, were prohibited. An older woman may have presided while younger women played games. Serpents or their representation accompanied the rites in the temple.

The better known ceremony occurred on the evening of December 3rd. Although a state event, the rituals were held in secret at the house of a high-level magistrate such as a consul. All males, including male animals, had to vacate the premises. Even the male ancestral portraits in the atrium were covered. The ceremony was led by the women of the magistrate's family, assisted by their female slaves and the Vestal Virgins. The room was decorated with vines and other plants. Wine was set out in a covered jar, but called milk and the jar a honey-pot. The Vestals first sacrificed a pig on behalf of the Roman people in the company of matrons. A libation was poured, followed by dancing and singing. In 62 BCE, the festival of the Bona Dea was held at the house of Julius Caesar. His mother, Aurelia, presided, aided by his wife Pompeia and his sister Julia. Disguised as a young woman, Clodius Pulcher, the brother of Clodia Metelli, infiltrated the secret rituals in an attempt to seduce Pompeia. Easily eluding detection with the aid of a slave woman, he was invited to play a game by an unsuspecting woman. When he refused, she led him before the others and demanded to know his identity. Once the women heard him speak, they knew instantly that he was a man disguised as a woman. Clodius was tried for desecrating the ritual and acquitted in a high-profile, much-discussed case. Caesar in turn divorced Pompeia, famously saying, "My wife must be beyond reproach" (Plut. *Caes.* 10.6).

A few other Roman festivals and temples were of particular significance for Roman women. The **Matronalia**, celebrated on the first of March, focused on childbirth and the family. On this day, matrons made offerings to Juno Lucina, goddess of childbirth, at her temple in Rome, and probably at her cult sites elsewhere. Reportedly dedicated in 375 BCE by a group of matrons wishing for sons, the temple from the earliest period had associations with matrons and ritual activities focusing on childbirth. The name Lucina may be derived from the Latin word for "light" (*lux*), because Juno presided over childbirth and brought children into the light and life, according to Ovid:

> Bring the goddess flowers: for this goddess loves flowering plants: garland your heads with fresh flowers, and say. "You, Lucina, have given us light," and say, "You hear the prayer of women in childbirth." But let her who is with child, let her pray with unbound hair, so the goddess may gently free her womb." (Ov. *Fast.* 3.253–8)

Husbands also prayed for the preservation of their wives and their marriages and offered them incense and flowers. After visiting the temple, the matrons served a special meal to their household slaves. Then husbands gave their wives gifts, some apparently lavish. The participation of the members of the household suggests that this religious occasion was not a women-only festival but rather a family celebration that focused on the domus and its welfare.

The festival of **Matralia**, held on the eleventh of June, honored Mater Matuta, an indigenous Roman goddess. Her cult promoted the role of women as mothers and the bonds between sisters. Only matrons in their first marriage could participate in her cult. Although slave women were not permitted in the temple, during the festival one was brought in, ritually slapped, and then expelled, perhaps to underscore the exclusion of women of low birth from the rites. The matrons brought not their own children but those of their sisters into the temple, held them in their arms, and prayed for their welfare. These rites may have been intended to emphasize ties between female family members. Recent excavations at the Temple of the Mater Matuta in Rome have uncovered several small votive offerings of the goddess holding or nursing an infant, underscoring the association of the goddess with infant care.

In contrast to these cults, the festival of **Fortuna Virilis** ("the Fortune of Men") involved women of all classes worshiping the deity "in the baths," according to one epigraphic calendar:

> The women make offerings to Fortuna Virilis; the lower class women even in the baths, because it was there that men bared that part of their anatomy with which they desired the favors of women. (*CIL* I 2.235)

According to this inscription, Fortuna Virilis helped women arouse their husbands' desire for them. Ovid connects her with a second goddess, Venus Verticordia, as well as gives a more detailed account of the sequence of rituals in which all women, prostitutes as well as matrons, participated. The women first bathed the cult statue of Venus Verticordia, she who "turns hearts" toward chastity and the faithful performance of marital duties. The image was then adorned with flowers and jewels. Wearing myrtle wreaths, a plant associated with sexuality, the women took hot baths, burned incense, and drank a special concoction of milk, honey, and poppies traditionally used to calm the nerves of new brides. It has been argued that the ceremony was organized around the rituals that preceded consummation of marriage. Venus Verticordia made sexual unions within marriage possible, assisted by Fortuna Virilis, who promised to make wives attractive to their husbands. Such public rituals directly related to women's roles as wives and mothers.

14.6 Women and Foreign Cults

Male authors portray Roman women as more susceptible than men to naturalized foreign cults, such as those associated with the Phrygian Magna Mater and Egyptian Isis (see Box 14.1). However, there is no concrete evidence that they had more power or dominated the membership of these cults. Women did figure prominently, however, in one notorious religious scandal involving the worship of a foreign god. The Bacchic affair of 186 BCE, which occurred just after the female protests against the Lex Oppia, is one of the most discussed episodes in Roman religion. The cult of Bacchus, the Roman name for Dionysus, was widespread throughout Italy. It cut across social categories, initiating men and women, slaves and ex-slaves, upper and lower classes. According to Livy, our primary source for the Bacchic affair, the cult originated in Greece and then rapidly spread – "like a plague" – throughout Italy. At first, initiation rites were restricted to women. Then a Campanian priestess named Paculla Annia reformed the cult. She began initiating men and introduced orgiastic rites that encouraged promiscuity and criminal activity:

> From the time that the rites were performed in common, men mingling with women and the freedom of darkness added, no form of crime, no sort of wrongdoing, was left untried. There were more lustful practices among men with one another than among women. If any of them shrank from submitting to violation or hesitated to violate others, they were sacrificed as victims. (Livy 39.13.10)

A frieze from the Villa of the Mysteries just outside Pompeii may depict some of the rites involved in Bacchic initiation. Probably painted around 55 BCE, it runs around the walls of a triclinium and shows a series of almost human scale figures. It depicts a drunken Dionysus with a female companion, probably Ariadne, his followers, two satyrs and a maenad, a young boy, and several women. One of the most arresting images is that of a kneeling, half-naked girl being flogged by a winged female figure (not shown) as she rests her head in the lap of a woman who seems to be comforting her (Figure 14.4). Why is the girl being whipped? Perhaps it is a form of ritual beating associated with the cult. Whatever the artist intended, the panels in the Villa of the Mysteries show multiple female actors engaging in secret ritual activity, much like the Bacchic cult.

In Livy's account, the exposure of scandal hinges on the actions of a "noble whore" (*scortum nobile*), a young freedwoman named Hispala Faecenia. Her concern for her lover, Publius Aebutius, and her shock at the depraved pursuits of the cult's initiates, despite her own questionable sexual status, set in motion the chain of events. Intending to corrupt or murder her son, Aebutius' mother, Duronia, already an initiate, and her husband encourage the youth to undergo the rites. When Hispala learns that he must abstain from sexual intercourse for 10 days beforehand, she tries to dissuade him by telling him about the cult's alarming practices, which she witnessed firsthand when she was initiated together with her mistress while still a slave. After her disclosure, Aebutius reports the illicit activities of the cult to the consul. Worried about public safety, the senate orders a criminal investigation. Seven thousand people of both sexes were reportedly implicated in performing Bacchic rites. Many committed suicide. A great number received the death penalty and were executed, including Duronia and her friends, and a few were imprisoned. Condemned women were handed over to relatives or to husbands, if in a manus marriage, to kill. Those not under male authority were publicly executed. The Roman senate in turn rewarded Hispala Faecenia, giving her a large cash payment and removing her status as an infamis. As a result, she had the right to dispose of her property, to marry a freeborn citizen, and to choose her guardian. The Bacchic scandal not only reveals

Figure 14.4 Detail from a wall painting in the room of the Villa of the Mysteries with scourged woman and dancing bacchante, 60–50 BCE, Pompeii. Heritage Image Partnership Ltd/Alamy Stock photo.

women's capacity for independent action, whatever their social status, it also demonstrates the perceived threat of foreign cults to the Roman state.

14.7 Conclusion

Civic-minded Roman women typically came from the highest levels of society, possessed great wealth, and enjoyed the respect of their communities. As benefactors, they funded the construction of temples, theaters, and aqueducts. They subsidized games, sponsored public banquets, and provided dowries for impoverished girls. Beneficiaries were in turn expected to acknowledge this generosity publicly with an honorific statue or inscription, thereby enhancing the prestige of the benefactor. For women, patronage was not without its risks: "favors" could be distorted and sexualized to damage a woman's reputation. The Roman brick industry surprisingly reveals a large number of female business owners and managers whose products facilitated the construction of some of the most important monuments of the empire. The importance of wealth display and financial control of property led aristocratic women to stage two demonstrations that led to a reversal of male proposals, the repeal of the Lex Oppia in 195 BCE and the reversal of the matronal tax in 42 BCE. These independent actions show that women could protest male policies without fear of physical harm and had the power to change men's minds. In the sphere of civic religion, Roman women played an active role as priestesses, participated in the expiation of prodigies, and celebrated the rites of matronal and other cults. The Vestal Virgins, in particular, demonstrate the need to incorporate female characteristics, such as purity, into the religious structure that perpetuated the Roman state. But the price of betraying their chastity was death.In the Bacchic scandal of 186 BCE, the heroic whore, Hispala, exposes a foreign cult and its secrets rites as potentially dangerous to the Roman state and receives as reward a release from her status as infamis. Although Livy's account is largely fictitious, it recognizes the potential for Roman women of all classes to act independently on behalf of their own interests and those of their loved ones.

Questions for Review

1   How did Roman patronage networks benefit women?

2   What impact did Domitia Lucilla have on her world?

3   Why did women protest the Lex Oppia?

4   Why was sexual purity, as represented by the Vestals, so important to the Roman state?

5   How does the Bona Dea resemble the Thesmophoria?

Further Reading

Primary Sources

Appian, *Civil Wars* 4.32-4 (Hortensia's speech)
Livy, *History of Rome* 34.1-8 (Lex Oppia), 39.8-19 (Bacchic scandal)
Pliny the Younger, *Letters* 2.7
Plutarch, *Life of Caesar* 9.1-10.3

Secondary Sources

Beard, Mary, North, John, and Price, Simon (1998). *Religions of Rome*, vol. 1 and 2. Cambridge: Cambridge University Press.
    A radical new survey of Roman religion, structured around a few central themes, including origins, politics, monuments, topography, community, and identity. Volume 1 provides an overview and Volume 2 contains translations of the primary sources.
Bauman, Richard (1992). *Women and Politics in Ancient Rome*. London and New York: Routledge.
    Explores women's involvement in law, government, and public affairs chronologically, with a focus on women's political interventions.
Diluzio, Meghan (2016). *A Place at the Altar: Priestesses in Republican Rome*. Princeton, NJ: Princeton University Press.
    A comprehensive examination of the role of female officials in the state cults of Rome that challenges traditional view of women's exclusion from religion.

Schultz, Celia (2006). *Women's Religious Activity in the Roman Republic*. Chapel Hill, NC: University of North Carolina Press.
   Explores the varieties women's religious engagement at Rome through literary, epigraphic, and material evidence to demonstrate female ritual practice focused not just on domestic concerns but also on gods unaffiliated with the household and family.
Takás, Sarolta (2008). *Vestal Virgins, Sybils, and Matrons*. Austin, TX: University of Texas Press.
   An overview of women's roles and functions in Roman religion, the major female deities and their cults to show not only their extensive involvement in religious structures but also their necessity for the health of the Roman state.
Wildfang, Robin Lorsch (2006). *Rome's Vestal Virgins: A Study of Rome's Vestal Priestesses in the Late Republic and Early Empire*. London and New York: Routledge.
   Investigates the rituals enacted by the Vestals, the relation between religion, state, and family structure, and their involvement in rites outside the domestic sphere through a detailed analysis of literary sources.

Glossary

Acropolis Greek name for the highest part of the Athenian city and important religious sanctuary

agnomen Latin term for the fourth name of a Roman man that called attention to a special achievement or characteristic

agora Greek word for marketplace

aidos Greek term for female modesty, expressed by covering the body and a downcast gaze

aischrologia Greek term for mockery and sexual joking by women in festivals of Demeter

amica Latin term for girlfriend

Amphidromia Greek term for the ritual of incorporation in the Greek family, which involved carrying the infant around the hearth

anakalypteria Greek term for the unveiling of the bride after the wedding feast

andreia Greek term for manly courage

andron Greek term for the male dining space within the house

Anodos Greek term meaning "the way up" that refers to the first day of the festival of the Thesmophoria

archon Greek term for a high-level Athenian magistrate responsible for political, religious, and military affairs

arete Greek term for excellence or virtue

arrhephoros (pl. arrhephoroi) Greek term for the ritual weaver in the Athenian festival of the Arrephoria

Assembly Name given to the deliberative body of the Athenian democracy, consisting of all adult male citizens

atrium The central entrance hall of a Roman villa

auletris Greek term for the female player of the aulos, a type of reed instrument often translated as flute

Bona Dea Latin term meaning Good Goddess, used as a euphemism for the unnamed goddess of a matronal cult in ancient Rome

bulla Latin term for a protective amulet worn by patrician boys in ancient Rome

captio Latin term for the formal ritual by which girls were selected and inducted into the Vestal order

chiton Greek term for a type of tunic worn both by women and men

chous (pl. choes) Greek term for a type of cup used for drinking wine at the Choes Festival

city Dionysia Greek name for the annual dramatic festival at Athens featuring both tragedy and comedy

cognomen Latin term for the third name denoting the branch of the clan to which the man belonged

Women in Classical Antiquity: From Birth to Death, First Edition. Laura K. McClure.
© 2020 John Wiley & Sons, Inc. Published 2020 by John Wiley & Sons, Inc.

concubina Latin term referring to cohabitation between two partners in which one member was ineligible to marry

cubiculum (pl. cubicula) Latin term for bedroom

cultus Latin term for neatness, adornment, bodily care, or refinement

deme Greek term for the Athenian political district

demotic Adjective derived from the Greek term deme, indicating the name of one's deme and comprising the third part of an Athenian man's name

dithyramb Greek term for a type of male choral performance that honored Dionysus

domus Latin term for house and the community it contained, including husband and wife, children, slaves, freed people, and other relatives

domina Latin term for mistress

ekphora (pl. ekphorai) Greek term for the funerary procession from the house to the cemetery

engye Greek pledge of betrothal between a groom and the bride's father

epikleros (pl. epikleroi) Greek term for heiress, a woman who transmitted her father's estate to a male relative in the absence of brothers

epinetron Greek term for a type of ceramic thigh guard used by women for working wool

epithalamium (pl. epithalamia) Greek term, also used by the Romans, for the wedding song sung at the door of the marriage chamber that later evolves into a poetic genre

erastes Greek term for lover, used of the older man in paiederastia

eromenos Greek term for beloved, term used of the younger party in paiederastia

exemplum (pl. exempla) Latin term for role model and a concept important to Roman historiography

familia Latin term for family, including the group of slaves connected to a husband and wife

flamen (pl. flamines) Latin term for priest

Flamen Dialis Latin name of the high priest of Jupiter

Flaminica Latin name of the wife of the Flamen Dialis and a model for wifely virtue in ancient Rome

flammeum Latin term for the bridal veil worn in ancient Rome

Fortuna Virilis Roman festival celebrated by lower-class women and prostitutes that honored the goddess Fortuna to attract men

genius Roman god symbolizing the procreative life force of the paterfamilias

gens Latin term for clan or extended family, including ancestors

genos Greek term for clan or extended family, including ancestors

gynaikonitis Greek term for the segregated space in the household reserved for women

gyne Greek term for woman and wife

Haloa Greek name of a women-only festival in honor of Athena held in Eleusis

hetaera Greek term for courtesan

himation Greek term for a type of cloak worn by both men and women

hoplite Greek term for the foot soldier who owned his own equipment

hybris Greek term for sexual violation of a free person, male or female

hydria Greek term for a type of vase used for carrying water

imago (pl. imagines) Latin term for the Roman ancestral masks used in ritual and religious festivals

incestum Latin term denoting a violation of religious chastity

infamis Latin term designating a lack or loss of reputation, a category that encompassed actresses, prostitutes, pimps, and the like

infula Latin term for the distinctive ritual headdress worn by a Vestal Virgin, composed of white and scarlet woolen bands

Julian Laws Name give to a set of Roman laws introduced by Augustus beginning in 18 BCE to encourage marriage and childbearing

juno The female version of the male genius or ancestral spirit of the Roman family

Kalligeneia Greek term meaning "beautiful birth" that refers to the third day of the Festival of the Thesmophoria

kanephoros Greek term for the adolescent girl who carried the basket of implements and led the sacrificial procession

katakhysmata Greek term for the offering of dried fruit and nuts to the bride and groom

kleos Greek term for fame, usually won in battle

kore Greek term for maiden also used for a type of statue of a clothed adolescent girl

krokotos Greek term for a saffron-dyed yellow garment worn by women on special occasions

kyrios Greek term for a woman's male guardian, usually a father or husband

Kypris Birthplace and epithet of Aphrodite

Lanificium Latin term for wool working in all its stages

Lararium Roman shrine of the family gods, located in the atrium

Lares Roman domestic gods, defenders of the boundaries between households and protectors of the family

lekythos Greek term for a type of vase used to hold oil and important in funerary ritual

Lex Oppia Name of a Roman law introduced in 215 BCE intended to prohibit women from owning or displaying an excessive amount of wealth

loutrophoros Greek term for a type of vase containing water used in wedding ritual

lupa Latin term for female wolf or prostitute

lupanar Latin term for "wolf den," usually denoting a brothel

lustratio Roman ceremony of purification that incorporated the infant into the family

manus Latin legal term meaning "hand" that designated the type of marriage into which a young woman entered. In a manus marriage, the bride passed from the control of her father to that of her husband. In a non-manus marriage, she did not fall under the legal authority of her husband but remained attached to her natal family.

Mater Matuta An indigenous Roman goddess associated with motherhood and ties between sisters

Materfamilias Latin honorific term meaning "mother of the family," referring to a wife in a manus marriage

Matralia Roman festival celebrated on June 11 in honor of the goddess Mater Matuta celebrated only by free women in their first marriage who offered prayers for their sisters' children

matrona (pl. matronae) Latin term for wife and mother

Matronalia Roman festival celebrated by Roman women on March 1, in honor of Juno Lucina, goddess of childbirth

meretrix (pl. meretrices) General Latin term for prostitute

miasma Greek term for religious pollution

mima Latin term for an actress-dancer who specialized in sexualized theatrical performances

moichos Greek term for adulterer who seduces another man's wife, mother, or sister

Nesteia Greek term meaning "fast" that refers to the second day of the of festival of the Thesmophoria

nomen Latin term for a man's second name, his hereditary name indicating his gens or clan

nymphe Greek term for bride, a girl ready for marriage

oikos Greek term for the household and family

optimas (pl. optimates) Latin political term for an aristocratic male and property owner

ornatrix (pl. ornatrices) Latin term for hairdresser

paiderastia Greek term for the sexual relationship between a male youth and an older man

palla Latin term for the veil or wrap worn by Roman matrons

pallake Greek term for concubine

Panathenaia The name of a Greek festival held in Athens every four years in honor of Athena

partheneia Greek term for the period of female adolescence

partheneion Greek term for a genre of poetry sung by a chorus of young women

parthenon Greek term for the segregated space in the house reserved for girls

parthenos Greek term for unmarried young woman

paterfamilias Latin term for the male head of household

patricians Designates the highest class of Romans descended from ancient clans

patronym Greek term for the practice of naming a son after his father

Pax Romana Latin phrase for the long period of peace and stability in the Roman empire begun under Augustus and lasting until Marcus Aurelius

Penates Roman domestic gods, keepers of the household's provisions

peplos Greek term for the loose, long Greek garment pinned at the shoulders

phratry Greek name of an Athenian social group based on hereditary membership

plebeians The name given to the nonpatrician class of Romans

polis (pl. poleis) Greek term for city-state

popularis (pl. populares) Latin political term for a man who sought popular support by advocating on behalf of the people

porne Greek term for brothel worker

potestas Latin term for the absolute, legal power wielded by the paterfamilias

potnia Greek term for mistress or queen, often applied to the goddess Artemis

praenomen Latin term for the first name of a Roman man, derived from short list of under twenty

princeps Latin term meaning "first citizen" chosen by Augustus to designate his political office

pronuba Latin term for the woman in Roman weddings who assisted the bride in a variety of ways

proscriptions Roman lists published with names of victims (usually political enemies) and a bounty offered to those who killed anyone on the list

prothesis Greek term for laying out of the corpse

pudicitia Latin term for female chastity and proper sexual conduct

puella Latin term for young girl, also "girlfriend" in Latin elegy

puer Latin term for boy

Pythia Greek name of the priestess of Apollo at Delphi

pyxis Greek term for cosmetic jar

scortum Derogatory Latin term for low-class prostitute

sex crines Latin term for the characteristic hairstyle worn by brides in ancient Rome

sponsa Latin term for fiancée

stele Greek term for the upright stone slab used as a grave marker and often ornamented with relief sculptures

stola Latin term for the sliplike garment with a deep V-shaped neckline worn by Roman matrons

stuprum Broad Latin term for sexual misconduct

symposium Greek term for the drinking party

Thesmophoria Name of a women-only festival in honor of Demeter at Athens

toga praetexta Latin term for the toga bordered by a purple stripe, worn by freeborn boys and girls

triclinium Latin term for dining room

tunica Latin term for the garment worn by all classes and genders

tunica recta Latin term for the simple, white woolen garment worn by brides in ancient Rome

tutor Latin term for male guardian, required for children and women lacking the legal rights and powers of the paterfamilias

univira Latin term for a woman who married only once

Venus Verticordia Epithet of Venus meaning "turner of hearts" worshipped by married Roman women on April 1

Vestal Virgins The name of the most important female priestly office in Rome, charged with celibacy and keeping alive the sacred fire of the Roman state

virgo (pl. virgines) Latin term for maiden or virgin

virtus Latin term for manly courage

vittae Latin term for the woolen ribbons worn by girls in ancient Rome

Index